Imagine Coexistence

Imagine Coexistence

Restoring Humanity After Violent Ethnic Conflict

Antonia Chayes and Martha Minow, Editors

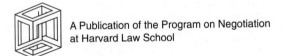

A Publication of the Program on Negotiation
at Harvard Law School

JOSSEY-BASS
A Wiley Imprint
www.josseybass.com

Published by Jossey-Bass
A Wiley Imprint
989 Market Street, San Francisco, CA 94103-1741   www.josseybass.com

Jossey-Bass books and products are available through most bookstores. To contact Jossey-Bass directly call our Customer Care Department within the U.S. at 800-956-7739, outside the U.S. at 317-572-3986 or fax 317-572-4002.

Jossey-Bass also publishes its books in a variety of electronic formats. Some content that appears in print may not be available in electronic books.

This book is not a substitute for counseling or legal, medical, or other professional advice, and the reader should be aware that Web sites mentioned or referenced may have changed or disappeared since this was written.

Library of Congress Cataloging-in-Publication Data

Imagine coexistence: restoring humanity after violent ethnic conflict /
    Antonia Chayes and Martha Minow, Editors.—1st ed.
        p. cm.
    Includes bibliographical references and index.
    ISBN 0-7879-6577-4 (alk. paper)
    1. Ethnic conflict. 2. Political violence. 3. Conflict management.
    4. Coexistence. I. Chayes, Antonia Handler, date. II. Minow, Martha, date.
HM1121.I42 2003
305.8—dc21

                                                     2002156551

Printed in the United States of America
FIRST EDITION
HB Printing   10 9 8 7 6 5 4 3 2 1

Contents

We dedicate this book to the memory of Abram Chayes, who helped so many people appreciate complexity and ambiguity in international law and politics.

Foreword

Imagining Coexistence in Conflict Communities

The Imagine Coexistence concept was an inspiration. As head of the United Nations agency for refugees, I grappled with the causes and consequences of conflict every day. On a Sunday afternoon in 1999, as I found myself browsing in a bookstore in Berkeley, California, my office was caring for nearly 12 million refugees and trying to assist some 2.5 million people who wanted to return home. A slim book, *Between Vengeance and Forgiveness: Facing History After Genocide and Mass Violence,* by Harvard professor Martha Minow, caught my eye. Minow was asking a simple and fundamental question. I wanted to find a way to answer that question and at the same time address the endemic cycle of insecurity faced by millions of men, women, and children displaced by war and conflicts.

Minow's question was, after mass atrocity, what can and should be faced about the past? I wanted to take this a step further and also ask, how can and should the past be faced? In many of the countries in which my staff and I worked, society itself had been rent into fragments. The vast majority of people had fled the cruelest of human inhumanity—had escaped genocide, ethnic cleansing, and the most massive violations of human rights—and were going back to their countries. No longer able to sustain a claim of persecution or the need to seek safety, refugee men, women, and children from Bosnia, Rwanda, East Timor, Kosovo, and Sierra Leone began to return home.

But home was now an impoverished community with no schools, no jobs, no festivals. Home was where your neighbour had killed your husband with a machete or had firebombed your house or had raped your daughter. My colleagues and I felt that to help refugees to return to these devastated communities, the fabric of the society would have to be stitched back together. This meant looking at individuals and their communities in the most holistic way and designing integrative projects that amalgamated social, economic, cultural, and spiritual aspects into a cohesive whole.

We were also concerned about the cycle of violence that could be repeated in unhealed communities. It was profoundly unsettling for governments to receive people who had been both the victims and the perpetrators of violence. As Minow wrote: "And if the longer-term goals include avoiding cycles of revenge, social integration of at least lower-level perpetrators should be pursued. In many circumstances, demonizing all on 'that side' means demonizing large segments of the society, including many individuals who believed they were acting for a larger good or who acted out of fear or who rationalize their conduct in other ways. To try to understand those beliefs is not a capitulation to evil or merely a pragmatic effort to avoid laying the foundation for further group conflicts."[1] Under these circumstances, the risk that we faced in many countries was that one side would prevail over the other and further conflict, killing, and ethnic cleansing would occur.

I also recognized that many of the activities that the United Nations High Commissioner for Refugees (UNHCR) attempted under the rubric of "reconciliation" were very difficult to implement in the immediate postconflict environments in which we were working. The concept of reconciliation was extremely sensitive for those who had fought so fiercely against each other. In Rwanda, for example, in the years immediately following the genocide, the government insisted on the need for justice, and the word *reconciliation* was never publicly used. Eventually, with the consolidation of the new "government of national unity and reconciliation," programs were established and a national commission was set up. By contrast, in Kosovo, even as I write this, the idea of reconciliation is untenable; the most that can be hoped for is coexistence.

To understand why this is so, and to aspire to the more modest aspiration of coexistence, it is crucial to have an understanding of the dynamics of the underlying conflict. Grounds for conflict persist when members of different groups assume ill intent in the acts of members of the other group. At the same time, the group members have no assurances that the others even concede their very right to exist. This hostility is capable of flaring into brutal violence, which can be temporarily intoxicating, even if ultimately toxic. When returnees and those they encounter each lack physical security and the opportunity to earn a livelihood, the temptation to hostility is great.

From this base, coexistence is an accomplishment. With coexistence, members of conflicting groups may indeed still mistrust one another, but they often undertake parallel or even joint activities. Ideally, by engaging in parallel activities and acknowledging these undertakings, members of conflicting groups can build a greater sense of security and a modicum of respect for others. Through the gradual recognition of increasing economic opportunity and human security, members of different groups can come to accept one another as participants in the society and interdependent actors. They can begin to imagine themselves living together in peace.

Clearly, the coexistence of groups who have had a recent history of communal violence is a matter very closely linked to refugee issues. Returnees—as repatriating refugees are termed—can be an obstacle to peace. Their return inevitably raises issues of property ownership, compensation, and unpunished crimes. They bring back real, fresh memories of the atrocities to which they were witness. For forty years, the Great Lakes region of Africa has unfortunately provided ample example of recurring refugee return and refugee flight. Promoting intercommunal coexistence is therefore essential for UNHCR.

During my ten years as the United Nations High Commissioner for Refugees, my agency was trying to find constructive, creative ways in which to address some of the most massive refugee and refugee repatriation situations. We started in Central America with what we termed "QUIPs," quick-impact projects. The idea was to start some productive engagements for returnees immediately after they returned. Later in Mozambique, we moved into more sophisticated methods, with community-based projects for the 1.7 million Mozambicans in six neighboring countries. We focused on community building—schools, water points, and health clinics and bringing those who were displaced and those who had never left together in the same community. There was little attempt in Mozambique to develop reconciliation, but that was not a focus until we got to Bosnia.

In Bosnia, we were groping for some way of bringing those who had come back to communities to face those with whom they had fought bitter wars. Neither my colleagues nor I had ever been exposed to so much hatred. This is when real interest in reconciliation started. In those days, the first answer was always justice, but that did not work. We would also be bringing in roofs, doors, and windows so that returnees could have shelter. But I noted that even after you go back and your house is repaired, it takes courage to be back in a community from which you were virtually expelled. I remember visiting a city where Serb women had gone back to a Bosnian-dominated community. One woman told me that when she returned, her house was intact, but what was frightening was that none of her former neighbors would talk to her. This was the reality of what one starts with as reconciliation.

In developing the conceptual framework for the coexistence projects, our starting point was with the people themselves. In situations of internal conflict, peace agreements sometimes succeed in stopping wars but rarely achieve the building of real peace. Peace must be built from the ground up, and in this UNHCR has a comparable advantage. Humanitarian, field-based organizations forge a direct link with the people they try to assist and enable—including nationals best suited to provide ongoing solutions to the nation's problems. UNHCR's mandate for refugee protection requires a presence with the refugees and the returnees on the ground. In situations of mass or forced displacement, UNHCR works with refugees in countries of asylum, helps them return across borders, and assists when they reintegrate in their home communities. Therefore, we determined to work with local communities and whenever possible with preexisting associations.

The second important element was to identify concrete sectors in which coexistence projects should be planned and implemented. The key idea was to define broad areas representing the fundamental activities of a community and convince people to carry out those activities together. We agreed to strive for combinations of the following domains: education; the media; psychosocial activities; business, income, and job creation; religion and spirituality; sports; literature; art, theater, and visual culture; mothers' and women's groups; activities for children and adolescents; and memorial or ritual activities.

On these two bases, the Imagine Coexistence pilot projects were launched in 2000 in Banja Luka in the Serb entity of the state of Bosnia and Herzegovina and in the Central African country of Rwanda. I hope that the Imagine Coexistence approach will some-day make the development agency people join in asking from this perspective: Where should we build a well? Where should we build a bridge? It does make a difference if you put it where you bring people together.

This book advances progress toward coexistence by presenting reports from field efforts to promote it, examination of approaches and obstacles, and initial evaluation efforts. I believe that the ideas presented here hold promise for many parts of the world.

Today I am cochairing the independent, international Commission on Human Security. One of the first tasks of this commission will be to define what is meant by "human security." I think the central concept that will emerge will be how to make coexistence work, not just for refugees but for all people. I think the territorial basis of state security may now be strengthened because in this age of globalization, the rapid movement of human beings, money, information, and goods cannot have a territorial basis. So, how can we strengthen security? By working at—not just imagining—coexistence.

March 2003   Sadako Ogata

Note

1. M. Minow, *Between Vengeance and Forgiveness: Facing History After Genocide and Mass Violence* (Boston: Beacon Press, 1998), pp. 121–122.

Introduction

How can people build peace after violent ethnic conflict? This extraordinary challenge, familiar across the globe, is heightened when displaced persons and refugees return home or move to regions where their very presence risks reopening the conflict. The challenge begins at the moment when international organizations and nongovernmental organizations (NGOs) enter the scenes of carnage. These organizations often emphasize expectations of reconciliation and reinforce local voices toward that end soon after conflict ends. The actions of these helping agencies too often ignore the simmering hatred that often persists after the gunfire has subsided. The distrust and tensions that linger call for immediate action in refugee camps and other places where fleeing people need food, shelter, and medicine. From the beginning, the choice of priorities by international and nongovernmental groups intending to help should reflect an understanding of the ongoing tensions so that even the most basic repairs to infrastructure and the most basic humanitarian assistance are immediately sensitive to the question of rebuilding a peaceful society.

Intercommunal tensions held in check by autocratic regimes during the Cold War exploded once the authority of those regimes began to crumble. Ambitious, corrupt, and greedy leaders preyed on distrust and fear by manipulating economic resentments and separating people and communities along crude ethnic or religious lines that can come to feel long-standing and authentic. Similar dynamics have occurred in Eastern Europe, in Africa, and in South Asia. Understanding this process of transforming genuine distrust into deeply believed myths of ethnic division is essential for any effort to repair the fabric of a war-torn society. Hatred, once stirred, has given rise to widespread violence and led to enduring nationalism and separatism, even after the violence has subsided.

Although each context of internal conflict is unique, certain recurring problems seem common to all and can be planned for and dealt with to help overcome the hatreds and tensions that fueled the conflict in the first place:

- New patterns of refugee movement are part of the ongoing ethnic conflicts that seek to expel or return people of a given group as the very means of expressing power. After basic peace is announced, these displaced people need food, shelter, protection, and resettlement.
- The country is likely to be devastated, without sewers, water, or electricity. Its communications and transportation infrastructure needs immediate repair and reconstruction or in some instances initial construction.
- Returning peoples need assistance to rebuild homes and lives; they also often need medical care and social services.
- Food, shelter, jobs, and health care may be lacking for displaced people and for many who remained in their home areas. Houses, schools, and hospitals are likely to have been destroyed.
- All residents need an assurance of safety and the restoration of law and order.
- The restoration of self-governance based on the rule of law and international human rights principles is likely to be a commitment demanded by the international community, along with efforts to disarm and demobilize combatants.
- The economy is likely to be devastated, with facilities and resources destroyed or impaired and prospects for international investment reduced or nonexistent.

These are just some of the recurring problems encountered in every internal conflict of the past dozen years. Each of them has demanded planning and urgent action on the part of the international community. Because of what are fairly described as urgent needs to meet basic human needs, those seeking to help seldom address systematically the devastated relationships between people who fell on opposite sides of the conflict. Yet if the methods of assistance, physical restoration, and governance do not also address these relationships, the prospects for restoring lasting peace are minimal. Indeed, it may be more satisfying emotionally for former combatants and victims to maintain hostile attitudes and pursue separation than to imagine the difficulties faced by others and to take the hard initial steps toward cooperation and collaboration. If helping agencies are inattentive to these dynamics, they may make matters worse. By handing out blankets and food or roofing materials and permits for vehicles without attention to the continuing tensions across groups, helping agencies may feed perceptions of unfairness and bias and therefore exacerbate resentment and mistrust. Through inattention, agencies can miss the chance to restore civility and begin the long journey to peace. The subject of intergroup relationships deserves as much priority as the efforts to ensure housing, food, medical care, and security.

Too often, issues such as reconciliation and the punishment of war criminals are treated as separate from rebuilding infrastructure, providing food and shelter, and ensuring security and the rule of law. Typically, reconciliation and accountability are deferred until after these initial steps of reconstruction have been taken. Yet whether addressed explicitly or not, the relationships across the lines of division will be profoundly affected by these initial stages of reconstruction. It is understandable to postpone formal processes of accountability, like war crimes trials or truth and reconciliation inquiries, yet inattention to the smoldering anger and resentments risks creating circumstances for new conflict or barriers to the basic steps of reconstructing the physical environment.

The argument embodied in this book is that the ruptured relationships cannot wait and that addressing them in terms of coexistence involves a goal that is both feasible and honest. Coexistence lends itself to immediate consideration. It also reflects an honest assessment of what is both possible and necessary immediately after conflict. It remains a difficult and complex challenge to bring civility and peace to a society at war with itself. Rebuilding homes and electrical grids looks more achievable—and such efforts, if pursued thoughtfully, may even strengthen the chances for civility and peace. Yet, pursued without attention to the remaining lines of conflict, even these basic steps may exacerbate the conflict and render prospects for long-term peace more remote. One of the major points of this book is that the concept of coexistence must infuse every effort to rebuild a society after conflict, both physically and institutionally. It cannot be postponed and thus must not be separated from other steps to help after ethnic conflict.

Another major point here is that coexistence may seem too small an aspiration in the face of calls for reconciliation; yet precisely because it is more modest, coexistence may be achieved while reconciliation may remain elusive or even an insulting notion to people still reeling from the murder of their loved ones or their own torture or rape. Reconciliation is certainly a worthy ultimate goal, but as Sadako Ogata points out in the Preface, she and her colleagues concluded that first "to help refugees return to . . . devastated communities, the fabric of the society would have to be stitched back together."

Under Ogata's courageous leadership, UNHCR, together with a group of academics and practitioners represented in this book, developed a cooperative project that this group called Imagine Coexistence. We chose the word *imagine* because in the early stages of recovery from intense violence, any attempt to bring parties together takes a leap of imagination. Promoting coexistence may seem a less ambitious goal than promoting reconciliation after interethnic conflict. But to be effective, it must pervade all areas of assistance, not merely those that focus on relationships, and in that respect, it is a tall ambition indeed.

Coexistence means more than simple peaceful living side by side. As we have conceived it, coexistence involves at least some degree of interaction and cooperation across the lines of ethnic division. International and nongovernmental initiatives can facilitate interactions and cooperation, but only by working assiduously to improve postconflict conditions while simultaneously working to restore communication and to avoid misunderstandings or work them through as they arise.

It has become clear that some efforts at assistance and restoration may make matters worse. Clumsy, premature attempts at reconciliation may do more harm than good. By contrast, strategically selected projects that build on shared interests rather than dividing people along the lines of prior conflicts may promote coexistence. The authors of this book seek to foster coexistence as a vital dimension of humanitarian practice and theory after intense ethnic conflict. Initiatives in the arts, dispute resolution, sports, new technologies, education, interfaith dialogue, and business can serve as such projects. Creating occasions for people from previously warring groups to work side by side or in parallel efforts toward common goals can be effective starting points for fostering coexistence. They may provide a better setting than dialogue alone in building trusting relationships, as several chapters based on field observations illustrate. It may often be more effective to promote coexistence indirectly, not by talking about it or by directly tackling intergroup tension but by building shared experiences, addressing pressing needs in ways that involve people from different groups, or enhancing the daily quality of life in ways to enlarge hope for the future. But these efforts cannot be isolated from either dialogue or community and national politics.

This volume represents an unusual effort to marry theory and practice in fostering coexistence. Our team includes scholars from many fields, NGO practitioners, and evaluators. They focus on approaches that will begin the process of rebuilding a peaceful society with the very first brick that is laid. Several authors explore antecedents in field practice for UNHCR's Imagine Coexistence project. The first chapters grow from field efforts of international organizations and NGOs in regions marked by violent ethnic conflict, including Bosnia and Herzegovina and Rwanda, the areas chosen for pilot projects by UNHCR. Some chapters reflect direct involvement with the Imagine Coexistence project. Like that initiative, these chapters invite people to imagine the possibility of coexistence and treat imagination as the first and essential ingredient for peaceful coexistence after conflict. They illustrate the scope of actual efforts undertaken over a large range of activities.

UNHCR wisely sought to evaluate the effectiveness of coexistence efforts, and UNHCR staff involved have worked with scholars to draw up an approach that will permit field personnel to assess the relative values of various projects as coexistence becomes a counterpoint theme in building peace. This is especially challenging as there are as yet no established evaluation tools in this area. Chapters in this volume synthesize and assess the bodies of potentially relevant evaluation approaches while also providing narrative accounts and case studies of coexistence efforts.

The very importance of coexistence has made it imperative to understand some of the obstacles that are thrown up to thwart such efforts. Some of the case studies describe the actual frustrations encountered. Three chapters examine in detail how widespread "state machinery" corruption is after conflict and how barriers to economic development are heightened by the very forces that have fanned the conflict, driven by economic greed. Efforts to mainstream coexistence are further frustrated by bureaucratic rigidities in the very agencies that aim to help, because it may deviate from standard operating procedures and interfere with carefully guarded organizational prerogatives. These problems persist and must be anticipated in the design and operation of coexistence initiatives.

The concrete areas addressed in depth, such as arts, education, and economic development, are illustrative of how coexistence efforts might be mainstreamed in rebuilding a war-torn society. The positive and negative role of religion is addressed. Other areas could have been be subjected to the same approaches—mental and physical health programs, sports, building a civil police force, disarmament, and civil society generally.

The theoretical approaches reflect research into some of the emotional and social dynamics of ethnic conflict that can build conditions for coexistence: narrative, myth, and identity are addressed both theoretically and in the context of cases. The human drive for repair itself provides hope, as one chapter explores.

All the contributors to this book hope that the experiences and ideas found in this collection will open fresh avenues for experiments in coexistence that increase the chances of success. In seeking to inform practice and research, the authors also express deep gratitude to the people at UNHCR and elsewhere in the field who have undertaken or enabled the work examined here and to the United States Institute of Peace for supporting this effort. It is a project of imagination that could kindle new hope after ethnic conflict.

Acknowledgments

The editors especially wish to thank Sadako Ogata for her initial idea and her continuing of our work promoting coexistence after ethnic conflict. All of the authors of this book became vital contributors to the collective undertaking, and many of them played instrumental roles in nurturing projects at the grassroots level. We thank the United States Institute of Peace for support for the conference and development of this book. We want to thank Filippo Grandi for his belief in this work, his deft skills, and his wisdom.

Tremendous thanks go also to Laurie Corzett, Jen Keats, Tim Mc-Intire, Jeannine Pao, Suzanne Katzenstein, and Naseem Khuri for help preparing the manuscript and most of all to Lauren Guth for her tireless and inspired work from the start of the project to the final period on the last page of the book.

March 2003   Antonia Chayes
                                                                Martha Minow

Imagine Coexistence

Part One

Concepts

Chapter One

Constructing Coexistence
A Survey of Coexistence Projects in Areas of Ethnic Conflict
Aneelah Afzali and Laura Colleton

The study and practice of coexistence is as varied as it is difficult. *Co-existence* is a broad term used to describe one general concept, but in differing degrees of intensity. While the most ambitious conno-tations envision completely integrated societies in which members of different ethnic, racial, or religious groups live in harmony with one another, the minimum concept of coexistence asks only that mem-bers of such groups live together without killing each other. While this issue affects virtually every society, its implementation is both most challenging and most imperative in societies where coexistence has broken down into widespread violence. This chapter examines various projects aimed at promoting coexistence in areas troubled by mass killing, genocide, or protracted ethnic conflict.

Even cursory research reveals literally thousands of coexistence projects around the world. The examples discussed in this chapter represent variations in the field—focusing especially on efforts to engage groups in hands-on activities—that appear successful enough to be potential models for future efforts. Some of the examples are simple projects with only a single concrete means of implement-ing this goal, while others are complex, interdisciplinary programs whose interrelated project components span many aspects of po-litical, economic, and social life.

This chapter's limited scope does not purport to solve the problem of achieving coexistence; rather, it pursues the narrower goals of sampling projects from various fields, offering a perspective on current coexistence initiatives, and presenting potential models for future efforts. The challenge of this overview is to give more form and content to *coexistence* as a meaningful term in inter-ethnic and international dialogue, as this idea has not yet been widely theorized, commonly debated, or universally implemented. This analysis meets that challenge by exploring a range of activities that can be understood through the concept of coexistence.

Various Paradigms of Coexistence Projects

In this chapter, we classify coexistence projects according to their activities or goals. However, not everyone follows this approach. Some organizations sort projects by target audience or geographical area; others cover many regions, populations, or types of activities; and still others just coordinate many other projects. An organization's choice of paradigm depends primarily on its focus, rather than on the relative merits of any one system over another.

Projects that target specific population groups usually distinguish their audience along gender or age, but not ethnic, lines. Like many others, these projects appeal to and emphasize their participants' commonalities but can do so in a more focused manner. Most popular examples of this approach are women's and children's groups, although some projects target adults, immigrants, or other groups.

A different typology separates projects created by local grass-roots groups from outside initiatives sponsored by governments, intergovernmental agencies, and nongovernmental organizations (NGOs). Each type has advantages and shortcomings: grassroots efforts are more in touch with the people involved, but they may lack the resources of larger organizations; outside intervention has the additional benefit of access to a large-scale public audience, particularly through media network, but local people may view the outside intervention with skepticism and suspicion. The source of funding can often influence the character or bias of the initiative. Government-funded projects may have ties to other political issues, but NGOs may have political agendas of their own. This dichotomy may nonetheless be useful to evaluators in revealing the specific perspectives and objectives of the project organizers.

Another approach to fostering coexistence is to embrace several disciplines and sectors and sponsor projects in each. The broad scope of this method renders it more responsive to the numerous and interrelated needs in postconflict societies. Integrating projects in the various fields helps offer a full range of services to address these needs in a comprehensive fashion. Organizations that implement these multi-faceted projects include Conflict Resolution Catalysts[1] in Kosovo and The Abraham Fund[2] in the Middle East.

Although cultural sensitivity and acknowledgment of regional differences remain important factors in building coexistence, multiregional projects benefit from their diverse experiences and can contribute much toward the development of universal strategies to promote coexistence. Umbrella projects, by contrast, usually confine themselves to one location, but they enjoy the advantages of a wider perspective on the needs of the community and the achievements of the projects so far. Thus they provide valuable input to potential funding organizations, identify deficiencies, and advise on the allocation of resources.

Each of these methods has its benefits and drawbacks, and a mixture of all of them is probably the best way to pursue the larger goal of coexistence. While recognizing the validity of all of these methods, a system that classifies the many projects according to their type of activity best suits the purposes of this chapter.

Dispute Resolution and Conflict Management

In a modern international culture that values the rule of law, the influence of laws and political participation on group interaction must not be underestimated. A necessary foundation for progressing from a society of ethnic domination and mass violence to a more fair and just one is an inculcation of the local legal system with common notions of equality and the rule of law. Such an effort involves reconstructing the judicial system, fostering political participation, and providing stable governments and domestic security. It also involves the development of effective techniques for dispute resolution and conflict management. This may take many forms: truth commissions, international criminal tribunals, domestic antidiscrimination laws, affirmative action programs, or citizens' groups that promote and embody political participation by ethnic and racial minorities. As the central aim of all of these methods is to foster both the reality and perception of justice and the rule of law, an integral aspect of coexistence is the presence and visibility of just laws as well as political processes that guarantee equal and nondiscriminatory treatment of members of all ethnic groups. Toward this end, NGOs and other national and international bodies, such as the United Nations Commission on Human Rights, the European Union, and the United States House of Representatives Committee on International Relations, have endorsed various antidiscrimination laws and affirmative action programs where necessary.[3] While many of these examples refer to affirmative action projects for women, analogous projects for ethnic minorities may also enhance a political environment conducive to coexistence.

Bringing a political end to the conflict provides closure, and a sense of resolution is essential before a society as a whole can move forward. While truth commissions and criminal tribunals address this issue on a large scale, citizens' groups and local NGOs confront the task of building coexistence using methods that are accessible to all citizens. Among their central goals are fostering dispute resolution, promoting reconciliation, and encouraging political participation. Moreover, "conflict prevention NGOs and other social actors are often better placed to work small changes, on both the political and personal level, that eventually transform head-on conflict into negotiable points of disagreement."[4]

The Network of East-West Women sponsors a project in Bosnia called Women to Women Citizen Association, an all-inclusive women's organization that reaches across religious, national, social, and ethnic boundaries to explore the role women can play through empowerment and a political voice in the reconstruction of society after conflict.[5] Activities of the organization include mobilization of women through joint projects, using nonnationalist language, the rule of law, and capacity building to promote political participation, peace building, and confidence building.

Through methods such as local councils and town meetings, another project, the Community Facilitators Project in Kosovo, aims to "move the society beyond a culture of disempowerment and violence, towards a culture of peace."[6] Likewise, the World Bank's Post-Conflict Unit sponsors the Rwandan government's Community and Reintegration Project,[7] which decentralizes government in order to involve citizens in political and administrative decision making on a local level and fosters ties between the local governments and the people they represent. These various approaches all seek to create a stable and just political environment for members of all ethnic groups, thereby satisfying a precedent for enduring coexistence.

Social Services

One of the most appropriate and effective forums for coexistence projects has been the social services sector. War, armed conflict, and the accompanying insecurity and displacement often disrupt the allocation of resources by governmental and nongovernmental institutions. In such situations, civilians lack access to necessary social services and ordinary recreation. Many projects have employed avenues such as education, health care, and cultural activities to foster coexistence while meeting immediate needs or providing opportunities for recreation and social activities.

Education

Multicultural schools, with bilingual (or trilingual) education and mixed staff, bring students of different ethnic and religious backgrounds together to learn core subjects while simultaneously bridging the gap between communities separated by conflict. Such a platform is conducive to making personal contacts across ethnic and religious divides, learning about the "other," and confronting stereotypes, without ever explicitly addressing coexistence or its corollaries, peace and tolerance. Indeed, simple proximity and the opportunity for creating friendships are major factors in breaking down prejudice and reducing stereotyping. Scientific research provides support for the "contact" hypothesis underlying this approach,[8] suggesting that cooperation and common goals in classrooms can lead to cross-ethnic friendships and then to changed attitudes.[9] Organizations sponsoring mixed schools can orient their programs to deemphasize individualism and competition while promoting cooperation among students.

The Center for Jewish-Arab Education exemplifies this approach through Hand in Hand, a program that "seeks to spark revolutionary change within Israeli education and society by establishing a new educational paradigm: integrated, bilingual schools where Jewish and Arab children and their families learn and grow together."[10] A number of other projects similarly endorse this type of coexistence model in education. A YMCA preschool in Jerusalem brings together Jewish and Arab children daily for recreational purposes. They visit each other to learn to speak each other's languages, celebrate each other's birthdays and holidays, hold monthly parent meetings, and engage in joint activities that promote friendships across ethnic and religious divides.[11]

This approach has been extended to many spheres, including computer courses,[12] language courses,[13] cultural education,[14] summer camps,[15] and youth leadership training.[16] In none of these situations is coexistence addressed per se. Leaders of such projects note that "coexistence, as such, actually appears nowhere in the program. The idea is to engage [participants] side by side in other, unrelated activities such as language instruction and cross-cultural events which, by virtue of the close proximity, promote coexistence."[17] Thus these projects can be an effective impetus for educating the population and simultaneously counteracting ethnic hatred.

Health Care

Health care is a universal basic need. Given the significance of this objective, even conflicting parties may cooperate to improve the health of all groups. Members of one community, for instance, recognized a deficiency in children's health and initiated a program, Immunization for Peace (IFP), after "peasant women requested that the health conditions of their children in the war zones be improved. This request prompted the IFP program's launch . . . by bringing together government, non-government and combatant groups that shared similar concerns toward the children. . . . IFP's goal was ensuring the 'survival, development and protection of children throughout the country by providing health services and achieving peaceful cooperation and coexistence among various groups affecting child welfare in conflict areas.'"[18]

Other health care projects in areas such as Sudan, Liberia, and Central America facilitated such initiatives as distribution of vitamins, vaccinations, and campaigns to raise awareness about diseases.[19] These efforts demonstrate how projects can meet basic human needs while healing the broader effects of ethnic conflict.

Arts

"Prose, poetry and art have through the ages proved themselves to be eloquent mirrors and ambassadors for the cause of peace, and for forming bridges among nations, even conflicting ones. . . . [They] can build up ideological, emotional and psychological motivation and knowledge that can help towards a foreseeable future of reconciliation. [They] can also convey the horrors of war and the atmosphere of fear, in a most immediate, profound and crucial way."[20]

In the field of music, Oći v Oći, a Bosnian NGO, sponsors an interreligious choir composed of Serbs, Croats, Muslims, and Jews, which sings the religious music of all four groups. This and similar projects, such as orchestras[21] and even guitar lessons,[22] provide their members with rich and diverse performance experiences while helping them appreciate the other groups' musical, cultural, and religious traditions.[23] As noted by another integrated choir project, "music is an international language which should be used to build bridges between the two communities."[24]

Visual arts, particularly photography and film production, present another forum for members of different groups to work side by side with former enemies in exercising their creativity and talents. These projects create anything from symbolic statements to simple expressions of artistic taste to substantial video productions.[25] In any case, participants can explore their own interests and realize a chance to interact with members of the other group in a nonadversarial atmosphere.

Dramatic entertainment has also proved to be an effective catalyst for coexistence by serving as a vehicle to bring members of different groups together in a specific common activity to promote mutual understanding.[26] Furthermore, role playing provides a unique opportunity for identification with the "other," facilitating better understanding and empathy, and in this context, drama can be used as a tool to heal actors.[27] In all of these fields, arts can facilitate greater understanding as well as fruitful expression of both serious and lighthearted themes.

Sports

"When one is active in sports, one does not commit genocide."[28]

Sports is another area in which children (or adults) can join in an organized activity that promotes coexistence without focusing on it directly, and some in the field consider "recreation and participation in sports an urgent priority for healing physical and emotional wounds."[29] This belief has sparked many activities in many regions, from volleyball in Rwanda[30] to basketball in Bosnia and Herzegovina[31] to dance in the Middle East.[32] Other projects sponsor mixed teams or camps for soccer, tennis, baseball, karate, and rugby.[33] For children who are not drawn to art or sports, several organizations sponsor general after-school programs and youth groups,[34] whose activities range from student newspapers[35] to chess matches.[36] Contact in all of these activities helps the members of different groups interact on a day-to-day, informal basis, allowing people to personalize the "other" and realize that they are more similar than different.

Income-Generating Projects

Economic restoration is undoubtedly an essential element of stable coexistence, for gainful employment and prosperity reduce tendencies to scapegoat and also generate general satisfaction. Furthermore, cooperation in entrepreneurial ventures encourages conflicting groups to work together toward joint goals for their mutual benefit. The correlation between conflict and abject poverty underscores the importance of economic development: "Fifteen of the world's twenty poorest countries have experienced major conflict during the past decade. Virtually *every low-income country* has either undergone a major conflict or borders one or more countries in conflict" (original emphasis).[37] The rebuilding of infrastructure, economic development, and agricultural restoration can serve as methods of rehabilitating the economy while also encouraging collaboration among former enemies. The World Bank,

USAID, and the European Union promote coexistence by taking active roles in these areas.

Rebuilding Infrastructure

Apart from preventing the return of displaced persons and the resumption of normal life, ruined infrastructure symbolically reflects the scars of society, serves as a constant reminder of the conflict, creates a general obstacle to hope for the future, and delays economic revitalization. Reconstruction is thus an elementary step toward restoring an overall sense of order.[38] The United Methodist Committee on Relief in Bosnia (UMCOR/Bosnia) has implemented, among other things, programs including "shelter and school rehabilitation, community infrastructure, and water-sewer system repair. . . . As basic elements of all of UMCOR/Bosnia's programs, reconciliation and conflict resolution are . . . creatively implemented in the sustainable agriculture, community development, income generation, and shelter programs." This is accomplished by establishing construction teams in neighborhoods that "will potentially produce ethnically mixed working groups, thus providing an opportunity for rebuilding trust between individuals who identify themselves as belonging to different ethnic/religious groups."[39]

In Rwanda, the Health Water and Sanitation Project has rehabilitated and installed new water systems and housing developments. Apart from the immediate benefit of physical construction, the Health Water and Sanitation Project has had an appreciable impact on developing positive relations between community members, Tutsis and Hutus, who have articulated a commitment to continue working together.[40] Organizers contribute their success to the following: "In order for people to reconcile and start working together again, they have to be organized around activities which mean something for them, activities which take care of their needs, which deal with their priorities. That's why we have to start with people at the grassroots, to look at their priorities and work with them, so they participate in their own development."[41]

The Working Group on Housing and Community Services as Peacebuilding Tools underscores that "physical rebuilding can be a valuable handmaiden to social and psychological rebuilding in post-conflict societies" in a variety of ways. For example, it is "one of the fastest means of stimulating a wide range of economic activities, producing jobs and new enterprises" and can serve as "an immediate way to generate trust in reformed institutions of government."[42]

These many projects, even as they address rudimentary needs, can also contribute to solving the longer-term problem of rebuilding interethnic tolerance. At a more fundamental level, the mere landscape of reconstruction can portray a secure physical environment.

Economic Development

For an increasingly global economy, economic development is one of the most important features of a functioning, growing society. Projects that foster economic development in postconflict situations, then, promote the overall health of the society along with the individual well-being of the participants. Like many of the other sectors, mixed composition in these projects can reinforce the notion that cooperation, not conflict, is in everyone's best interest. The more small businesses develop, the more vibrant the economy becomes, thereby lessening the importance of interethnic competition or rivalries. Although economic security does not guarantee peaceful coexistence, it can nonetheless reduce the tension and serve as a disincentive to engaging in armed conflict, which impedes economic growth and development. Projects in this area promote economic development through loans for small businesses, assistance in setting up such businesses, and training in business skills.[43]

One project, the Income Generation Program, sponsored by UMCOR/Bosnia, provides "support to local economies through small loans and business training," which have been used to establish businesses in "tailoring, pasta making, carpentry, printing, beekeeping, and fish farms."[44] Another example of an economic assistance project is the Center for Jewish-Arab Economic Development. This program aims to provide entrepreneurial training and management skills to Israeli Arab and Jewish professionals and to "create investment and networking opportunities, as well as facilitate joint ventures between Israeli Arabs and Jews."[45]

On a larger scale, the World Bank has facilitated economic revival in many areas of the world. One project in the Balkans described its progress in the following terms: "The reconstruction effort—including targeted programs to jump-start economic activity—has also fueled high growth rates and brought a tangible re-start of economic activity. The achievements in this area are moderated, however, by the fact that recovery is fragile. Unemployment remains high [and] economic growth continues to be linked primarily to reconstruction. . . ."[46] Clearly much remains to be done, but projects such as this pave the way to economic recovery.

Agriculture

Agriculture, a crucial means of sustenance in many postconflict areas, can also be used to foster coexistence. One project whose name appropriately captures the dual objectives in this domain is Cultivating Coexistence, supported by the Abraham Fund.[47] Other projects similarly offer opportunities for populations in postconflict regions to achieve coexistence by working together to provide agricultural products for the community. For example, UMCOR/Bosnia "provides agribusiness seminars and training programs to small farmers . . . [and] loans to local farmers and individuals who want to start up or expand an agribusiness" through the Technical Assistance Project and the Agricultural Credit Project.[48]

These kinds of efforts can help restore the society as a whole by initiating progress toward self-sustainability. Because generating income is a staple of modern growth and progress, projects that promote small business and agriculture are elementary in a society's recovery from conflict. Together with physical reconstruction, economic development constitutes an essential aspect of genuine coexistence.

Reconciliation and Dealing with Trauma

Interethnic violence traumatizes the population and precipitates inevitable psychological consequences. Programs that address this trauma and initiate coexistence education in postconflict societies reflect a worthy and well-placed effort to remedy these effects and to establish a more lasting peace among the parties. Several different disciplines, including psychiatry and psychology, religion, and the arts, can be useful in finding various ways to begin the healing process, either directly or indirectly.

Some direct attempts to deal with collective trauma involve the individuals who witnessed or even participated in the ethnic violence. Many projects undertake the task of bringing people together from both sides to address the effects of the violence through mixed-group encounters. These may take the form of after-school programs,[49] youth groups, or discussion groups for adults.[50] Sharing their experiences of the conflict and acknowledging their own wrongdoing can lead people on both sides of the ethnic divide to appreciate the other's suffering, identify their common plight, and recognize the crucial importance of postconflict coexistence.[51] This narrative approach to healing permits victims and witnesses to understand the damage the conflict caused and to offer sympathy and comfort to one another.

Although religion has often been cited as a cause of interethnic conflict, it can be part of the solution as well as the problem. The Abraham Fund sponsors two projects related to religion and coexistence. In Yakar's Beit-Midrash-Madrasa Curriculum Implementation Project, Jewish and Muslim teachers develop and implement a coexistence curriculum on how to convey lessons about the shared values of Judaism and Islam.[52] The other project, Stepping Stone to Peace: Religious Coexistence, utilizes role playing, shared holiday celebrations, and visits to religious sites and institutions to encourage teenagers to tolerate other religious viewpoints.[53] Still, given the divisive potential of religion, project creators and funders may be understandably reluctant to embrace such an idea.

Other projects aimed at promoting peace approach the task of initiating communal healing by bringing their message to a more general audience, without direct participation from victims or wrongdoers.[54] As mentioned earlier, art can be a particularly expressive way of communicating one's feelings following the shock and suffering of interethnic violence. One group notes: "Art can help the individual in various ways: as a mirror of his [or her] own feelings, thoughts and desires, as well as those of [the] society, as a catalyst of self-clarification and renewed points of view, and in realizing past and present limitations to peaceful coexistence."[55]

More indirect efforts to foster tolerance and peace include teacher training and school courses on coexistence. While the teachers and students involved may or may not have been directly affected by past violence, programs emphasizing the importance of co-existence aim to create a general culture that is more tolerant and consequently less prone to ethnic violence. One such project is Education for Peace and Coexistence, a two-semester course that studies the various "historical, cultural, sociological, psychological, educational and didactic aspects of coexistence. . . . [It] aims to teach—and teach educators how to teach—pluralism, tolerance, humanism, and democracy, and to further understanding, respect and peace. . . ."[56] In sum, coexistence education, in all its forms, fulfills a requisite for changing intergroup relations and increasing tolerance.[57]

Conclusion

The overview in this chapter highlights creative ways to promote coexistence, directly or indirectly, in different fields. Although not all methods will fit all contexts, some of these ideas can be applied to each society facing postconflict reconstruction. Such projects generate economic, social, and cultural benefits and provide a powerful impetus for constructing coexistence. Unfortunately, this survey also reveals the inherent difficulty of any effort to reduce intolerance and deep-seated hatred and to improve relations between groups recently embroiled in ethnic conflict.

Projects such as these will be in vain if they neglect underlying causes of interethnic conflict. More realistic and more promising efforts would target the roots of the problems: political wrongs and inequitable distribution of resources. Another essential element is time—time to implement these changes and time to heal the scars from the wounds of these injustices. As top-down efforts resolve the fundamental political and legal concerns, bottom-up efforts can provide vital reinforcement and actualization of coexistence on a more immediate and more personal level.

The descriptions of coexistence projects offered here do not supply complete normative answers, but they may, by way of an overview of current programs, propose a framework for future initiatives and help define its contours. Despite its shortcomings and limitations, this study provides a starting point for deeper analyses, such as those in subsequent chapters of this book, and lays a foundation for future work to realize the promise of coexistence.

Notes

1. See Conflict Resolutions Catalysts, "The People Connection Project" [http://www.crcvt.org/connection.html]; B. Hemmer, "Bottom-Up Peacebuilding in Bosnia," Spring 1997 [http://www.crcvt.org/parcnews.html]; Conflict Resolution Catalysts, "The Community Facilitators Project in Kosovo" [http://www.crcvt.org/community.html].

2. Abraham Fund and Ahavat Hagalil, "*Shchenim* (Neighbors) and Coexistence" [http://www.abrahamfund.org].

3. See United Nations Commission on Human Rights, "Report of the United Nations High Commissioner for Human Rights and Follow-Up to the World Conference on Human Rights," Dec. 28, 1999 [http://www.unhchr.ch/huridocda/huridoca.nsf/(Symbol)/E.CN.4.2000.12.En?OpenDocument]; "International Convention on the Elimination of All Forms of Racial Discrimination," Sept. 3, 1981, art. 2, 1249 UNTS 20378. [http://www.unhchr.ch/html/menu3/b/d_icerd.htm]; F. Cameron, "EU Law and Policy Overview: International Conflict Resolution: Challenges and Strategies," June 2000 [http://www.eurunion.org/legislat/Defense/FCSpeechConfPrev.htm]; Subcommittee on International Operations and Human Rights, "Human Rights and the Peace Process in Northern Ireland," 105th Cong., Oct. 9, 1997 [http://commdocs.house.gov/committees/intlrel/hfa45500.000/hfa455000.htm]; Flamme African Sisters Online [http://www.flamme.org/documents/afrngorep.html].

4. P. van Tongeren, "Exploring the Local Capacity for Peace: The Role of NGOs," Mar.-Apr. 1998 [http://www.euforic.org/courier/168e_ton.htm.

5. Network of East-West Women, "Women to Women Citizen Association" [http://www.neww.org/countries/Bosnia/women_to_women.htm].

6. Conflict Resolution Catalysts, "Community Facilitators Project."

7. See World Bank Group. "Building Trust to Rebuild Rwanda: World Bank Supports Community Reintegration and Development," News Release no. 99/2003/AFR, Dec. 1, 1998 [http://www.worldbank.org/html/extdr/extme/2003.htm].

8. See G. Allport, *The Nature of Prejudice* (Boston: Beacon Press, 1954); see also R. Ben-Ari and Y. Amir, "Contact Between Arab and Jewish Youth in Israel: Reality and Potential," in M. Hewstone and R. Brown (eds.), *Contact and Conflict in Intergroup Encounters* (New York: Oxford University Press, 1986); M. B. Brewer and N. Miller, *Groups in Contact: The Psychology of Desegregation* (Orlando, Fla.: Academic Press, 1984); and W. G. Stephan and C. W. Stephan, *Intergroup Relations* (Boulder, Colo.: Westview Press, 1996).

9. See, for example, R. Slavin, "Enhancing Intergroup Relations in Schools: Cooperative Learning and Other Strategies," in W. D. Hawley and A. W. Jackson (eds.), *Toward a Common Destiny: Improving Race Relations in America* (San Francisco: Jossey-Bass, 1995); J. F. Dovidio, G. Maruyama, and M. G. Alexander, "A Social Psychology of National and International Group Relations," *Journal of Social Issues,* 1998, *54,* 831–846; R. E. Slavin and R. Cooper, "Improving Intergroup Relations: Lessons Learned From Cooperative Learning Programs," *Journal of Social Issues,* Winter 1999, *55*(4), 647–663 (providing an

overview of research and evaluation of cooperative learning approach); and Y. Amir, "The Role of Intergroup Contact in Change of Prejudice and Ethnic Relations," in P. Katz (ed.), *Towards the Elimination of Racism* (New York: Pergamon, 1976). But see also R. Halabi and N. Sonnenschein, "School for Peace, *Neve Shalom/Wahat al Salam,*" in *Improving Arab-Jewish Relations in Israel: Theory and Practice in Coexistence Program* (proposed special issue of the *Journal of Social Issues* prepared by Rachel Hertz-Lazarowitz, Tamar Zelniker, Walter G. Stephan, and Cookie White Stephan), provided by Walter G. Stephan through electronic communication, Mar. 13, 2001 (indicating that the contact hypothesis in the Jewish-Arab context may simply perpetuate the status quo. "At the School for Peace . . . there was frustration and dissatisfaction with this model on the part of participants and facilitators alike, especially the Arabs. . . . The model was perceived as artificial and not authentic and as representing the interests of the Jewish participants" [Halabi and Sonnenschein, personal communication with Walter G. Stephan, Mar. 13, 2001]).

10. Center for Jewish-Arab Education in Israel, "The Hand in Hand Mission" [http://www.handinhand12.org/TheCente/TheCente.html].

11. See Abraham Fund and YMCA International [http://www.abrahamfund. org/?oid=708]. See also Shemesh: The Organization for Jewish-Arab Friendship and Coexistence in the Galilee. See either of the following Web sites for a description of the Shemesh project: http:/www.usisrael.org/jsource/bridges/ three.html; http://www.abrahamfund.org/?oid=692.

12. See, for example, integrated computer courses offered by the Leo Baeck Education Center, sponsored by Building Bridges, at http://www.usisrael. org/jsource/bridges/three.html, pages 7 and 8. The Shemesh project, also sponsored by Building Bridges and described on pages 14 through 16 of the same Web site, offers computer courses as well (listed as part of "Chugim" on page 15).

13. See, for example, Abraham Fund and Beit Shmuel, "Language Training Program" (a component of the Jewish-Arab Coexistence Project) [http://www. usisrael.org/jsource.bridges/three.html]. ("The objectives of the classes are far broader than 'mere' language acquisition. Also important—and meant to be transmitted through the language courses—is the understanding of another ethnic group's religious, historical, cultural and social foundations. . . . The study of language can be used as a bridge for coexistence" (pp. 3, 4).

14. See, for example, Abraham Fund and Association of Italian Jews, "Art and Culture for Coexistence" [http://www.abrahamfund.org].

15. See, for example, Shemesh, "Good Neighbors' Summer Camp," p. 15 of the Building Bridges Web site, and the Leo Baeck Education Center summer camp, pp. 1 and 8, also on the Building Bridges Web site: [http://www. usisrael.org/jsource/bridges/three.html].

16. Shemesh, "Youth Leadership Training" [http://www.usisrael.org/jsource/ bridges/three.html], p. 15.

17. Jewish-Arab Coexistence Project, quotation on page 4 of the Building Bridges Web site [http://www.usisrael.org/jsource/bridges/three.html].

18. R. A. Shankar, "Analyzing Health Initiatives as Bridges Towards Peace During

Complex Humanitarian Emergencies and the Roles of Actors and Economic Aid in Making These Bridges Sustainable," 1998 [http://www.who.int/disasters/hbp/Thesis.pdf].

19. Shankar, "Analyzing Health Initiatives."
20. "Seeking Arab-Israeli Peacemaking and Reconciliation Through Culture" [http://listserv.ac.il/~ada/h_seek.html].
21. See music workshops offered by the House of Arts, Emek Yizrael, pictured and described at http://www.abrahamfund.org/?oid=1310.
22. See Hemmer, "Bottom-Up Peacebuilding in Bosnia."
23. See Abraham Fund and Israel Association of Community Centers, "Music as a Language to Promote Coexistence" referenced in a Shabbat Sermon by Rabbi Mitchell Wohlberg at Parshat Bereishit on October 28, 2000, available at the Beth Tfiloh Web site [http://www.btfiloh.org/mwohlberg10282000.htm].
24. See the Building Bridges Web site [http://www.usisrael.org/jsource/bridges/three.html], p. 16.
25. See, for example, Abraham Fund and Rosh Pina Mainstreaming Network, "In the Lens of the Camera" [http://www.abrahamfund.org/?oid=1255]; Leo Baeck Education Center, "Film for Thought" [http://www.usisrael.org/jsource/bridges/three.html#leo]; Abraham Fund and Barrer Arts Center, "Through Art We Communicate" [http://www.abrahamfund.org/?oid=680]; Abraham Fund and Jerusalem Association of Community Councils and Centers, "Through the Camera" referenced in a Shabbat Sermon by Rabbi Mitchell Wohlberg at Parshat Bereishit on October 28, 2000, available at the Beth Tfiloh Web site [http://www.btfiloh.org/mwohlberg10282000.htm].
26. Abraham Fund and Daliat el Carmel Community Center, "Multicultural Drama" [http://www.abrahamfund.org/oid?=725].
27. See, for example, Abraham Fund and Peace Child Israel, "Dramatic Cooperation" [http://www.abrahamfund.org/html/grants%20booklet.pdf].
28. Statement by Christine Nukanurangira, participant in a Dutch-sponsored volleyball-training project in Rwanda), in European Centre for Conflict Prevention, "Volleyball as Response to Rwanda's Trauma" [http://www.xs4all.nl/~conflic1/pbp/8/4_volley.htm].
29. War Child Projects, "Let Us Play: Peace and Reconciliation Through Sports" [http://www.warchild.org/projects/letsplay.html].
30. See European Centre for Conflict Prevention, "Volleyball . . ."
31. See War Child Projects, "Let Us Play."
32. See Abraham Fund and Ramle Community Center, "Arab-Jewish Dance Troupe" [http://www.salam-shalom.net/dance-troupe.html].
33. See, for example, Interns for Peace, "Programs/Projects" [http://www.internsforpeace.org/ifpprog.htm]; Abraham Fund and Organization for the Support of Sport, "Tennis, 2000" referenced in a Shabbat Sermon by Rabbi Mitchell Wohlberg at Parshat Bereishit on October 28, 2000, available at the Beth Tfiloh Web site [http://www.btfiloh.org/mwohlberg10282000.htm]; Abraham Fund and Jewish-Arab Community Association, "Community Building" referenced in a Shabbat Sermon by Rabbi Mitchell Wohlberg at Parshat Bereishit on October 28, 2000, available at the Beth Tfiloh Web site [http://www.btfiloh.org/mwohlberg10282000.htm].

34. See, for example, Abraham Fund and Friendship's Way, "The Neighborhood Home" [http://www.usisrael.org/jsource/bridges/three/html], pp. 1 and 25; United Methodist Committee on Relief in Bosnia, "Community Development: Youth House Project" [http://gbgm-umc.org/umcor/ngo/bosnia. cfm].

35. See Shemesh, [http://www.shemesh.org].

36. See Conflict Resolution Catalysts, "Community Facilitators Project" [http:// www.crcvt.org/community.html].

37. World Bank Group, "Supporting Peace: The World Bank's Role in Post-Conflict Reconstruction" [http://www.worldbank.org/html/extdr/backgrd/ ibrd/peace.htm]. *Note:* Web site no longer active; hard copy on file with authors.

38. The World Bank is heavily involved in postconflict reconstruction in many areas of the world, including Bosnia-Herzegovina, the West Bank and Gaza, Haiti, and Africa.

39. General Board of Global Ministries, United Methodist Committee on Relief in Bosnia, "Shelter Reconstruction" [http://gbgm-umc.org/umcor/ngo/ bosnia.cfm].

40. See S. Ann, "Rwandan Women with Hope," *Focus,* Dec. 1997, pp. 12–15. [http://www.ausaid.gov.au/publications/focus/focuspdfs/1297/129712–15. pdf].

41. John Muyenzi, Oxfam program officer, in Ann, "Rwandan Women with Hope," p. 15.

42. Canadian Peacebuilding Coordinating Committee, "Working Group on Housing and Community Services as Peacebuilding Tools" [http://www. cpcc.ottawa.on.ca/wghousing-e.htm].

43. See, for example, United Methodist Committee on Relief in Bosnia, "Income Generation" [http://gbgm-umc.org/umcor/ngo/bosnia.cfm]; Center for Jewish-Arab Economic Development, "About CJAED" [http://www. cjaed.org.il].

44. See United Methodist Committee, "Income Generation."

45. Center for Jewish-Arab Economic Development, "About CJAED" [http://www. cjaed.org.il/about.html].

46. World Bank Group, "Lessons for Rebuilding Southeast Europe: The Bosnia and Herzegovina Experience" [http://wbln0018.worldbank.org/eca/eca. ns.35b06f845e98525688f007f1e92?OpenDocument].

47. Abraham Fund and Yoav, "Cultivating Coexistence" [http://www.abraham-fund.org/?oid=718].

48. General Board of Global Ministries, United Methodist Committee, "Agri-culture."

49. For a more detailed description of after-school programs, see the section sub-headed "Sports" earlier in this chapter.

50. See, for example, Conflict Resolution Catalysts, "People Connection Project"; Beit Hagefen, "Arab/Jewish Encounters: Meetings" [http://www.haifa.gov.il/ beit-hagefen/meetings.html]; American-Israeli Cooperative Enterprise, "Building Bridges: The Experiential Approach" [http://www.usisrael.org/ jsource/bridges/three.html].

51. See L. A. Pearlman and E. Staub, "Understanding Basic Human Needs" [http://www-unix.oit.umass.edu/%7egubin/rwanda/lec1.htm].
52. See the Beit Midrash-Madrasa Curriculum Implementation Project, available at http://www.abrahamfund.org/?oid=693.
53. Abraham Fund and Defense for Children International—Israel, "Stepping Stone to Peace: Religious Coexistence" [http://www.abrahamfund.org]. *Note:* no longer available on-line; hard copy on file with authors.
54. This is not to say that those making these efforts, be they organizations or schools or individuals, may not be victims or wrongdoers themselves, but they need not be.
55. "Seeking Arab-Israeli Peacemaking and Reconciliation Through Culture" [http://tx.technion.ac.il/~ada/h_seek.html].
56. Janusz Korczak Educational Center for Peace and Coexistence, "Education for Peace and Coexistence" [http://www.usisrael.org/jsource/bridges/three. html]. Sponsored by David Yellin Teachers College.
57. Daniel Bar-Tal, professor of psychology in the School of Education, Tel Aviv University, argues that "in case of intractable intergroup conflict, education for co-existence is a necessary, but not sufficient factor for changing intergroup relations." D. Bar-Tal, "The Nature, the Reasons, and the Effectiveness of Education for Coexistence," in *Improving Arab-Jewish Relations in Israel: Theory and Practice in Coexistence Programs* (proposed special issue of the *Journal of Social Issues* prepared by Rachel Hertz-Lazarowitz, Tamar Zelniker, Walter G. Stephan, and Cookie White Stephan), provided by Walter G. Stephan through electronic communication, Mar. 13, 2001.

Chapter Two

The Process Toward Reconciliation

Carlos E. Sluzki

The winding pathway "between vengeance and forgiveness,"[1] between confrontational zero-sum and collaborative non-zero-sum games,[2] may be paved with good intentions but is filled with countless obstacles.

To start with, that process of transformation is frustratingly slow, moving at a pace that may collide against the pressing hopes and needs of the parties involved, thereby increasing the chances of accusations of ill will toward the other party and risking a collapse of the process. In fact, studies of the real-time estimate of postwar socioeconomic recovery indicate that it "typically requires at least two decades of sustained effort."[3] Second, while the threat of renewed conflict may loom on and off at different moments, its progress is extremely unstable. The evolution of a conflict is extremely sensitive to, if not contingent upon, multiple variables. They may be relational, stemming from changes in the "spiral of reciprocal perspectives"[4] of the parties in terms of each one's evolving perception of the other. The variables may be derived from contextual phenomena, suprarelational or extrarelational factors, be they "acts of God" such as a drought in the region or an economic collapse of a potential ally (or, in a couple in conflict, a disease in one of their children).[5] And they may depend on the internal vicissitudes of the parties, such as the need of a given government to galvanize public opinion so as to distract the population from internal foibles. An example of this is the out-of-the-blue engineering of the ill-fated

1982 Falkland Wars by the military junta in power in Argentina, whose popularity waned as the country's economy disintegrated. Third, the complex nature of human and political systems ensures that there will be some specific areas or sectors in which change, evolution, and progress are more viable than in others, with greater or fewer opportunities for shifts from adversarial to collaborative activities. For instance, neighboring countries in conflict may be able to develop some minimal cooperation in the agricultural activities but not in an industrial sector (and a couple in conflict may be able to share a civilized conversation during dinner but not to engage in a tender sexual encounter—or vice versa).

From Confrontation to Integration: A Sequence of Stages

A fourth and perhaps less discussed, if not unrecognized, variable is the fact that the process from open conflict to constructive collaboration is not a smooth continuum but rather is characterized by a set of discrete intermediary stepping stones, stages, or stations. These stages constitute an evolutionary progression or sequencing (although, as noted, at any given moment in any complex scenario, different stages may be expressed). Each stage depicts or is characteristic of a specific period of a given relationship in the process and therefore gauges progress in the process of change. It should also be highlighted that several intermediary steps in the evolutionary sequence may in fact become desirable goals within the process or even the end of the line.

The specific traits that characterize each of these configurations are, of course, contingent upon the nature of the relationship being considered (are we talking about a marital couple in conflict, a management-labor dispute, an interethnic escalation, or two countries at war?). They are also contingent upon the nature of the conflict (is it about reciprocal responsibilities, about control of a territory, about saving face, about finances?), as well as on countless variables of context, be they cultural or circumstantial.

When analyzing the vicissitudes of this pathway, the transition between any two of these steps appears sometimes seamless and sometimes agonizingly complex. A poignant example of this assertion can be found in the detailed insider's account of the Irish "Good Friday Agreement" that George Mitchell helped forge.[6]

Moreover, two steps forward are sometimes followed by one or more steps back. However, the mere fact that progression toward constructive collaboration takes place one step at a time and in a predictable order or sequence indicates that we are in the presence of a normative process.

My presentation here aims at specifying the sequence of familiar but discrete steps or stances that characterize the long pathway from one extreme, open conflict, to the other extreme, full integration, and to explore some of the most salient traits of each of these stages. The sequential elements of this evolutionary model may provide a framework for the design of interventions and evaluation processes while exposing the strong possibility that bypassing some of these steps in the planning and implementation of peace and reconciliation processes decreases the probability of their success (see Table 2.1).

Conflict

This stage entails an active involvement in hostilities intending to damage the other party's life, livelihood, or well-being. Each party assumes and attributes ill intent to any act of the other. The basic tenets to establish or maintain a dialogue are broken, and communication is sometimes tentatively achieved only through the

Table 2.1. The Process Toward Reconciliation.

Stage	Narrative	Emotion
Conflict	"Hostility is the only option."	Hostility, contempt, elation
Coexistence	"We are ready for hostile acts when needed."	Resentment, anger, mistrust
Collaboration	"Hostilities are a fall-back option."	Ambivalence
Cooperation	"Hostilities would be a major disadvantage."	Cautious empathy
Interdependence	"We need each other."	Acceptance of past, cautious trust
Integration	"We are one."	Solidarity, friendly trust

good offices of "neutral" third parties. The narrative that dominates conversations within each group, as well as among each group's spokespersons or controlled media, could be summarized in the statement "Hostility is the only option." The participants' emotions include hostility, contempt for the opponent, and elation in the empowerment of the confrontation. The rules of engagement in this stage are unambiguously those of a zero-sum game: "Your loss is my gain."

Coexistence

This stage is marked by the ability of the parties to coexist without open acts of violence. Sometimes they live side by side as two neighboring countries or two neighboring families; sometimes they live at a distance, such as a wife who takes refuge in a shelter after an act of physical abuse by her husband. This stage remains dominated by behaviors that denote an assumption of ill intent behind any act by the other. An example of these assumptions in action could be seen during the June 2002 escalation and deescalation phases of the confrontation between India and Pakistan over Kashmir, during which negative interpretations and open mistrust was expressed about what could otherwise be seen as conciliatory gestures displayed by both parties. The enactment of hostility is curtailed only by the presence of a real or virtual "neutral zone," strongly pressured, patrolled, or controlled by a powerful independent party (such as U.S. diplomacy, active physical separation, or the presence of a third family member in the case of marital conflicts with potential for violence.)[7] The dominant narratives in this stage are variations of the motto "We are ready for hostile acts when needed." The dominant emotions that sustain and are sustained by this stage are resentment—a sentiment characterized by rumination on past victimizations and old and new grudges; anger—kept active by those ruminations and at times by the media; and mistrust of the other party. The rules of engagement between the parties still follow the principles of zero-sum games.

Collaboration

While assumptions of ill intent still loom as a background, the scenario changes when some activities in common are initiated, joint projects such as sharecropping of neighboring boundary lands, rebuilding a bridge, reestablishing a railroad across boundary lines, or even sharing a river where women from the two parties wash clothes. The external regulatory presence of the third party becomes less visible, and its role may become one of witness or verifier of the process and occasionally acting as a cybernetic governor to minimize the deviations from the parameters of a given agreement. The cautionary banner that underlies the narratives that dominate this stage reads "Hostilities are a fall-back option," and a calmer ambivalence begins to reduce the clouds of mistrust as a dominant emotion. Some rules characteristic of non-zero-sum games can begin to be noticed in the processes between the parties, as this is a stage in which the first inklings of a civil society appear (or reappear).

Cooperation

The planning of certain activities in common (cooperation), such as designing a dam to facilitate irrigation in both territories, is accompanied by a shift in the dominant assumption toward an attribution of neutral intent ("They may not be our friends, but they aren't acting like our foes. The interests they are pursuing fit our own"). The presence of the external buffer is no longer necessary, and those forces are experienced as an almost inconvenient reminder of past hostilities. At this stage, emergency relief agencies such as the United Nations High Commissioner for Refugees (UNHCR) and the World Food Programme (WFP) complete their withdrawal from the field, being replaced by self-reliance. In fact, the motto underlying narratives at this stage seems to evolve toward "Hostilities would be a major disadvantage . . . for both of us. Peace is desirable." The relational field moves toward the enactment of non-zero-sum rules of partnership, and the dominant emotions appear to shift away from ambivalence toward the possibility of a cautious empathy.

Interdependence

In this stage, the materialization of the common goals overshadow the remnants of assumptions of ill intent as the parties engage in joint planning and actions toward the collective good. The dominant narratives display a consensus that "We need each other. Hostility would be foolish," and the constructive nature of the relationship is carefully maintained and signaled again and again in an active display of non-zero-sum ritual reminders. The dominant emotions may include acceptance of the past and even forgiveness for prior misdeeds, with cautious trust and open attachment.

Integration

At this end of the spectrum, all relational moves are based on an implicit assumption of good intent attributed to any act of the other, as well as an active involvement in planning and actions toward the common good (full non-zero sum). Furthermore, conflict management strategies and systems are built into the relational infrastructure, so as problems arise, and they do, they are reformulated, attributing positive intent to the other party. Moreover, each party supports the other's growth. Narratives are inspired by the banner "We are one. Hostilities do not even enter into consideration." The dominant emotions are solidarity, friendly trust, and perhaps even love. Achieving this step, which occurs occasionally in interpersonal relations and much more rarely in other large systems, entails a second-order (qualitative) change in the relationship.

Most conflictive relations can be predicted to move through these six configurations. The process can stagnate at any stage, as well as deteriorate toward more conflictive stages if not enticed in the opposite direction by circumstances, best interests, or leadership. Equally important, it is *sequential:* stages tend not to be skipped; one follows the other, and each contains experiences that when consolidated constitute the seed of the next one. However, the evolution from one evolutionary stage to the next is hard; slippage is frequent and may lead to a tumbling back to a previous stage. In addition, the reward for active efforts toward reaching the "top" appears to be, as in any mountain climbing during the ascent, far away. And what is more disheartening to many participants, a long-range view is not possible until reaching the vicinities of the final summit.

Movement and Equilibrium

Each stage has not only distinctive traits but also its own inertia. Complex systems do not evolve linearly but by stages, alternating qualitative changes with unsteady but stable stages (what von

Foerster called the *eigenvalues* of a system),[8] with complex processes that tend to keep the system operating within specific thresholds. However, no unstable-but-steady system remains indefinitely in any given stage. In fact, the unstable nature of any complex processes may lead in the long run to increasing (quantitative) oscillations, which may override their established threshold. When that happens, fitting Gladwell's notion of "tipping points,"[9] the whole system shifts to a new and qualitatively different level of equilibrium, where again the system coalesces . . . until new oscillations destabilize it. This evolutionary process of fluctuations that at a given moment pass a threshold after which new baselines—new values, new rules of the game—are established has been described as characteristic of all complex systems in unstable equilibrium.[10]

The value of understanding these processes, from open conflict to reconciliation, from a systemic perspective, and following an optic of unstable steady states, lies in the possibility of assuming that qualitative changes occur following unstable processes of any given stage. Further, seeds of the next stage can be sown at any given stage but cannot be imposed, as complex systems follow these quantitative-qualitative dynamics. At the same time, random (in the sense of unpredictable) contextual variables introduce multiple perturbations that affect the future processes and actions of the system, reducing the precision in timetables for these evolutionary changes.

Confrontation and Integration as Attractors

Each end of the proposed sequence operates as a "powerful attractor," in that processes near that sphere of influence tend to be pulled in its direction. And as stated earlier, although intermediary stages can acquire stability through consistent practices, they are comparatively unstable. In addition, the climb toward interdependence is time-consuming, and the parties frequently experience the process as extremely slow, with a low level of gratification, unlike the moves toward conflict, which are potentially quicker and therefore tempting in their potential for immediate gratification. This explains the risk of short circuits in the evolutionary process and the danger of the dreaded "slippery slope."

At one end of the spectrum, the fumes of conflict have an intoxicating effect ("I love the smell of napalm in the morning. It smells like . . . victory!").[11] As William Ury states, "War is contagious."[12] In fact, in the beginning, conflict

- Reaffirms the self ("They see us; therefore we exist")
- Expands the self (generates a sense of power and righteousness)
- Creates affiliation (fosters a sense of togetherness: "*Il fascio*")
- Gives meaning to life (creates a story of optimism and protagonism)
- Creates hope (opens an alternative future)
- Fosters business (generates microeconomies, black markets, bartering, reconstruction)

However, in the long run, if persistent, it has a toxic effect ("The horror! The horror!")[13] as it exhausts resources and fosters hopelessness, an experience that unravels the prior process. As Mitchell observed, in reference to Irish public opinion after years of protracted conflict, "The people long for peace. They are sick of war, weary of anxiety and fear. They still have differences, but they want to settle them through democratic dialogue."[14]

In turn, the pole of integration attracts, for it enhances

- Predictability and prospection (planning can be done with some degree of certainty)
- Civility (the rules of interpersonal and institutional relations are guaranteed by collectively enacted behaviors and collectively agreed-upon enforcement agencies)
- Personal and relational well-being (in contrast with the exhausting stress stemming from violence)

Some Final Comments on Narratives

As briefly pointed out, each stage is characterized by a set of narratives, by stories that people tell about the situation (the "good guys" and "bad guys," the protagonists and deuteragonists, the parties with noble and ignoble intentions, the ultimate motivations and hidden intents of the others, and so forth). And each set of stories will tend to reconstitute (that is, to solidify and anchor) their respective stage. Thus the whole process toward reconciliation entails, and may even be centrally focused in, a progressive shift of dominant narratives, from stories of victimization to stories of evolution and empowerment. This process of shifting dominant narratives (and therefore facilitating changes toward more developed stages) is difficult because dominant stories get entrenched over time, anchored in (and anchoring) the individual and collective identity. That is why the passage between stages toward constructive collaboration becomes more viable when changes are simultaneously enacted and anchored by activities at multiple levels, such as the economics, education, sports, and artistic domains that contribute (unequally) to building a civil society.

Subsequent steps in the development of this model may include further specifying the traits ("symptoms") that characterize each stage, in order to be able to identify ("diagnose") more accurately the locus of the evolutionary stalemate in different situations of malaise or conflict. For the time being, we will have to rely on intuition in order to pinpoint, with some degree of approximation, the specific stage in which a given process may be stuck.

One valuable and perhaps key task of a mediator, facilitator, or consultant consists in destabilizing and transforming the story brought forth by the parties in favor of a "better" one and facilitating its consensual adoption by all parties. An example of a desirable shift in the transformations of stories is the passage from a passive to an active stance (from people as powerless recipients of acts by others toward people as agents of change). However—and this is the reason why it is highlighted here—this shift has the potential of becoming a double-edged sword, as the early incorporation of agency (that is, of people as active protagonists in their own story) into a narrative previously characterized by passive victimization may push the participants toward violent revenge rather than toward constructive collaboration. (In clinical psychiatry, if the physical passivity that accompanies depression is neutralized with medications before the patient's mood improves, the risk of suicide increases!)

Embedded in this discussion lies another important issue: stories live in the interpersonal space (in addition to the iconic space of symbols and rituals). Hence the minimal unit of analysis should not be the individual but the "social network" as a key interpersonal space of daily life—including but not limited to the family, affinity groups, community organizations, and interest-related aggregates—where old and new stories circulate and are reconstituted and then either reconfirmed and anchored or changed. Needless to say, many highly structured networks (such as armies, political parties, and religious groups) may be invested in self-sustaining narratives that may push toward conflict, and that may be difficult to challenge because of the dense and homogeneous nature of the collective.

"Narratives," it may be clear by now, are both the dominant stories and the daily practices that intertwine and support each other, both within each party in a conflict and between parties, in the vicious cycle of conflict as well as in the virtuous cycle toward reconciliation. Hence the difficult task of destabilizing the rather entrenched dominant stories of the parties in conflict may start by challenging and changing those practices that are rooted in the dominant conflict-sustaining narratives and contribute to further anchor them: a project done in common may make possible the development of stories of commonality, and vice versa. In fact, attempting to determine a sequential order in a shift in stories and in action may be more a need of the observer than a pragmatic reality: they are two sides of the same process of mediation, where conflict-based narratives as well as daily practices are destabilized and transformed, in an effort to nudge the conflict system toward constructive coexistence.

It is hoped that the map introduced here will provide a useful orientation for planning this complex journey.

Notes

1. M. Minow, *Between Vengeance and Forgiveness: Facing History After Genocide and Mass Violence* (Boston: Beacon Press, 1998).
2. R. Axelrod, *The Evolution of Cooperation* (New York: Basic Books, 1984).
3. A. Kreimer, P. Collier, C. Scott, and M. Arnold, *Uganda: Post-Conflict Reconstruction* (Washington, D.C.: World Bank, 2000), p. 67.
4. R. D. Laing, H. Phillipson, and A. R. Lee, *Interpersonal Perception: A Theory and a Method of Research* (London: Tavistock, 1966).
5. As conflict scenarios range from the interpersonal to the intercontinental, from relations between individual people to relations between blocs of nations, examples will be provided that sometimes refer to couples (such as a marriage on the rocks) and sometimes to socioeconomic and ethnopolitical entities (such as countries in dispute or disputes within countries).
6. G. J. Mitchell, *Making Peace* (Berkeley: University of California Press, 1999).

7. W. Ury, *The Third Side*, rev. ed. (New York: Penguin, 2000). (First published as *Getting to Peace*).

8. H. von Foerster, "Objects: Tokens for (Eigen-) Behaviors." *Cybernetic Forum*, 1976, *8*(3–4), 91–96. Also in H. von Foerster, *Observing Systems* (Seaside, Calif.: Intersystems Publications, 1981). The original in French was included as a chapter in B. Inhelder, R. Garcia, and J. Voneche (eds.), *Épistémologie Génétique et Équilibration* (Neuchâtel, Switzerland: Delachaux et Nistle, 1978).

9. M. Gladwell, *The Tipping Point: How Little Things Can Make a Big Difference* (New York: Little, Brown, 2000).

10. Prigogine and Stengers assert the universality of these processes, defining them as the essence of all evolutionary or coevolutionary dynamics. Complex systems, they assert, pass through periods of stability or equilibrium within fixed parameters, but they evolve toward parametric fluctuations that progressively push the system away from equilibrium until, reaching a threshold or "point of bifurcation," new baselines are set, and the cycle repeats itself, but at a different evolutionary stage. I. Prigogine and I. Stengers, *Order out of Chaos: Man's New Dialogue with Nature* (New York: Bantam Books, 1984).

11. Joyfully exclaimed by a military commander in the middle of violent carnage in Francis Ford Coppola's 1979 film *Apocalypse Now*, with screenplay by John Milius and Francis Ford Coppola.

12. Ury, *The Third Side*.

13. Utterance murmured in despair by the burned-out, doomed, suicidal Colonel Kurtz in Francis Ford Coppola's *Apocalypse Now*. The script was inspired by Joseph Conrad's 1899 novella *Heart of Darkness*, in which a character by the same name mumbles the same words.

14. Mitchell, *Making Peace*, p. xii.

Part Two

Practice

Chapter Three

On Hidden Ground
One Coexistence Strategy in Central Africa
Marc Sommers and Elizabeth McClintock

Early in 2001, a series of meetings between a delegation of women from Burundi and Burundi refugee women leaders in Dar es Salaam, Tanzania, dramatized the difficulties of achieving peaceful coexistence in Central Africa. As survivors of a genocide that had targeted all educated Burundian Hutu for extermination in 1972,[1] the refugee women were dumbfounded to learn that their Hutu and Tutsi guests were actually sharing hotel rooms. "Don't you realize those Tutsi could kill you in your sleep?" they asked the Hutu women from Burundi. Most of the meeting time was directed at persuading the refugee women to remain in the same room with the Tutsi visitors from their homeland. The delegation returned to Burundi discouraged and shaken.

Prospects for coexistence in Rwanda, which suffered a genocide in 1994 during which approximately 86 percent of all Tutsi citizens were killed, can be equally discouraging. A former Tutsi member of the ruling Rwandan Patriotic Front (RPF) described the response of women involved in an economic development project. During one meeting, some of the women openly detailed their involvement in genocidal activities. All the women attending the meeting were Hutu, and all of them stated that they would respond to a second call to help kill Tutsi neighbors just as they had in 1994.

The impact of such killing and hatred extends not only across borders but also across generations of Central Africans. The concept of cultural fear was devised to explain why second-generation

survivors of genocide in Burundi acted as if they had witnessed massacres that in reality took place before they were born.[2] And in
1998, drawings by refugee children who were among those who
fled Burundi following the outbreak of civil war in 1993 contained
depictions of the *igihume*, a phantomlike figure present in Central
African folk tales. The *igihume* is considered dangerous because it
treads in forests, haunts villages at night, and cannot be reasoned
with. It is also thought to yield terrible luck, such as cursing preg-
nant women who disobey community behavior codes and causing
them to give birth to deformed children. Refugee children, even
those who had been away from Burundi for several years, identified
the *igihume* as the source of their fears and the cause of regular
nightmares.[3] In many of the drawings, the *igihume* is drawn wearing
a beret—the trademark of Burundian government soldiers, nearly
all of whom are Tutsi.

Fear and distrust is endemic to much of Central Africa. Its reach
is much broader and more intimate than just ethnic animosity. It
is the "hidden ground." The threat of poisoning is considered very
real. A beer in a bar must be opened in front of the customer to ensure that it had not been poisoned. A woman from Burundi reported that the fear of poisoning is so widespread that "some people
will take their food to the latrine with them" rather than leave it
on the family table during meals. It is considered entirely plausible that even one's child or spouse may actually be plotting one's
destruction.

Against a background of ethnic animosity, widespread distrust,
a diversity of fears, and extreme violence, the coexistence challenge in Central Africa is daunting. Nonetheless, some efforts are
moving ahead in both Burundi and Rwanda. International support
for these efforts has been inconsistent and inadequate, but Central Africans have not given up. Many activities, even those considered unsuccessful, offer interesting lessons about the nature of
identity and its implications for violence and for coexistence.

Notes on an Ethnic Obsession

The Rwandan genocide has produced an extraordinary outpour-
ing of publications on ethnicity and violence.[4] Burundi's torturous
past and present, sadly, has received considerably less attention.[5]

In nearly all of this writing, authors underscore the difficulty of distinguishing between two ethnic groups that are closely intermingled. Ethnicity in Central Africa, indeed, has been a source of considerable speculation: just how can supposedly distinct groups share the same history, geography, language, culture, and nearly every other characteristic thought to lend uniqueness to an ethnic identity yet still be considered separate ethnic groups?

It is widely believed that ethnic Tutsi entered the geographical area that is now Burundi and Rwanda centuries ago, gradually assuming roles in the upper tiers of society and power. But it is also true that those who are known as Hutu also migrated into the area many centuries ago. Des Forges states, "Forerunners of the people who are now known as Hutu and Tutsi settled in the region over a period of two thousand years."[6] The population thought to have the longest tenure in Central Africa are the Twa, who are smaller in stature than the Hutu and Tutsi and have intermarried with others in Rwanda and Burundi much less frequently. The Twa are thought to be related to forest dwellers in the modern-day Democratic Republic of the Congo (formerly Zaïre).[7] Part of the mythology of these three groups is the size of their respective populations in Rwanda and Burundi: the Hutu at 85 percent, the Tutsi at 14 percent, and the Twa at 1 percent. These figures, though, are mere approximations.

Steps toward a "racialization of consciousness" that transformed class or caste distinctions into ethnic and racial categories[8] began with the entrance of one of Europe's earliest visitors to the region, the British explorer John Hanning Speke. While passing through present-day Uganda, Speke had an inspiration: that the Tutsi-like rulers he was visiting had originally hailed from Ethiopia.[9] Soon it was commonly held among what Prunier has termed "racially obsessed nineteenth-century Europeans"[10] that Ethiopians and their Central African descendants had a distant but nonetheless important biological connection to Europe's Aryans. The Belgian colonialists, missionaries, and anthropologists residing in Burundi and Rwanda eventually conjured Hutu and Tutsi as races. Based on flimsy evidence, they relied heavily on pronounced stereotyping to reinvent Central African society with a rigid, immutable social structure consisting of Bazungu (white Europeans) at the top, followed by, in order, the Tutsi (categorized by Europeans as Hamites), who helped them rule and were heavily favored; the Hutu (considered African Bantu), who carried out grunt work and were considered distinctly dull and in all ways inferior to the Tutsi save for their physical abilities (but most particularly in intellectual and emotional terms); and at the bottom, the oft-forgotten Twa (labeled Pygmoid), who were thought to be peculiar but intriguing primitives. The Western absorption with ethnicities, tribes, and races has never faltered, and it continues to influence some coexistence efforts in the region.

Since colonial culture perceived society as vertical and necessarily unequal, and Tutsi were thought to be superior to Hutu, Europeans concluded that the Tutsi should be entitled to authority, responsibility, and opportunities for enrichment. That theme eventually helped inspire what Uvin has called "forces of exclusion"[11] in postcolonial Rwanda. It has also applied to life in Burundi, and its power to sculpt and influence social life has been consistently underestimated by foreigners in both countries.

In reality, the haziness between Hutu and Tutsi remains so great that it might seem best to set the entire endeavor aside. But this has not proved possible because of the depth of belief in and intensity of emotion about ethnicity. Ethnic difference is as much a part of the landscape as the extreme fear, profound distrust, and lacerating memories of brutality and injustice that nourish it. Ideas of Hutu and Tutsi live in stereotypes so vivid that their connection to reality is far less important than their power to explain the unseen. These ideas can define the hidden thoughts of one's ethnic adversary, unsettle all ground that is shared, and inspire dreadful, desperate actions.[12]

Yet in some ways, the ground beneath these ethnic stereotypes is shifting. New alliances are being formed, particularly in Rwanda, while old identities have retained their meaning. At the same time, the ideas underlying Tutsi and Hutu stereotypes—one characterized by cunning and superiority (Tutsi), the other by brutishness and debasement (Hutu)—live on in other identities.

Distinctions by class are present and powerful in Burundi and Rwanda. The idea of the "High People" (*Watu wa Juu* in Swahili) attempts to categorize upper-class, educated elites generally. This class is considered superior in terms of skill and stature to the "Ignorant People" (*Watu Wahuni*) or "Very Low People" (*Watu wa Chinichini*), who are characterized as dim, crude followers.

Distinctions according to regional stereotypes also retain their significance. Northern Rwanda, for example, has historically been a mainly Hutu area on the periphery of power, influence, and prestige. All of this changed when Juvénal Habyarimana, a northerner (from the northwest, specifically), rose to power. During his reign, the sort of clout and spoils that Belgian colonials had awarded to favored Tutsi was instead given to Hutu. But not just any Hutu rose through the government's ranks. Increasingly, elites from the "'blessed region,' that is, the northwest,"[13] were the primary beneficiaries. The Habyarimana regime's regional favoritism aimed to redress past wrongs while at the same time cloaking the change as an ethnic, not regional, "revolution." Many, if not most, of those who organized the 1994 genocide were Hutu from the northwest. To terrify and incite masses of impoverished Rwandans to join in the slaughter, however, the organizers summoned the power of ethnic difference. Regional rivalries were intentionally overlooked.

Yet other stereotypes persist. Northern Rwanda is still referred to as Urukiga, an area thought to contain backward, primitive people. Urukiga is also related to conceptions of the Bakiga, who live on both sides of the Rwanda-Uganda border. Rukiga (Kiga language) is widely considered a dialect of Kinyarwanda (Rwanda language), but in cultural terms many Bakiga consider themselves distinct from other Rwandans. Prunier even calls them "hill-dwellers who belong to a completely different tribe."[14] A European Catholic "White Father" reported that they were Rwanda's equivalent to "hillbillies" in the United States. Their reputation, however, is similar to the Urukiga. Southern Rwanda can still be referred to as Nduga, where the allegedly sophisticated, wise, and refined Abanduga people live. It is also an area containing a mixture of Tutsi and Hutu Rwandans who were among the first to convert to Christianity and to have access to education during the colonial era.

A similar distinction has arisen in Burundi refugee camps to describe differences in Burundi. The Imbo people, who originally lived in Cibitoke Province and along the lowland shores of Lake Tanganyika, speak a slightly different dialect of Kirundi (Rundi language) and consider themselves "pure" Hutu because "Imboland" was Hutu-dominated in the past. On the other hand, the Banyaruguru are considered the highland people containing Hutu and Tutsi, some of whom have intermarried. The Imbo consider the

Banyaruguru less "pure," while the Banyaruguru, in turn, castigate the Imbo as being detached from mainstream Burundian culture.[15]

Still other examples can be cited. The Tutsi Hima in Burundi are thought to be cruder and less refined (a Hutu-like characterization) than the Tutsi Banyaruguru. The so-called Gisaka people of Kibungo Prefecture in Rwanda are thought to be expert at poisoning and deception and have magic powers (qualities that are part of the Tutsi stereotype), while the Abaganza are thought to avoid long conversations, preferring to conceal their thoughts behind short answers (another characteristic associated with the Tutsi stereotype).

The religious dimension of this superiority-debasement duality is complex and neither well researched nor understood. The alignment of Satan with one's ethnic adversary has been noted, however,[16] and it is certainly plausible that massacres in churches during the Rwandan genocide were part of the *génocidaires'* strategy to demonstrate that not even God Himself could protect Tutsi victims from slaughter.

Other alliances and identities have arisen that do not necessarily cut along the familiar divides. For example, popular nicknames of Rwandan (largely Tutsi) refugees from the 1959–1964 massacres have surfaced since the refugees' return. *Waragi* (adapted from a Ugandan liquor of the same name) is used to describe returnees from Uganda. According to the stereotype, they are thought to be unsophisticated, rough, poorly educated peasants—a Hutu-like stereotype affixed to a highly influential population segment. The *Dubai* label (referring to a Middle Eastern duty-free zone) refers to returnees from Congo who may seem impressive in appearance but are rather shallow within. Returnees from Burundi are known as G.P. (the initials of the *Garde Présidentielle*) and are thought to be rough and crude (a stereotypical Hutu characteristic) while simultaneously deceptive (part of the Tutsi stereotype). Finally, there are the *Sopekiya*, which refers to a well-known Kigali gas station that never closed during the 1994 genocide and served anyone who could pay for gasoline: people involved in genocidal activity, people fleeing the genocide, and foreigners. This term is used to apply to Tutsi survivors of the genocide, who were often defenseless during and after the genocide and did whatever they could to survive, including prostitution.

The purpose of this elaboration has been to suggest how creative and changeable identities in Central Africa can be. At the same time, ideas arising from ethnic stereotypes have been applied to a wealth of other distinctions, retaining some of the power of ethnic identification. Addressing underlying ethnic issues is made all the more complicated by the fact that explicit mention of ethnicity is, for the most part, disdained in Rwanda. Burundi, on the other hand, is currently undergoing a negotiated government transition. Part of the agreement between the Tutsi-dominated government and opposing Hutu groups is a publicized formula for ethnic balance in government. The minority model of governance, so vigilantly and ruthlessly practiced by Burundian Tutsi in power following the 1972 "selective genocide,"[17] shuns overt mention of ethnicity and makes public discussions of ethnic identity and violence difficult if not illegal. This is the opposite of the majority governance model practiced by the Hutu-dominated Habyarimana regime in Rwanda and embraced by the international donor community,[18] which applied the colonial practice of requiring every Rwandan citizen to carry an identification card listing ethnic affiliation. Today, genocide can be discussed in Rwanda but ethnicity, at least in most situations, cannot. The reasoning seems logical and persuasive to Rwandans: Why emphasize something that has proved so poisonous and caused such profound destruction? But limiting talk about ethnicity does not eradicate its potency. It might just send it underground.

One way to observe change in ethnic attitudes despite the silence is to observe how the hierarchy of Central African societies has tended to remain constant. Although current governments in both Burundi and Rwanda are taking significant steps toward enlarging participation in government, interviews with Central Africans strongly suggest that nonelites nonetheless feel alternatively watched, quashed, or silenced by "the Authorities" or the "High People" above them. Fear of some sort of retribution continues, and authoritarianism and social control remain components of the governance model in Central Africa. A hierarchical or vertical society, combined with enveloping poverty, a legacy of terrible violence, and extreme unease about the future, give rise to a view shared by most Central Africans that their world is divided into those who have power and the powerless, who are affected by power but wield none.[19] The fact that war and insecurity persist in both countries also means that traditions of authoritarianism and social control continue to dominate everyday life.

In this larger social context, ethnic identities remain the most potent symbol of inequality and verticality. The power of ethnic stereotypes extends far beyond the bounds of mere Hutu and Tutsi labels, however. As we have attempted to suggest, they have inspired a world of other identities, inferences, suggestions, ideas, and lifestyles that also separate Rwandans and Burundians into polarized, opposing groups. The various meanings underlying Hutu and Tutsi stereotypes generated in an authoritarian social environment have given rise to a variety of ways to perceive society as divided between the controllers and the controlled, the superior and the inferior, the confident and the self-hating, the blessed and the damned, the clever and the stupid, and the privileged and the desperate.

Reconciliation and Coexistence Efforts in Central Africa

If ethnicity is a moving target in Central Africa, then so are ideas like coexistence and reconciliation. Dealing with ethnic rifts alone will not ensure that violent conflict will not recur. The potential causes of new conflict are more varied and persistent. One Rwandan *préfet,* for example, recently called the land shortage problem "our time bomb." Soil erosion, population pressure, severe poverty, unemployment, and a general absence of credit and investment reduce prospects for opportunity and give many Rwandans a feeling of powerlessness. Treading water may be the very best they can hope for. For most, it is not a new predicament.[20]

Basic social and economic problems are not being addressed. Grinding poverty and inequality are magnified by the severe loss and trauma caused by civil war, flight, and appallingly effective genocide. Widows and children-headed households populate the countryside. Orphaned children occupy every urban area. Civil society is still being developed, and nongovernmental organizations are mostly to be found in the capital. Many people simply resort to the Central African tradition of maintaining a low profile. Avoiding notice is a time-honored way to deal with "the Authorities." But ignored problems do not disappear. Approximately 130,000 genocide suspects, many of whom have yet to be formally charged, remain in Rwanda's prisons, soon to be tried by recently trained local court officials under a reinvented Gacaca (pronounced "ga-cha-cha"), the traditional dispute resolution system (which will be detailed later). Civil war pitting Hutu and Tutsi militias and armies has continued in neighboring Burundi since it began in late 1993, despite the negotiated political transition that began on November 1, 2001. Rwanda's direct military involvement in the war in Congo continues, and the threat of attack by the genocide's foot soldiers, the notorious Interahamwe, persists. The situation in Rwanda, in short, does not appear to provide very fertile ground for coexistence.

Nonetheless, on many different fronts, coexistence efforts continue. Most of them are considered programs of reconciliation. Even though coexistence is less demanding than reconciliation, the conflation in Central Africa is not surprising. Reconciliation and justice, *not* coexistence, are concepts that are part and parcel of Rwandan government policy. Reconciliation connotes forgiveness and is generally associated with spiritual concerns in Rwanda. In Rwanda, reconciliation remains a hard challenge: many genocide survivors have asked, "How can I forgive people who have not asked for forgiveness?" The less demanding concept of coexistence connotes a spirit of getting on with life and indeed was the spirit that *appeared* to exist in Rwanda, particularly to many outside observers, just before the 1994 genocide occurred. Coexistence might be easier to achieve, but as the genocide suggests, it may be more challenging to make permanent. We shall describe a few of the many programs conceived to promote coexistence or reconciliation in the complex and vast landscape of Rwanda.

Imidugudu

The Imidugudu concept of community development, a planned village model, was developed by RPF social and economic experts during the civil war period (late 1990 to early 1994) and implemented after the genocide. Hundreds of thousands of returnees from what was then Zaïre, Burundi, Uganda, and Tanzania created a massive housing shortage. In this situation, the United Nations High Commissioner for Refugees (UNHCR) spearheaded the building of Imidugudu housing across the country, usually erecting new homes on the tops of hills in ordered lines that resembled refugee camp arrangements.[21] Whether this new way of "coexisting" can succeed, especially as Rwandans have traditionally lived on their family plots a good distance from each other, remains to be seen.

The National Unity and Reconciliation Commission (NURC)

The NURC has been given the responsibility of leading Rwandans past the legacy of genocide to a situation where genocide can no longer take place in Rwanda. The assignment is massive, and plans and capacities are still being developed even as reconciliation efforts are undertaken. The focus of the NURC efforts has been threefold: "to speed up the process of justice, help find new homes for 300,000 orphans from the genocide and run programs to bring Rwanda's Hutu and Tutsi communities together."[22]

Contact Programs

Contact programs bring former genocide victims and perpetrators together and try to facilitate open dialogue about participant involvement in atrocities and broader ethnic issues. While many seem to consider these retreats positive, few rural Rwandans have had either the means or the opportunity to attend. Some who have participated were not in the country during the civil war and genocide, having grown up as refugees elsewhere. In addition, workshop organizers have a limited capacity for following up either to evaluate impact or to help participants deal with the lasting trauma of genocide.[23]

Gacaca

The Rwandan court system and the international war crimes tribunal have such a backlog that with more than 130,000 genocide suspects behind bars, the government was forced to experiment with other means to expedite cases. It has chosen to reinvent the traditional dispute resolution system to handle "low to moderate" crimes against humanity. The concept of "low to moderate" is relative, given the enormity of genocidal crimes in 1994. The United Nations has described Gacaca: "Over 250,000 judges, elected by their own communities on the basis of their 'integrity,' will hear the cases of the 115,000 prison detainees accused of genocide-related crimes. Each detainee will be brought back to the scene of the alleged crime, and local residents who witnessed the events will be invited to make accusations, or defend the person, in order to reveal 'the truth' about what happened."[24] Given the overwhelming judicial challenge faced by the Rwandan government, Gacaca has received considerable attention. There is much support for this reinvented system, both inside and outside Rwanda. The system is not without its detractors, however. According to an Amnesty International official, "The abbreviated training they have received is grossly inadequate to the task at hand, given the complex nature and context of the crimes committed during the genocide." According to the same official, "Pre-Gacaca trial sessions they observed in 2001 were marked by 'intimidation and haranguing' of defendants, defense witnesses and local populations."[25]

Significantly, crimes that may have taken place during the civil war period prior to the genocide and subsequent conflicts in Congo will not be part of Gacaca deliberations. In many parts of Rwanda, the focus on the hundred days of genocide does not represent the complete story of violence and repression during the past thirty years, although it could be considered the most significant event. Though many Rwandans are upbeat and hopeful, it remains to be seen the degree to which the Gacaca system will ultimately contribute to reconciliation or coexistence or to further violence.

United Nations and International Nongovernmental Organization Efforts

Many international organizations and both local and international NGOs address a wide range of concrete and abstract issues—for example, health education that includes efforts to combat the increasing incidence of AIDS and maternal and child health; a variety of educational efforts at all levels; economic development and job creation; and the coexistence projects of UNHCR (described in Chapter Five).[26]

UNICEF's Rwanda program emphasizes girls' education. Its work includes improving opportunities for vocational and psychosocial skill development for both Hutu and Tutsi girls out of school. These children include working girls, juvenile girls in conflict with the law, girls who live on the street, those who are sexually exploited, heads of households, and AIDS and genocide orphans.[27]

United Nations Development Programme initiatives include several conflict prevention and resolution efforts. The objective of the "Women and Peace" program include reinforcing the capacity of women's organizations to prevent and resolve conflict, particularly at the local level, as well as the promotion of a national network of women's coalitions who work for peace.[28]

Catholic Relief Services' youth program in Rwanda provides a dialogue and education effort. The program aims to educate young people to create an environment conducive to national reconciliation. Activities are centered around solidarity camps where youth learn about Rwandan history, nonviolence, human rights, and small project development.[29]

Trócaire's Civil Society Programme supports eight partners promoting and protecting human rights, peace, and reconciliation at community level and local income generating activities.[30]

NGO efforts in Burundi have reflected similar goals. Search for Common Ground's Youth Project is designed to promote "unity and opportunity" among Burundian young adults; the International Foundation for Election Systems has launched a program to "increase the capacity of Burundi's civil society and promote reconciliation"; and the Canadian Centre for Education and International Cooperation's PREVCONB project trains trainers and supports the education projects of local NGOs. This is just a selection of the many ongoing efforts in the region. Many of these initiatives are increasingly incorporating a conflict resolution and conflict management framework and embody the underlying premise that the reconstruction of communities emerging from violence cannot take place without addressing how communities will work together in the future. Some are designed to develop skills; others focus primarily on dialogue. However, because many of these efforts are at an early stage of development, evaluative data are lacking. The effectiveness of these programs remains difficult to determine.

A New Way Forward?

In designing a program to deal with the aftermath of genocide, Conflict Management Group (CMG), with considerable experience in Africa, examined many programs that featured some aspects of conflict management or resolution. Our impressions—and they are only impressions, given the lack of evaluative data—support many of the conclusions presented in Chapters Four and Six. In addition to the need to link conflict management skill development with concrete programs, the CMG Central Africa Project concluded that wider inclusion of a particular community is necessary to have lasting impact. Moreover, ongoing evaluation is essential to make midcourse corrections.

Including the Marginalized

The goal of CMG's Central Africa Project has been to develop and document a new learning process by extending the skills of conflict resolution, negotiation, and joint problem solving to traditionally marginalized populations. Initially, the program was not linked to a concrete development program. However, evaluation data revealed the need for a midcourse correction, and the program is now focused on providing conflict resolution skills in the context of income-generating cooperatives. The program tests three important hypotheses: (1) coexistence in a community requires including the most marginalized citizens as well as elites in developing conflict resolution skills; (2) it is possible to provide a method for negotiating conflict without direct reference to ethnic divisions; and (3) ongoing program evaluation provides significant lessons, offers the opportunity for midcourse correction, and generates effective new approaches.

This program comes at a crucial time in Rwanda. The Rwandan government has embarked on a decentralization program that dramatically expands participation of women and youth in the decision-making structures of their communities. This sudden expansion of local government activity has left many new government officials without the skills necessary to help manage relationships in their communities. By targeting marginalized women and youth, as well as leaders, CMG hopes to enhance the capacity of the entire community for peaceful development. These hypotheses differ markedly from other programs in Rwanda that target elites or educated people or focus on a small community segment.

It is important to note here that by "elite" we are referring not just to individuals in the highest income brackets or holding national office. In Central Africa, the frame of reference would also include anyone who has had access to secondary education or has achieved a degree of community prominence. This larger group of elites would include religious leaders, women's leaders, and youth leaders. An implicit assumption of training elites, broadly defined, is that it facilitates the spread of conflict resolution skills to the wider society and will result in a more enlightened power structure. These are the "spillover" and "trickle-up" effects rejected by Chigas and Ganson in Chapter Four. Our view from the outset has been that singling out elites excludes the majority of the population from access to an important capacity-building opportunity. In Rwanda, where at least 70 percent of the population lives below the poverty level,[31] such selectivity would reinforce existing patterns of exclusion and promote the perception of further empowering the powerful at the expense of the powerless. It is hard to imagine how a conflict resolution and negotiation program can yield a lasting positive impact if it does not feature the participation of poor Rwandans. Therefore, the aim of the CMG Central Africa Project has been to reach the poorest of the poor—the majority. In addition, it is designed to include community members that tend to be the most overlooked, such as young women who are underrepresented in both youth and women's groups. The project's pedagogy and approach are also explicitly designed to include illiterate Rwandans as equal participants in training. The illiterate constitute a considerable proportion of impoverished Rwandans and are rarely able to participate in conflict management work.

Community Selection

CMG conducted an extensive diagnostic analysis to determine a community in which the project might have significant impact. The Sector of Muranzi, in Kisaro District, Byumba Province, suffered greatly during the Rwandan civil war, although the community members claimed that the genocidal killings so pervasive in other parts of Rwanda never took place there in 1994. Various reasons were offered, ranging from the presence of UN troops in the area to the community's strong faith in God. Regardless of reasons, all those interviewed reported that community violence did not occur either during the recent civil war or genocide periods, even when Muranzi residents hosted tens of thousands of internally displaced Rwandans from nearby areas. These findings suggested that Muranzi community members had developed fairly effective problem-solving skills and therefore constituted a promising testing ground for applying the new program model. At the same time, since the end of the genocide, international organizations had made few investments to alleviate poverty and suffering in Muranzi. As one of very few programs of any kind present in the Province of Byumba, CMG has received strong and consistent support for this effort from local institutions and government representatives from the outset of its work.

Dealing with Government

The challenge confronting most organizations involved in conflict prevention, peace building, or conflict resolution activities in Central Africa is striking a balance between gaining government support (critical to the success of any organization's activities) and effectively reaching out to the people. The perception that government is highly authoritarian—even when that is not the government's intention—can incite fear or unease in many corners of the population. Marginalized Rwandans in particular might be unwilling to participate in a program that they regard as too closely associated with government for fear of being monitored by officials. This would in turn compromise the project's effectiveness.

At the same time, recognizing that the project's success relies on support from the government, extensive contacts had to be maintained with both national and local leaders. Local leaders were included in the initial training sessions and in the participant selection process for subsequent trainings. However, the program aims to remain, as much as possible, below the national government's radar, with few efforts made to publicize the work. This low-profile approach is in keeping with the needs and concerns of poor participants.

The dual approach to reaching the population—providing local leaders with training while ensuring that most training is available to the poorest community members—is not a widely applied program feature in Rwanda. Here, however, it is considered a key to program success. There was concern initially that conflict resolution programs might be interpreted as a threat to government officials, especially as the program has succeeded in empowering participants to solve their own problems and reduce their dependence on government. The inclusion of local leaders in the training process is designed to ensure that community leaders and marginalized members alike share a conflict management language and approach and can work together to address present and future community conflicts. Inclusion of all levels of the community was designed to reduce any threat the program might appear to present and facilitate its success.

Ethnicity

Another feature that distinguishes the CMG program from many other programs in Rwanda is the fact that it does not make explicit reference to the issue of ethnicity. It does not necessarily assume that the Hutu-Tutsi divide is the most important challenge to coexistence. Ethnicity is a contentious issue that can attract unwanted attention to those who may raise it in public. Instead, the curriculum focuses on day-to-day problems and the skills needed to manage those problems effectively. It also presents conflict management skills as tools that can be applied to any conflict (including, by implication, those with an ethnic base). Conflicts arising from the severe land shortage in the area where the program operated have proved to be the dominant concern of participants. Avoiding specific reference to ethnic conflict may have increased the comfort level of participants both with the workshop content and with the facilitators. It certainly helped the program maintain a low public profile. Very occasionally, issues of ethnicity have arisen during training, though only at the initiation of participants.

The Importance of Evaluation

The program's emphasis on evaluation began with the collection of baseline data prior to project implementation. Evaluation continues throughout the life of the program. This process has led to program modifications. The curriculum was redesigned on the basis of input from Rwandan colleagues and feedback from participants. Some findings were unexpected—but readily accepted. Evaluations by participants and Rwandan colleagues are what led to the inclusion of equitable numbers of young women to the training sessions. Other findings led to the introduction of economic development issues.

Learning from Ongoing Evaluation

The largely hidden emotional landscape and the legacy of explosive, extreme violence in Central Africa mask the effectiveness of efforts to promote coexistence. Our experience has reinforced our original idea that in the context and culture of Central Africa, coexistence efforts can succeed only if they include the marginalized and the poor. The evaluations and experience have brought up many other useful insights, and the learning process never ends.

Congruence

Considerable experimentation was required to reach the most marginalized—those who were illiterate and those lacking any schooling. It became clear that a way must be found to align programmatic structure with pedagogical goals. It was evident that the methodology must empower participants from the outset—avoiding even a hint of traditional authoritarian methods. To do this, the project had to create a learning environment congruent with the participants' own experiences. Members of the training team would be observed closely and thus must model the skills imparted both inside and outside the classroom to convey their legitimacy and usefulness. Both American and Rwandan trainers were used, the Rwandan partner having been trained in advance and then slowly integrated into the training team as a "second." The translators were also trained in advance, as their stance would be crucial to successfully conveying the conceptual messages.

Every opportunity was taken to provide a mode for participants— sometimes at a risk. During one evaluation visit, the CMG evaluator was asked to serve as an *umuhuza*—a third-party intervener—to resolve a long-simmering feud between two leaders involved in organizing the first series of CMG training sessions. There were risks in either accepting or rejecting the unanticipated *umuhuza* role. It proved useful in providing an opportunity to demonstrate how conflict resolution techniques introduced in the workshops could be used in ordinary life. It gave CMG the further opportunity to examine the ways in which those participants who had witnessed the dispute had learned skills from the training. It revealed more about community dynamics and suggested ways to integrate CMG's approach with culturally based negotiation techniques. The ability to model the conflict negotiation skills we teach is an important demonstration of congruence. It also serves as a very concrete example of how the skills might contribute to coexistence.

In addition to the risk of failure, the concern about encouraging community passivity made us hesitate to mediate as *umuhuza*. However, the evaluation data supported the move to do so. Participants inside and outside the government structure now report that they regularly use lessons arising from the training sessions to help them solve problems—both their own and those of others.

The use of local culture—an array of sayings and proverbs—was essential to congruence. "Those who collect firewood together work together" was a favorite. Participants said that they regularly used the illustrations provided in the curriculum to help themselves and other people involved in conflict attempt to understand the perspectives of the other side and to illustrate the importance of "coming together" and listening to the views of others. These concepts were significant to trainees because they suggested that people could solve conflicts without always resorting to an *umuhuza* or seeking redress farther up the power structure.

Balancing Local Ways and New Models

A criticism often leveled at conflict resolution programs in the developing world is that the lack of local knowledge in program design destroys its effectiveness. In this view, "exporting" Western values to these contexts is doomed to fail because the programs introduce new ideas without honoring local customs. While it is important to honor local knowledge and local conflict resolution strategies, evaluation data from Rwanda have shown that there is real value in offering new ideas and concepts for consideration. What is important is the *way* in which these ideas are offered and whether the participants are permitted to participate in a dialogue about the selection and use of new ideas. The approach must seem relevant to their experience: congruence must be apparent.

Program design requires a critical balance between promoting new ideas and honoring local traditions. As a training team, we had to be willing to adopt a stance of inquiry and openness to learning and a willingness to consider changing our design. The original curriculum was based on an abstract presentation of concepts. The inquiry process, first with Rwandan partners and translators and then with participants themselves, led to several revisions and alterations, which resulted in a more culturally appropriate collection of stories and proverbs and the broader application of conflict resolution skills to issues such as economic development, which have a direct impact on the lives of participants.

But we learned that inquiry should be balanced with courage. For example, the CMG methodology emphasizes that "no one person is wrong in a conflict." This is a very powerful idea and seemed contrary to local knowledge. In Rwanda, the conflict resolution process is as much about assigning blame as it is about resolving the problem. However, CMG facilitators chose simply to present the concept, knowing that it might not be accepted, while adopting a learning stance rather than an authoritative methodology.

As a result, joint contribution seems to be one of the most powerful lessons taken away from the training workshops by participants. During the evaluation, participants reported to have learned from the program that understanding the perspectives of both sides in a conflict facilitates dispute resolution, can reveal misunderstandings between opposing parties, and can help minimize the potential for ongoing, unresolved feuds.

Refining the Focus on Gender

Many projects in the developing world place specific emphasis on women. Others target youth. Given the burdens that women bear in supporting their rural communities and their lack of opportunity, this emphasis is important. However, one crucial portion of the population is not consistently considered in either women's or youth programming: young women. Youth programming most often focuses on young men, particularly with providing them with economic opportunities or education. In programs targeted at women, the young women are marginalized, whether because of the competition they represent to older women (the threat of the "co-wife") or the burden they represent as unmarried members of the household. If the success of coexistence efforts is in part predicated on reaching the poorest of the poor, then particular attention must be paid to acknowledging and dealing with the needs of these adolescent girls and young women—often the most vulnerable members of a community.

Rapid Acceptance of the Program

One surprising result of the program was the alacrity with which both leaders and participants bought into a program designed predominantly for the poor. Though possibly threatening because of its potential to empower the poor, the program was instead embraced by leaders, for two reasons. First, it allowed more people to gain skills to address conflicts quickly, before problems became unmanageable. Second, the idea that people could solve their own problems lessened the burden on local leaders, who are overwhelmed with disputes and responsibilities, especially in the newly decentralized government system. The inclusion of marginalized community members was also perceived as a way to reduce the burdens on the overwhelmed formal justice system. The system of government justice is deemed slow, expensive, and frequently unjust. Poor farmers interviewed during field evaluations reported that the CMG trainings provided a new and valued empowerment tool, which enabled them to solve problems themselves and thus avoid the "High People" in the government structure. When conflicts went "up" to the "High People," they explained, final resolutions were thought to be arbitrary, unpredictable, or subject to influence from one side or the other. Thus even cases that seemed clear and resolvable could be extended and bring surprising results. Avoiding this system is an explicit goal of many of Muranzi's poor.

Participant buy-in was reinforced by the heightened prominence as community problem solvers that they continued to receive long after they had concluded their CMG training. Participants are regularly invited to serve as *umuhuza* or advisers to *umuhuza*. Key people at the sector and district levels ask CMG trainees to contribute. The CMG certificate they receive signals their expertise as problem solvers and is now included as one of the many identification cards and papers that Rwandans carry with them at all times.

Conclusion

As evaluation data trickle in, there is support for the view that systematic efforts to help more people—particularly the poorest of the poor—solve at least some of their problems peacefully can contribute to a climate of reduced social tension, self-empowerment, and nonviolence. Most of those in the target groups were functionally illiterate, and at least one had never been inside a school classroom before. Designing and modifying a curriculum and an approach that was accessible to the illiterate and overlooked was one of the highly unusual features of the CMG program in Rwanda.

In evaluating coexistence efforts in Central Africa and the challenges they face, it is important to reflect more broadly on whether the skills gained have a wider impact on the social structure of society. CMG's Central Africa program had limited goals. It sought to provide the same skills and concepts both to leaders and to the impoverished. But it is *how* "the Authorities" and "the Very Low People" have ended up applying their new skills that sheds light on the limits of social movement in Rwandan society and has exposed the distance between powerful and weak society members, ultimately revealing the constraints within which coexistence efforts must operate.

Poor women and youth who received the CMG training sought to apply their new skills to avoid the established dispute resolution system and hope to use the skills to more effectively exploit economic opportunities offered by local cooperatives. Away from the wealthiest and most influential members of local society, surrounded by other poor families on the slopes and in the valleys of Muranzi, poor trainees shared their new information on problem-solving techniques with relatives and neighbors and assumed new roles for themselves—joint problem solvers and third-party *umuhuza*. They believed that sharing their new knowledge and skills would help them minimize the number of disputes that surfaced and help resolve those that did emerge more quickly. Most of these disputes involved the dual problem of land scarcity and desperate economic conditions.

This belief did not surprise the "High People" living, quite literally, above the "Very Low." They viewed the growing ability of the poor people in the valleys to solve their own problems as a good thing. The desire of the marginalized to avoid "the Authorities" was not a threat. Many leaders also reported that the CMG skills also helped them resolve disputes more effectively. Additionally, the trainings facilitated the involvement of more people as problem solvers, notably poor women and youth. In the end, CMG's program certainly seems to have helped Muranzi residents solve problems more effectively.

At the same time, the program has underscored the distance that coexistence programs have yet to travel in supporting stable and lasting peace in Rwandan communities. The trainings may have helped "High" and "Low" people in one community in significant ways, but they do not appear to have markedly improved Muranzi's social cohesion. The distance between the two groups remains great, and bridging the gap seems virtually impossible, given the problems of land scarcity, population growth, grinding poverty, the legacy of extreme violence, authoritarian traditions, and a still-dramatic separation between the relatively few haves and multitude of have-nots. Uvin has noted how peasant life in rural Rwanda prior to the genocide "was perceived as a prison without escape in which poverty, infantilization, social inferiority, and powerlessness combined to create a sense of personal failure."[32] How far most Rwandans have traveled since that time remains an open question.

Notes

1. See M. Sommers, "Epilogue: The Forgotten People," *Fear in Bongoland: Burundi Refugees in Urban Tanzania*. Studies in Forced Migration Series, vol. 8 (New York: Berghahn Books, 2001).

2. M. Sommers, "Epilogue."

3. M. Sommers, *A Child's Nightmare: Burundian Children at Risk* (New York: Women's Commission for Refugee Women and Children, 1998).

4. The list is long. See, for example, special editions of journals such as *Issue: A Journal of Opinion* (1995) and the *Journal of Refugee Studies* (1996); African Rights, *Rwanda: Death, Despair and Defiance* (London: African Rights, 1995); C. Braeckman, "Rwanda: Histoire d'un génocide" (Paris: Éditions Fayard, 1994); B. Davidson, "On Rwanda," *London Review of Books*, Aug. 18, 1994; J.-P. Chrétien and others, *Rwanda: Les Médias du Génocide* (Paris: Karthala, 1995); A. Destexhe, *Rwanda and Genocide in the Twentieth Century* (East Haven, Conn.: Pluto Press, 1995); A. de Waal, "The Genocidal State: Hutu Extremism and the Origins of the 'Final Solution' in Rwanda," *Anthropology*, July 1994; P. Gourevitch, *We Wish to Inform You That Tomorrow We Will Be Killed with Our Families: Stories from Rwanda* (New York: Farrar, Straus & Giroux, 1998); A. J.

Kuperman, *The Limits of Humanitarian Intervention: Genocide in Rwanda* (Washington, D.C.: Brookings Institution, 2001); R. Lemarchand, "Rwanda: The Rationality of Genocide," *Issue*, 1995, *23*(3), 8–11; M. Mamdani, *When Victims Become Killers: Colonialism, Nativism, and the Genocide in Rwanda* (Princeton, N.J.: Princeton University Press, 2001); M. Sommers, "Representing Refugees: Assessing the Role of Elites in Burundi Refugee Society," *Disasters*, 1995, *19*(1), 19–25; F. Reyntjens, "Rwanda: Background to a Genocide," *Bulletin des Séances, Académie Royale des Sciences d'Outre-Mer, Brussels*, 1995, p. 4; C. C. Taylor, *Sacrifice as Terror: The Rwandan Genocide of 1994* (New York: Berg, 1999); and P. Watson, "Purging the Evil," *Africa Report*, 1994.

5. Significant works include Human Rights Watch, *Proxy Targets: Civilians in the War in Burundi* (New York: Human Rights Watch, 1998); R. Lemarchand, *Burundi: Ethnic Conflict and Genocide* (Cambridge: Woodrow Wilson Center Press/ Cambridge University Press, 1996); A. Ould-Abdallah, *Burundi on the Brink, 1993–95: A UN Special Envoy Reflects on Preventive Diplomacy* (Washington, D.C.: United States Institute of Peace Press, 2000); F. Reyntjens, *Burundi: Breaking the Cycle of Violence* (London: Minority Rights Group International, 1995); and W. Weinstein with R. Schrire, *Political Conflict and Ethnic Strategies: A Case Study of Burundi* (Syracuse, N.Y.: Maxwell School of Citizenship and Public Affairs, Syracuse University, 1976).

6. A. L. Des Forges, *Leave None to Tell the Story: Genocide in Rwanda* (New York: Human Rights Watch, 1999), p. 31.

7. Per the *United Nations World Factbook 2002*.

8. G. Prunier, *The Rwanda Crisis: History of a Genocide* (New York: Columbia University Press, 1995), p. 38.

9. J. H. Speke, *Journal of the Discovery of the Source of the Nile* (London: Dent, 1969). (Originally published 1864.)

10. Prunier, *Rwanda Crisis*, p. 6.

11. P. Uvin, *Aiding Violence: The Development Enterprise in Rwanda* (West Hartford, Conn.: Kumarian Press, 1998), p. 118.

12. These ideas are detailed in Sommers, "Epilogue."

13. Des Forges, *Leave None*, p. 46.

14. Prunier, *Rwanda Crisis*, p. 69.

15. The Imbo-Banyaruguru distinction is detailed at length in Sommers, "Epilogue." See also M. Sommers, "Young, Male and Pentecostal: Urban Refugees in Dar es Salaam, Tanzania," *Journal of Refugee Studies*, 2001, *14*(4).

16. Somers, "Epilogue." See also M. Sommers, *Reconciliation and Religion: Refugee Churches in the Rwandan Camps* (Uppsala, Sweden: Life and Peace Institute, 1998).

17. R. Lemarchand and D. Martin, *Selective Genocide in Burundi* (London: Minority Rights Group, 1974).

18. Uvin, *Aiding Violence*.

19. This distinction regarding power is described in M. Sommers, "Power and the Powerless," *New Routes: A Journal of Peace Research and Action*, 1998, *2*(4), 11–12.

20. Uvin, *Aiding Violence*.

21. Imidugudu triggered a vibrant debate in the years immediately following the 1994 genocide. This version of events is adapted from private interviews gathered since 2000.
22. United Nations Integrated Regional Information Networks (IRIN), "Rwanda: Rwandan Reconciliation Commission Making Progress, Says Official." June 27, 2001. On-line at http://www.irinnews.org/report.asp?ReportID=8872& SelectRegion=Great_Lakes&SelectCountry=Rwanda.
23. Information gathered from private interviews, 2000–2001.
24. IRIN, "Rwanda: Gacaca Courts Get Under Way." June 21, 2002. On-line at http://www.irinnews.org/report.asp?ReportID=28453&SelectRegion=Great_ Lakes&SelectCountry=Rwanda.
25. IRIN, "Rwanda: Gacaca Courts Get Under Way."
26. Organizations working in Rwanda include the World Bank, USAID, and other bilateral donors such as the Norwegian and British governments, United Nations agencies, international NGOs such as Catholic Relief Services, Trócaire and the International Rescue Committee, and local NGOs like Profemme and IWACU.
27. UNICEF, "Girls' Education in Rwanda," 2002 [http://www.unicef.org/ programme/girlseducation/action/cases/rwanda.htm].
28. United Nations Development Programme, "Femmes et Paix," 2002 [http: //www.bi.undp.org/html/projet/fempai.htm].
29. Catholic Relief Services, "Peacebuilding Programming," 2002 [http:// www.catholicrelief.org/where_we_work/africa/rwanda/peace/index.cfm].
30. Trócaire, "Rwanda," 2002 [http://www.trocaire.org/overseas/africa/rwanda. htm].
31. Central Intelligence Agency, *The World Factbook, 2002* [http://www.cia. gov/cia/publications/factbook/geos/rw.html#Econ].
32. Uvin, *Aiding Violence,* p. 117.

Chapter Four

Grand Visions and Small Projects

Coexistence Efforts in Southeastern Europe

Diana Chigas and Brian Ganson

A prodigious amount of political, financial, and human resources has been invested in bringing together divided communities in southeastern Europe through community reconstruction, economic development, and joint activities in education, employment, the arts, and sports. Conflict resolution skills training, dialogue, and psychosocial interventions are also employed to allow neighbors once again to work with one another and cope with trauma. Many relief and development projects attempt to create incentives for cooperation, or at least "do no harm" by not exacerbating existing divisions.

Most coexistence projects are small and local. They cannot address every contributing factor to conflict. They can only touch a limited number of people. Their impact depends largely on personal participation and the experience of a different kind of relationship with the "other." Even when initiatives are designed to reach a broad spectrum of the population, the change generated by a project represents only a part of the daily experience of its beneficiaries. Funders generally expect, however, that social contact, by changing the relationships and attitudes of the general population, will help build a broad "peace constituency" that will pressure elites to strengthen a fragile or cold peace.[1]

Coexistence initiatives consequently need to be examined on two levels, by responding to the following questions:

1. Do the projects achieve their "micro-level" goals of fostering co-existence among participants? Are they sustained long enough to effect a lasting change in attitude and action?
2. Do the projects affect the course of the conflict beyond the participants themselves? Is the potential of individual projects to contribute to broader social change maximized?[2]

Our experience suggests that most projects are not sustained long enough to succeed even at the micro level. In addition, both the spillover into participants' broader experience of the other and the "trickle-up" from the grassroots to the governance level are far less than assumed by donors. Indicators and evidence on the measurement of impact at the micro level are frequently positive, but the significance of the changes measured for the dynamics of the larger conflict remains unproven.

This suggests that the major challenge of coexistence may be less of invention than of rigor—in particular, leveraging the interventions to be real catalysts for change. We explore these questions in the context of three coexistence field initiatives in southeastern Europe: (1) a multiyear conflict resolution training and dialogue project in Cyprus, (2) a project assessment and "best practices" evaluation in Bosnia and Herzegovina, and (3) an economic development project promoting structural interdependence in eastern Kosovo.

Cyprus: Dialogue for Coexistence

Cyprus belongs to a class of protracted conflicts that have stubbornly resisted resolution even after the end of the Cold War and despite continued international efforts to mediate a settlement. International—especially American—frustration with the intractability of the official negotiation process in this decades-old conflict has led to significant investment of resources in unofficial bicommunal coexistence efforts.

Until 1993, dialogue between Greek and Turkish Cypriots was limited and sporadic. That year was a turning point for bicommunal rapprochement: two highly positive pilot efforts that included the children of the communities' two leaders and withstood vicious attacks in the media. Based on this success, the following year,

USAID provided significant funds to the Conflict Management Group (CMG) and the Institute for Multi-Track Diplomacy (IMTD) to launch the Cyprus Consortium, a five-year intensive effort to bring the communities together through conflict resolution training. Its goals were to help change attitudes, provide opportunities and processes for meaningful dialogue to build mutual understanding and trust, and improve communication and joint problem-solving skills and capacities. The project envisioned empowering a network of local change agents.

The workshops brought Greek and Turkish Cypriots together in a neutral space (outside of Cyprus or in the buffer zone separating the two communities) to learn and practice skills of communication, conflict analysis, and cooperative problem-solving to create new possibilities for dealing with the conflict. The workshops (supplemented by social interaction and visits to each side of the island) were directed to a wide range of sectors: ordinary citizens, professionals, youth, women, and others. Significantly, political leaders from all the major parties on both sides were also targeted for the first time, in order to enhance the legitimacy of bicommunal conflict resolution. By the end of 1994, several hundred people had been trained, a corps of thirty Greek Cypriot and Turkish Cypriot trainers was providing introductory conflict resolution training to bicommunal groups, and an office in the buffer zone had been created specifically for these local trainers to manage the expanding bicommunal activities.

Since 1994, more than eight hundred people were trained by the Cyprus Consortium, countless more were instructed by local Greek and Turkish Cypriot trainers, and a series of U.S.-sponsored programs brought together hundreds more for dialogue, joint projects, and joint study tours. The Trainers Group, as the local trainers called themselves, supported by a number of U.S.-sponsored resident Fulbright scholars, has spawned dozens of bicommunal projects, including lawyers who translated post-1974 legislation passed on both sides, a bicommunal management center, a bicommunal choir, bicommunal cultural events, several youth groups, a women's group, and educators' groups working on examining history texts.[3] By 1997, it was fair to say that a genuine bicommunal peacebuilding movement involving thousands of people from both sides had been formed. And despite the formidable obstacles put in place by political authorities in late 1997 (when permissions for Turkish Cypriots to participate in bicommunal activities were cut off following the European Union's decision to accept Cyprus's application for membership), bicommunal activities have continued in a wide variety of sectors, including a significant effort directed toward assisting the political negotiation process.

Bosnia and Herzegovina: Coexistence in Everyday Life

The 1995 Dayton Accords brought an end to the bloodshed and wholesale atrocities in Bosnia and Herzegovina, but the peace enforced by NATO troops has proved elusive in the political realm. The country remains divided along ethnic lines. While a return to war seems thankfully remote, few people in the new country believe that the internationally imposed political order will prove viable. Yet the international community and some citizens entertain hope that if positive interethnic experiences are reintroduced, perhaps a vision of a viable multiethnic state can also be made believable to the population. Donors have invested heavily in initiatives to provide experiences of peaceful interethnic coexistence in work, school, sports, the arts, and civic life.

The projects we investigated in detail were directed by the Office of the United Nations High Commissioner for Refugees (UNHCR) as part of the Imagine Coexistence initiative.[4] UNHCR hoped to reduce friction in communities where return was already beginning to occur and to encourage refugees who were considering return by demonstrating the viability of interethnic coexistence at the grassroots level. Based on a survey of similar initiatives across Bosnia and Herzegovina, we can state that the UNHCR initiative is reasonably typical of other efforts taking place across the country.

UNHCR targeted two particularly difficult communities for its pilot efforts. The first, the municipality of Prijedor in the Republika Srpska, was the site of murder, rape, and the systematic destruction of the Bosniak community found by the UN Commission of Experts to meet the definition of genocide.[5] Here was an attempt to reintegrate neighbors who had turned on neighbors. The second municipality targeted by UNHCR, Drvar, in the Croat-Muslim Federation, represents the problem of integrating populations that had no prewar history whatsoever. Ninety-seven percent Serb before the war, Drvar was abandoned by the Serb army as indefensible. It became 100 percent Croat, primarily displaced populations from central Bosnia promised a permanent home.

In both municipalities, widespread, organized rioting and violence against returnees was commonplace. Steps were taken by nationalists in each place to maintain economic and political monopolies, even as return accelerated. In Drvar, for example, the Croat authorities shifted much of the responsibility for government property and finances from the municipal to the canton level—keeping the purse strings in Croat hands even as Drvar slowly re-establishes a Serb majority—and selling the main state economic enterprise in Drvar to a Croatian company reported to have close ties to the family of Franjo Tudjman, the main funder of extremist nationalist Croats in the region. Return in both places is largely to outlying villages, rather than to the city center. Shops and cafés are separated along ethnic lines, and groups largely go about their separate lives.

Faced with daunting nationalist opposition to return, UNHCR set out to sponsor a series of projects in Prijedor and Drvar that would demonstrate the feasibility of coexistence in a variety of everyday activities. UNHCR chose a local implementing partner, Genesis, in part for its cross-ethnic and psychosocial expertise. Genesis recruited project leaders of each nationality and offered them support on the condition that they involve roughly equal numbers of participants from each community in their activities. UNHCR decided to "depoliticize" its coexistence initiative as much as possible, attempting to stay away from projects that would be likely to become embroiled in local politics and from project leaders considered political.

Genesis reported that the decision to participate in a coexistence initiative was often harder for participants than the actual experience of participation itself. Given the social divide across ethnic lines, the process of launching the initiatives required a slow and careful process of identifying project leaders with courage, open minds, and acceptance that coexistence might be possible and desirable in their community; of recruiting willing participants from each ethnic community; and of overcoming the practical barriers to project success. To meet these challenges, project leaders of each nationality were supported with a series of joint training sessions that gradually approached core issues of ethnic division.

After six months of laying the groundwork, a café was opened in Drvar where the staff is biethnic and all people are welcome. Children in each community were invited to engage in joint arts and sports activities. Small-scale enterprises were supported where Croats and Serbs and Muslims (though rarely, if ever, Roma [or gypsies, as they have been called]) work side by side. At least some level of grassroots collaboration, cooperation, and interaction was set in motion.

Kosovo: Creating Structural Linkages

After the war in 1999, Serb return to Kosovo, desired by many in the international community, was determined to be likely to endanger the lives of both returnees and international workers, threatening to turn an already volatile situation into a dangerous, explosive one. Mercy Corps (MC), a nongovernmental humanitarian organization, suggested to the U.S. State Department's Bureau of Population, Refugees and Migration (PRM) that it instead begin by promoting interethnic "stabilization." MC, working in collaboration with CMG, proposed an economic development program in the agricultural sector to promote structural interdependence between Albanians and remaining Serbs and to create a forum for cross-communal dialogue. MC chose eastern Kosovo—the Gnjilane/Gjilan and Vitina/Viti areas—because historically they were mixed communities that had not been as badly affected by the war as other areas of Kosovo and also still had a significant Serb population.

The concept was to create a chain of interethnic agricultural market linkages among producers, intermediary suppliers, and processors to increase market access and expansion. The Eastern Kosovo Stabilization Program (EKSP) would provide Albanians and Serbs with tangible rewards for working together and make it "bad business to harm your neighbor."[6] A typical project is the Dairy Seven, an Albanian-owned dairy in a mixed village that produces yogurt and, with MC help, expanded with a line of cheese products. By linking Dairy Seven with Serb milk producers in surrounding communities, MC helped both gain a new market outlet. The process of overcoming economic challenges was designed to become the impetus for cross-ethnic dialogue and eventually joint business problem solving.

Initially, MC did not openly describe the project as an interethnic stabilization effort. MC understood that revealing such goals would invite extremists to obstruct implementation and undermine the coexistence that might develop. It was only after six months that MC staff began to speak openly to applicants of the project's coexistence goals. Yet from the beginning, MC sought to model coexistence by its own practices. It employed an interethnic local staff who openly worked together in both Albanian and Serb villages. MC also provided a neutral space through its agricultural Resource Center, which offered information, training, and other support.

Unsurprisingly, formidable barriers emerged that forced some shifts in implementation plans. Intimidation tactics increased the security concerns of participants. Serb enclaves were isolated; Serbs lacked freedom of movement. Moreover, the absence of a facilitating legal framework and professional institutions hampered project success and still impedes a broader sector transformation. It has been difficult enough to identify individuals willing and able to develop projects. The goal of also fostering extensive cross-community dialogue was impossible within the year allotted to the project. Even intracommunity problem solving and consensus building were difficult. Despite these obstacles, the mixed local staff played a crucial role in helping applicants develop business plans, identify partners from the other community, and in Serb communities especially, overcome suspicions and fears of working with Americans and Albanians.

The project team believed that merely providing economic incentives would not, in and of itself, lead to stable and sustainable cross-communal coexistence. The team needed to help participants deal directly with the sources of intergroup tension. Participant interviews suggested that unresolved issues of the past and suspicions about future intent posed significant barriers to cooperation. MC and CMG therefore decided to bring participants together for discussion of deeper issues. In May 2001, thirteen Albanians and ten Serbs met at a conference in Macedonia. They discussed the realities, challenges, and opportunities of working cross-ethnically. The conference provided an opportunity for Serbs and Albanians to hear each other's experiences before, during, and after the war and to develop strategies for overcoming obstacles to future business sustainability. Relationships were strengthened, difficult topics tackled, and plans made for future expansion of cooperation.

Mercy Corps continued to build on the initial EKSP program in 2002. An expanded stabilization program encouraged rural development and ethnic tolerance in mixed communities throughout Kosovo with a blend of technical and financial assistance, including training and support for development of associations. MC also continued to provide opportunities for ongoing dialogue for participants, with several additional off-site conferences.

Impact of the Programs in Comparative Perspective

These projects are also only a small sampling of the multiple coexistence initiatives in southeastern Europe and therefore not a basis for drawing definitive conclusions. Nonetheless, some common themes may provide insights into the value and limitations of coexistence projects.

Micro-Level Successes

The cases illustrate demonstrable success in bringing participants of hostile communities together. In Cyprus, evaluations suggest that the project met and exceeded its micro-level goals and the goals articulated by the participants.[7] The evaluations suggested that workshops had an enormous impact on individual participants in the following ways:

• Breaking down stereotypes and the "enemy image"
• Developing a shared perception of common humanity
• Correcting misinformation each side had about the other
• Developing trust and friendships
• Beginning to feel empathy for the other side
• Developing skills in communication, conflict resolution, and problem solving that came to be used in their personal and professional lives, especially among Turkish Cypriots

- Building confidence that they could deal with differences and work through problems together

There were dramatic stories that illustrate these findings, including the nationalist who became a supporter of bicommunal activities and the journalist who had at first locked his door in fear of Turkish Cypriots and was later suspended from his job for refusing to use offensive language against them.

The Kosovo evaluation results are still in progress, but preliminary assessments of the EKSP suggest that it handily met its objective, "to provide members of all ethnic groups with a positive experience of working together and help overcome mutual hostility and suspicion."[8] In the first year, fifty-four businesses or associations with significant cross-ethnic linkages were developed and supported, far beyond the initial goal of twelve. EKSP raised income levels for more than 959 families and created more than 165 jobs in southeastern Kosovo.

The impact of EKSP is most impressive in the qualitative results, which are difficult to document in statistical terms. Relationships formed among participants have continued outside the auspices of the program and have moved beyond project boundaries. Secondary relationships among Albanian vendors and Serb clients, originating mainly when MC purchased inputs or supplies for a specific project, also continued after funding concluded.[9] Some of the changed attitudes found by staff are reflected in this comment of a Serb refrigeration plant manager: "Last year's conference had a very positive effect on me personally. I met many Serbs and Albanians, and it changed my opinions about them and gave me greater knowledge about them and their situation. . . ."[10] A Serb greenhouse operator stated, "I learned that we actually could live together."[11]

Early observations on UNHCR's coexistence initiative in Bosnia and Herzegovina show similar impacts. The modest projects seem to work effectively in establishing positive contacts. The story of one returning Muslim woman from Prijedor mirrors many others. She had been driven out by Serbs and lost her family to concentration camps. Unwilling to make the first overture to her neighbors upon her return, she was greeted by silence from people with whom she had shared holidays and family celebrations before the war. At a joint training on strawberry production, she and her Serb neighbors were "reintroduced" by the trainer and have since then been able to talk as neighbors. In this way, the micro-level projects have been able to jump-start interaction between people who were otherwise unable to reestablish basic contact.

As people came to work together in the various community initiatives, many reported that they came to trust individuals involved in their projects from other ethnic groups. The "contact theory" of coexistence seems to be at play here: people who spend productive time together come to see each other as reliable and trustworthy. But they have not yet generalized trust of individuals to trust of the other ethnic group. Participants remained deeply entrenched both in their suspicions about coexistence and about the other ethnic group. They retained their views about economic and political power. Many participants reported that successful project-level coexistence was possible only because of a tacit agreement not to discuss difficult issues—war experiences or hopes and fears for the future of the country.[12] While the intensity and relevance of project experience might deepen over time, there appear to be parallel influences against coexistence in daily life outside the projects.

Macro-Level Successes and Limitations

We have observed some wider impact of the small coexistence projects beyond immediate participants, but too much should not be expected from them. They remain fragile. In Cyprus, bicommunal groups have proliferated from a handful of participants to thousands by 1997. Projects developed by training participants evolved from social and cultural activities to joint dialogue and advocacy on issues central to the conflict. The program also generated public discussion and considerable media coverage. Attendance at United Nations functions in the buffer zone and applications for new bicommunal training programs grew exponentially. Slowly efforts were institutionalized, despite formidable odds after 1997. This suggests that the initial work helped build a peace constituency, even if it remains fragile and vulnerable. Relationships, skills, and networks are in place to consolidate a future peace agreement. Even a fledgling capacity for preemptive action against conflict escalation had been developed. For example, following violent incidents at the line of separation or Green Line in 1996, the bicommunal trainers were able to bring together participants in a counterdemonstration to a belligerent nationalist demonstration.[13] This led UN officials to organize a UN Day event that attracted several thousand people and prevented a potentially explosive border clash from escalating.

The EKSP agribusiness linkages have also had some impact on the local communities, especially since the government in Belgrade changed and the security situation improved. Mercy Corps reports increased interethnic communication. Attitudes in the broader communities have also been affected as more and more project beneficiaries have displayed publicly their participation in cross-communal activities.[14]

It is too early to see a broader impact of coexistence in the Bosnia project or even the development of a peace constituency. Early signs are not very encouraging. As elsewhere, other factors are exerting contrary pressures. While we have observed that these small coexistence projects can have a wider impact on communities beyond the participants alone, they represent only one thread in a complex tapestry that constrains their macro-level impact. In each case, several factors have worked against progress toward coexistence:

- A hostile political environment encouraged ethnic separation and prevented the projects from growing.
- Antagonistic ethnic identities were heavily reinforced in communities and other networks and limited attitudinal and behavioral change even among participants themselves.
- The projects were expected to have wide impact with inadequate funds, time, and follow-up.

Hostile Political Environment

Coexistence efforts in southeastern Europe, as in other war-torn societies, tend to run against the current of local and national politics (for more on this, see Chapter Seven). These efforts are vulnerable to "spoilers," often political and opinion leaders themselves. In Kosovo, participants were subjected to harassment, intimidation, and violence from ex–Kosovo Liberation Army guerrillas. In Cyprus, participants were attacked by opinion leaders in the media and politics. Less overt hostile bureaucratic actions by political authorities also made implementation difficult.[15] For example, in Drvar, a Croat school principal refused to permit the use of the school for biethnic programs. The Croat-controlled cantonal government restricted the use of public space for a "mixed" social project. In Prijedor, the ruling Serb bureaucracy denied a simple construction permit to a Bosniak-led coexistence project. In Cyprus, the Greek Cypriot government refused to protect coexistence participants from physical harassment by demonstrating nationalists, and the Turkish Cypriot government prosecuted civil servants participating in bicommunal activities under a law forbidding such contact. The constant and unrelenting attacks on the political space for cooperation and coexistence have had a harsh and deterrent effect on morale and have discouraged all but the most intrepid. How many people are willing to bear the social, economic, and sometimes even physical costs of openly engaging in opposition to community or political leaders who have the power to affect their lives?

Community Reinforcement of Antagonistic Ethnic Identities

Closely connected to politics were forces, both in the design of the projects and in the operating context, that reinforced ethnic separation. The projects examined in this chapter, all based on promoting coexistence through providing direct experience and connection with the "other," seem to have had a limited impact on broader ethnic attitudes and, in particular, on the political views of participants. To a large extent, the trust, relationships, and willingness to cooperate were limited to the other participants and the activities in which they were engaged together. Participants differentiated colleagues from another ethnic group in the coexistence project as "different" from their larger ethnic group. The relationships were based largely on interpersonal experience, with few generalizations made. Attitudes and stereotypes about the ethnic categories themselves remained intact.

Participants exhibited limited change in their relationships as members of their national community. Coexistence work—like the ethnonational projects it is trying to counteract—engages several levels of participants' identity, both personal (the individuated self-concept) and social (our individual perception of what defines "us").[16] Whereas personal identity is stable (although not unchanging) across different contexts, social identity is multiple. Different contexts trigger an individual to think, feel, and behave on the basis of the particular identity that is salient in that situation, whether family, regional, occupational, partisan, or national. In Bosnia, twelve Croat girls left the folkloric dance troupe with which they had been training for months, for example, rather than perform ethnic Serb dances (along with Croat, Muslim, and other Balkan dances) in public. In Cyprus, powerful personal and relational transformations achieved in the workshops were not reflected in many participants' political views or behavior. A new and meaningful social identity may have been activated for a participant in these cross-communal projects, but many other social contexts reinforced that participant's identity as a member of a particular ethnic or national group—with all the attendant prejudices, stereotypes, and fears.

Contrary to the assumptions of donors and implementers in Bosnia, cooperative activities in the social or economic realm did not automatically lead to significant transformations in stereotypes, perceptions, or enemy images. Similarly, in Cyprus, we found that even carefully developed intercommunity dialogue exploring perceptions and attitudes did not necessarily lead organically thereafter to broader cooperative action or behavior. There was insufficient reinforcement to ensure the sustainability of the programs and their ability to have a broader social influence. Participants in dialogue are influenced by new information about the "other" (and indirectly about themselves). This can lead to private acceptance and internalization of new attitudes and images. But they are also subject to normative influences from their own communities, where the pressure to conform to prevailing attitudes exerts a powerful contrary pull.[17] Thus even if dialogue does lead to personal transformation, participants may conform to monoethnic social norms to retain standing in their own groups. And we have also observed that participants are able to work together in a group whose norms are to try to be hospitable and please others in the joint group, yet their original attitudes remain unchanged.[18] Coexistence efforts must take account of these identity issues.

Donor Agendas and Timelines

A third factor limiting coexistence projects is the agendas of donors and their timelines. For large international and regional organizations especially, funding cycles are short, often only a year in duration. Their start date is often long after promises have been made. This has been particularly true of the European Union, frequently a year and a half behind commitments. Moreover, NGOs also move on to the next crisis, especially when their funding support dries up.

Each donor has its own implicit theory about peace building. A predominant one in our experience in southeastern Europe has been that simple contact on an issue of common concern would promote broader coexistence. If large sectors of the population can be included, the theory goes, they will exert pressure on political leaders to soften their opposition to cross-community rapprochement. In Cyprus and Bosnia, this led to funding only joint activities and going "wide" instead of "deep"—trying to reach large numbers in many domains. While these policies have had the advantage of demonstrating the relevance of coexistence in many areas of life and of touching many people, they also made projects vulnerable to fluctuations in the political and social climate.

It is noteworthy that in Cyprus, the period of greatest impact and growth of the bicommunal movement was in the period 1994–1996, when efforts were focused on building local capacity, on bringing the various bicommunal groups and projects into a network with each other, and on building institutional processes for ongoing networking. In later years, as the groups grew, the donors' preference for exposing new people to the bicommunal experience over efforts to deepen and institutionalize existing networks undermined the groups' ability to organize in the face of hostility. Unfortunately, the bicommunal movement became increasingly marginalized as the political and social debate about the future of Cyprus intensified.

The experience in Bosnia has been similar. The diffusion of social experiences and target populations has also dispersed the resources and focus of the Imagine Coexistence initiative in ways that prevented projects from receiving sustained attention. The breadth of the program, coupled with a stringent time limit for implementation, has thus far limited its impact. Many projects simply ended when UNHCR funding ended. Others, suffering from lack of depth of engagement, are proving to be unsustainable on their own. Project leaders, convened through trainings designed by UNHCR's implementing partner, had just begun to discuss openly the critical underlying barriers to coexistence in their communities. This group seemed capable of transforming itself into an effective network of coexistence leaders in their communities. But time and resource constraints have limited their development as a more general voice for coexistence.

Sustained funding is needed to strengthen the "coalitions across conflict lines" formed in these projects.[19] Assistance must be ongoing and sensitive to the fact that participants' ability to influence their own communities depends to a large extent on how they are perceived when they "return home." Coexistence coalitions remain uneasy because of the strong bonds of the participants to their communities and ethnic groups. If a coalition becomes so cohesive that participants begin to ignore the ethnic divide, their effectiveness in their own communities will likely be undermined.[20] At the same time, the coalition must be robust enough to survive the inevitable ups and downs of the political and psychological climate. Coexistence initiatives in Cyprus, and thus far as structured and funded in Bosnia and Kosovo, have not been sufficient to fully counteract the pull toward conflict and violence during flash-point periods.[21] The policies and timelines of the donors have not afforded an adequate investment in processes and structures that would allow participants to maintain their coalition and become a voice for coexistence in the face of enduring political hostility. The failure of the projects in Cyprus and Bosnia to invest in the further development of participants as community leaders and the failure to invest in participants' capacities and resources to manage relationships with their own national communities or to help institutionalize networks that could serve to prevent conflict have undermined the international goal of creating a strong coexistence constituency.

Implications and Conclusions

It is possible to point out only a few salient insights from a small sample. The projects studied here have all been implemented in a single geographical region—southeastern Europe—where a unique historical background, great uncertainty about the future, continuing ethnonationalist narratives, and a large, unique international presence in a European context all influence the development and impact of coexistence projects. Nonetheless, the emergence of common themes in these experiences may help in the future design and implementation of coexistence interventions more broadly.

The Lack of Expected "Spillover"

Donors and organizations seem to premise funding and implementation of coexistence projects on some implicit assumptions. First, if enough people have positive experiences of the "other," the impact will spill over into other domains by changing attitudes and providing a model for coexistence. Second, improved cooperation and social relationships at the grassroots level will also "trickle up" to the political leadership by creating a constituency for peace that will put pressure on the elites. Government will become responsive to an increasingly tolerant and cooperative population. Indeed, in Cyprus, the U.S. government made these assumptions explicit in funding bicommunal activities. The official peace process had stalled, and coexistence initiatives were, as one official put it, an attempt to put pressure on the leaders and disprove the nationalist contentions of the political leadership by demonstrating that Greek and Turkish Cypriots could live together.[22]

Yet in our experience in Cyprus, Bosnia, and Kosovo, profound personal changes, successful cooperative activities, and changes in relationships across conflict lines did not lead to changes in political attitudes or have a demonstrable impact on the peace process. In the cases of Bosnia and Kosovo, it may be too early to measure the broader impact of these initiatives. However, it is also worth reflecting that the implicit assumption that changes in one dimension of life or experience will naturally spread into others may prove inadequate.

Our experience suggests that living peacefully and respectfully[23] with former enemies requires fundamental shifts in several dimensions of relationships among participants in order to produce sustainable change beyond the project boundaries. These dimensions are depicted in Figure 4.1.

At each level of society—grassroots, middle, and elite—coexistence requires changes in the emotional, psychological, and perceptual attitudes of individuals who have lived through unthinkable trauma and who still live in fear and hatred of the "enemy"

Figure 4.1. Necessary Integration.

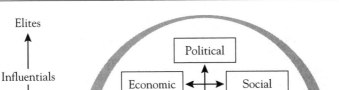

that has caused this pain. Coexistence also requires changes in the way people interact across conflict lines. These interactions are not one-dimensional. Our experience suggests that a robust peace-building process requires transformation in several distinct domains of relationship. Individual changes are needed and are the first to be accomplished. The social dimension addresses broader transformations in relationships with the other community—from confrontation and violence to more constructive communication and mutual understanding, trust, and interdependence. The structural dimension—institutional, legal, and economic—can effect changes in systems of behavior in ways that support coexistence. The complex political dimension suffuses the entire context of the parties' relationship, including their power relations, ideologies, decision-making structures, and processes.[24] Politics, in small and large ways, can undermine the development of any form of cooperation among the former enemies. Without conscious effort, coexistence projects are unlikely to affect the dominant political tone but are very much affected by it.

No project or activity can, of course, deal with every aspect of coexistence at once; there are too many interrelated causes of conflict and forces for coexistence. Yet in the coexistence initiatives examined here, the assumption was that gains in one domain would spill over into others and that the effects of activities in many domains would come together somehow to add up to peace. This assumption was not borne out by the facts. As noted previously, we saw little evidence that social experience would spread into political or economic relationships or that practical cooperation would automatically change attitudes.

Nor did we see evidence that grassroots experience would trickle up and automatically change the dominant political tone. On the contrary, in Cyprus and Bosnia, in particular, the linkage was negative. Once the level of activity reached a certain threshold, it was explicitly perceived as a threat, and the authorities (or other spoilers) took action to undermine it. The reported reaction of the Turkish Cypriot president to the growing bicommunal movement reflects the attitude of leading community and nationally based political forces in all three sites: noting that "this is getting out of control," he ordered contacts to be stopped, lest the people believe they can live together and then become "hoodwinked" into an agreement that will not protect them.

The Political Dimension: The Inseparability of Coexistence and Politics

It is difficult to depoliticize coexistence. Coexistence projects are intended to communicate a different vision for society—a vision of shifting the social norm from one of ethnonational exclusion to one of tolerance, coexistence, cooperation, and in some cases multiethnicity. In southeastern Europe, coexistence activities are therefore by their very nature political. In each case, the initiatives were limited and often actively undermined by the very political forces from which they were presumably insulated.

Yet coexistence is being promoted in highly volatile political situations, where unresolved issues of power, political status, and questions of an imposed "peace" and of "victor's justice" permeate social, economic, and political life. And "coexistence" reflects a highly controversial international mandate for multiethnicity and pluralism—a mandate for which there is little domestic will, political or popular. In this context, every intervention can be seen as an effort to tip the balance toward one political solution or another. To the extent that political and economic power is based on the continuation of separation and hostility, coexistence efforts will be actively undermined because they decrease or end that power. Coexistence initiatives effectively put the people in direct confrontation with their political leaders, who in all three cases are the major proponents of the nationalist framework. These initiatives are a direct challenge to the definitions of identity, narratives, and exclusionary visions of nationalist factions vying for dominance. Intense policing of ethnic boundaries by those who have a more ethnonationally based vision for the future is to be expected.[25] It should be no surprise that politicians undermine coexistence activities.

Furthermore, it is important to recognize that people themselves, often enthusiastic participants in coexistence projects, remain enmeshed in political conflict. Even where people increasingly believe in the right of the "other" to exist and secure a livelihood, they may feel deeply divided by issues of political identity and power: Whose interests does the country exist to serve? Who should be a full-fledged member of society? Doubt remains about sharing the power to make decisions about the economic and political future. These unresolved issues create currents of tension within coexistence projects that, if unmanaged, can make even seemingly innocuous decisions highly charged politically. If ignored, the projects will become microcosms of the larger conflict.

This does not suggest that efforts to depoliticize contact are without value. Indeed, in Cyprus, as well as in Kosovo, our direct experience suggests that initial efforts to insulate efforts from the surrounding political debate and relationships by limiting contact to the social or professional level were essential to the success of the projects. It does mean that programming at the project level must take account of the vulnerability of coexistence to hostile political forces and recognize the internal political conflicts that project participants may themselves be facing. It must plan for the protection of space and the safety of participants. In our projects in Bosnia, Kosovo, and Cyprus, international third parties—the international NGOs and the bilateral and international donors supporting the projects—supplied this protection. The question remains, what happens when the third parties leave? They rarely stay until the political situation changes. How will the parties engaged in coexistence work be able to manage the political pressure and become an effective voice for coexistence in their communities? What kinds of institutional structures, networks, and skills are needed to ensure a preemptive or conflict prevention capacity? What kind of support is needed to develop and nurture coexistence leadership? And if participants are not to lose credibility or potential influence as agents for coexistence in their own ethnic communities, how will they retain their credibility and still reconnect to the larger political environment? These questions need to be addressed in the design of any coexistence effort.

An enduring transformative community impact will demand more than careful project design and implementation. It requires far more conscious cooperation with other international authorities—those providing security, helping to create governance structures, and attending to rule of law and democratization issues. No coexistence project can thrive in a political vacuum.

The Social and Structural Dimensions and Limitations of Trickle-Up

Two conclusions emerge from the limited spillover among dimensions of relationship. First, as indicated earlier, many influences affect the people's experience of their identity on various personal and social levels. Where the prevailing dynamic is one of division and antagonism, and where powerful incentives exist to create roadblocks against coexistence politically and socially, the impact of small grassroots coexistence initiatives will be limited and will not overcome other forces unless a conscious effort is made to deal with other levels of identity too. Many coexistence efforts seem to succeed in decreasing the salience of ethnic identity within the boundaries of the project, but the transfer to other domains of participants' lives is likely to happen only if reinforcement occurs in the other important arenas too—social, political, economic, professional, and personal. Moreover, given the remarkable stability of partisan and ethnic identities as compared with other social identities,[26] transfer will also require greater attention in the projects themselves to transformations in people's experience of their collective identities. More thought must be given to understanding the norms and characteristics of each group.[27] Shifts are needed at all levels of identity for coexistence to become embedded in the social fabric.

Second, small community efforts will have an impact at higher political levels only if interveners either incorporate activity at different levels of society—adding elites and officials—or plan *explicitly* how to link their activities with other activities at each level of society. Such linkages could help create safe political space for coexistence activities and also expand the impact of the project beyond the participants directly involved. In Cyprus, Bosnia, and Kosovo, these linkages did not occur organically; projects and initiatives had only a limited cumulative effect. It is no coincidence that the Cyprus project experienced its most successful phase in 1994–1996, when the multiple interveners (official and unofficial) established linkages among themselves and their varied programs and worked to facilitate the establishment of strong networks among the variety of bicommunal projects and groups at different levels of society, from grassroots to political elites, and least effective when the interveners and the groups with which they worked pursued their activities in parallel.

Implications for Programming

It is not our intent here to devalue the importance of grassroots or citizen-based coexistence initiatives or to put on them the entire burden of resolving complex, intractable political problems. No coexistence project can or should address all dimensions of a relationship, nor can it involve all levels of society. However, our experience suggests that an individual initiative in one domain must explicitly and proactively incorporate into its program design linkages to other dimensions and other levels of society in at least two important ways.

Linking Activity and Dialogue

Neither dialogue nor activity alone seems to accomplish coexistence goals. Both are needed in tandem. Project designers would be well advised to plan for connecting activity with increasingly deep dialogue. In Cyprus, dialogue led to powerful personal transformations, but although many joint projects were spawned by participants, it was nearly impossible to implement them. Few concrete benefits flowed from the spirit of cooperation that was generated. The political situation stymied economic and other joint action. For example, the installation of twenty phone lines, agreed to by a bicommunal business group facilitated by Richard Holbrooke in 1996, was blocked by the Turkish Cypriot authorities. The three UN lines that had connected the two sides of the island were disconnected, and exorbitant international rates to connect the two communities led to lack of use, leaving communication channels worse than before. Many other initiatives for joint business ventures were blocked by the Cyprus government's ban on trade with Turkish Cypriots. Legal barriers were erected to prevent doing business with a "nonentity." The resulting frustration for participants in coexistence initiatives led to discouragement and loss of momentum.

In Bosnia, by contrast, there was a rush to visible and tangible multiethnic activity, with considerably less investment in relationship building and dialogue. The focus on activity at the expense of perceptual and trust-building dialogue led to a similar loss of commitment on the part of participants. One person in a biethnic agricultural project summed up broader attitudes: "I go to work, I do my job, that's all."[28] The lack of dialogue and reflection also left participants vulnerable to internal conflicts over their feelings about coexistence. The projects, particularly in Drvar, are showing a dwindling interest in continuing participation and maintaining relationships with the other side.

The Kosovo initiative suggests the value of providing relationship-building dialogue together with cooperative activities. Mercy Corps chose a narrow focus for activity—agricultural linkages—and a narrow target population. The projects had to be economically promising to gain support. Participants could be brought into dialogue on the basis of deep common interest and a preexisting common language and in some cases prior relationships. Yet the business relationships were not promoted merely as a tool for interethnic contact. Cooperation emerged when it was seen as a useful path to economic gain. This gave a solid and sustainable base for cooperation. MC later supplemented the business cooperation by providing project leaders with skills to begin to deal with relational issues. This twinned effort culminated in the first highly successful conference on agribusiness in eastern Kosovo. The relationships built in these dialogue processes have in turn allowed participants to strengthen their business cooperation—in many cases moving toward institutionalization.

Connecting the Grassroots with the Broader Political Context

What can be done about the political roadblocks that nationalist governments at all levels place in the way of enduring coexistence projects? Our experience, that of others, and much of the theoretical work suggest two approaches: (1) that donors provide adequate funding and a long enough time period to permit coexistence projects to become institutionalized and a strong community coexistence constituency to grow and (2) that coexistence project sponsors continue to put pressure on the rest of the international community to foster a facilitative political climate. It is not possible to insulate coexistence projects and expect them to endure.

With a theoretical framework that supports our experience that neither spillover nor trickle-up occurs automatically, John Paul Lederach proposes a "nested paradigm" of peace-building activity that takes account of the fact that immediate or concrete issues are embedded within a broader relationship among the parties and within the broader sociopolitical environment that perpetuates conflict. This can and should be done within the individual initiatives through a project design that explores systemic concerns and problematic relationships as well as immediate concrete issues.[29]

But "nesting" must also take place more broadly, by connecting peace building at the different levels of society—at the grassroots, in the middle, and among political decision makers.[30] First, with adequate funding and time, the projects can identify and develop some participants as leaders and "change agents." This would require special program support. Many participants are trailblazers: their activities provide narratives of "profiles in courage." Project success has depended on participant courage, commitment, and leadership. Leadership traits need conscious development to help create the coexistence constituency that might have an impact at least on local government. Moreover, project designers should seek ways to select people who are "connectors"[31] and encourage them to link with others working toward the same overarching goals, at both the grassroots and political elite levels, in order to build a robust pro-coexistence community that can provide mutual support.

Second, the international community must realize that coexistence is no substitute for governance. In the face of a difficult, even intransigent, political environment, international actors have at times turned to more grassroots coexistence initiatives instead of continuing to push for broader political change. Small coexistence projects can—and indeed are designed to—help prepare a fertile ground for the achievement of coexistence in the society at large. But such small projects remain vulnerable to hostile political forces.

The three cases described in this chapter underscore the need for the international community to foster a more facilitative environment for coexistence efforts. If necessary permits to operate are stalled, if bicommunal telephone service is interrupted, or if intimidation is tolerated, coexistence will wither. Since projects cannot flourish without security, freedom of movement, basic protection of human rights, and the beginnings of facilitative legal and administrative frameworks, their designers must press hard to make and keep strong connections with the international actors working on those issues.

Coexistence projects cannot bear the full burden of creating an entire peaceful environment where a constituency for coexistence will develop. Such a change requires concerted, coordinated efforts by international actors to help the nation work toward an enduring peace.

Notes

1. L. Olson, "Measuring Peace: Indicators of Impact for Peace Practice," Reflecting on Peace Practice Issue Paper, Collaborative for Development Action, July 2001 [http://www.cdainc.com].
2. Olson, "Measuring Peace."
3. For an extensive description of the development of the citizens' peace-building movement and a list of past and present bicommunal projects, see O. Wolleh, "Cyprus: A Civil Society Caught Up in the Question of Recognition," in *Searching for Peace in Europe, the Caucasus and Central Asia* (Utrecht, Netherlands: European Platform for Conflict Prevention and Transformation, 2001); O. Wolleh, *Local Peace Constituencies in Cyprus,* Berghof Report no. 8 (Berlin: Berghof Center for Constructive Conflict Management, 2001); Technology for Peace, "Peace Groups and Initiatives," June 2002 [http://www/tech4peace.org].
4. An evaluation of the Imagine Coexistence initiative in Bosnia and Rwanda was commissioned by UNHCR and implemented by the Center for Human Rights and Conflict Resolution at Tufts University's Fletcher School of Law and Diplomacy, under the direction of Assistant Professor Eileen Babbitt. The observations and conclusions reached in this chapter on UNHCR's initiative in Bosnia are based on this study, which was conducted in Bosnia by coauthor Brian Ganson, but are solely those of the authors.
5. United Nations, *Final Report of the United Nations Commission of Experts, Established Pursuant to Security Council Resolution 780* (New York: United Nations, 1992); S/1994674/Add.2 (Vol.), Dec. 28, 1994, Annex V, Part 2, Section IX, Subsection D.
6. Mercy Corps Kosovo Mission Director James White, personal communication, Nov. 2000.

7. Evaluations were undertaken in 1994 by a separate evaluation team and were ongoing through to the closure of the Cyprus Consortium's second grant in 1997. D. Klein, *Evaluation Report: Cyprus Conflict Management Project* (Cambridge, Mass.: Conflict Management Group, 1994); Conflict Management Group. *Final Report to AMIDEAST: Cyprus Conflict Management Project* (Cambridge, Mass.: Conflict Management Group, 1994, 1997).

8. Mercy Corps, *Eastern Kosovo Stabilization Program: Proposal to the Bureau of Population, Refugees and Migration, U.S. Department of State* (Washington, D.C.: Mercy Corps, 2000).

9. Mercy Corps, *Eastern Kosovo Stabilization Program, Year 1 Final Report, August 1, 2000–August 31, 2001* (Washington, D.C.: Mercy Corps, 2001).

10. Mercy Corps, *Interviews with Participants in Agribusiness in Eastern Kosovo: Stability, Opportunity and Sustainability Conferences (2001–2002)* (Washington, D.C.: Mercy Corps, June 2002).

11. Mercy Corps, *Interviews.*

12. B. Ganson, interviews with community members and participants in the Imagine Coexistence initiative, Drvar and Prijedor, 2001–2002.

13. Wolleh, *Local Peace Constituencies*, p. 17.

14. Mercy Corps, *Eastern Kosovo Stabilization Program.*

15. See Wolleh, *Local Peace Constituencies.*

16. J. D. Fearon, "What Is Identity (as We Now Use the Word)?" Unpublished manuscript. [http://www.wcfia.harvard.edu/misc/initiative/identity/Identity Workshop/fearon2.pdf]. Nov. 3, 1999, p. 11; M. B. Brewer and W. Gardner, "Who Is This 'We'? Levels of Collective Identity and Self-Representations," *Journal of Personality and Social Psychology*, 1996, 71(1), 83–93.

17. J. C. Turner, *Social Influence* (Pacific Grove, Calif.: Brooks/Cole, 1991).

18. See D. D. Laitin, *Identity in Formation: The Russian-Speaking Populations in the Near Abroad* (Ithaca, N.Y.: Cornell University Press, 1998), p. 24. Laitin suggests that identity shifts occur in a kind of "tipping game" or cascade based on individuals' weighing alternative social identities through comparison with others in their community. This dynamic works against coexistence "spillover," as the status quo ante is one of division and antagonism, and anti-coexistence forces raise roadblocks to cues for a "cascade" toward coexistence.

19. H. Kelman, "Coalitions Across Conflict Lines: The Interplay of Conflicts Within and Between the Israeli and Palestinian Communities," in S. Worchel and J. A. Simpson (eds.), *Conflict Between People and Groups: Causes, Processes, and Resolutions* (Chicago: Nelson-Hall, 1993).

20. Kelman, "Coalitions Across Conflict Lines."

21. J. Bock, "The Exercise of Authority to Prevent Communal Conflict," *Peace and Change*, 2001, 26, 188–190.

22. A United States embassy official, personal communication, 1996.

23. See Coexistence Initiative, July 2002 [http://www.coexistence.net/coexistence/index.asp?page_id=164&catid=79].

24. L. Diamond, *What Is Peacebuilding?* (Washington, D.C.: Institute for Multi-Track Diplomacy, 1993).

25. J. D. Fearon and D. D. Laitin, "Explaining Interethnic Cooperation," *American*

Political Science Review, 1996, *90,* 715–735. Fearon and Laitin suggest that in-group policing of ethnic boundaries can in fact offer an equilibrium support-ing cooperation if the group sanctions its own members for cross-group violations. But if captured by ethnic entrepreneurs with an interest in mobi-lizing ethnic groups for conflict, it can fuel conflict escalation.

26. L. Huddy, "From Social to Political Identity: A Critical Examination of Social Identity Theory," *Political Psychology,* 2001, *22*(1), 121–156.

27. See Brewer and Gardner, "Who Is This 'We'?"

28. Interviews with community members and participants in the Imagine Coex-istence initiative, Drvar and Prijedor, 2001–2002.

29. J. P. Lederach, *Building Peace: Sustainable Reconciliation in Divided Societies* (Washington, D.C.: United States Institute of Peace Press, 1997).

30. See Lederach, *Building Peace,* pp. 37–55.

31. M. Gladwell, *The Tipping Point: How Little Things Can Make a Big Difference* (New York: Little, Brown, 2000).

Chapter Five

Imagine Coexistence Pilot Projects in Rwanda and Bosnia

Cynthia Burns, Laura McGrew, and Ilija Todorovic

The field staff of the United Nations High Commissioner for Refugees (UNHCR) has both a special responsibility for coexistence projects and a special perspective on them. As former High Commissioner for Refugees Sadako Ogata has explained, coexistence seems to provide an approach to the daunting problem of reintegrating refugees into their communities after violence and war. It has been up to field staff to undertake the translation of a concept into an effective UN program on the ground. This chapter presents a description of our beginnings, the questions that our initial work has raised, and our hopes for the future.

The Imagine Coexistence Project in Rwanda

Rwanda, located in the heart of Africa, is a small country of rolling hills and valleys. Today it seems quiet and calm. But in 1994, almost one million men, women, and children were brutally murdered in a ninety-day frenzy that generated shock waves around the globe, the effects of which are still felt in Rwanda today. It is in this context that UNHCR began the Imagine Coexistence project in Rwanda.

Background

UNHCR began its work with Rwandan refugees in 1959, assisting individuals fleeing ethnic conflict in the region. Several other waves of refugees occurred over the years, but the largest was following the genocide of Tutsi and massacre of moderate Hutu that started in April 1994. By July of that year, nearly half of Rwanda's population had either been killed or fled.[1] The Rwandans who remained were internally displaced, survivors of genocide, or otherwise traumatized. The country's infrastructure was in ruins, and the majority of its trained and educated personnel were dead or in exile. Between 1994 and 1996, UNHCR assisted in repatriating 1.3 million Rwandans. In late 1996, within a matter of a few weeks, an additional 1.1 million refugees returned from Zaïre (now known as the Democratic Republic of the Congo, or DRC) and Tanzania. It is currently estimated that one hundred thousand Rwandans remain outside the country and that forty-five thousand soldiers remain to be demobilized. The security situation in Rwanda remains tenuous because of continued fighting in the DRC and the fragility of neighboring Burundi's ongoing peace process. Continued peace and stability will depend on the successful reintegration of present and future returnees and overall geopolitical evolution of the Great Lakes region of Africa.

In July 1994, a new government composed mainly of Rwandans who had been in exile took control. From the beginning, the new Rwandan government called for the return of all refugees, arguing that the only way to solve the nation's long-standing problems was to bring all Rwandan people home to work out their differences regardless of their ethnic background. As an indication of the government's commitment to reintegration and reconciliation, the National Unity and Reconciliation Commission (NURC) was created in 1999. The Imagine Coexistence project works closely with the NURC, and on a global level, the NURC is providing an important model for postconflict national reconciliation.

Project Sites: Butare, Ruhengeri, and Umutara Provinces

Three distinct areas of the country were selected for the Imagine Coexistence pilot projects. Butare Province is considered the intellectual capital of the country because it houses the National University of Rwanda, the first and largest of the few universities in the nation, and its Center for Conflict Management (CCM). Historically, Butare also had a reputation for tolerance, and there was a greater degree of intermarriage between Hutu and Tutsi there than in other prefectures. It was also where many atrocities took place during the 1994 genocide because so many Tutsi and moderate Hutu mistakenly fled there seeking sanctuary. Butare continues to play a major role in the economic and legal development of Rwanda.

Two other provinces also host the Imagine Coexistence project, providing important comparisons and contrasts to Butare. Ruhengeri, with a primarily Hutu population, is in the northwest of the country, sharing borders with Uganda and the DRC. Given its proximity to the instability of these regions, the area remains insecure and inhospitable to rehabilitation efforts. Because of the insecurity, there are many internally displaced people. The bulk of the region's inhabitants live without adequate shelter and have lost their livestock; food shortages and poverty rack the area. Ruhengeri has received probably the least amount of assistance since the massive repatriation. The population of Ruhengeri suffered less from the genocide than from war between government soldiers and insurgents, which often affected the local civilian populations and bred simmering resentment against the government.

Umutara is a newly created province in the northeast, bordering Uganda and Tanzania, which has been relatively peaceful since 1995. Umutara is less mountainous than the other two provinces, with wide swatches of grazing land sprinkled with round houses used by traditional cattle grazers, many of whom are returnees from Uganda.

The Partners and the Projects

The Imagine Coexistence pilot projects in Rwanda are developed at the community level and generally revolve around an economic activity. Cash grants for the purchase of materials and services are distributed through an implementing partner. A key issue for the implementing partners is the process by which the projects are chosen and the capacity-building aspects inherent in the decision-making and monitoring processes for the projects. UNHCR's Imagine Coexistence implementing partners in Rwanda are Oxfam

Great Britain and Norwegian People's Aid (NPA). Joint work on the Imagine Coexistence initiative began in earnest in July 2001.

Oxfam Great Britain

Oxfam has been active in Rwanda for many years, working with communities primarily on water and reconstruction projects. Its collaboration with Imagine Coexistence began in early 2001 after a lengthy assessment of the communities with which it had worked since 1994. In these selected communities, Oxfam facilitated a process whereby the community chose a representative committee of twenty-five to thirty persons to participate in training sessions designed to enhance conflict resolution skills. Once they had been chosen, Oxfam began the first of three sessions, focusing on capacity building, communication and listening skills, and joint problem solving. After completing these training sessions, the committees identified community projects that Oxfam would help support. In Ruhengeri, the groups have chosen forty-three projects to date, the majority of which are livestock-breeding projects. In Umutara, twenty projects have been chosen in the domains of the arts, agriculture, credit funds, and livestock breeding.

Norwegian People's Aid

NPA used a different approach in choosing local collaborators with whom to work. Rather than create new committees, NPA instead partnered with associations or groups already working on coexistence issues. They have to date chosen three local partner groups: CECULUNGO, a youth arts and culture group; Abarahuje, a women's group on the Rotary Club model; and Équipes de Vie, a large group of eighteen hundred women divided into approximately eighty associations, including widows of the genocide and women whose husbands are in prison on charges of genocide. NPA is also following a capacity-building approach, providing small group meetings and more formal training to assist the groups to do project selection and microproject description development.

UNHCR and the Coexistence Network

As a basis for survey work, to gather information for lessons learned, and to fill an identified gap in coordination, a Rwandan "coexistence network" was developed by UNHCR. Working closely with the NURC as well as the CCM at the National University of Rwanda, UNHCR has coordinated and facilitated monthly meetings on topics of common interest to a group of NGOs and others focusing on coexistence.[2] Topics include the effects on coexistence in Rwanda of the reintegration of accused and convicted prisoners, the NURC, youth, women, land issues, HIV/AIDS, and the reintegration of demobilized soldiers.

Surprisingly, in many cases, these network meetings provided the first opportunity for participants to meet one another, learn of other coexistence work in the region, and create links between organizations and individuals with similar goals. The connections made through this network have also facilitated a parallel initiative created by a local NGO, the Friends Peace House, which hosts monthly "peace lunches" and a film series that serve to strengthen the network.

Coexistence Workshops

UNHCR has convened several participatory workshops with key partners in the coexistence network. These workshops have served a team-building purpose and also provide important information on lessons learned or what might be called the best practices of coexistence. Topics of discussion have included concepts of coexistence, project selection criteria, and indicators of coexistence and of project success.

Constraints

Security problems in certain areas of the country constrain implementation of the pilot projects. The limited availability of local staff and local partner groups in Rwanda has also been a constraint. Given the years of turmoil and the decimation of the population, there are few people with skills in project implementation. Trauma resulting from the genocide and years of war has resulted in a lack of trust and confidence and increased fear.

Perhaps most important, there is a disconnect between the national focus on reconciliation and the inability of the majority of Rwandans to speak about ethnicity or the group differences that led to conflict in 1994. In the aftermath of the genocide, ethnicity has been taken off identity cards, and it is no longer "politically correct" to speak of ethnicity. Barring discussion of ethnicity has greatly hindered the ability of the NGOs to address the causes of recent violence in Rwanda and facilitate the beginning of healing.

Transitional Justice in Rwanda

Transitional justice is an issue of tremendous importance in Rwanda in that it affects the ability of Rwandans to reintegrate and coexist. Believing peace, justice, mercy, and reconciliation to be linked, many Rwandans declare that in order to have coexistence, some sort of justice must be achieved. But in Rwanda, the process of justice is complicated, due to both the tremendous numbers of perpetrators involved in the genocide and the current disarray in the legal system. In response to these constraints, the government of Rwanda is in the process of introducing a traditional judicial system wherein individuals accused of certain crimes related to the genocide can be tried at the community level by peers. Given the high degree of community participation required, the delicate subjects that must be discussed, and the inevitable unearthing of past traumas, there is a fear among many observers that this Gacaca process, while addressing important issues, will inadvertently heighten mistrust and conflict in the community (see Chapter Three). This will most certainly have a direct impact on the reintegration of Rwandan society and affect the possibility of coexistence in Rwanda. The Gacaca process is thus being observed and discussed within the context of the project.

The Imagine Coexistence Project in Bosnia and Herzegovina

The state of Bosnia and Herzegovina (BiH), recognized in 1992 as an independent country, was one of six republics that once formed the former Socialist Federal Republic of Yugoslavia (SFRY).[3] Located geographically at the center of the federation, Bosnia's population was made up of all the ethnic groups that made up the SFRY, with Bosniaks (or Muslims), Serbs, and Croats accounting for the vast majority.

Given this mixture of different ethnic communities, BiH had the highest number of interethnic marriages and was in many ways a microcosm of the harmonious relations between the main ethnic communities in the SFRY at large. All this changed in 1992 when the civil war broke out in BiH on the heels of the conflict in Slovenia and Croatia. Within weeks, all notions of ethnic coexistence were lost. The ensuing three and a half years of war left some two hundred thousand dead, while an estimated 1.2 million persons fled abroad and an additional million people became internally displaced. The conflict added the expression "ethnic cleansing" to the world's vocabulary.

The result, by the end of 1995, was a newly recognized country, separated like oil and vinegar by its ethnic mixture. Serbs lived in the northern Republika Srpska entity while Croats unwillingly shared with Bosniaks a divided southern federation entity. The nation was in ruins physically, socially, and economically. The only way to combat a renewal of "ethnic cleansing" was to aid in reconstruction and rehabilitation—to help individuals return home and start anew—and the international community reconstruction effort assisted thousands of people to do just that. Now UNHCR's coexistence project has turned its attention to the question, How can the returns be sustained in an ethnically mixed postconflict environment as a step in the reestablishment of coexistence?

Aftermath of the Conflict

Since 1996, UNHCR has helped minorities return to their prewar homes either through efforts to reconstruct destroyed properties or by pressuring local authorities to reinstate returnees into their former homes, temporarily occupied by others. Since 1998, when minority returns started to be recorded, a total of 287,000 persons have returned to their homes in BiH. Despite these encouraging figures, UNHCR estimates that some 600,000 Bosnian refugees and displaced persons remain in the region, for whom a durable solution has yet to be found.

The Dayton Accords did not provide any political framework for the process of coexistence, let alone the more difficult goal of reconciliation. The notion of justice was left to the International Criminal Tribunal for the Former Yugoslavia (ICTY). It is important to note that none of the national, entity, or local authorities in Bosnia and Herzegovina have undertaken any significant steps toward opening up a dialogue on what happened during the conflict. Hence there has been to date no governmental leadership to foster reconciliation efforts between the warring ethnic groups. If anything, coexistence activities in the country are grassroots initiatives financed and initiated in general by the international community. These initiatives have served as the model for implementation of the Imagine Coexistence project in Bosnia.

Project Sites: Drvar and Prijedor (Kozarac)

UNHCR selected two areas in Bosnia as pilot sites for the Imagine Coexistence project. These are Drvar and Kozarac, a suburb of Prijedor.

Drvar, a logging town, is located in the western part of the country known as the Bosnian Krajina. Before the war, Drvar had approximately sixteen thousand inhabitants, 97 percent of whom were of Serb ethnicity. In 1995, the vast majority of the Bosnian Serbs in Drvar were forcefully expelled by Croatian forces and the area was subsequently repopulated by Bosnian Croats. Though the environment remained very fragile, the first Serb returns to Drvar began in 1997. The conditions conducive to return have been adversely affected on several occasions, punctuated by occasional violence and riots, but Bosnian Serbs have returned to Drvar in fairly considerable numbers. At the same time, a number of the displaced Croats began to move from Drvar to their prewar municipalities, enabling the return of Bosnian Serbs and repossession of their property. Today the population of Drvar is estimated to be nine thousand persons, with an approximately equal split between displaced Croats and Serb returnees. Although more Serbs are likely to return, it is estimated that nearly 80 percent of the displaced Croats wish to remain in Drvar.

Unfortunately, the political and economic power in Drvar is still in the hands of the Bosnian Croats. The main prewar employer, a lumber mill called Finvest, is run by Bosnian Croats and employs only Croats. Croats also fill the majority of the municipal jobs. Moreover, the Bosnian Croat army (the HVO) still maintains a presence in the center of the town.

Prijedor, the second largest town in the Republika Srpska, is located fifty kilometers northwest of Banja Luka. Before the war, the population of the Prijedor municipality was approximately 120,000 inhabitants, split nearly equally between Bosniaks and Serbs. During the war, as Serb forces set up three internment camps in the area, Bosniaks fled, and Prijedor became a Serb stronghold. As Bosniaks fled, displaced Serbs moved en masse to inhabit Prijedor and its surrounding suburbs, including the town of Kozarac. Since 1998, the greater Kozarac area has witnessed the return of twenty-five hundred minorities (mostly Muslims) to their homes as a result of large-scale reconstruction efforts made by the international community. At the same time, approximately thirteen hundred of the displaced Serbs remain in Kozarac. Although significant attention and assistance by the international community in housing reconstruction and infrastructure have created the basic conditions for a relatively normal life for returnees, the economic infrastructure was ruined by the war, and the area still lacks job opportunities.

The Genesis Project: UNHCR Implementing Partner

Genesis was a direct implementing partner for UNHCR in 1996 through one of its Bosnian Women's Initiative projects and has sponsored a project for community residents, schoolchildren, and other beneficiaries selected by UNHCR, known as the Video Bus and Mobile Library. Genesis is itself a model of coexistence, made up of staff members coming from different ethnic backgrounds.

The Projects

Since the coexistence efforts are all designed to be at the grassroots level, Genesis has been quite active at the two BiH sites, meeting with local authorities, NGOs, associations, and prominent community leaders. It helped identify the needs in the community and develop a network of coexistence-oriented groups to address these needs through the local initiatives. UNHCR and Genesis consultants have since identified nineteen formal and informal local NGOs willing to assist UNHCR and Genesis in the process of implementing twenty-six coexistence projects in Drvar and Kozarac. Approximately half of these are income-generating projects; the remainder are cultural, educational, psychosocial, or sports-centered initiatives. Several of the activities chosen are being carried out by local NGOs or groups that have developed a reputation for coexistence, while others are newly formed and will require some capacity building to make them effective.

The basic criteria applied during the two selection rounds for projects and groups concentrated on several key issues. The microprojects must

- Be at the community level, with local NGOs and groups fully supporting the initiative, which would include joint activities among the conflict groups at the beneficiary level
- Create a context where relationships can be built and where healing of trauma is likely to occur
- Embody the principle of nondiscriminatory treatment
- Be capable of replication or adaptation elsewhere
- Promise sustainable effects and impact beyond the life of the subproject
- Have variable points of entry on which coexistence activities can be structured

Coexistence Workshops

Genesis, with the advice of UNHCR, has been involved in organizing several workshops for the potential and selected participants in the Imagine Coexistence project. Issues raised in these workshops have included the definition of coexistence, ways to achieve it through proposed community-based activities, possible indicators to measure its progress, and project selection criteria.

One result of these workshops has been a bond among ethnic groups as they share the constraints and successes of the projects within and outside the community. It has also allowed some project organizers to view cooperation with other groups as a positive way to further their own abilities to achieve their project goals. In any case, it brought the Serbs and Bosniaks in Kozarac and the Serbs and Croats in Drvar closer by opening avenues for dialogue and shared work experiences.

Justice Through ICTY

During its formation, the International Criminal Tribunal for the Former Yugoslavia was considered by the international community

as a step forward in the process of punishing the guilty and in helping victims find closure in connection with terrible crimes. This
has so far proved not to be the case. Most groups in the region believe that the court is too political and biased, laying the blame for
the war primarily on the Serbs. Many Bosniaks feel that ICTY has
only targeted the top leaders and has not dealt with the regular
army soldiers, local authorities, and policemen who participated
in and committed war crimes during the conflict. In general, Bosnian inhabitants are unified in their view that ICTY's notion of reconciliation does not work. This failure, in addition to the lack of
government-sponsored reconciliation dialogue, has left the various ethnic groups still firm in their differing views of how the war
started, its aftermath, and the concept of collective and individual
responsibilities for actions taken in it.

Initial Observations on Lessons Learned in Rwanda and Bosnia

The following observations are part of the field perspective that
fed into the initial research design described in Chapter Six. In
turn, field operations are being modified by the ongoing research
and evaluation efforts that UNHCR has underwritten.

Definition and Measurement of Coexistence

In the development stage of the Imagine Coexistence project, coexistence had not been clearly defined. However, as the project
progressed, the UNHCR Bosnia office realized that the concept in
practice was the same as what had been done for many years since
Dayton under the guise of reintegration or assistance projects.

In Rwanda, there has been much discussion on the definition of
coexistence. Defining the concept has been difficult given the linguistic and cultural divides in the country, and translating the idea
of coexistence into Kinyarwanda has been especially problematic.
Throughout the Rwandan workshops and meetings, various definitions of coexistence were put forward, the most comprehensive of
which is as follows: *Coexistence is the process whereby reconciliation is
achieved, and it combines equally the concepts of peace, truth, justice, and
forgiveness.*

Another issue raised at both sites involved the difficulty of defining and measuring success in achieving coexistence. While some project milestones are easier to determine, the real test of coexistence is in the changing attitudes of the population, and these are difficult to codify.

Short-Term Focus of the Project Versus Long-Term Process of Coexistence

In Rwanda and Bosnia, as in most countries emerging from conflict, the development of trust is key to coexistence. Given the shattered social networks, the building of trust and the development of community activities will necessarily take a very long time, in stark contrast to UNHCR's short-term mandate in emergency situations. Repatriations processes must begin quickly, with only a six-month period to follow up on returnees; UNHCR must simultaneously focus on the initial steps needed for the building of the kind of trust required to achieve coexistence.

Training in Conflict Resolution and Transformation

Consensus seems to be that training in conflict resolution, which we believe is integral to promoting coexistence, cannot be separated from projects in economic development or humanitarian assistance. Partners have often stated that when training alone is offered, "hungry people can't concentrate." However, they also have observed that economic activities alone can perpetuate conflictual relationships or even lead to violence, as noted by Mary Anderson's "Do No Harm" model.[4]

Capacity-Building Approach Versus Traditional Project Implementation Approach

Both implementing partners have focused on the process of selecting and defining the microprojects and included such capacity-building aspects as conflict analysis, problem-solving skills, and communication skills. The underlying belief is that these skills are necessary for coexistence and that unless done properly, the project by itself cannot lead to coexistence.

Role of Religion in Rwanda

The majority of the groups working on coexistence or reconciliation in Rwanda are either NGOs with religious ties or established religious structures. This religious base raises two important issues affecting the work of the Imagine Coexistence project. First of all, the UN is a secular organization, and the Bible-based focus of many of the groups makes work difficult on occasion. Second, the role of the churches before and during the genocide is a subject not often discussed in society. Since at times the church itself and, more often, individuals in the church have been implicated (and some of them convicted in the various tribunals), there are many sensitive issues related to this topic that need further study.

Selection of Implementing Partners

The community-based projects require a great deal of time, a number of resources, and special expertise. Given UNHCR's far-reaching mandate and responsibilities, local or international partners are needed to manage the day-to-day implementation of the projects.

Selection of Project Sites in BiH

The selection of Drvar and Prijedor (Kozarac) is proving to be problematic. Although both were ethnically mixed at the time of selection in late 2000, the two areas are now becoming increasingly more monoethnic, due to more effective implementation of property legislation throughout BiH. Increasing monoethnicism will continue to be the trend in the coming years. One must wonder how successful coexistence projects can exist in increasingly monoethnic regions.

Selection of the Recipients of the Grants

UNHCR discovered that the selection process for both partners and projects was not easy. Because communities recovering from mass violence generally remain polarized for some time after the cessation of hostilities, everything can be seen as politicized. A careful balance must be struck in selecting organizations representing the various ethnic groups as well as those representing displaced and returning persons.

Importance of Income-Generating Projects

Another tremendous factor compounding the process of promoting coexistence, in the case of Bosnia, is the country's economic malaise. BiH has an unemployment rate of more than 50 percent. Can a divided community reconcile after a war when so many of its people are unemployed, left idle to carry on the hatreds of the past? Given this environment, any well-intentioned coexistence project will have problems developing and flourishing in the long run, and what is needed is a national program of reconciliation coupled with vast economic investment and development to create more jobs. In Rwanda, all but one of the microproject grants were income-generating, also showing that economic issues were at the forefront of beneficiary concerns.

National Reconciliation Efforts in Bosnia and Rwanda

An additional lesson we must heed is that only so much coexistence can be achieved through small-scale grassroots efforts. ICTY seems to have had no effect on fostering reconciliation, and BiH has no statewide program for that purpose, given a lack of political will at all levels of government. In BiH, a sprinkling of grassroots projects can have only a minimal influence on a community that lacks a national peace-oriented program in politics, employment, education, and the media. In Rwanda, the state-sponsored NURC has been an integral partner to UNHCR in promoting coexistence. Although one of the stated purposes of the International Criminal Tribunal for Rwanda (ICTR) is to promote national reconciliation, ICTR, similar to ICTY, has also been reported to have had little positive effect on reconciliation so far.

Evaluating Coexistence

The Bosnia and Rwanda pilot projects have been and will continue to be evaluated, and lessons will be drawn from their design and implementation. The very different postconflict environments of

Bosnia and Rwanda proved to be rich terrain for these pilot projects. Capacity, culture, infrastructure, and the prevailing economic and social conditions in each location provided great contrasts. Yet the one commonality was a deep-rooted hatred both causing and caused by brutality: genocide in one case, ethnically motivated murder in another.

The decision to build the majority of these efforts around an economic activity will be reviewed. In designing the projects, we were conscious of the extreme poverty and deprivation that both societies faced and how that would detract from reconciliation efforts. We were reminded repeatedly that a hungry belly thinks of little more than eating. We were also aware that in both conflicts, the issue of property—its ownership, occupation, and recuperation—was central before, during, and after the conflict. Economics has certainly had a bearing on relationships.

Most of the grassroots projects noted here have been implemented by women's groups in both countries. The role of women as peacemakers and in reconstructing their lives and societies will also have to be evaluated in the context of these pilot projects. The role and contributions of youth have also been important and should be investigated, as well as those of the elderly where they are implicated in projects.

Another important element to the success of this project has been the need to devote considerable time to the process itself. Implementation of the projects is not nearly as important as the steps required to get there. Training, developing the relationship between group members, designing and selecting the projects, and coming to a consensus on the roles of the group members are at the heart of the coexistence intent. Project implementation is really the test of whether the re-creation of a collaborative relationship works.

The coexistence network that was successfully established in Rwanda has been a source of a great deal of good thought and exchanges on peace, reconciliation, and conflict resolution. One factor that facilitated the implementation of the projects in Rwanda was the national government's sponsorship of reconciliation, institutionalized in the National Unity and Reconciliation Commission. This factor was not present in Bosnia, and the effect of this difference will also form part of the evaluation.

Several important topics for further study have been identified, including the following:

- What are the commonalties and differences between the approaches of the implementing partners in Rwanda and in Bosnia?
- What is the role of conflict resolution training in economic development and humanitarian projects? Which tools are most effective for training?
- What is the role of change agents—dynamic, committed, aware individuals who have done great works? The project has not yet been able to fully explore this concept in the field context.
- What is the influence of various internal and external processes and events on prospects for coexistence? The project has so far identified several key topics. In Rwanda, Gacaca will play an extremely important role in the process of promoting coexistence—both the legal process itself and issues related to the reintegration of accused and convicted prisoners. Land scarcity, development, and use; poverty; decentralization; demobilized soldiers; high unemployment rates; and an increasingly disenfranchised youth population all have a bearing on the return to a state of coexistence.
- What are the specific roles of women, UNHCR and NGO staff, and other key outside individuals influencing reconciliation? A study of these factors would also be informative.

These and many more questions will be posed as the research component, currently under way, brings out important lessons for UNHCR and other humanitarian practitioners. [5]

Perhaps at first glance the Imagine Coexistence approach to re-constructing and reconciling societies does not seem very novel. Humanitarian organizations such as UNHCR have been implementing small-scale assistance projects in postconflict situations for decades. What it does do, however, is require us to ask one more question and make one further analysis in project implementation than perhaps we might otherwise do: Does this project, small though it may be, foster coexistence between conflicted communities?

The pilot projects may indeed raise more questions than they answer. But inquiry is a necessary requirement for an organization such as UNHCR to remain dynamic, responsive, and proactive. Every day we face challenges caused by inhumanity and the need to find a human solution. We need to imagine—just imagine—what more could be done.

Notes

1. United Nations High Commissioner for Refugees, *Rwanda Recovery: UNHCR's Repatriation and Reintegration Activities in Rwanda from 1994–1999* (Geneva, Switzerland: Office of the United National High Commissioner for Refugees, 2000).

2. The initial group consisted primarily of the key international NGOs or "key partners": Catholic Relief Services, Trócaire, Norwegian People's Aid, Oxfam, GTZ, and World Vision. Gradually donors and international and local NGOs were added.

3. The six republics in SFRY were Croatia, Slovenia, Bosnia and Herzegovina, Serbia, Montenegro, and Macedonia. Serbia contained two autonomous provinces, Kosovo-Metohija and Vojvodina.

4. See Mary B. Anderson, *Do No Harm: How Aid Can Support Peace—or War* (Boulder, Colo.: Rienner, 1999).

5. The research component is being conducted by a team from the Fletcher School, Tufts University, Medford, Mass.

Chapter Six

Evaluating Coexistence
Insights and Challenges
Eileen F. Babbitt

Coexistence projects have existed for many decades, although they are often referred to by other names (see Chapter One). With the upsurge of civil wars in the 1990s, the former UN High Commissioner for Refugees (UNHCR), Sadako Ogata, became interested in coexistence work as a possible way for UNHCR to manage the reintegration of refugees into communities where they were no longer wanted and from which they had in many cases been violently rejected. As described in Chapter Five, UNHCR launched the Imagine Coexistence initiative in 1999 and chose Bosnia and Rwanda as the locations for coexistence pilot projects. To ensure their effectiveness, UNHCR also wanted ongoing evaluation of these efforts, based on up-to-date knowledge of both the theory and the practice of coexistence work. This was a great challenge, as the evaluation of such efforts has been fragmented, and there is no consensus on how it should be done. However, a team of researchers from the Fletcher School at Tufts University agreed to take on this task.[1]

In this chapter, I will examine the assumptions we made as we began our study and review some of our major findings. I will then describe the methods we used to arrive at our results, in the hope that our methodology might lead to improved standards of practice. It is important to note here that our methods were developed for practical use by field staff of a large international organization, not for social scientists trained in the rigors of academic data collection. Finally, I will comment on the changes we would now make to that methodology, based on our experiences in this study.

Assumptions Going In

We began the study with the following hypotheses, based on our previous experiences working with coexistence efforts and on the expectations we heard from UNHCR:

1. It is important to explore how members of divided communities define coexistence, in order to frame this initiative in ways that will resonate with local participants.
2. It is also important to explore how outside interveners define coexistence, to find out what kinds of predispositions and biases they might be bringing into their work.
3. Bringing internally displaced persons or people from returnee groups together with the domicile population for activities of various kinds is a good way to help them develop relationships with each other.
4. Because of the lack of economic opportunities in divided communities, income-generating projects are the most effective type of activity to foster coexistence.
5. All activities should be augmented with conflict resolution training, to improve skills in communication, negotiation, and problem solving.
6. Since many of the people in these divided communities have been traumatized by the violence in their country, encouraging people to talk about their past experiences is a helpful way to humanize relationships and promote healing.
7. Activities should be especially targeted for women and youth, as women are more likely to be the "bridge builders" in their communities and youth are the hope for the future.
8. Leadership matters in coexistence activities and the way in which projects are managed should model the kinds of values that coexistence seeks to foster.
9. The larger context within which coexistence work is done has a significant impact on the success of the activities in each location.
10. Evaluation of project successes should focus on the process by which results are achieved, as well as on the results themselves.

11. Sustainability of the impacts will result from the relationships that are built during the initial one-year pilot period.
12. UNHCR can be a change agent in these communities, by providing the resources and the initial institutional support to jump-start coexistence efforts.

To assess the validity of these assumptions, we compared three sets of data: context analyses of the five pilot regions (Prijedor and Drvar in Bosnia; Ruhengeri, Umutara, and Butare provinces in Rwanda); the approaches used by the three implementing partners to organize the interventions (Genesis in Bosnia; Oxfam GB and Norwegian People's Aid in Rwanda); and the development and implementation of forty projects launched by the communities in these regions.

Significant Findings

Although these findings are only preliminary, given the short amount of time for the implementation of the projects, we were surprised at some of the results.

Importance of the Implementing Partners

We had not anticipated the significance of the implementing partners, which were clearly the most crucial element in the success of the coexistence work. In collaboration with the UNHCR field staff, they determined the strategy to follow in each implementing community, they provided the front line of oversight and support to the coexistence activities, and they were looked to as a model for the coexistence attitudes and behaviors the initiative hoped to instill in the target communities. They also provided an important lens through which to see and interpret local events, issues, attitudes, and perceptions that were critical for coexistence efforts. Two of the most important strategic decisions implementing partners would make were, first, how to engage the community and, second, how to establish criteria for project selection.

Genesis: A Bosnian NGO and UNHCR's Implementary Partner

Genesis brought potential applicants in each community together, to introduce the project and explain its definition of coexistence:

communication, interaction, cooperation, trust. The group invited community leaders, heads of other NGOs, and other community organizations. Individuals and groups in each community who were interested in applying for a grant then attended a second workshop, in which Genesis helped them develop their ideas, encouraged and clarified the coexistence elements in each proposal, and worked to weed out overlapping ideas. Also at this stage, Genesis began to assess who, in their words, were the "real believers" in coexistence, rather than entities just wanting to get funds. In addition, it was looking for applicants who could set realistic goals within the time frame allotted, could clearly demonstrate a coexistence component in their project, and had the ability to manage the activity they were proposing.

The strategy of UNHCR Bosnia was to work in a variety of social domains and with a variety of target groups. Genesis therefore consciously sought out projects in sports, employment, education, social settings, and therapeutic settings. It also involved different target groups in the coexistence initiative, including men and women, older and younger people, rural and urban populations, and of course, people of different ethnic backgrounds. This had the advantage of demonstrating the possibility of coexistence work in a variety of social interactions and with diverse populations, and it also gave the research team a rich array of material to analyze. It had the possible disadvantage of dispersing the initiative's resources and focus in ways that prevented any one of these domains from receiving concentrated attention.

Norwegian People's Aid

UNHCR asked Norwegian People's Aid (NPA) to launch the initiative in Rwanda's Butare Province, and NPA decided to implement the project through existing local associations that had explicit coexistence goals. It identified several of these, conducted interviews with staff and beneficiaries of these organizations, and finally chose three with which to work, eliciting the organizations' assessment of community needs and helping them develop project proposals that contained a coexistence component. NPA had no previous experience working in Butare (though it had conducted programs elsewhere in Rwanda), and this lack of relationship and deep local knowledge compromised its effectiveness, particularly in situations where political access would have helped move projects along.

Oxfam Great Britain

In the summer of 2000, Oxfam had launched its own coexistence initiative, after a long internal review process of its entire program in Rwanda. The results of that review were a reorientation of its focus in Rwanda to community-based decision making and conflict management.[2]

To do this, Oxfam decided to work with whole communities rather than groups within those communities. The organization questioned the assumption that the best entry point for coexistence work is through projects in established associations, based on feedback from the community and having observed that in certain contexts, these associations can themselves be sources of division (they are generally targeted at a specific group and therefore do not benefit the community as a whole).

Oxfam therefore identified specific "cellules" in Ruhengeri and Umutara provinces and worked with the community development councils (CDCs) in each cellule. First, Oxfam staff attended several community meetings. At those meetings, Oxfam outlined the project goals and criteria and told each community that it would receive a set amount of money. The important step was that the community itself, as a whole rather than just its leadership, had to decide how the money would be allocated. As Oxfam noted in its October 2001 report, "Meetings in the targeted communities have demonstrated that they are looking for ways to make the small grants funds work for the community rather than individuals. In Ruhengeri, for example, communities have proposed that rather than implement the grants through associations that focus on specific populations or interests (for example, farmers' associations or widows' associations), the funds should be provided for community projects implemented by traditional systems that are designed to benefit the entire community. The traditional 'ambulance' system is an example of this idea—it is a structure already in existence that reaches everyone in the community." The fact that the community was made aware that the grants were for the benefit of the entire community also contributed to increasing participation in community meetings and in subsequent decision making.

These very different approaches and capacities exerted more influence than any other single element in determining the effect of the coexistence projects in each region. Each had strengths and weaknesses. The Oxfam program, with its focus on whole communities, laid the most solid foundations for enduring change.

Inadequacy of the Contact Hypothesis and Income Generation

Two of our initial hypotheses related to the kinds of activities most likely to facilitate coexistence. One said that bringing returnees together with the domicile population in various ways would promote relationships, and another argued that income-generating activities would be most effective in this regard. Neither has proved to be true.

Bringing People Together to Jump-Start Relationships

This is a form of the well-known contact hypothesis, in which the key assumption is that simply putting people together in some way will create change; they will talk, drink coffee, laugh, and find out that they have interests in common and that they are all human beings rather than monsters. Based on this hypothesis, projects were sought that created conditions for people to get together around some kind of activity. Conflict in return communities would then be reduced by "normalized" contact with the "other."

Our findings were that contact did not facilitate coexistence unless the activity was specifically designed and implemented to do so. For example, activities such as bringing people together to watch films or learn about childbirth did not, by themselves, spur the development of relationships. Something more had to be introduced—facilitated discussions, conflict management training, shared decision making—for relationships to be established and improved.

Income-Generating Projects

Income-generating projects were of particular interest to UNHCR, as it was one of the operating assumptions that the best strategy would be to use such projects as an incentive for people from different identity groups to come in contact with each other. Such projects would thus achieve two important goals at once: coexistence and economic development. We were therefore particularly interested in testing this assumption. We found that in the short time available for project implementation, none of the income-generating projects attained financial self-sufficiency, although many have some potential to do so. In addition, income generation was neither necessary nor sufficient for coexistence efforts to be successful. It was not necessary for coexistence because there were many nonincome projects that produced positive coexistence results, and it was not sufficient for coexistence to occur because the income projects with a coexistence benefit were supplemented with activities other than the work environment itself that created the conditions for improved relationships.

Even with a short time frame and a small universe of projects, Table 6.1 indicates that there were many nonincome projects that had positive coexistence impacts, while some income-generating projects did not. This suggests strongly that income generation is not a necessary component of success. It is also not sufficient, as a closer look at the list of income-generating projects with positive coexistence benefits illustrates.

In Bosnia, two of the income-generating projects that showed some positive signs of coexistence (Internet café, mushroom cultivation) did so because of the project leaders. In the Internet café, the leader took a hands-off approach to running the café, and therefore the staff had lots of opportunity to pitch in. This established much better working relations than other projects in which staff were more tightly controlled and viewed the workplace as merely a job. In the mushroom-growing project, the leader (a Croat) was clearly committed to an equal relationship with her employee (a Serb). Both felt comfortable with each other, and the leader is handing over the business to her employee when she leaves Drvar.

In the coffeeshop project, coexistence was not strong among employees, but the shop itself attracted a mix of patrons from both Serb and Croat communities, unlike most of the other commercial ventures in the town. In large part, this was due to its identity as a safe, family-oriented environment that drew both parents and children. This coffeeshop stands out in contrast to the other places in town where people gather. It does not serve alcohol and is not rowdy. The child-friendly atmosphere seemed to help coexistence.

In Rwanda, livestock and agriculture projects were implemented in Ruhengeri and Umutara, as part of the communitywide decision process put in place by Oxfam. These included goat rearing, sheep breeding, marketing of vegetables, and grain milling. Therefore, the projects themselves grew out of a very participatory

Table 6.1. Relationship of Income Generation and Coexistence Benefits.

Coexistence Benefits	Income-Generating Projects Currently Producing Assets for Beneficiaries		Non-Income-Generating Projects
	Positive Assets	No Assets	
Positive benefits	*Bosnia* Coffeeshop	*Bosnia* Greenhouse[a] Mushroom growing Internet café	*Bosnia* Journalism training Psychosocial programs for children, women, and the elderly
	Rwanda Livestock (goat rearing, sheep breeding) Agriculture (marketing of vegetables, milling of grain) Microcredit Bus (for paid transport to town)	*Rwanda* Public phone Health club	Handball Band (entertainment) Basketball Folk dance club Community newspaper Judo club Computer class
No benefits	*Bosnia* Plastic bag factory Chicken raising Strawberry cultivation	*Bosnia* Nail production Herb drying[a] Apple cultivation *Rwanda* Brick manufacture	*Bosnia* Pregnancy information classes Films for community viewing

[a]Projected to generate income in year two or three of operation.

process and did not stand alone. As the Oxfam director stated, "Specifying the aim of 'improving livelihoods' as an expected outcome of the grants would contradict our goal. The goal is to have the community decide on its priorities—be they livelihoods, income generation, building a school, human rights training, or whatever. Our goal is not to decide this for the people—actually, it is the decision-making process that is key. If we insist that the aim be directed at livelihoods per se, we believe that we would be undermining this process."

The remaining projects in Rwanda, chosen by NPA, were implemented by two existing local NGOs—one a youth group and the other a women's group—already committed to coexistence work. Both existed before the income-generating projects were launched, and the difficulties they encountered in making these successful in fact only strengthened their already strong internal relationships.

We also identified additional cautions that made us question the priority that income projects were given by UNHCR. First, income-generating projects seem to be more expensive, on a per capita basis, than nonincome projects. In Bosnia, the average cost per beneficiary of the income-generating projects was 3,469 convertible marks (KM), or $1,734. The average cost per beneficiary of the non-income-generating projects was only 589 KM, or $294, less than 20 percent of the income projects. Of course, the hope for these income projects is that they will become self-sustaining, making the higher initial investment worthwhile. This premise will have to be tested at a later stage to see if it holds. It was not possible to do so in the four months of project operations.

It will also be important to determine whether these businesses continue to employ a multiethnic staff. In Bosnia, some of the project leaders seemed resentful at having to conform to this requirement in order to receive the funding. When and if their businesses become self-sufficient, or even out of the range of monitoring by Genesis, it will be interesting to note whether they retain their diversity. In Rwanda, the crucial question for the Oxfam-supported projects is whether the communities continue to be inclusive in their decision making and power sharing. With the NPA projects, the associations sponsoring these projects are themselves multiethnic, so ongoing assessment would include the extent to which both the projects and the associations remain diverse.

The third caution is that income projects sometimes reach far fewer beneficiaries than nonincome projects. In Bosnia, the average number of beneficiaries for the income projects was 10, with a range from 2 to 26 and a total of 104 beneficiaries over ten projects. The nonincome projects reached an average of 102 beneficiaries, with a range from 4 to 730 participants and a total of 1,537 beneficiaries over fifteen projects. This is a significant difference. The Oxfam data are a counterpoint, however; because their design encompassed entire communities, the income-generating work reached fairly large numbers. Again, we do not yet know how sustainable any of these projects are economically or in terms of coexistence. That can only be ascertained with ongoing assessment over the next three to five years.

More troublesome was our observation that in Bosnia, income projects may actually perpetuate divisions rather than heal them. It puts UNHCR in the position of providing jobs in circumstances where employment is not just a livelihood but also very politicized. The politics of job creation cannot be ignored. We found that hiring choices even in small enterprises is a function of patronage and party affiliation; interveners can unwittingly make things worse for members of minority or returnee groups if job placement is not handled sensitively.

In many cases, creating a multiethnic work environment can also be complex and troublesome, especially where a person from one group has sole management control and offers nothing but a salary to members of other groups to join as employees. Without more effort at fostering coexistence, we question long-term viability. But without longer-term follow-up on these projects, it is impossible to know if these situations eventually work themselves out over time or simply get worse. Oxfam and NPA present an alternative, in which income generation was incorporated into a broader set of activities or accompanied by dialogue and joint problem solving. This did not prevent conflict within projects completely but allowed for it to be managed constructively.

Finally, as noted, it was difficult to generate projects that both enjoyed financial success and yielded coexistence benefits. In Bosnia, only the coffeeshop project in Drvar demonstrated some financial success as well as some coexistence benefits in the community. As pointed out, thus far the coexistence benefits were primarily among customers rather than within staff.

In Rwanda, many of the Oxfam projects have seemed able to both create income and foster coexistence because of the nature of project implementation. Success in terms of wealth creation (for example, the purchase and care of livestock) was possible only if the communities found a way to work together; otherwise they would not get the grants to purchase their goats. In Bosnia, UNHCR's approach was to look for project leaders with interests in coexistence, even if they had no previous business experience. The thought was that it would be easier to teach business skills than to instill coexistence values into someone with lots of business expertise but no interest in coexistence. Our research did not investigate whether this strategy worked, and it would be an important question to include in future studies.

One thing we did learn from the projects in Butare, Rwanda, is that there must be a sound process for evaluating the viability of income-generating projects before they are funded. For example, one of the projects proposed by a women's organization involved the purchase and running of a shuttle bus between their village and the major town nearby. The intent was that by providing a much needed community service, the woman would also generate work and income for themselves. However, during the rainy season, the road between their village and the town becomes impassable by anything other than a large four-wheel-drive vehicle. The bus has been purchased, but it cannot run on the route where the women intended until the road is repaired. A more careful analysis beforehand might have helped correct the deficiencies in their planning, which would have made the project more financially viable.

In the income-generating projects in particular, transparency in project management was an important key to the emergence of coexistence. There is a great deal of suspicion in both countries that people who manage projects keep implementation money for themselves and the beneficiaries never see it. A lack of transparency or accountability as to the way decisions about project resources are made or how project funds are managed can exacerbate distrust and undermine coexistence goals. The Oxfam projects, for example, as well as some of the projects in Butare, were high on the coexistence dimension in large part because of the management structure and the equal participation of all beneficiaries. This created the required transparency and accountability and made everyone involved feel equally responsible for success or failure.

The Insufficiency of Small Projects

In both countries, it was also clear that microprojects alone could not address the underlying forces that continued to generate ongoing conflict and intergroup tensions in communities. There are larger structural forces at work, and activities would have to be specifically designed to tackle these forces in order to have an impact on them. Moreover, as Chapter Four illustrates, the microprojects themselves might be eroded by these larger forces. We observed that several projects in Drvar, Prijedor, and Butare were undermined by a lack of political cooperation. In both Bosnia and Rwanda, we asked implementing partners and project leaders if they thought their activities had created relationships that could withstand the pressure if violence were again to escalate. All of them answered in the negative—it would take much more for relationships to progress to that point. One person in Bosnia said that even forty-five years of living together had not prevented the Yugoslav wars and that this extended period of "enforced coexistence" was actually what led to the conflicts of the 1990s. Clearly, more than time is needed now as well.

Research Methodology

The dependent variable in our study, the element we were most interested in explaining, was improved relationships between members of previously warring groups within so-called divided communities. These are communities in which two or more identity groups reside but often have very little contact with each other. They patronize different businesses, work in different places, send their children to different schools, worship in different religious traditions, and live on different streets. Therefore, our working definition of coexistence became the following:

> *A relationship between two or more identity groups living in close proximity to one another that is more than merely living side by side and includes some degree of communication, interaction, and cooperation.*

With this emphasis in mind, we reviewed the evaluation approaches commonly used by international development agencies and by nongovernmental organizations involved in conflict resolution, economic development, and humanitarian assistance. Drawing on and adapting these approaches, we decided on two complementary ways to assess the value of the Imagine Coexistence initiative—process tracing and project impact analysis via the use of effectiveness criteria.

Process Tracing

We determined that process tracing was a key methodology for providing results within project parameters. It is defined as a method ". . . to generate and analyze data on the causal mechanisms, or processes, events, actions, expectations, and other intervening variables, that link putative causes to observed effects."[3] It has grown out of the increasing concern that statistical and other methods that assess correlations ". . . do not provide a solid basis for inferring underlying causality."[4] In other words, they can measure the extent to which we can observe correlation between independent and dependent variables, but they are not good at discerning *how* the causality operates. Process tracing fills this gap in understanding by looking at things such as the ". . . intentions, expectations, information, small-group and bureaucratic decision-making dynamics, coalition dynamics, [and] strategic interaction" that make up the complex chain of events leading to the observed outcomes.[5]

The diagram of the system pathways along which we conducted the process tracing is shown in Figure 6.1. It included UNHCR headquarters in Geneva; the UNHCR field offices in Kigali, Rwanda, Banja Luka, and Bosnia that were choosing the implementing partners and overseeing their work; the three implementing partners (two international NGOs in Rwanda and one local NGO in Bosnia); the five communities in which pilot projects were launched; the local NGOs who designed the projects; and the multiple projects that were ultimately implemented.

Drawing on the literature in conflict analysis and resolution, trauma and healing, systems and organizational theory, political and economic development, and evaluation methodology, our fundamental belief was that coexistence between previously warring groups requires significant social change at both the individual and the institutional level. We therefore wanted our process tracing to analyze several broad categories of change. First, and most important, was tracking relationships between individuals and groups. Our premise was that positive changes in attitudes and perceptions of the "other" are one of the primary mechanisms by which coexistence develops;[6] in the absence of being able to test for attitude change directly (due to time and resource constraints), we reasoned that observable changes in the quality of relationships was a good

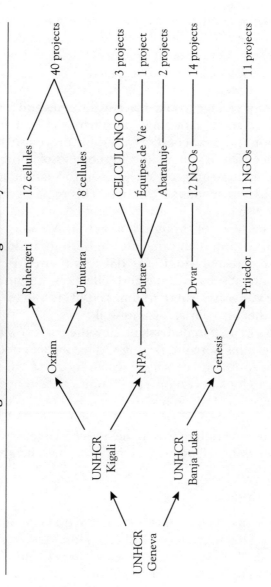

Figure 6.1. Process-Tracing Pathways.

proxy. In order to generate as many observations as possible, as well as to capture the complexity of relationships inherent in such a project, we included data on specific kinds of interactions such as decision making, conflict management strategies, and leadership dynamics. Presumably, as the capacity for coexistence develops, such relationships undergo a qualitative improvement, and we were looking for indications that this had occurred.

Our second overarching category was self-reflection and learning. In order for change to take place in attitudes and perceptions, both individuals and organizations must have some capacity to take in information that may conflict with their previously held (conscious or unconscious) biases and stereotypes of another group, be willing to analyze and test such new information, and adjust their thoughts and actions accordingly. This requires openness to learning and also interest in observing and possibly changing one's established patterns of thought and action. We were therefore interested in tracing such capacities in both individuals and organizations connected with the UNHCR initiative. We knew that trauma can inhibit such learning and reflection, and since we were operating in war zones where trauma was likely to have occurred, we factored that into our analysis as well.

Finally, we wanted to understand how the context within which people and groups were interacting was having an effect on their relationships and their capacity to learn. In this study, we had an opportunity to look at two different countries and five different communities, each of which had experienced both violence and its aftermath in quite distinct social and political ways. We therefore wanted to use these differences to see how the larger system affects changes that may be taking place at the individual and group levels.

Effectiveness Criteria

In addition to process tracing, we wanted to evaluate what impacts on coexistence, if any, the individual community projects produced in and of themselves. We reviewed the existing literature on impact assessment and found the most promising to be the Reflecting on Peace Practice (RPP) project, directed by Mary Anderson of the Collaborative for Development Action.

This project is examining an extensive set of case studies that document peace-building work as it is practiced by nongovernmental organizations worldwide. From these cases, the RPP research team has culled a set of six criteria used in the field to evaluate effectiveness, and we in turn used five of these. We adopted the RPP terminology of "criteria for effectiveness," as opposed to "indicators of impact." We found, as the RPP did, that *indicators* are very context-specific, whereas *criteria for effectiveness* are framed more generically.[7]

This point is worth elaborating, as it has been our experience as well as that of the RPP project that "indicators" are used extensively by many assistance and development organizations for evaluating their field operations. However, by separating criteria from indicators, an organization can set more *general* and replicable goals for evaluation (criteria) while allowing the *specific* goals (indicators) to be developed locally in context. Ideally, the indicators should be developed in partnership with the implementing NGOs and with the communities themselves. This ensures that success is measured in terms that are locally meaningful, and hence the community can document any progress that is being made in ways that make sense to them. Attempting to develop and use generic coexistence indicators could actually jeopardize attempts to promote coexistence and to understand the impact of local projects, because generic indicators might have no relevance to the community being evaluated.

Building and repairing relationships, especially in the aftermath of significant violence, is a long-term process. In the short amount of time that was available to plan and implement activities in the five pilot communities, we expected to see only modest progress. We were looking to track how far these communities had come from where they had begun at the start of the intervention, not whether they had reached some predetermined end point. To do this, we relied on the following fifteen criteria for effectiveness:[8]

1. It increased the number of people actively working or speaking out for coexistence (or reduced the number of people actively engaged in or promoting conflict).
2. It influenced community leaders to act on behalf of coexistence.
3. It promoted activities, networks, and organizations that, when

violence worsened or threats were made, were able to sustain their efforts and maintain their membership.

4. It established links between leaders and the general public that made it possible for them to communicate more effectively about how to foster coexistence.
5. Specific acts of violence stopped, or specific causes of conflict were resolved.
6. The project made progress toward or achieved its stated goals.
7. The leadership, implementation, and management of the project were shared by people from different identity groups.
8. The project was perceived as a joint endeavor by the project staff.
9. The project staff felt that the project was valuable (worth their time and effort to work together).
10. The project broadened social connections among the beneficiaries.
11. A shift occurred toward a more positive perception of members of groups toward other groups.
12. The project has hosted or helped generate other joint activities.
13. The project has been used as a resource or support for others wanting to engage in joint activities.
14. Project staff or beneficiaries (or both) developed problem-solving, planning, or communication skills.
15. Project staff or beneficiaries (or both) developed an increased level of trust in their relationships with each other.

In applying these criteria to the forty projects implemented in the initiative, we encountered several overarching challenges. The first was that the period of implementation was too brief to notice any lasting change in any of the parameters. We could identify small steps taken but had no way of judging, without follow-up over time, which of these might be permanent. However, even small steps in some cases were significant. For example, in Rwanda, there were shifts in the relationship of communities to local mayors such that the community members themselves were handling family disputes and not looking to the authorities to do this for them. The authorities actually welcomed this development, as it relieved them of some of their backlog of work and also gave them a feeling of pride in "their" community's skills and abilities. While this in and of itself will not stop genocide, it is the beginning of a shift from the passivity that allowed such violence to occur.

The second challenge was overcoming the belief held by UNHCR (and many other funders of international projects) that the outcome is the only thing worth evaluating. However, based on our experience and on the evaluative literature in conflict resolution, development, and trauma recovery work, the process itself—the *way* things are done—is as important as *what* is done. This is primarily because people are explicitly and implicitly learning about relationships as they interact with each other. The result is that the many complex interactions—in our example, among UNHCR, its implementing partners, project leaders, beneficiaries, local authorities, and the larger community—are all key component of coexistence work. Therefore, process-tracing analysis is as important as outcome analysis in understanding the impact of the coexistence initiative. We did not want that point to get lost in the discussion of criteria and indicators.

Finally, there is the challenge mentioned earlier of separating *criteria for effectiveness* from *indicators of success*. Some of the most interesting evaluation discussions were with the implementing partners as they grappled with how to translate the criteria into locally relevant indicators. An example is shown in a section of a planning chart developed by Oxfam for its work in Rwanda, displayed in Exhibit 6.1. As can be seen, the indicators that are chosen are themselves an important window into how coexistence is viewed in a given culture and community. Without getting down to such a level of detail, it is easy to miss significant data about project outcomes.

However, to generate such indicators, time and effort were needed to structure a process for doing so. In our initiative, the implementing partners were committed to making the time and importing the expertise to do this well. It paid off, in terms of quality of data and also in terms of enhancing local interest in the projects.

Assessing the Evaluation Design

The following methods were used to create an evaluation design. Although imperfect in some ways, they were practical because they could be applied within the time and resource constraints of the project.

Exhibit 6.1. Oxfam GB.

Results	Measurable Indicators	Means of Verification	Assumptions
1.1 Result 1.1a: Useful understanding of social dynamics in relation to conflict management at the community level	Identification of at least 8 actors, 4 interests of each actor (2 hidden, 2 open), 5 conflicts in each province, 5 common responses to conflict	Provincial Research Reports (Umutara, Ruhengeri) Comprehensive Analysis Chart	
Result 1.1b: Contribution to the establishment of "Best Practice" for data collection for the useful understanding of social dynamics in relation to conflict management at the community level	Two practical techniques identified, adapted, piloted and analysed Production of base-line data		
2.1 Result 2.1: Development of a conflict management Pilot Project with participation of all stakeholders	Official approval of the project by 2 provinces, 5 districts and 20 cellules Selection of 20 cellules by district authorities according to selection criteria Verbal approval of the project by 20 njyanamas that participated in the research	Provincial and district activity plans Local registration letter District meetings minutes District statistics Interviews with community members Minutes of njyanama meetings	• (A 2.1) The pilot approach is accepted by communities in non-selected zones without a long-term negative impact • (A 2.2) The trained individuals are prepared to use their

	Indicators	Means of verification	Assumptions
			new skills in the face of potential opposition from their community members and the authorities
2.2 Result 2.2: Improvement of skills and practices of key people in the community in relation to conflict management	Trained community members are capable of managing certain personal, family and community conflicts Change in attitude of local authorities towards local conflict management	Trainers reports Training Evaluation Report Observations of Oxfam Team	
2.3 Result 2.3: Application of non-violent conflict management methods by civil society and local authority representatives in community forums	Observation of use of techniques by trained people during njyanama meetings: (a) active listening; (b) process not cause; (c) process not result; (d) action, time and resources	Conflict management tool monitoring form	• (A 2.3) The people chosen to attend the training are sufficiently respected by and credible to the communities to lead conflict management
2.4 Result 2.4: Functioning decentralisation mechanisms in relation to Micro-Projects funded by the Pilot Project grants	At least 60% of households are represented at njyanama meetings All projects are approved by the njyanama, not CDC/CPA[a] 80% of projects begin within 3 weeks of receipt of funds Funds released with cellule-level authorisation[b] The progress of 50% of the projects implemented is documented and reported to seceur and district levels Development of a project evaluation/accountability and closure mechanism for the njyanama	Njyanama participation form Project Monitoring form Monthly njyanama reports	• (A 2.3) The training transforms individuals to lead conflict management and the communities allow themselves to be led by the trained individuals • (A 2.3) The njyanamas are an appropriate community forum

Exhibit 6.1. *(Continued)*

Results	Measurable Indicators	Means of Verification	Assumptions
3.1 Result 3.1: Verification that the implementation strategy (training/grants) provides a positive impact towards non-violent conflict management	Specific objective 2 is X% achieved	External evaluation	• (A 3.3) The process of decentralisation is transparent and information is available and accessible
3.2 Result 3.2: Increased awareness of actors capable of responding to the conflict situation in Rwanda	Increased requests for (a) information; (b) project visits; (c) participation in meetings/conferences on conflict management	Monthly reports	
3.3 Result 3.3: Better understanding of the practical application of decentralisation policies in two provinces of Rwanda	Development of 5 recommendations that respond to key problems identified in the application of the decentralisation policy	External consultation report	

[a]CDC is the elected community development committee made up of 6 sectoral representatives. The CPA is the elected community political administration made up of 4 administration authorities.

[b]The cellule is the most grassroots unit of administrative authority in Rwanda: a number of cellules make up a sector, a number of sectors make up a district, while several districts make up a province. There are a total of 18 provinces in Rwanda.

Process Tracing

We found this methodology to be useful and usable by researchers, with the appropriate training, and would therefore recommend it to field personnel with prior instruction. As with the projects themselves, however, a longer, ongoing use of this method is needed in order to be confident of results.

Effectiveness Criteria

Having used the fifteen criteria as written, we would now modify them in several ways. First, we would change those that presume that activities have to be "joint" to be coexistence work. Our observation was that under some circumstances, coexistence work might be better done separately with identity groups before bringing them together. This might occur when one or both parties are still too angry or hostile toward the other to even agree to come together. For example, it could involve projects with refugees still in countries of asylum before they return and then separately with the communities to which they are likely to return.

Second, as our report was being prepared, the RPP drafted a revised set of criteria for effectiveness, which are still under review as of this writing. This demonstrates the continuing learning and updating of data available in this evaluation work. We might incorporate these updates into future revisions.[9]

We also analyzed the overall design of the study and whether the approaches we used to evaluate the initiative were effective. We came to the following conclusions.

Countrywide Surveys

We conducted a survey of coexistence projects being done throughout each of the two pilot countries. In Bosnia there were one hundred respondents, and in Rwanda there were fifty. The surveys were conducted by local research teams in each country, who consulted with us on the survey design and on the wording of questions.

The country surveys helped us in three ways. They did give a view of other ongoing coexistence projects. They told us something of how coexistence is being evaluated by other organizations on the ground, and they allowed us to see if there are identifiable impacts of projects that have been in operation for a long period of time, especially those that are similar to the ones in our pilot communities.

The countrywide surveys were a good effort in a short span of time but would have elicited much more useful data with a larger sample, more randomly determined, with a longer period for training and working with the researchers. Also, follow-up was needed to fill in more information in many cases, and there was insufficient time to do this. The questions worked well, but the interviewers needed more orientation on the techniques involved in semistructured interviewing. It is clear that on sensitive issues such as coexistence, a structured survey may well not be the best tool for eliciting information. More time was needed to train the researchers and develop appropriate tools for gathering information.

Baseline Studies

In both countries, we sought out baseline studies to map the range of attitudes, perceptions, and emotions that each identity group holds of the "other," in each of our pilot communities. In Rwanda, Oxfam GB had already done an extensive assessment in Ruhengeri and Umutara, focusing on conflicts in the communities and how these were being handled. In Bosnia, no comparable study had been done, so we retained a local research team to conduct interviews in Drvar and Prijedor. No comparable study was done in Butare, due to lack of time and capacity on the part of the implementing partner.

The baseline study in Bosnia was done too far along in the process to be a valid "before" measure. Also, we used existing studies in Rwanda that asked different questions than the ones we designed; although they provided very useful information, we did not have consistency of baseline data across all of the pilot communities. We therefore need the same instrument administered in each location, probably with a larger sample.

Journals

We asked project leaders and implementing partners to keep journals in order to trace their personal learning process throughout the implementation phase. These were not very successful. Genesis staff did a great job keeping journals, but the project leaders did not. In Rwanda, the implementing partners tried to incorporate their reflections into their monthly reports, but these were not as extensive as we would have liked. In both countries, committing thoughts and feelings to writing is not commonly done. In Bosnia, there was reluctance to have any such information documented in writing; and in Rwanda, many of the project participants were not literate and there was a fear of documentation and what it might be used for. We hired our Bosnian research team to conduct interviews with project leaders, but the results were not very illuminating. In Rwanda, we worked with Oxfam to help develop techniques for tracking and gathering information on changes in coexistence in the communities; that process is still continuing as of this writing, so there are no definitive results. We therefore need to continue developing effective ways to capture the interim perceptions and attitudes of project leaders and beneficiaries.

Research as Educational Intervention

When our mandate was drawn up in May 2001, it was envisioned that we would not be designing any interventions but rather only assessing what UNHCR was implementing through its partners. However, we did learn that in the process of collecting data, we were also providing an educational function by helping the implementing partners in particular to think about what data to collect, how to collect them, and how to develop processes for analysis. The feedback that we received from the three partners is that this educational component was extremely useful for them, and we would want to incorporate this element much more systematically in any future research effort.

Conclusion

In conducting this study, our learning was both substantive and methodological. We were able to begin an assessment of many of the assumptions driving coexistence work, a process that will hopefully continue in both Rwanda and Bosnia as the projects proceed. We also built upon some existing evaluation tools and created others, adding to the growing literature on coexistence assessment and moving the field one step further in understanding this most important postsettlement intervention.

Notes

1. The members of the team in addition to myself were Rebecca Dale, senior researcher for Rwanda; Brian Ganson, JD, senior researcher for Bosnia; Ivana Vuco, senior research associate; Branka Peuraca, research assistant; Holly Benner, research assistant; Odette Nyirakabyare, Rwanda research assistant.

2. Oxfam's thinking is summarized in its original project proposal submitted to UNHCR in June 2002:

> . . . Oxfam believes that there is a need to focus on the current issues that perpetuate divisions and conflict within Rwanda while working towards transforming this environment into one where sustainable peace can be fostered. As outlined in the conditions leading to the geno-politicide, one of the key factors that still exists in Rwanda is the prevalence of centralised leadership structures that do not allow for participation in decision-making. In the past, this disenfranchisement led to abusive power relationships, as well as highly inequitable resource distribution resulting in a deepening of the level of poverty and frustration for the majority of Rwandans—with disastrous consequences.
>
> Thus, Oxfam GB in Rwanda is the only organisation to specifically propose reinforcing decentralisation structures for the dual purposes of promoting participatory decision-making in the pursuit of community development and managing destructive conflict in a way that is inclusive of all community members.

3. A. Bennett and A. L. George, "Process Tracing in Case Study Research," paper presented at the MacArthur Foundation Workshop on Case Study Methods, Belfer Center for Science and International Affairs, Harvard University, Oct. 17–19, 1997. [http://www.georgetown.edu/bennett].

4. Bennett and George, "Process Tracing."

5. Bennett and George, "Process Tracing."

6. The other primary mechanism for promoting coexistence is through law, as was the case with civil rights legislation in the United States.

7. Collaborative for Development Action, Reflecting on Peace Practice Issue Paper, "Effectiveness Criteria: Difference Between Criteria of Effectiveness and Indicators of Impacts," 2002. [www.cdainc.com].

8. The first five of our criteria were adapted from the RPP project, as noted. An earlier incarnation of the Imagine Coexistence research group, chaired by Martha Minow of the Harvard Law School from fall 1999 to spring 2001, developed criteria 6 through 14; criterion 15 was added later. The list can be further grouped into two categories: criteria that reflect behavior, perceptions, and attitudes within the projects themselves (criteria 6–11, 14, and 15) and criteria that capture behavior, perceptions, and attitudes of the broader communities within which the projects operate (criteria 1–5, 12, and 13).

9. The RPP's evidence to date suggests that peace programs are more effective—that is, they are able to make an impact on peace writ large—if the following conditions hold true:

- The effort is marked by participants' sustained engagement over time. The involvement of people is not one-off and is sustained in the face of difficulty or even threats and overt pressure to discontinue.
- The effort has a linking dynamic. It links upward (to bring in people with existing influence on the political process or support new alternative leaders) or downward (to bring in larger numbers of people and build public support at the grassroots level). It links key people to more people or more people to key people.
- The effort does something substantive about root and proximate causes of conflict. It does not simply talk about peace but also seeks and finds solutions to the key problems driving the conflict.
- The effort is geared toward creating institutional solutions. It is not sustained only by ephemeral personal relationships or ad hoc initiatives but is institutionalized and enduring.
- The effort causes people to respond differently from before in relation to conflict. This can involve increasing people's ability to resist manipulation or to undertake proactive efforts. This can occur through increased skills for analyzing, managing, and responding to conflict or changed values and attitudes.

The experience gathered through RPP to date suggests that these criteria are additive. If a single effort meets all five, it is more effective than one that accomplishes only one.

Part Three

Obstacles

Chapter Seven

Freedom's Hidden Price
Framing the Obstacles to Economic Coexistence
Sven M. Spengemann

To imagine coexistence is to assume a highly complex, difficult task in the effort to reconstruct a war-torn society. Internal conflicts and their aftermaths continue to take their toll across the globe, in Africa, the Middle East, the Balkans, and Latin America, while the complexities of postconflict reconstruction challenge scholars and practitioners alike. The term *coexistence* offers a *modus* for the resumption of a secure, productive life, a social order under which members of formerly warring factions can live and work together without destroying each other. Coexistence is a process that must be managed carefully to avoid the renewal of hostilities. In some circumstances, it may take the form of a relatively stable but nonintegrative end state; other cases may offer prospects for achieving deeper social and economic integration.

This chapter argues that in itself, economic interaction among former antagonists and victims does not guarantee coexistence, nor does it form a precondition. This conclusion is based on an analysis and reconciliation of two alternative accounts of the nature and origin of internal armed conflict, which, for these purposes, includes civil war. For lack of better labels, I call these approaches the "political" and "economic" hypotheses. They are neither conceptually inconsistent nor mutually exclusive in their operation but tend to interact as complex causal explanations. Their relative contributions are highly case-specific. Part of the objective, therefore,

is to develop a cognitive map of relevant factors and their anticipated impact. Each hypothesis ultimately points to a strategy for coexistence. However, the meaning of coexistence takes on distinct
overtones under each approach. In the first three sections, this chapter will draw particular attention to the impact of economic incentives for violence on the prospects for coexistence. Using the case
of Mitrovica, in the Kosovo region of Yugoslavia, it will then outline
a concrete, multifactoral framework for the development and evaluation of employment programs in postconflict zones.

Political Origins of Conflict

The political hypothesis offers the classical account of war and civil
strife, whereby war is a continuation of politics through the use of
additional means.[1] Political conflict can take place along ideological, ethnic, cultural, linguistic, religious, class-based, and territorial divisions, and it generally evokes images of competing parties
attempting to settle a dispute, albeit through violence rather than
through bargaining or deliberation. While political disputes typically involve grievances about equality, human rights, or self-
determination, violence is seen as mindless, disruptive, and irrational, a breakdown of the social order that must be resolved
quickly through an effective transition to peace.[2]

Interstate wars are seen as the result of (1) informational constraints that prevent parties from making the correct tactical
and strategic choices; (2) commitment problems; or (3) issue indi-
visibility that precludes effective negotiation. Alternative explanations, including the temptation to engage in preventive war or in
wars with a "positive expected utility," are challenged, at least in theory, by claims that better negotiated alternatives always exist.[3]
Thanks to its realist heritage, classical political analysis is premised
on the nation-state as the principal, unitary actor in international
relations, and proponents of this branch of social science tend to
focus on the aggregate costs of war. On this basis, war is inefficient
in virtually all circumstances. Aside from direct military and civilian
casualties, including deaths, injuries, and displacements, the physical and social infrastructure of participating nations is damaged;
inter- and intrastate mistrust rises to maximum levels; competitive

trade flows are disrupted or distorted; alliances, military operations, and armament strategies put pressure on national resources and populations; and the protection of human and civil rights suffers.

Until intrastate civil wars began to proliferate during the 1990s, social-scientific analysis framed political conflicts and their resolution as top-down or aggregate political problems involving systemic, institutional, or governmental explanations. As such, efforts to examine war as a function of ethnic hatred also fall into the political framework.[4] Ethnic conflict has been treated as a commitment problem, in that ethnic minorities cannot trust a majority government of a different ethnicity to grant them adequate protection. During the Cold War, the superpowers, as third parties, could guarantee political agreements between ethnic populations.[5] In the absence of stabilizing external influence, however, mistrust and hatred have developed freely along ethnic divisions and have led to unspeakable violence over the past decade (see the Preface to this volume). While ethnic hatred can lead to social breakdown and war, ethnicity in itself may not offer a sufficient explanation. The political model must explain why war breaks out in some cases involving ethnic division but not in others. Coexistence work, in turn, is seen as a facilitating device for bottom-up, political agreement in the aftermath of violent conflict. Reconstruction strategies are expected to compensate for weak external protection and to mitigate the persistent impact of high levels of mistrust.

Even more nuanced political analyses that do account for individual incentives or preferences point to flaws in a strictly political approach to policy development. The principal constraint under the political or "grievance" model is that of free-riding. Individuals aggrieved by human rights violations may want to see their government overthrown, but, as Paul Collier explains, they prefer that someone else fight on their behalf. At the same time, since the likelihood of success of a rebellion depends on its size, people will be more inclined to join large rebel movements than small ones. Moreover, opposition leaders operate under the shadow of the future, and potential followers recognize that promises made to them may be impossible to keep. The combined effect of these collective action and coordination problems is the failure of most politically motivated rebel movements to gain enough momentum to account for the outbreak and persistence of civil wars.[6] These constraints are less significant, however, when economic incentives are added to the analysis.

Economic Origins of Conflict

The competing view to the political hypothesis claims that the inclusion of economic motivations provides a more persuasive explanation of civil violence. This insight may be masked by a selective focus on political factors, such as ethnic hatred and institutional breakdown. Simply put, the economic hypothesis would argue that certain actors in civil conflicts have vested economic interests in their continuation.[7] In the context of globalization, trade liberalization, and networked states, war and peace are not seen as distinct phases but as concepts that stand in a relative position to each other: Domestic or regional *war* economies reveal commonalities with both the *global* economy and the respective national or regional *peace* economies.[8] A war economy, for example, may operate under the effective suspension of criminal justice, but it draws upon subsets of preexisting trading patterns and relationships and on the international financial architecture. This two-dimensional anchoring of the war economy helps explain both the continuity of conflict and its relatively tempered nature: Civil conflicts will only rarely rise to a level of violence that threatens the underlying economies themselves. In short, the economic hypothesis challenges two common conclusions: that conflict only has negative consequences and that winning is the overall aim of the combatants.[9]

This analysis moves away from the conceptualization of states as the principal, unitary participants in conflict toward a more nuanced approach that privileges individuals and substate groups.[10] When the United States and the former Soviet bloc effectively terminated alliance or proxy relationships with a number of weak states, these states inherited both greater political freedom and increased economic vulnerability.[11] The change confronted former protégés with the alternatives of developing into strong states or remaining weak. Strength, in this sense, does not reflect military capacity but measures the capacity of a government to provide public goods through a functional bureaucracy and infrastructure and fair and effective representation of the population under the rule of law.[12] Leaders of weak states, in turn, provide protection, services, and preferential access on a discriminate, personal basis in exchange for political loyalty. Since they must control sufficient sources of revenue to sustain this power base, these rulers tend to accumulate vast fortunes in order to sustain and expand political loyalties.[13] Typically, the sources of these appropriations include major economic entities, such as factories or smelters, and natural resources, which can be protected through decentralized violence but also by civil society in general. The frequency of direct, discriminate bargains and patronage relationships between government leaders and "warlords" obliterates the distinction between public and private competences and effectively causes the weak state to forfeit its claim to a legitimate monopoly on the use of force.

Although the outcome of each case is shaped by its individual context, certain factors support the political inertia of weak states and the pathways to economic violence. First, weak states are generally unable to transform themselves into strong states without a viable national economy, a significant resource base, or substantial external assistance. Second, in choosing to strengthen the state, the current leadership would have to cede power to political and administrative institutions. Strong states are funded by an effective taxation system under which politicians, operating within a relatively clearly defined public realm, must protect a decentralized productive sphere. A strong state depends on legitimacy for its political power and thereby prevents leaders from securing the loyalty of individual followers through patronage and from exercising unchecked personal control over state assets.

Additional disincentives to the development of a strong state can be found in different contexts. But the cessation of external support is perhaps the single most significant catalyst.[14] When the West and the Soviet bloc offered support to a range of countries, or sympathetic factions within them, they paid little attention to the manner in which these governments or rebel groups treated their citizens.[15] Following the withdrawal of strategic political support, the United States began to substitute humanitarian aid, conditioned on progress in matters of democracy and human rights. Contrary to expectations, violence increased in the post–Cold War era, particularly in the form of intrastate civil war.[16] Other reinforcing factors were made possible by the withdrawal of the East-West patrons, such as the trafficking of drugs and prostitutes.

The pathways to economic violence flow from a fairly discrete set of conditions. Many states involved in recent civil wars had been recognized as sovereign, even if they utterly lacked the capacity to distribute public goods. Sovereignty played a pivotal role in attracting the sustained interest of the superpowers. First, it facilitated alliance relationships. The leaders of weak allied states, in turn, enjoyed the formal protection of sovereignty but relied on external support rather than having to develop and extract public resources internally.[17] Second, most states that had attracted superpower support before 1991 had also acquired some level of military capacity. Both the former USSR and the West had shipped substantial amounts of cheap, light weapons to their governmental or nonstate allies, along with operational training. These weapons gave rise to a flourishing interstate trade that to this day helps arm factions and may even provide external markets. Military command structures were also put in place, with many governments being led by "strongmen," a designation that ironically complements the weak state. Military commanders were able to reward their soldiers by maintaining an environment of impunity with respect to the theft of certain public resources and private property.

In an environment where the military leadership and individual combatants have ample opportunity to engage in short-term accumulation, particularly where lucrative drug smuggling or resource extraction is involved,[18] there are insufficient incentives for the regime to substitute the uncertainties of legitimate representative power and a bureaucratic administration for military strength and patronage. In such circumstances, economic violence remains the more likely outcome.

Levels of Violence, Shadow States, and Free-Riding

David Keen distinguishes economic top-down violence from bottom-up violence: Weak governments engage in top-down violence to enhance their resources or spheres of influence or to delay the onset of democracy. The incitement of ethnic strife as a cover for repressive, self-preserving actions is not uncommon in this context; neither is the encouragement of violence by purported adversaries. Government leaders and rebel groups engaged in top-down violence both benefit from hiding behind what is often a fabricated "war" that publicly excuses their own human rights violations.[19] Seven conditions facilitate this type of violence:

- A weak state
- Rebel movements without significant external financial support
- An undemocratic or noninclusive regime under threat
- Economic crisis
- Ethnic divisions that cut across class lines
- The presence of valuable raw materials
- Prolonged conflict[20]

The likelihood that a regime will engage in economic violence increases in the presence of combinations of these conditions, particularly when the government of a weak state is threatened by an insurgency but has insufficient resources at its immediate disposal to defend itself.[21] The seventh factor, the length of the conflict, yields several important subhypotheses. First, it determines the degree to which present and future generations of citizens are socialized into accepting ethnic divisions as the purported source of civil violence. Moreover, prolonged conflict allows war economies to become inert. The longer a conflict prevails, the more widespread will be the displacement of alternative sources of income by the war economy. Governments and rebel groups will have a progressively easier time finding new recruits for their armed forces as interethnic hatred grows and civil society faces diminished commercial and agricultural employment opportunities.[22]

In addition to identifying the conditions that facilitate economic "top-down" violence, Keen proposes multiple modes of violent appropriation of resources and property. These include pillage, forced payment of protection money, monopolistic control of trade, facilitation of the exploitation of labor, staking a direct claim to land, extraction of benefits from foreign aid, and the accrual of institutionalized benefits to the military.[23] Similarly, Collier distinguishes four "groups of opportunities" for profit during civil wars. First, civil wars reduce the predictability of social behavior by compelling people to discount the future more heavily. Second, criminal behavior will increase as resources are shifted toward military spending and away from civil police forces and other law enforcement mechanisms. As a result, criminals will attempt to remove assets from the country, thereby further eroding the resource base that can sustain armies and rebel groups and placing increased economic pressure on trade networks and civilian populations. Third, market efficiency will be disrupted. Violent conflict leads to decreased commercial competition as information becomes more costly to obtain. At the same time, monopolistic activities and other distortions will develop, particularly with respect to the export of natural resources.[24] Finally, rent-seeking predation on trade will increase in an environment characterized by lowered scrutiny, if not impunity. Ultimately, this condition may give rise to the "sobel" phenomenon, whereby regular government soldiers become rebels at night and prey on state assets and civil society.[25]

"Bottom-up" violence is the result of a particular reaction by individuals to economic scarcity, uncertainty, and physical insecurity. It is conditioned, in part, by some of the same factors that facilitate top-down violence. Prolonged conflict, for example, is particularly likely to trigger bottom-up violence: Young men in conflict zones are likely to take up arms as members of government forces or armed rebel groups once alternative economic prospects have diminished. Not only may participation in armed conflict be a path to greater physical security and autonomy, but it may also provide the best assurance of economic survival within the dynamics of a civil war. Second, as violent appropriations by combatants put civilian populations under increasing pressure, individuals will likely arm and defend themselves.[26]

Three additional factors encourage bottom-up violence: (1) significant social and economic exclusion, (2) a lack of strong revolutionary organizations, and (3) impunity with respect to violent crime.[27] Rebellions that involve violence against particular ethnic groups can be rewarded by economic gain, power, and an opportunity to act on feelings of anger or hatred toward members of another ethnicity. The collective action problem that, according to Collier, accounts for the absence of strong, politically driven rebel movements may lead to the strategic choice to attack individual civilians rather than the regime.

Impunity from criminal sanctions can in turn stem from a lack of top-down enforcement capacity due to a lack of training, resources, or resource allocation that favors military strength. At the bottom-up level, by contrast, impunity tends to reflect a lack of ideological commitment and coherence on the part of rebel movements. Ideologically motivated opposition, in order to attract sufficient numbers of followers, must remain legitimate in the eyes of the public. It must therefore prohibit and punish the very same types of human rights abuses that it seeks to eliminate at the government level. When this discipline breaks down, bottom-up economic violence is a likely consequence, particularly where it is encouraged by the government in power through discriminatory dispossession or other reductions of the rebel movement's resource base.[28]

The economic hypothesis exposes the basic complementarity of incentives for violence at the top-down and bottom-up levels: Weak states and ideologically strong opposition movements faced each other during the Cold War, armed and financially supported by their respective superpower allies. As the ideological and strategic bases of this constellation collapsed, the resulting power vacuum and decline in external economic support opened up an opportunity for personal, elite-level enrichment that is best nurtured in a state somewhere between war and peace. All-out war threatens the very existence of elites on both sides—within the government and among rebel movements—while complete peace fails to sustain the required impunity and the cover of war that permits the suspension of human rights.

The duration of an economically driven civil war would then depend partly on the level of collusion between government and rebel forces. If the parties to the conflict take a longer-term view of the benefits that flow from their exploitation of civilians, the economic hypothesis suggests that participants may actively seek to maintain a balanced level of violence. Alternatively, if participants discount the future more heavily, competition for economic appropriation and the desire to occupy or reclaim tracts of land may lead to higher levels of violence. This dynamic plays itself out on two levels: shadow state rulers must control free-riding on the "absent welfare state" to prevent a loss of personal power to competing warlords.[29] Conversely, in areas where the state is unwilling to provide or incapable of providing public goods, entrepreneurs manage their own economic and security environment through violence and may gain political power in the process.[30]

The Case of Mitrovica

In at least one respect, Mitrovica, in northern Kosovo, presents a complex challenge to coexistence policy. The city is neatly divided along ethnic lines by the Ibar River. The northern section is ethnically more heterogeneous but Serb-dominated, while the southern portion, containing the majority of the city's overall population, is primarily ethnic Albanian. Small populations of each ethnic group live in the opposite section, such as the small enclave of Serbs living under the protection of NATO's Kosovo Force (KFOR) near the Orthodox church south of the Ibar.[31] Mitrovica has a high overall rate of unemployment, primarily since the largest local employer, the Trepca industrial and mining complex, has ceased to operate.[32] Not surprisingly, a shadow economy has developed, sustained in part by organized crime. Comparatively speaking, the Albanian side of Mitrovica enjoys a more vibrant economy consisting of shops and small businesses, while business in north Mitrovica has been depressed by sanctions imposed against Serbia.[33] Some of the larger operational industries in Mitrovica include flour and bread, public utilities, and public transit.[34]

The Serb and Albanian populations in Mitrovica clearly mistrust each other, and regular outbreaks of violence are reported. Absent the required political, ground-level incentives, the United Nations Mission in Kosovo (UNMIK) has failed to establish effective multiethnic institutions. The Serbs therefore also distrust the UN presence and have established a parallel municipal structure in north Mitrovica as well an informal security force. The "bridgewatchers," a group of Serbs whose description ranges from mere thugs to a quasi-security presence made up of plainclothes employees of various Serbian agencies, patrol the northern side of Mitrovica's Ibar bridges.[35] Bridgewatchers guard against Albanian incursions and are funded through criminal activities, including the solicitation of protection money from local businesses and restaurants. At the same time, Belgrade exerts substantial administrative control over this portion of the city, in the form of criminal justice, education, and health services, as well as telecommunications, public payroll structure, taxation, and pension payments.[36] Public services in north Mitrovica, however, remain poor.[37]

The Fragmentation of Serbian Interests

Politicians in Belgrade hold conflicting viewpoints on Mitrovica. On the one hand, there are those who consider northern Kosovo to be part of Serbia and who favor some form of formal geographical and ethnic segregation from Albanian-controlled areas. This faction is interested in covertly undermining the institution-building efforts of UNMIK and KFOR in order to sustain the argument that non-Albanians do not receive sufficient protection in Kosovo and are thus forced to live in segregated communities. At the same time, the weak economy of the Mitrovica region, combined with Serbia's inability to provide financial backing, has led to a continuing net outflow of Serbs even from districts that remain populated by a Serbian majority.[38] On the other hand, many observers in Belgrade focus on the autonomy and interests of Serbs still living among an Albanian majority and whose options are either to live in some form of peaceful coexistence or to leave Kosovo altogether. This faction criticizes Belgrade's involvement as adverse to Serb interests in the electoral process and as obstructionist with respect to the central administration of Kosovo.[39]

The interests of the north Mitrovica Serbs themselves tend to diverge from the administration in Belgrade. Several local, informal governing bodies have been established, including the Serb National Council (SNC). The key political leaders, Marko Jaksic, Milan Ivanovic, and SNC head Oliver Ivanovic, serve as UNMIK's "Northern Advisory Group" but, according to the International Crisis Group (ICG), are also linked to organized crime among radical Mitrovica Serbs, including cigarette smuggling and protection rackets. Jaksic and Milan Ivanovic are dissatisfied with the small proportion of Mitrovica that is under Serb control and with the lack of autonomy that north Mitrovica enjoys vis-à-vis Belgrade. It appears to be their aspiration to partition northern Kosovo and to cantonize the remainder. Although Oliver Ivanovic has displayed a more conciliatory approach toward UNMIK, he maintains strong ties to Belgrade and will likely support the government's claim that Kosovo forms part of Serbia.[40] He has engaged in open, inflammatory anti-NATO rhetoric and appears to control the bridgewatchers very closely. There have also been reports that this group has assaulted Serbian residents who refused to demonstrate against Albanians.[41]

Albanian Perspectives

The Mitrovica Albanians denounce UNMIK's inability to establish a solid presence in the northern section. They claim that the establishment of parallel municipal bodies in the Serbian portion represents a failure on the part of UNMIK and KFOR to protect the moral right of Albanians to a safe, integrated society. UNMIK's acquiescence in the new status quo, combined with disparate treatment of the Albanians in weapons searches and disarmament, continue to fuel significant dissatisfaction. In April 2002, the Albanian leadership issued a list of demands through the Albanian-controlled municipal assembly of Mitrovica, including "secure and free movement throughout the city, the return of [internally displaced persons] to five neighborhoods in the North, a corridor for free movement from an Albanian area to the main bridge, an open hospital under international management, and urgent action to disband the Bridgewatchers."[42] Albanian politicians are also concerned about the rather nontransparent nature of UNMIK's operations. There are rumors that UNMIK has agreed to Serb requests for an official, new municipality in north Mitrovica as well as to concessions regarding the release of prisoners.[43] Because Mitrovica is regarded as a key indicator of the province's future, any formal recognition of the city's separation would also create a favorable environment for the separation of northern Kosovo, which in turn would likely be met with violence on the part of the Albanians.[44]

The Kosovo Albanians do not hold a unified view any more than the Serbs do. Bajram Rexhepi, currently prime minister of Kosovo and a former mayor of Mitrovica who was supported by the Kosovo Liberation Army (KLA) elements, delivered a sharp indictment of the international community's actions in Mitrovica after the 1999 war, describing the peacekeeping efforts as consisting of "a rapid rotation at the top, lack of coordination, and mutual finger-pointing when trouble breaks out."[45] Despite political rhetoric, however, the incentives of the former KLA and its successor groups do not seem to line up neatly with UNMIK and KFOR ambitions for a stable, united Kosovo. While various factions prevail within the Kosovo Protection Corps (KPC), the permitted successor to the KLA, Mitrovica itself belongs to the "historic core" of the KLA and is therefore closely aligned with the direction of Hashim Thaçi.[46]

KLA opposition to UNMIK and NATO surfaced when the KLA concluded that the international interveners remained steadfast in opposing independence. In February 2000, NATO peacekeepers clashed with ethnic Albanian militants, and in June of that year, Thaçi boycotted the Interim Administrative Council. Thaçi's decision was seen by some as the rejection of a forthcoming memorandum whereby the UN would offer special protective measures to the Serbs, a move that would signal an ethnic segregation of Kosovo. However, there was also speculation that Thaçi's action reflected his own growing frustration with the intervention force, which prevented him from consolidating his own power and moving Kosovo toward independence.[47]

The KLA's involvement with organized crime since the mid-1990s, notably pan-European drug trafficking, is well documented.[48] After the withdrawal of Serbian forces from Kosovo in June 1999, and contrary to sharing the Western conception of a democratic Kosovo committed to human rights, the KLA systematically drove Serbs and other non-Albanians out, seized property and businesses, extorted money, and intimidated moderate ethnic Albanians and political opponents.[49] Shortly after the KLA had been officially replaced by the KPC in early 2000, the ICG nevertheless reported that the KLA, "in its various manifestations . . . remains a powerful and active element in almost every element in Kosovo," and while "some parts of the old KLA operate openly and essentially as before, . . . others have been transformed; some new elements have been added; and much remains underground."[50] According to a UN report, KPC members detained, tortured, and killed local citizens; conducted law enforcement activities without legitimate authority; forced local business owners to pay "liberation taxes"; and threatened UN police forces who sought to intervene.[51] The newspaper *Koha Ditore* proclaimed that KLA factions were engaged in illegal enterprise, the exploitation of position and power for private gain, intrusions into the privacy of individuals, and "political developments" in general.[52] Other incidents of extortion and the collection of illicit taxes, fees, and customs duties, and the involvement of former KLA members in "protection rackets, prostitution, corruption and bribery,"[53] appear to have contributed to the conclusion of one account that "the harsh reality . . . was and still is that NATO and UN officials find themselves not with a peacekeeping operation in Kosovo, but with a KLA management operation."[54]

Conclusion: Building a Multifactoral Policy Framework

Donor countries, focused on the common good of the war-torn region, tend to supply humanitarian assistance evenhandedly to equally exhausted factions of combatants and civilians and to focus on the repair and general restoration of infrastructure. But the "firefighting" approach to reconstruction, under which aid is indiscriminately sprinkled on the recipient area, can clearly do more harm than good. A coexistence policy, then, places greater demands on economic development and employment than on mere subsistence. It must operate simultaneously on several levels and draw upon multiple causal factors, which fall into two categories. The first consists of top-down actions that are aimed at breaking the war economy and hence the cycle of violence. To be successful, these steps must remove the incentives of the beneficiaries of a prolonged conflict, both in the government and among armed rebel movements. The second directs the corresponding transformation of bottom-up incentives that guide people's decision to leave or to remain in the region. A coexistence policy must treat ethnic hatred as both a potential cause and a consequence of economic disparity and violence, and lest one accepts stagnation or even regression as a permissible outcome, it must be sufficiently progressive to support economic diversification and expansion from agriculture and light manufacturing into supporting industries and services, such as education, finance, and the professions.

The Macro Level: Breaking the War Economy

The cycle of self-sustaining economic violence will collapse under two conditions: economic exhaustion and reduced incentives. First, the population would have to be too economically exhausted to support further violent appropriation by government and rebel forces. Second, vital, regime-supporting trade would have to be disrupted. On the one hand, the mere infusion of economic aid can stabilize a postconflict zone, since even the theft of goods can lead to lower market prices and reduced levels of violence.[55] However, without a fundamental change in incentives or a change in leadership, the likely outcome will be an "armed peace" under which warlords and government strongmen retain their spheres of control but limit outright conflict in order to attract foreign aid.[56] When aid flows ultimately diminish or cease, conditions may quickly return to the status quo ante. Coexistence projects that strengthen the economic capacity of civil society through small business development, market exchanges, farming, and employment projects without eliminating the structural, top-level incentives for violence may therefore foster, rather than reduce, the potential for continued civil conflict.

On the other hand, the transformation to a strong state calls for politically tough, expensive choices to reduce incentives for economic violence. In cases involving profitable, long-term conflict, it is unlikely that the principal beneficiaries can be persuaded to give up military power for salaried positions within a bureaucratic state, nor is it clear that these individuals could function effectively as representatives in such institutions without prior restitution or return of stolen property and a parallel effort of reconciliation with civil society. A successful coexistence policy, therefore, cannot rule out the forcible replacement of individual rulers and warlords, some of whom may previously have been supported by intervening nations. As these rulers are replaced with representative politicians, small arms trade and possession, narcotics trafficking, and other means of funding economic violence must also be eliminated. The replacement of the leadership will help break the cycle of ethnic hatred, which served as a primary cover for top-down economic violence. But institution building and the implementation of the rule of law are complex, costly projects that must be carefully timed and sustained. Although positive incentives may be generated through the creation of well-paid, equally accessible civil service positions in local and regional interim administrations, a lag in the establishment of a strong state, combined with leaks in arms embargoes or other sanctions, may promote a resurgence of warlord rule.

The transition from a weak to a strong state requires significant infusions of aid and subsidies, infrastructural development, and technical expertise. Developments in Mitrovica illustrate that the delivery of such assistance through the international community can create an additional level of popular mistrust and, from the perspective of competing warlords or strongmen, even a common enemy. The dilemma is completed by the recognition that full-scale economic development cannot take place until the primary political question, that of Kosovo's status, is settled. Civil service positions, for example, cannot be fairly allocated until the arrangements that will govern daily life in a mixed ethnic community, such as proportional representation, arithmetic equality, or affirmative action, have been agreed on. Similarly, large foreign investors are reluctant to enter the region until the equivalent of a constitutional order, capable of guaranteeing the rule of law, has been created. This step, in turn, is premised on the resolution of the status question.

Nevertheless, a viable interim approach is possible. It is based on the implementation of a ground-level employment program that is logistically small enough to operate in a region with a limited initial capacity to absorb aid but that provides sufficient incentives for individuals to remain in the region. Although such a program remains several steps away from political integration, it can create an initial breathing space following repeated cycles of violence and exploitation. Its initial focus should be on individual entrepreneurship or light industrial, artisanal, or agricultural opportunities in order to avoid distributive problems raised by a concentration of jobs among large employers that were formerly controlled by a single ethnic group. In this way, the development program also supports the formation of an endogenous, inclusive constituency to determine the territory's political future, rather than allowing this question and its timing to be hijacked by those who benefit most from continued instability. As a central precondition to a successful economic development program, impunity against violence must be eliminated, along with the practices of removing stolen assets from the region and soliciting protection money. This condition, in turn, requires the establishment of an effective interim police force and the cooperation of neighboring countries in the imposition and enforcement of criminal sanctions. A more ambitious project, which will nonetheless be crucial to long-term economic growth, is the development of an effective system of real and personal property law. The rule of law, under this approach, will replace military force as the primary way of protecting property, and it will allow property owners to leverage their assets in the capital markets and to build individual and national wealth.[57]

The Micro Level: Developing Dignity, Satisfaction, and Tolerance

At the level of the individual, the sources of hatred are varied. Hatred may build up through political domination and oppression, economic disparities between ethnic groups, top-down political or religious indoctrination or intergenerational narratives, social exclusion, or as in the case of Serbian and Albanian forces in Mitrovica, previous incidents of violence committed by members of one group against its own citizens. Although the restoration of economic opportunity cannot be expected to remove general feelings of hatred, it is a tool to refocus the energies of the population toward positive objectives that in turn reestablish individual dignity and autonomy, as Chigas and Ganson illustrate in Chapter Four.

Even as the first element of a coexistence policy removes the most immediate set of incentives for the perpetuation of violence, animosity and hatred will likely persist, particularly if the situation involves a history of prolonged conflict. Initially, citizens may simply choose to leave, even if, as in north Mitrovica, their immediate surroundings are controlled by their own ethnic group. Much will depend on the general state of the economy subsequent to the conflict. However, a coexistence policy must always provide more than the basic means of survival; it must offer an opportunity to earn a livelihood at a level that provides sufficient motivation for new initiative and entrepreneurship. For some residents, this will mean a better job than mere subsistence farming; for others, it may demand the courage to work alongside members of the other ethnic community. Hatred and fear must be managed to an extent that people belonging to different ethnic groups can functionally interact with each other in the workplace. In less heterogeneous cities or villages, the aspirations may be more modest due to the lesser intensity of interaction. In those places, an early success might be the restoration of intervillage trade flows through a common, weekly market.

Through the same psychological channels that link employment to feelings of self-worth and dignity, systematic economic inequality can perpetuate hatred and violence. Economic aid can in turn amplify or reduce preexisting disparities, particularly if external assistance takes the form of employment projects that adjust income levels and social status in tangible ways. Local perceptions of equality and fairness must therefore be carefully managed across two cleavages that do not necessarily overlap: former militants and civilian victims of violence, on the one hand, and ethnic majorities and minorities, on the other. Specific attention must be given to fair and impartial treatment in access to public positions, salary structures, supervisory positions, and promotional opportunities. Similarly, contract awards, transitional licensing requirements, business and income taxation, and other regulatory processes must be nondiscriminatory, both on their face and in their application. Close micro-level monitoring, coupled with the flexibility to make adjustments, will determine success or failure.

Persistent animosity and hatred require effective community-based policing, as repeated acts of small-scale violence against civilians undermine coexistence efforts as much as continued top-down oppression. Particularly during the time immediately following the end of large-scale violence, security forces must be capable of addressing diverse scenarios, including threats or attacks in the workplace itself or along commuting routes through ethnically hostile areas. At the same time, successful disarmament and the reconciliation of property theft cases may become preconditions to the acceptance and reintegration of former militants into the local economy. The importance of this issue will depend in part on the number of former combatants to be integrated. After prolonged conflict, a majority of the potential workforce may consist of former soldiers or guerrillas, while a corresponding majority of civilians would have fallen prey to economic violence.

Even an initially modest coexistence policy should be flexible and progressive enough to support subsequent transformations. In particular, continued economic growth will depend on the level of education available to present and future generations. Strong economies, for example, are characterized by extensive and dynamic relationships between postsecondary institutions and industry. A coexistence policy can begin to lay the groundwork for later stages of development by encouraging parties to formulate guidelines for the mutual recognition of professional degrees from universities located in neighboring regions or countries and by implementing external scholarship, exchange, and internship programs to enable young professionals of different ethnic backgrounds to return to and practice in the postconflict territory. More specific projects seeking to explore cognitive interactions in such settings as joint interethnic medical teams have not delivered immediate results against deeply rooted antagonism and prejudice.[58] Well-planned external assistance, however, can transform the economic and security environment to provide a crucial respite from oppression and violence. At the same time, if one accepts that true transformation in a wartorn society must be endogenous, efforts to engage the members of an emerging intellectual community in the challenges of their homeland will improve the conditions for mutual understanding, greater levels of tolerance, and the development of a common vision of the future.

Notes

1. C. von Clausewitz, *On War* (M. Howard and P. Paret, eds. and trans.) (Princeton, N.J.: Princeton University Press, 1984).

2. D. Keen, *The Economic Functions of Violence in Civil Wars* (Oxford: Oxford University Press, 1998).

3. J. D. Fearon, "Rationalist Explanations for War," *International Organization,* 1995, *49,* 379.

4. See P. Collier, "Doing Well out of War: An Economic Perspective," in M. Berdal and D. M. Malone (eds.), *Greed and Grievance: Economic Agendas in Civil Wars* (Boulder, Colo.: Rienner, 2000).

5. J. D. Fearon, "Commitment Problems and the Spread of Ethnic Conflict, " in D. A. Lake and D. Rothschild (eds.), *The International Spread of Ethnic Conflict: Fear, Diffusion, and Escalation* (Princeton, N.J.: Princeton University Press, 1998).

6. Collier, "Doing Well out of War."

7. W. Reno, "Shadow States and the Political Economy of Civil Wars," in Berdal and Malone, *Greed and Grievance.*

8. M. Duffield, "Globalization, Transborder Trade, and War Economies," in Berdal and Malone, *Greed and Grievance.*

9. Keen, *Economic Functions of Violence.*

10. This approach is consistent with liberal international relations theory. See A. Moravcsik, "Taking Preferences Seriously: A Liberal Theory of International Politics." *International Organization,* 1997, *51,* 513. See also A. Slaughter, "International Law in a World of Liberal States," *European Journal of International Law,* 1995, *6,* 503.

11. Duffield, "Globalization."

12. Even an ultraliberal, minimal state is defined as a "strong state," as the rule of law forms the central pillar on which a liberal society is built.

13. Reno, "Shadow States."

14. Whereas twelve major internal wars (with casualties in excess of one thousand people) took place in the former Soviet bloc and postcolonial states in 1989, that number had risen to thirty-seven by 1997. Reno, "Shadow States," p. 43.

15. Keen, *Economic Functions of Violence.*

16. Keen, *Economic Functions of Violence.*

17. Reno, "Shadow States."

18. Keen, *Economic Functions of Violence.*

19. Keen, *Economic Functions of Violence.*

20. Keen, *Economic Functions of Violence,* p. 24.

21. Keen, *Economic Functions of Violence.*

22. Keen, *Economic Functions of Violence.*

23. Keen, *Economic Functions of Violence.*

24. Collier, "Doing Well out of War"; see also Indra de Soysa, "The Resource Curse: Are Civil Wars Driven by Rapacity or Paucity?" in Berdal and Malone, *Greed and Grievance.*

25. A. Abraham, "War and Transition to Peace: A Study of State Conspiracy in Perpetrating Armed Conflict," *Africa Development,* 1997, *22,* 103.

26. Keen, *Economic Functions of War.*

27. Keen, *Economic Functions of War.*

28. Keen, *Economic Functions of War.*

29. Reno, "Shadow States."

30. Reno, "Shadow States."

31. International Crisis Group, "Kosovo's Linchpin: Overcoming Division in Mitrovica." Balkans Report no. 96, May 31, 2000. [http://www.crisisweb.org/projects/showreport.cfm?reportid=13].

32. International Crisis Group (ICG), "UNMIK's Kosovo Albatross: Tackling Division in Mitrovica." Balkans Report no. 131, June 3, 2002. [http://www.crisisweb.org/projects/showreport.cfm?reportid=672].

33. International Crisis Group, "Kosovo's Linchpin."

34. Organization for Security and Cooperation in Europe, "Municipal Profile (Mitrovica)" Report, Department of Democratization, Aug. 2001. [http://

www.osce.org/kosovo/documents/reports/municipal_profiles/Municipal_prof_Mitrovica_final.pdf].

35. ICG, "Kosovo's Linchpin"; ICG, "UNMIK's Kovoso Albatross.

36. ICG, "UNMIK's Kosovo Albatross."

37. ICG, "UNMIK's Kosovo Albatross."

38. ICG, "UNMIK's Kosovo Albatross."

39. ICG, "UNMIK's Kosovo Albatross."

40. ICG, "UNMIK's Kosovo Albatross."

41. ICG, "Kosovo's Linchpin."

42. ICG, "UNMIK's Kosovo Albatross," p. 10.

43. ICG, "UNMIK's Kosovo Albatross."

44. ICG, "UNMIK's Kosovo Albatross."

45. ICG, "Kosovo's Linchpin," p. 7.

46. International Crisis Group, "What Happened to the KLA?" Balkans Report no. 88, Mar. 3, 2000. [http://www.crisisweb.org/projects/showreport.cfm?reportid=24].

47. G. T. Dempsey and R. W. Fontaine, *Fool's Errands: America's Recent Encounters with Nation Building* (Washington, D.C.: CATO Institute, 2001).

48. Dempsey and Fontaine, *Fool's Errands;* see particularly the sources listed in note 88.

49. Dempsey and Fontaine, *Fool's Errands;* footnotes omitted.

50. ICF, "What Happened to the KLA?" p. 4. See also Dempsey and Fontaine, *Fool's Errands.*

51. Dempsey and Fontaine, *Fool's Errands.*

52. "Kosovo Protection Corps and Its Involvement in Incidents in Kosovo," *Koha Ditore* (Prishtina), July 11, 2000, p. 3.

53. Dempsey and Fontaine, *Fool's Errands,* p. 149.

54. Dempsey and Fontaine, *Fool's Errands,* p. 144.

55. D. Keen, "Incentives and Disincentives for Violence," in Berdal and Malone, *Greed and Grievance.*

56. Keen, "Incentives and Disincentives"; see also K. Menkhaus and J. Prendergast, "Political Economy of Post-Intervention Somalia, " Somalia Task Force Issue Paper no. 3, Apr. 1995. [http://www.netnomad.com/menkhaus.html].

57. See H. de Soto, *The Mystery of Capital* (New York: Basic Books, 2000).

58. H. S. Desivilya, "Jewish-Arab Coexistence in Israel: The Role of Joint Professional Teams," *Journal of Peace Research,* 1998, *35,* 429.

Chapter Eight

Bureaucratic Obstacles to Imagining Coexistence

Antonia Chayes

Reconciliation among previously warring parties within a nation has proved to be a long and painstaking process. When the international community began to intervene in internal conflicts in the early 1990s, it had unrealistic hopes that intervention would be swift and withdrawal rapid. It expected to help new democratic societies emerge from the devastation within a few years. But these "minor wars" have turned out to be more complex and difficult. In most of the violent internal religious and ethnic conflicts of recent years, the parties have been too intermingled to permit complete separation, even though breakup remains the aspiration. International intervention thus seems to bring with it an obligation to help heal the rift among those who have done violence to one another. The effort to find a coherent frame of reference for societal reconstruction is a critical task. Even in areas where geographical delineation is possible, the solution—whether some form of confederation or total separation—may require international attention to effect peaceful coexistence. Despite previous American distaste for the notion of nation building, it has gradually become clear that conflicts cannot be resolved or recurrence prevented unless careful thought is given to how societies are put back together.

In the Imagine Coexistence project, we have focused on societies where ethnic conflicts cannot be resolved by geographical segregation and hence some degree of peaceful interaction will be required. We have defined coexistence as more than "living peacefully side by side but involving some degree of communication, interaction, and even some degree of cooperation." In a situation where "direct violence may be halted only by the presence of powerful third parties or a political shift to cabin but not curtail the conflict, . . . movement to a stage of coexistence is an accomplishment."[1] Our premise has been that systematic implementation of the concept has the potential, in many postconflict situations, to help decimated societies recover. It is a far less ambitious goal than reconciliation. But it offers the next steps after a cease-fire and a signed agreement. It may provide a bridge to ultimate reconciliation. Yet it also leaves the parties with their options, while stemming the recurrence of violence. A focus on the concept of coexistence by international interveners can offer the tattered population experience with the "other" that might begin to loosen some of the stereotypes of evil that had developed by demagoguery, incitement to violence, and the mayhem that occurred. It provides breathing room for gradual shifts in attitudes. It recognizes the reality of how long the healing process takes while offering some measure of education in tolerance.

If the concept of coexistence is to be useful and used, it must be become a guiding principle for international interveners. It must be an integral part of the framework and criteria guiding the selection of actual programs in the field for physical and institutional reconstruction and the way they are managed. The same question must be asked each time: "If we support this program, will it promote coexistence?" When that question is answered in the affirmative, hard choices may be forced. To find a positive answer may slow physical reconstruction. This has been the case of the German governmental corporation, THW, in Prijedor, in the northeast part of the Republika Srpska in Bosnia. In interviewing construction managers, I found that they had resolved the dilemma of building houses rapidly for Muslim refugees by relying on trained Bosnian Serb crews, since few Muslim internally displaced persons (IDPs) had yet returned to an area of wartime atrocities. By the time the Muslims came trickling back, construction crews were working well, and the German overseers were reluctant to disrupt a functioning operation that was providing shelter efficiently. In this and many other cases, the application of a coexistence principle does create dilemmas and may rub up against other values.

However, if coexistence is articulated as a principle of policy both centrally and in the field, some of the dilemmas that may arise can be articulated and dealt with early. In the United States, affirmative action in response to racial segregation met resistance in the name of efficiency and compatibility of workforce. Nonetheless, over the years, it became a workable policy, and many of the arguments seemed less cogent as people were educated and began to understand the intrinsic fairness of the policy. In the case of war-torn societies, the simple goal to rebuild physical infrastructure and provide shelter quickly may require tempering by social goals.

A policy of coexistence plays out in very small concrete ways. If providing telephone communication in both Srpska and the Bosnian Federation meant that the separate entities of Bosnia would not be connected, because to do so would be too arduous a negotiation, was it worth the patience to delay the project to develop interentity cooperation, or were internal sector connectivity and jobs the more important goal? If schools can only be built with an understanding that the parties will be rigidly separated because their religion and their view of history diverge so sharply, would a coexistence policy permit that separation and build separate schools or require some common ground so that the children do interact?

If the coexistence question is asked, the resolution of dilemmas posed will at least be mindful, and the consequences of decisions will be understood. Applying the coexistence principle, especially in the first few years after war ends, may slow the process of reconstruction but help ensure that the peace is sustainable. The principle is easy to recite. Its concrete application becomes difficult and complex to execute. Rhetoric from organizational leadership is useful as inspiration, but if it is not related to budget and decision making in the field, it is a chimera.

This chapter discusses some of the obstacles to implementing a policy of coexistence both within and among assisting international organizations and then attempts to find ways to overcome the obstacles and to provide examples of successful efforts. Much of the research and analysis has been drawn from *Planning for Intervention*,[2] written with Abram Chayes, and from subsequent interviews and discussions in Bosnia.

Obstacles to Implementing the Principle of Coexistence

For a major shift in the orientation of international interveners to occur, there must be a greater degree of cooperation and collaboration among them. Traditional approaches to coordination have not worked well. Umbrella organizations do not keep out the rain. Designated "lead organizations" are not always followed, although we have seen structural and other improvements in Kosovo[3] and East Timor.[4] Nevertheless, the following obstacles still occur:

1. An unwieldy number of actors intervene in every conflict. They perform a wide variety of tasks and operate with differing perspectives, different agendas, and often overlapping or contradictory activities. Each of them is likely to deal with parties and stakeholders to the conflict and to express these differences. Arriving at coherence is never simple.

The typical array of participants include the United Nations and some of its departments; its specialized intergovernmental agencies, such as the World Health Organization (WHO) and UN's the Food and Agricultural Organization (FAO); international financial organizations, particularly the World Bank; regional organizations like Organization for Security and Cooperation in Europe (OSCE) or the Organization for African Unity (OAU); the powerful European Union, whose reach extends beyond Europe; nation-states, both as political actors and as donors in bilateral aid programs; military organizations; and a host of NGOs, both international and local. These organizations have different mandates (often embodied in their own charters), funding sources, constituencies, and needs, not fully appreciated by the others. NGOs large and small operate within a tradition of fierce independence and autonomy. There is scant opportunity to harmonize the different approaches ahead of time, and control from headquarters makes collaboration on the ground even more difficult.

2. Bureaucratic rigidity and jealousy pervade this multiplicity of interveners. Even a bare-bones listing of players makes it evident that there is no official or organization with the legal authority, let alone the practical power or political and economic resources, to impose order. Exhortations for clear leadership are applauded but

go unheeded. In comparison with the early 1990s, I have recently noticed some recognition and appreciation of different bureaucratic approaches and a slight softening of the rigidities, especially on the ground. But "turf consciousness" and jealousy are magnified as donor fatigue sets in. Competition for scarce resources is fierce. Civilian organizations compete for priority and visibility. Military forces are overstretched, and some nations, such as the United States, want to limit their duration and commitment. Others lack the resources to make a significant long-term contribution to peace operations.

3. Perhaps the worst obstacle—and one that structural or institutional change does not fix—is the lack of clear political direction from powerful and other involved states. Political leaders and policy analysts call for clear, consistent mandates and well-defined missions to guide and organize interventions. But states, acting on their own and within the international organizations of which they are members, pursue divergent agendas in response to their different interests. Conflicting policies struggle for predominance within a single international organization and even within a single government. The machinery by which the international community decides to intervene is incapable of producing more than vague and ambiguous compromise as to the scope and purpose of intervention.

These fundamental political disagreements are exemplified by examining almost any set of UN Security Council resolutions with respect to a single conflict. They are compromises that often paper over deep policy differences (the wartime Bosnia resolutions are a prime example). Many are also written for domestic constituencies and may be internally inconsistent. This ambiguity is inherent in the political conditions under which international organizations and even states make decisions. It cannot be cured by exhortation. It is true that intrepid and wise leadership on the ground may sometimes limit an impracticable mandate from the Security Council, as Yasushi Akashi did for a time in Cambodia, but it is hard to work around policy confusion in a fast-moving crisis.

4. Finally, the international community wants low-cost fixes and seems to lack the patience and persistence to ensure that a conflict will be unlikely to recur. Lack of funding is a major problem, particularly as new crises emerge and drain funds from "old

wars." Trained manpower is in short supply. Unwelcome danger to civilians and military personnel adversely affects domestic political constituencies. It has taken years to absorb some of the lessons of the lack of response to the Rwandan genocide, but Sierra Leone kidnappings may increase reluctance once again.

In recent years, the international community has recognized these obstacles and begun to address them. But the same old mistakes are also repeated by new people in new situations.

Bureaucratic Rigidity and Resistance to Change

The first point—multiplicity of actors—is a recognized fact of life in conflict intervention.[5] Current solutions have helped somewhat, but not sufficiently. Differing goals and agendas present obstacles. These are compounded by the bureaucratic rigidity of large international organizations and their resistance to change of any kind. Both experience and organizational research indicate that even though the logic may be compelling for major organizational change, the actual process turns out to be slow and painstakingly difficult.[6] Analysts across the range of organizational studies, from business to public bureaucracies, agree. Major cultural change is painful, disruptive, and is likely to be resisted at all levels of the organization.

Even though the chief executive may provide the impetus for change, the rest of senior management may be less enthusiastic, perceiving risks both to the organization and their positions. Alfred Chandler, in his classic study of business, *Strategy and Structure,* discusses the obstacles to implementing major structural change in four large companies. He concludes that "one of the primary reasons structure was slow to follow strategy was that existing management was unable to change its ways."[7] There is always a fear that results may not be as intended and that change may give rise to new and unanticipated problems. Even though it may be clear that the external operational environment has changed radically, the exact form of adaptation to the new environment is not apparent. Thus responsible management may lack confidence that a particular form of nonincremental change may improve the situation. Whatever else is doubtful, there will surely be "discontinuity, disorder and distraction,"[8] and the organization may seem out of control. "Even when institutions do not conform to the demands of a given environment, they may nevertheless endure because . . . the prospective gains from altering them are outweighed by the costs of making the changes."[9]

For international organizations, the difficulties are compounded. The same traits that make it so difficult for them to respond to the demands of fast-moving post–Cold War emergencies are sources of resistance to internal cultural change. Most of our present array of international organizations were created in the wake of World War II, the heyday of the centralized organization, when the ideal form was a smooth pyramid with strong senior management. This form of organization has managed to persist in most public bureaucracies, especially in international organizations. Each of them was set up with a specific function and purpose. Each focused on its special contribution and on performing its task well. The downside was parochialism, tunnel vision, and, worse, bureaucratic jealousies and information hoarding that developed over the years. Functional specialization led over time to institutional insularity. The ethos of the era was that "each tub rests on its own bottom." Communication and coordination with others were not ideals to be pursued.

With the demands of conflict intervention missions in the post–Cold War era, international organizations have had to operate on common tasks in the same arena. In fact, their very limitations should be a greater source of strength than it is. They are specialized and experienced. No organization has the skills to do all the tasks needed, but together they come close. At a high level of abstraction they share common goals—preventing or ending conflict, providing assistance to the people who have suffered, rebuilding the physical structures, and helping establish democratic institutions that can deal with conflict. This commonality ought to provide a basis for cooperative action.

Yet the insistence on preserving bureaucratic domains has, if anything, hardened with scarce funds. Each organization has sought to carve its niche on the world scene, develop its own external support and sources of funding, and establish its identity in order to survive. The inward focus has therefore become stronger. Bureaucratic competition for primacy has not yielded to a recognition of the necessary interdependence of all interveners, civilian and military. It has not seemed important for senior managers of most international organizations to make the effort to fully appreciate the skills of the other organizational players, the contribution they could make, their views of the problem, or their conceptions of their roles, much less their organizational goals. Thus UN Secretary General Kofi Annan was prompted to state to the special meeting of the General Assembly on reform in July 1997, "Where we should have been flexible and adaptable, we have all too often been bureaucratic. Where we should have reached across sectoral lines and institutional barriers, we have stayed within rigid structures, working in isolation, with little or no coordination."[10]

Despite these words, the conception that cooperation is the *only* means of attaining shared goals of successful conflict management is not yet embedded in the corporate cultures of most intervening organizations.[11] The imperative of each organization often remains its own performance, its bureaucratic position, and its funding goals.

The threatening aspects of organizational change loom especially large in a climate of cost cutting and downsizing in all organizations, where "reengineering" often seems to be translated into personnel cuts. In such a climate, radical changes that may be undertaken primarily for other purposes will nevertheless be perceived as job elimination and resisted on that ground. If the change takes the shape of a personal and imminent threat, the immediate losses will outweigh the benefits in the minds of the very people who must implement it. The resistance to change that could be normally expected will be even fiercer. Change feels like loss—and people need time to mourn before they can adapt.[12]

The personnel practices pursued by international organizations create a special problem. Staffing policies have traditionally responded to member states' demands for equity of representation by increasing personnel at all levels, especially prestigious management positions. As new positions have built up, accusations of bloated bureaucracy have multiplied. As a consequence, a major focus of reform, especially in the UN system, has been personnel reductions.[13] Kofi Annan, in one of his early acts as secretary general, bowed to the pressure for cost cutting and sought the elimination of one thousand positions (about 2 percent) in his July 1997 report.[14] Remaining staff tend to "circle the wagons" to protect their own positions. That has not led to the acceptance of new ideas or redirection of policy.[15]

Added to all these problems is the fact that organizational change must be accommodated while meeting the urgent new demands of ongoing conflict intervention. Given the shortages of personnel and funding, the intensive internal efforts necessary to bring about organizational change are likely to seem an annoying distraction. It is difficult to mobilize the people in the organization for the hard work of change when officials are constantly being pulled off to deal with urgent crises. This has been the experience of broad UN reform efforts. In *Planning for Intervention,* we applauded the efforts of the United Nations High Commissioner for Refugees (UNHCR) to decentralize its operations, a requirement we concluded was essential to effective cooperation and collaboration in the field. In revisiting the accomplishments of the Delphi Plan several years later, we found that implementation had gone very slowly, and the tradition of central micromanagement was still being asserted.

Finally, resistance to cooperation even in the field is reinforced by the welter of other players, each with strong traditions of organizational independence. NGOs are fierce defenders of their independence. Some organizations, such as the International Committee of the Red Cross, remain aloof because they believe their access to the people they are committed to helping requires uncompromising neutrality and distance from political activities. Yet despite centrifugal inclinations, many of these NGOs must be brought into team operations. In the earlier post–Cold War interventions, they arrived on the scene on their own initiative with their own resources and missions. No one could tell them to leave. In the intervening years, they have become essential operational elements of conflict intervention in a more formal sense. Much of the assistance provided by international and national organizations—UNHCR, the Disaster Assistance and Response Team (DART) of the U.S. Office of Foreign Disaster Assistance (OFDA) within the U.S. Agency for International Development (USAID), the European Community Humanitarian Office (ECHO)—is given through NGOs under contract. Thus they have become dependent on the large international organizations for financial support and often on the military for logistics, and so the dependence is mutual.

Lack of Clarity in Policy and Direction

The lack of clear political direction from powerful and other involved states remains the most profound obstacle, one that structural or institutional change does not fix. Political leaders and policy analysts call for clear, consistent mandates and well-defined missions to guide and organize interventions. Clarity, coherence, and agreement within the international community, particularly within the UN Security Council, may help establish a policy of coexistence. However, only in rare cases is that likely to occur.

Even if unity of purpose should result in a clear mandate, it can be considered a necessary but not sufficient condition for an implementable policy of coexistence. The effort to obtain a clear mandate is certainly an important first step, but it is not a panacea. It must be followed by sustained effort on the part of the relevant states that provide guidance to international organizations, together with adequate resources of money, goods, and trained personnel to ensure that the policy does not go off track. So long as ultimate separation of the conflicting groups remains a realistic goal of the parties, it may be very difficult for the international community to promote coexistence without a permanent military interposition force. Coexistence is unlikely to be workable unless the parties have some recognition that ultimate separation is physically infeasible. Education and experience are large parts of a coexistence effort. Moreover, some history of peaceful coexistence at some level may be essential to re-creating that frame. Three cases sketched here illustrate the complexities of obtaining clear policy guidance.

Bosnia

The Dayton Accords of December 1995 signed by representatives of the parties to the Bosnian conflict met the entry conditions for coexistence. It is true that capitulation of the Bosnian Serbs may have resulted from near-defeat from both NATO and Croatian ground forces and that international consensus was imposed more by the United States than developed collaboratively within the UN Security Council or even NATO. Nevertheless, all parties did acquiesce, and the UN Security Council subsequently affirmed the detailed scheme of the Dayton Accords and spelled out respective obligations of the parties and international organizations.[16] A policy of coexistence is inherent in the scheme of governance. It reaffirmed specifically the awkward structure of a tripartite presidency and the "development of a Bosnian state based on the principles of democracy and consisting of two Entities: the Federation of Bosnia and Herzegovina and the Republika Srpska. . . ." The Dayton Accords also set forth the exact boundaries of each entity and the joint and separate institutions to be created. It further provides a constitution prepared by the Americans.[17]

The history of Bosnia since 1996 has not been a smooth development of coexistence, as many subsequent writings demonstrate (see Chapter Four).[18] The parties to the conflict did accept the fact of coexistence reluctantly, although the Bosnian Serbs have not given up hope of eventually becoming part of Serbia. More recently, the international transitional authority, the Office of the High Representative (OHR), has had to deal with an incipient attempt of Bosnian Croats to withdraw from the accords to create their own entity.[19]

Nonetheless, even though outbreaks of violence have occurred throughout Bosnia since 1996, they have lessened in intensity and number, enabling an increase in refugee return. The numbers of refugees returning in minority status to their homes have increased to 778,651 (just over half of the 1.5 million refugees), with an exponential increase since 2000.[20] Returnees are adequately protected by the 17,500 members of SFOR (NATO's Stabilization Forces),[21] but their continuing presence will be needed for a long time to come.

The obstacles to reconciliation in Bosnia are enormous, despite clarity of mandate. Yet there are examples now of coexistence—something more than hostile but parallel action. There are small-scale examples of real cooperation on the ground among the parties in small projects. One can speculate that the process would have gone more quickly and smoothly if encouraged by a better-planned international authority that could have hit the ground running.[22]

Not only did the newly appointed high representative—a position created by the Dayton Accords—have to start from scratch, his office had no budget until the Peace Implementation Conference held after the accords were signed and donations solicited. The organization had to assemble a staff, physical space, and funds, all in a hostile environment where violence was recurring daily. Other, more experienced agencies such as UNHCR understood its mandate. OSCE, inexperienced in running elections, at least had experience working in conflict areas and an existing staff on which to call. But there was no comprehensive whole. Despite that, the specificity and detail of the peace agreement and the international support for it seem to have been helpful. The accords and the Security Council resolutions provided guidance to both an experienced military force and the inexperienced ad hoc governing civilian authority.

In comparison with many other peace agreements and other postconflict mandates of the Security Council, the Dayton Accords for Bosnia laid out the intentions of the international interveners with as much clear direction and precision as could be negotiated. In fact, one could say that the agreement comes close to compelling a policy of coexistence. But as discussed later in the chapter, large obstacles remain, and they are bureaucratic, political, and practical.

Cyprus

If we look back forty years, Cyprus offers a more typical example of a mandate that does not set forth international policy with clarity. It is far more typical of what usually results from intense differences among members of the international community who see a situation through different lenses. Cyprus had a history of geographically mixed communities during the colonial era. The British acquired the island from Turkey in 1875 and ruled it until 1960. Independence was granted pursuant to a tripartite agreement negotiated by Great Britain, Greece, and Turkey to which the two Cypriot communities adhered. The agreement established a power-sharing constitution and government based on the principle of mutual vetoes for the two communities. The scheme actually worked for three years but then broke down when each community refused to accept important proposals by the other. Fighting broke out on the island in December 1963, and calls for a cease-fire were unavailing. After violence and civil war, the experiment in joint governance failed. Greek and Turkish troops of the international security force provided by the 1960 agreement became involved in the conflict and did not restore peace.

The British convened a conference of the three guarantor powers after hearing rumors of an imminent Turkish invasion. It became clear that differences could not be easily resolved, and there was a need for a broader international peacekeeping force. British suggestions of NATO were rejected, and the fighting continued into February 1964, when heated UN Security Council debates finally concluded with a resolution that called for the restoration of law and order. The resolution of March 4, 1964, provided for the creation of a peacekeeping force, with the consent of the government of Cyprus. It did not spell out the power or objectives of the peacekeeping force and provided no civilian authority to provide a transition to peace. It exhorted the government of Cyprus "to take all additional measures necessary to stop violence and bloodshed" and admonished all member states "to refrain from any action or threat of action likely to worsen the situation. . . ." And it recommended that the newly created force "use its best efforts" to restore law and order and "a return to normal conditions."[23]

Four decades of separation between Greek and Turkish Cypriots has been enforced by a UN peacekeeping force and a rigid "green line." It has led to a relatively tense peace without progress toward either a united government or two separate nations. While many informal connections have been made between the two communities, and only occasional violence erupts, there is not much in the way of coexistence. Many official efforts and efforts by NGOs have been made to bring Greek and Turkish Cypriots together,[24] but separation remains. Whether a Dayton-type mandate might have worked remains a question. Given the ongoing hostility between Greece and Turkey, such an agreement would not have gained sufficient international support as a political matter. Without much deeper study, it is hard to say whether coexistence would have been more likely if the international players had a clearer, more coherent international political policy expressed not only in mandates but also by earlier coherent and forceful mediation efforts and stronger incentives and disincentives, such as more stringent criteria for EU membership consideration. Certainly Greece and Turkey, both NATO members, have had a polarizing impact.

Kosovo

In Kosovo, the entry conditions for coexistence barely exist. Before the war, the population was nearly 90 percent Albanian and 7 percent Serb. Each group had nationalist aspirations that date far back into history.[25] Before violence erupted, the Albanians suffered legal discrimination, job and property loss, human rights abuses, and violence at the hands of Serbs whose nationalism was fueled by the rise of Slobodan Milosevic and cemented by his revocation of autonomy for Kosovo in 1990. After a long period of passive resistance, nonviolence, and the construction of parallel institutions, a younger generation of Albanians began to express their resistance through militancy. By 1991, Albanian Kosovars not only demanded constitutional and legal rights but were also calling for independence.[26] They were reinforced by the recognition of other states broken from the former Yugoslavia.

Nonviolent tactics gave way to more violent confrontation with the advent of the Kosovo Liberation Army (KLA). Belated efforts first by unofficial and then by international mediators did not stem the deterioration. The violence escalated as Serb punishment grew harsher. Internal military and paramilitary action grew increasingly violent with little more than exhortations from the international community. A UN Security Council demand for a cease-fire in September 1998 had little effect,[27] nor did the stronger step of an arms embargo.[28] Finally, the West, led aggressively by Richard Holbrooke of the United States, negotiated an agreement with Milosevic in October 1998 for a reduction of Yugoslav troops and police in Kosovo, the insertion of verification monitors, and NATO air surveillance to ensure that the agreement was carried out. Initial compliance with the agreement and accompanying Security Council resolutions[29] soon deteriorated, with KLA and Serb ambushes, Serb wholesale detentions, and KLA kidnappings.

The "Contact Group" of Western states called for further negotiations and produced a plan in early 1999 that called for the withdrawal of Serb forces, disarming the KLA, and the introduction of a NATO peacekeeping force of thirty thousand. The plan called for a restoration of Kosovo's autonomy but left open the question of independence for three years. Intense negotiations during February and March 1999, culminating in an international conference in Rambouillet, France, did not succeed in halting the violent civil war. The Kosovar Albanians acquiesced in the March accords, but the Serbs refused to do so. The West, now heavily involved, left itself with few options other than military intervention after the aborted Rambouillet conference. NATO bombing began in April, and simultaneously, the systematic expulsion of Albanians occurred.

According to the Kosovo Commission report, 863,000 Albanians became refugees, and an additional 590,000 were internally displaced. Neither the length of the war nor the magnitude of refugee flows was anticipated. About 10,000 Albanians were killed.

Milosevic capitulated in June, seventy-eight days after the war started. Martti Ahtisaari of Finland and Viktor Chernomyrdin of Russia negotiated an agreement after intense G-8 discussions.[30] It provided the basis for the Military Technical Agreement and the UN Security Council resolution that followed. Unsurprisingly, given strong basic differences in views within the alliance that brought the war to an end, the future of Kosovo was not settled—it was merely stated that the people of Kosovo would enjoy "substantial autonomy" within the Republic of Yugoslavia. Unlike the Dayton Accords, the Ahtisaari-Chernomyrdin agreement and the military technical agreement did not spell out the future political status of Kosovo. The subsequent UN Security Council resolution, no. 1244, set forth the design, tasks, and role of the transitional administration for Kosovo but continued the ambiguity of "substantial autonomy" and the concept of "substantial self-government" but created a political process and timetable whereby ultimate status would be determined three years in the future.[31]

By 2000, half the Serb population had left,[32] with the remaining Serbs isolated in hostile enclaves in the north, such as Mitrovica. The transitional UN administration and NATO (KFOR) forces have tried to minimize the retaliatory violence and the skirmishes that have occurred. The United Nations Mission in Kosovo (UNMIK) has had a policy of coexistence and attempted to bring Serbs and Albanians into transitional self-governance arrangements. The Serbs have been most reluctant, and popular support among Albanians is weak. A few isolated economic development projects have fared somewhat better, but the picture has not been encouraging.

Thus the Kosovo Commission, in assessing the bitter situation that remained, considered five options for the future of Kosovo: (1) continuing a protectorate, (2) partition, (3) full independence, (4) autonomy within a democratic Republic of Yugoslavia, and (5) conditional independence. It concluded that conditional independence was the best solution, to occur after UNMIK consulted fully with all factions and a referendum is carefully framed. It envisaged a long and secure transition, protected by international military and police, and the critical condition of majority acceptance and inclusion of minorities. Part of the reason for the report's conclusion was the continuing hostility that time had not begun to heal and the continued repressiveness of the Milosevic regime.

It is hard to say now that the conditions for coexistence exist in Kosovo. Although the stated objective of the special representative of the secretary general is coexistence, success has been elusive. The Serbs have refused to participate in the election process or transitional institutions created by UNMIK. Its efforts and those of many international organizations have not brought about much interaction or cooperation between the groups, but the time necessary for healing has not yet occurred, nor has the full impact of the fall and subsequent indictment of Milosevic by the International Criminal Tribunal for the former Yugoslavia (ICTY) and his delivery to The Hague. Even ultimate independence does not settle that question. The international community, having finally taken a stand against ethnic cleansing and other forms of ethnic violence, is not going to tolerate it with respect to the Serb minority in Kosovo. It is likely that some resolution involving complete or nearly total confederated separation from Yugoslavia will occur peacefully within the next few years, but even then, some Serbs will remain in Kosovo, and their treatment will remain a concern of the international community.

Would a clear international policy and mandate have made a difference to the outcome? As a practical matter, international agreement could not have been secured for either complete integration or complete separation. Separatism remains a huge threat to Russia and China, and sympathies differed among the other three permanent Security Council members. Apart from political realities, Kosovo presents a case for separation almost as compelling as that of the Baltic states. Nevertheless, even if separation were to occur, the need for coexistence remains. Minorities will remain within the borders. Even in Israel, if a Palestinian state is accomplished, there will be minorities on both sides of the border. Border contact implies some degree of cooperation, and economic reality requires it.

Yet despite the difficulties of forming and maintaining a coalition for the whole range of actions exemplified by these three cases, the calls for a "clear and practicable mandate" continue unabated.[33]

In most of the internal civil violence we have been studying, the nations that comprise the international community perceive both the situation and their interests differently. Even the terrorist attack on the World Trade Center on September 11, 2001, has required artful coalition building, despite immediate overwhelming international support for the United States. Within a month, it began to erode as domestic opposition to military action against Afghanistan became more vocal and even violent, and threatened action against Iraq has fractured the coalition further. Forging a coalition is difficult and painstaking work, particularly when military forces are required or high costs imposed. Maintaining a coalition is even harder, in the light of continuing sacrifices, as we have seen over the years of sanctions against Iraq.

States face opposition at home, and the words used publicly must take account of domestic political vulnerability. Legitimacy in such situations requires the one form of joint statement that international law has to offer—the UN Security Council resolution invoking Chapter VII of the UN Charter. The UN Charter requires at least a broad agreement among the five permanent members of the council to avoid a veto, and bridging the differences often requires the very vagueness complained about as a "fuzzy mandate."[34]

A search for greater clarity is worth the effort, but it should be understood that in most complex cases, interveners will have to settle for only broad policy, and other ways must be developed to harmonize efforts on the ground. Unfortunately, this often leads to timidity and indecisiveness on the part of international bureaucrats. It is "Jell-O bureaucracy," as one senior diplomat dubbed it: "These organizations strive for the lowest common denominator to avoid making waves."[35] Given this fact of life, international organizations, like domestic administrative agencies, should be more forthcoming in spelling out clear policy guidelines and take the risk of member state rebuke.

Lack of Funding and Donor Fatigue

Inadequate funds and insufficient commitment to help a war-torn nation can cause difficulties for the nation's transition into a functioning and peaceful member of the international community. Generally, the international community has backed lofty ambitions with low-cost action. In addition, the constant emergence of new crises diverts funds and experienced personnel from finishing the job of helping a society reconstruct itself.

Even before September 11, 2001, the United States—a leader in funding internal crises and societal reconstruction—had made some small movement away from a pure "exit strategy" since the early 1990s. The original notion was that commitment of military forces would remain until a (premature) "democratic" election, after which, presumably, a democratic government would be in place and the military could depart. Our expectations have been constantly disappointed from Bosnia onward, and rhetoric about exits has been decreasing. The United States failed to pay its UN dues for years and only recently began to reduce its debt, though it has been a generous donor in other ways. The EU, the other source of postconflict funding, is so bound up in complex bureaucratic procedures that it cannot and does not meet obligations and promises. It remains to be seen whether the current rhetoric of patience and persistence in combating terrorism will be followed by strong international support for the slow, painstaking process of rebuilding devastated societies. Afghanistan is an unpromising example.

Unfortunately, when faced with declining funding, many NGOs move on to the next dramatic crisis because today's drama attracts both capable staff and donors. In *Planning for Intervention,* we advanced the following argument:

> The most powerful inducement for fundamental change in the international machinery for dealing with the practical requirements of conflict intervention is the record of the past decade. The conflicts that have occupied the international community since 1990 have nearly overwhelmed it. At the same time, if the bureaucratic leadership at headquarters has been unresponsive, . . . the changing availability of political, material and human resources creates powerful incentives to compel greater cooperation. In the private sector, it is said, the discipline of the "bottom line" is what forces organizations to abandon strategies that are not succeeding and to embrace cultural change. It is argued that no similar motive operates on international organizations and NGOs. The constituency of these organizations is diffuse and conflicting. The contradictory voices of dissatisfaction and support [and] the clashing viewpoints of member states, donors and publics may operate to

cancel one another out, leaving the organizations with a false sense of freedom and autonomy. Since the conflicts are themselves so complex and intractable, it is hard to pinpoint the reasons for lack of success.[36]

In *Planning for Intervention,* we went on to argue in greater detail that there was a powerful analogy between the need for business to respond to changed economic conditions and that of international organizations to do the same. It was our expectation that the widespread criticism of the UN and other international organizations that has led in large part to erosion of support and credibility would lead to better, more efficient performance—to better training, less red tape, and improved performance overall. We were too optimistic.

The process has proved to be far slower than anticipated. The connections between erosion of support and poor performance do not seem to be made agency by agency, even though recognized in the UN Secretariat. We did not fully appreciate the escape that disappointing or dramatically bad results offer an organization because the causes of bad results are so complex. It is easier to become defensive after failures such as the UNOSOM II phase of Somalia or the conduct of operations during the war in Bosnia than to examine the role that organizational inadequacy may have played. Mixed political signals obscure the connection between inadequate performance and declining financial support.

What we have observed is that organizations, when facing a shortage of funds coupled with requirements to take on new missions elsewhere, tend to hunker down, cut staff across the board, send their most experienced staff to deal with new crises, extend the workload of those who remain, and replace employees with temporary workers. Next they cut programs. Temporary staff, although well-meaning, are often inadequately briefed about the situation and make mistakes that might have been avoided with more continuity. The constant need for start-up time is wasteful and often destructive. While the immediate task of repatriation has slowed, the entire strategy of coexistence depends on the resettlement of IDPs and assurance that they will lead normal lives once more.

Even though the similarities between business and international organizations should not be exaggerated, no business organization would survive without making the connection between its performance and reduced revenues. Even though there are multiple causes for reduced resources, it is far too easy to blame "donor fatigue" and new demands on international resources, rather than dealing with internal bureaucratic rigidity that resists change at every level. The linkage of reduced budgets to ineffective performance needs to be made with thoughtfulness, precision, and persistence. Loss of relevance, which has occurred in many organizations, is the "moral equivalent" of the bottom line.

Implications for Coexistence and Possible Solutions

The concept of coexistence does not call for a large burden of radical change among international organizations that operate in the field. The concept is already accepted by international organizations and NGOs in many projects in Bosnia and Rwanda.

However, two important systemic processes that are much harder to effect as a matter of organizational change are still lacking: creation of a culture of *joint or interorganizational planning* and an increased policy of *planned decentralization*. These organizational changes rub up against all the bureaucratic resistance discussed in this chapter but may be necessary to help provide the key to more effective performance and to stem the loss of resources. There is no question that the fight against terrorism has begun to shake up traditional bureaucratic patterns not only in the United States but also in all the nations joining in the coalition. The need for something more than loose coordination of disparate organizations has long been necessary in postconflict reconstruction. How might it be developed?

Joint Planning

In societies that have suffered violent conflict, there are many simultaneous actions that interveners must take to help the society recover and to prevent recurrence. Welding multiple actors and actions into a coherent whole is a huge undertaking. Crisis response without a comprehensive understanding of what the consequences of any intervention might be can do more harm than good. Internal organizational planning is important, but it is not enough. Intended effects are bound to be distorted by the actions of others. Comprehensive civil-military planning that begins early and is ongoing provides the best hope for effective physical and social reconstruction.

A number of questions emerge. Where and when should collaborative planning take place? Who should be involved? What type of process is effective? First, planning must be an ongoing process, taking place early and continuing as a situation unfolds, so that officials are not merely reacting to surprises as they occur.

Planning is needed at different levels, and the emphasis is somewhat different for each level.

1. Strategic policy planning is needed at the highest level among the major actors—states, international organizations, and NGOs. This should be the major emphasis of the headquarters level in any operation that is undertaken. The most available model is the military. But in the sort of conflicts that the past decade has witnessed, even the most effective and sophisticated military planning has not been adequate because it excluded the necessary civil component. And less planning appears to be done for the postconflict phases, despite the risk of recurrence.

2. Operational planning in the field is just as necessary and also in the spirit of the military approach. Detailed day-to-day operations cannot be anticipated in advance or at the highest levels but have to be dealt with locally, on a shorter-range basis, with flexibility and foresight. Issues that might require major shifts in policy or the overall strategic approach go up to a higher level. Thus there is constant reciprocity among field and headquarters in the planning process. This need for planning locally is what led us to our recommendation (to be discussed shortly) in favor of decentralization. It is at the local level that the affected populations should be involved. If they are not, the consequences of action remain unknown, and a transitional administration is not doing its job of helping pass governmental authority to the local population.

3. Key also is intraorganizational planning—the planning that permits each organization to undertake specific tasks with competence and adequate resources to do the job. This level of planning will reassure policymakers that the larger strategic planning process is workable and enable policymakers to use the perspectives of

each participating group to anticipate the gaps and the overlaps that a successful operation must overcome.

It is beyond the scope of this chapter to describe the planning process in detail, but it should begin with military planning, grow to include what corporations do, and further link civil and military planning.

The object of such planning is not to predict the future but to develop options for dealing with a broad range of possible contingencies. The process itself teaches people to pay attention to different perspectives and to work together more cooperatively. It is far more effective than simple coordination. It can identify the overlaps and the gaps. When officials from different units within an organization or from different organizations try to work through the demands of a problem that they must address jointly, they come to know each other, to understand the unique capabilities of individuals and organizations, and to develop a degree of collaboration in action that no process of coordination can achieve. Differences of viewpoint between individuals and organizations can be dealt with in the planning process, rather than in the course of the operation. In the best case, the beginnings of trust will emerge, a sense that each component can be relied on to do its part. The situations we face in postconflict societies such as Bosnia and Rwanda do not present the same urgency as a country in crisis. There is time for an ongoing planning process to bring postconflict societies out of high risk and into the international community. In the Balkans, "jointness" must continue to be civil-military. Rwanda faces limited funds and a greater NGO presence than that of the international organizations. The process may be harder to make effective under these circumstances. Afghanistan is proving even more complex. Although some UN planning has been done among its agencies, a civil-military process has not developed.

The tradition of planning so familiar to Western and Eastern military organizations has only begun to be seen even in well-staffed foreign ministries—and is still regarded with some disdain by NGOs, whose participants often resist strategic analysis and planning because they prefer responding to crises. Some say, "The issues are so complex and fast-moving that it is essential to be on the ground quickly to understand them" or "We need to move in early—that is when we are most needed—so there is no time to engage in a planning process" or "We just don't have the funds and staff to plan and act." These comments may reflect realities, but they may lead to a rapid response that does more harm than good.

Planning for response to a crisis may be more accepted than a decade ago, but advance contingency planning still remains a remote goal. Particularly for civilian organizations, it seems to be a luxury or a waste of time and money to plan for a contingency that may never occur when there are so many crises that need immediate attention. But planning for such contingencies may be the key to crisis intervention. Even though contingency is different from what ultimately occurs, initial thinking about analogous situations has helped train people and organizations to act coherently. The planning process is not only the best form of interorganizational coordination but may also be the most cost effective form of staff training.

A more difficult problem is the international political sensitivity about planning in the absence of international consensus, which is rarely achieved before a crisis has erupted. "We can only intervene when we have a consensus of our members. This takes a long time to develop," stated one high UN official.[37] The Rwanda genocide is a glaring case of failure. When a crisis seems to be brewing, officials fear that even theoretical discussions of international involvement could adversely affect possible peaceful settlement. The fact is that relevant military organizations are likely to be involved in contingency planning at that time, but because there are so many scenarios out there—for the Americans, Iraq, North Korea, Colombia, and Kosovo, to name only a few—the sensitivity of any one is not heightened by what is known to be standard (and highly classified) activity.

Civil management reluctance is accentuated by the issue of jurisdiction and control at the highest levels of international organizations, particularly the UN. Security Council members do not take kindly to an initiative that might usurp their prerogatives. States are reluctant to relinquish to the international organizations any suggestion of power to control the fact, timing, or extent of intervention. Political unwillingness of the members to relinquish or compromise control makes it more difficult for an organization to engage in systematic planning. Nor is this a UN problem only. In the OSCE, the consensus decision rule, deliberate understaffing, and the reluctance of members to create a strong secretariat all reflect an unwillingness to empower the organization to act forcefully and early.[38] But an effective cooperative planning effort would go far to lay out the options for ultimate decision makers.

The military has not historically facilitated the process of civil-military joint efforts, although greater understanding of interdependence emerges in the UK Civil Military Committee (CIMIC) work. The tradition of secrecy that serves the military so well in preserving the advantage of surprise and protecting the safety of the force erects barriers against opening the planning process to civilians. Moreover, for many nations, the desire to protect intelligence sources and methods imposes a further constraint on sharing of operational planning data. Even in the Gulf War—a far more typical military engagement than Bosnia—this was a problem within the purely military coalition against Iraq.[39] Yet the disastrous ambush of the U.S. Rangers in Somalia argues forcefully for more collaborative civilian-military planning, even on the narrow grounds of safety of military personnel. The rationale for failure to plan is less persuasive in a postconflict situation, especially where tensions run high. The international community is already in place. Some form of interorganizational relationship has already begun. Yet the efforts are far less effective than they might be, even today. The United States learned some important lessons after the failure to anticipate the consequences of its actions in Somalia. The postconflict effort in Haiti in 1993 was a definite improvement but represented only a rudimentary civil-military planning process.

Bosnia in its early postwar stages illustrates the costs of a lack of cooperative planning. The military aspects of Bosnia had been planned meticulously by well-oiled NATO planning staff who had been working on the Bosnian problem years before Dayton. The nature and specific contours of NATO involvement were defined in advance. Clearly circumscribed commitments had been hammered out in the North Atlantic Council (NAC). Despite the large size of the intervention force (IFOR), the military goals were modest and well within the bounds of traditional peacekeeping, although unlike "classical" peacekeeping efforts, IFOR was authorized to use force under Chapter VII of the UN Charter. As a result, the military intervention went off without a hitch. The military objectives were secured within a few weeks, well in advance of the scheduled time frame.

The contrast with the civil side of the Bosnian intervention could hardly be starker. The problems that plagued the early reconstruction effort in Bosnia illustrate many of the consequences of the absence of interorganizational planning.[40] True, no one knew just when and how the war would end. But everyone knew that it *would* end, almost certainly before the century ended, from sheer exhaustion if nothing else. It was also predictable that the outcome would be some kind of brokered peace, however precarious, not one imposed by the military victory of one side or the other. It was also possible, on the basis of the experience in other post–Cold War internal conflicts, to anticipate the physical and social elements that would be involved in rebuilding a peaceful society:

- Refugees and internally displaced persons would have to be fed, sheltered, protected, and ultimately resettled. Some of these requirements were already being addressed during the conflict.
- Basic human needs for food, shelter, and medical care for the larger population became apparent as the conflict raged on.
- Infrastructure would need repair—water, power, roads, transportation, and the like. Communications would have to be restored.
- A major construction requirement for housing and public buildings could be anticipated.
- The local civil police, who were dispersed or corrupted during the war, would have to be retrained or replaced.[41]
- Skilled mediators would be needed to deal with crises that would inevitably arise even under "peacetime" conditions, to settle disputes and to help restore communication among the parties.
- Some efforts at demilitarization and disarmament would undoubtedly be mandated in any peace agreement. There would be mines to clear. And as elsewhere, former military combatants would have to be integrated into society.[42]

- Jobs and training were needed to provide a livelihood in a society where the prewar economy was destroyed. Economic development was a key to sustained peace.
- Given the commitment of the major Western powers to democratization, elections would be mounted. And efforts would be made to build a democratic legal structure and civil society.

All these activities require careful planning and training. The international community demonstrated some organizational learning as they responded to the crises in Kosovo and East Timor. Some improvements were made—certainly in creating a structure for civil administration. But in the Kosovo case, civil and military planners did not work together in advance. Perhaps they could not have appreciated all the possible effects of military action, but if a joint planning process, allowing for security requirements, is well entrenched in the international community, the options and choices will be clearer. Now that we realize that well-meaning efforts may have unintended consequences and may create new problems, it should be obvious that a concerted planning process that helps anticipate results has real value.

In the early days of the Bosnia crisis, these elements were not just knowable but known and widely discussed.[43] Some of them were addressed by ongoing planning within some key organizations. Preparation within all the agencies with urgently needed core competences was completely lacking. Even the plans for raising the sums to cement an uneasy peace were far from complete, although it was clear that an immediate infusion of funds would be needed. As for collaborative planning, there was none at all. The collaborative aspects of the process were simply disregarded, and so there was no attempt to push the traditional NATO planning envelope to include civil-military planning. Efforts to reach across the civil-military divide and to work out a sensible division of labor among the many civil organizations on the scene once the operation was under way were helpful, but it was hard to play catchup after initial expectations had formed. In the beginning, coordination at ground level was lacking—joint coordination meetings were not convened until months into the operation.

Barely six years after Dayton, many lessons have been learned. The OHR does function in its coordinating role; country-level planning is done through the periodic meetings of the Reconstruction and Return Task Force (RRTF). To the extent that funds become available, new problems are dealt with, if not fully anticipated. For example, there has been growing concern that the economy was not growing fast enough to sustain the gradual withdrawal of foreign assistance funds, and the international organizations have redoubled their efforts to establish small enterprises. This need has been accelerated by the exponential increase in the rate of refugee and IDP return since OHR insisted on tough property rights laws in both Bosnian entities. There are other successes in joint planning—the civil police and military (SFOR) now function in a smoother interface. But corruption and customs issues are just beginning to be addressed. Six years is a long time, and donor fatigue set in long ago.

The international presence is very large. The UN Mission in Bosnia and Herzegovina (UNMIBH) has had some 340 international and 1,600 local personnel, as well as approximately 1,800 International Police Task Force officers, and a large headquarters building in Sarajevo on loan from the University of Sarajevo. OHR has developed a large apparatus to fill its missions with nearly 700 people and nineteen field offices. The RRTF does function to coordinate efforts and to establish priorities, but it does not represent a very comprehensive planning effort.[44] For example, although USAID, British CIMIC projects, and other organizations all deal with small-scale economic development projects and inform one another, there have been no comprehensive planning efforts to bring those involved in job creation together with agencies working on such matters as housing for returnees, housing and jobs for IDPs who do not wish to return to their original homes, public health workers, education, and corruption and customs reform.

As mentioned, a similar analysis of Kosovo shows that there has been some institutional learning since Bosnia, but not enough. There was joint planning in the UN Secretariat, but it was not civil-military. Representatives of the secretary general and some UN agencies were engaged in a very quiet joint planning process before the NATO bombing in the spring of 1999, and it accomplished the creation of a more workable civilian structure than in Bosnia. NATO engaged in a planning process that did not include the UN. In my view, the early troublesome differences about the respective functions of civil police and military could have been resolved earlier in a joint planning process. Initially, Kosovo was a repetition of Bosnia and other conflicts.[45]

Joint planning needs to take place early and on a continuing basis. Organizations must be more skilled at planning for the postwar period when a country is in chaos or splintered and its people are wounded, hungry, and poor. As indicated, although every situation is unique, there are predictable problems and needs after violent conflict. And as we have seen, we have models now. Under U.S. Presidential Decision Directive 56, interagency planning among relevant U.S. departments, both civil and military, at a high level, were triggered by a National Security Council decision. This has been modified by the Bush administration, but the theme is being sounded strongly in the fight against terrorism after September 11, 2001. It built on the traditional planning process evolved by Western militaries over generations as well as more recent experience in political-military gaming and simulations. It defines a specific and detailed process for interagency planning and cooperation in conflict intervention. It is an ambitious attempt to institutionalize joint planning and joint operations. It has evolved over several years, and corrections have been made to the accompanying training to fit American needs. However, it is not an international effort and is therefore very limited.

The UN has developed a process that is quite similar to the U.S. PDD 56 planning process. Joint planning is conducted under interdepartmental task forces that bring together all the elements needed for planning a comprehensive peace operation, including postconflict reconstruction. They can be created at the suggestion of a desk officer in a UN department or agency that has clear warning signals of a brewing crisis. More likely, the initiative will come from the secretary general himself or the Executive Committee on Peace and Security, created in February 1997 as part of the secretary general's initial structural reforms.[46] It is improving with experience but remains timid, incomplete, and underfunded. It is insufficiently inclusive. It has not included the World Bank, which must play a major role in reconstruction. It has not included regional organizations until after designations of roles and responsibilities are made, and that is usually after a peace agreement has been achieved, whereas work must start at once. Most important, it has not worked with military organizations. If NATO is to be the military group, as in Kosovo, joint planning should occur early. If it is to be a pickup UN force, then political consensus for such a force must be in place, and the force assembled, before joint planning can occur. That is late in the day. Moreover, the planning and intelligence capacities of the Department of Peacekeeping Operations (DPKO) have been decimated at various times by budget cuts and political refusal to permit seconding by wealthy Western states. The refusal to implement the Brahimi Report's recommendation to create a strategy and analysis entity (the Information and Strategic Analysis Secretariat) is a further missed opportunity to create an expert planning capability.[47]

But planning for coexistence should not be a difficult problem. The policy must be set at the highest international levels in an interorganizational planning process. The value and possible outcome of devoting resources to coexistence in particular war-torn societies needs assessment. What priority should such a policy be given, in comparison with other strategies? Should it be made an integral part of other strategies such as providing shelter, protecting refugees, economic development, or education, even if its implementation slows them down? What are the costs and benefits? If these policy considerations are not discussed at the highest level, they are not likely to be implemented on the ground in a systematic way.

Planning for coexistence at the field level also requires a systematic effort. In Bosnia, the story of the German housing construction stands in contrast to British SFOR coexistence work with the British economic development agency, DFID. The British military selects small economic development projects and conditions funding on local willingness to employ workers from the minority groups who are returning to the area. This policy is not uniform throughout Bosnia. There are good and less good examples of coexistence, but a joint planning process would implement policy into a more coherent whole. And its effectiveness would be constantly under scrutiny in a robust joint planning process. Most important, such a planning process must begin to involve the local populations so that their views become part of a process that they can ultimately assume if there is to be real coexistence.

Planned Decentralization

The idea that decentralization might prove a better approach to achieving collaboration and cooperation among the multiplicity of interveners in conflict developed both from observations in the field and from business experience. In this conception, operational responsibility is delegated to the field. But its success depends on a number of factors, starting with policy direction that results from a joint strategic planning process at the headquarters level. This means that a broad strategy has been established and there are some policy guidelines, even though national differences are papered over. It also is important that a structure has been established for cooperation and ongoing planning on the ground, even though in some of the most impressive examples a structure emerged from felt need. Even though there has been little progress on real policy planning thus far, there has been some improvement in understanding that a structure for cooperation and collaboration is important.

Because the policy differences among states at the top are not going to disappear by exhortation, a planning effort must clarify to state members of international and regional organizations what the implications are for the policies they espouse—to expose unworkability, pitfalls, and unintended negative consequences. But planning is not a cure for policy defects—no political process is ever wholly rational. One can only hope for greater rationality and consequential thinking. When the Dayton Peace Accords were imposed, primarily by the Americans, there were strong state differences about the feasibility of restoring a multiethnic state in Bosnia. Yet five years later, there is some movement toward peaceful coexistence, if not reconciliation. After a very slow start, organizations on the ground have worked hard and quite well, even cooperatively, to make Dayton work. Bosnia is not a viable state yet, but in the field, officials have persuaded the highest level that the process takes longer than earlier thought, and both the military and civilian presence is being sustained.

The argument for considerable delegation to the field for operations is based in part on the near impossibility of centralized micromanagement. Only staff on the ground fully appreciate the uniqueness of the problems and the fit of international efforts to a fluid situation. Even though the broad needs are understood at headquarters, implementation can adapt more readily to the subtleties that any community presents. Moreover, it can begin to include the local populations and listen to their perceptions and interests.

In the literature of corporate change,[48] business theorists had been preaching since the early 1970s on the need to move away from rigid, hierarchical organizations to flexible, more lateral, and more decentralized forms. As the business environment shifted, with many companies becoming less competitive and less profitable in an increasingly global market, business organizations began to question the way they were structured and operated. Many were prepared to make fundamental changes in their corporate culture to meet the challenges of rapid technological change, increasing competition in the world market, and loss of market share.

What academic organization theorists preached, American business has put into practice over the past three decades. This period has seen radical shifts in the organizational form of U.S. businesses, from highly centralized functional organizations to decentralized units and cross-functional teams, in response to the demands of intensified global competition, rapidly changing markets, and changing technology. They began to develop innovative modes of responding to the complexities they faced, usually by moving toward structures that could adapt quickly to constantly changing business demands. Despite fits and starts and a good deal of experimentation over a fifteen-year period, the change is now well seated. For corporations, the dominant motivation was the "bottom line" and the ability to position themselves to adjust to rapid market and technology change or risk failure. Some companies succeeded; others went under. It has become clear that policy direction for the organization remains at the top, but creativity in reaching broad goals is decentralized.

International bureaucrats with whom we spoke early in our research were hard pressed to see the parallels with business organizations, but it should be clear to them that there may be a "bottom line" in this arena as well. International organizations have witnessed the drying up of funds and the unwillingness of donors to keep contributing to the slow process of reconstruction and redevelopment after violence has ended, although they do not fully perceive a connection with donor fatigue. They have seen their reputations tarnished and have been subject to severe criticism. UN Secretary General Kofi Annan responded to some of that criticism in a reform report that said, "Where we should have been flexible and adaptable, we have all too often been bureaucratic. Where we should have reached across sectoral lines and institutional barriers, we have stayed within rigid structures, working in isolation, with little or no coordination."[49]

UNHCR was the first international agency to mount a serious effort at decentralization, through the Delphi Project. It has not been wholly successful and does illustrate the power of institutional resistance. Nevertheless, it is a start. And where the bureaucratic leadership at headquarters has been unresponsive, the need for concerted action continues to be recognized in the field, in reaction to the immediacy of issues that must be dealt with on the ground. Smaller units that are flexible and hospitable to innovation are much better able to mount creative response to complex, fast-moving situations.[50]

In most situations, cooperation on the ground does surpass coordination at headquarters. While there is still "turf" or jurisdictional competition that is often imposed from above, bureaucratic rigidities seem less important than needs on the ground. Of course, this is regrettably less the case when the conflict is no longer acute. Organizations tend to revert to the bureaucratic battles that have dominated their relationships over the years. But entrenched bureaucratic jealousies can yield to pragmatic needs, although this is not always the case. While lack of adequate funds will not be met in the field, it is possible to avoid some duplication by field cooperation on the ground. This may, in some small measure, alleviate donor fatigue, which seems to be composed of both weariness of conflict proliferation and ineffectual responses. Policy incoherence among major states, however, can only be helped somewhat by better field workarounds. Neither planning nor decentralization will totally cure that problem.

Effective models of decentralized coordinated action emerged not by policy design but by superb in-country consensus-building leadership in the United Task Force (UNITAF) phase of the Somalia intervention. For some months in early 1993, a loosely organized set of venues on the ground in Somalia succeeded in coordinating what was an extraordinarily complex and multifaceted humanitarian assistance operation. The hub of this network was the Humanitarian Operations Center (HOC), which became the central clearinghouse for all humanitarian assistance in Somalia. The HOC knitted these two components together into an effective coordinating mechanism. The principal instrumentality was the institution of regular meetings held each morning.[51] Within weeks, the meetings were drawing crowds of a hundred people, including representatives of NGOs, UN agencies, the United Nations Operation in Somalia (UNOSOM), and the military, as well as Somalis working for UNITAF and the relief community.[52]

The meetings began with basic military briefings on security and the weather. Thereafter, the NGOs would provide information on their activities, locations, needs, and observations in the field. Everyone was given an opportunity to speak as discussion worked its way around the room following particular topics, locations, and relief activities. In the process, there was also an opportunity to voice criticisms and concerns. A consensus would emerge on what needed to be done and in what order. The large meeting would then break down into smaller groups for discussion of specific tasks. These smaller, task-specific meetings were facilitated by a floating USAID representative, who maintained an overall sense of the planning process, passing information from one group to another, and setting up spot conferences among representatives of different groups as needed. Thus the HOC was able to sustain a rolling consensus on the overall humanitarian operation as well as specific day-to-day assignments.

Military participation in and liaison with the HOC was carried out by the Civil Military Operations Center (CMOC), colocated with it. The CMOC grew out of an ad hoc arrangement developed after the Gulf War for coordinating military and humanitarian operations to provide relief to the Kurds.[53] This instrumentality created a sense of shared purpose and generated a specific agenda, if only a few days in advance. Humanitarian workers, HOC personnel, and military officers knew who was doing what and what the needs and requirements of the situation were. Frequent face-to-face contacts and shared efforts to address needs fostered good working relationships among the people directly involved. People from dramatically different organizations—the UN, the military, the NGO community—developed an understanding of each other's perspectives and the sense that they were all in it together. All that changed when UNOSOM II took over: there was a failure of learning from experience, and the disasters that ensued, when eighteen U.S. soldiers were killed, can be traced to the lack of collaborative effort.[54]

Similar mechanisms were developed in some aspects of the peace process in El Salvador, in the humanitarian effort to assist the Kurds in northern Iraq, and in other cases.[55] In all these situations, there was an ad hoc forum at ground level in which all the actors met frequently and regularly, face to face. It was informal, open to all, unstructured, and transparent. There was little hierarchy. The principal activities were information sharing and consensus building, and these led to coherent responses and even efficient use of available resources in extraordinarily difficult and demanding circumstances. Superiors at headquarters in New York or national capitals were too remote from the actual situation to give useful guidance and in any case were usually engaged in arcane and unresolvable struggles about overall policy.

The model has since been formalized and extended as a vehicle for civil-military coordination in humanitarian interventions when Western troops are involved. The British military has developed the concept even further, and the model is well understood and used by NATO. Indeed, the CMOC itself is an example of a decentralized team, responding flexibly to requirements for coordination and action on the ground in fast-moving intervention situations.

Planned decentralization is designed as a systematic way to replicate these successes in the field. As the early organizational chaos in Bosnia demonstrates, it is not a sure thing that this form of cooperation will self-generate. If it does, it takes a long time. It is best if a structure is established to make sure that it does. The organization of UNMIK in Kosovo represents, in part, a structural response, as it does in East Timor. There has been some institutional learning. However, the kind of consensus leadership exercised by U.S. diplomat Robert Oakley is not always available, and no structure can generate collaboration on a foolproof basis.

The business model of decentralization (such as product development teams) in fact shows parallels to the kind of consensus leadership exercised by Ambassador Oakley. All members of the team, with their various skills, were essential to effective functioning. The further lesson from business is that lead roles necessarily change over time, as the work evolves. For example, the designers predominate in the early phase, manufacturing in the next, and so on. In a war-torn society, groups concerned with security, infrastructure repair, and refugees may predominate first; economic opportunity comes later. Timing and flexibility to meet emerging needs can be best responded to in the field, not at headquarters. This is the broad logic of planned decentralization.

Conclusion

Coexistence may be a valuable, worthy, and useful tool for the international community to use in the process of helping heal and reconstruct societies decimated by internal conflict. The concept is neither mysterious nor difficult to grasp. Coexistence is now approached on a case-by-case and project-by-project basis. It is likely to continue that way. If that happens, its power and usefulness will be limited. This chapter asks for more. It asks for insisting on processes that will provide the international community with far more than the ability to implement a coexistence policy. The move to a culture of joint planning will empower international organizations to make better choices because they have a better understanding of the issues and the likely impact of what they do. Moreover, if they begin to move away from the top-heavy centralized structures that lead to micromanagement, they will be better able to implement their policies with sensitivity. But they will need strong and persistent leadership and adequate training to replace an entrenched culture with one that is more flexible, adroit, and responsive.

Notes

1. M. Minow, "Imagine Coexistence: Working with People Who Return to Divided Communities." Memorandum for UNHCR Conference 10, Cambridge, Mass., 2001.
2. A. H. Chayes and A. Chayes, *Planning for Intervention: International Cooperation in Conflict Management* (Cambridge, Mass.: Kluwer Law International, 1999).
3. S.C. Res. 1244, UN SCOR, 54th sess., 4011th mtg., UN Doc. no. S/RES/1244 (1999).

4. Interview with Peter Galbraith, minister of political affairs and Timor Sea, Oct. 10, 2001.

5. Much of the discussion in this section is based on Chayes and Chayes, *Planning for Intervention.*

6. D. A. Nadler, "Concepts for the Management of Organizational Change," in J. R Hackman, E. E. Lawler III, and L. W. Porter (eds.), *Perspectives on Behavior in Organizations,* 2nd ed. (New York: McGraw-Hill, 1983).

7. A. D. Chandler Jr., *Strategy and Structure: Chapters in the History of the American Industrial Enterprise* (Cambridge, Mass.: MIT Press, 1962), p. 320.

8. R. M. Kanter, B. A. Stein, and T. D. Jick, *The Challenge of Organizational Change: How Companies Experience It and Leaders Guide It* (New York: Free Press, 1992), p. 216.

9. W. W. Powell and P. J. DiMaggion, "Introduction," in W. W. Powell and P. J. DiMaggio (eds.), *The New Institutionalism in Organizational Analysis* (Chicago: University of Chicago Press, 1991).

10. K. Annan, statement to the Special Meeting of the UN General Assembly on Reform, New York, July 16, 1997. [http://www.un.org/reform/track2/sgstatmn.htm].

11. As discussed later in this chapter, perhaps the most notable exception is UNHCR, which is systematically trying to change its approach and self-image by moving to regional joint planning, early cooperation with other organizations, and significant decentralization to the field as part of reform efforts in its Delphi Plan.

12. Nadler, "Concepts."

13. See W. Gordon, *The United Nations at the Crossroads of Reform* (Armonk, N.Y.: Sharpe, 1994).

14. K. Annan, *Renewing the United Nations: A Programme for Reform,* UN Doc. no. A/51/950 (New York: United Nations, 1997).

15. See K. Annan, *Report of the Secretary General on the Implementation of the Recommendations of the Special Committee on Peacekeeping Operations and the Panel on United Nations Peace Operations,* UN Doc. no. A/55/977 (New York: United Nations, 2001).

16. S.C. Res. 1088. UN SCOR, 51st sess., 3723rd mtg., UN Doc. no. S/RES/1088 (1996).

17. Dayton Accords, U.S. Department of State Supplement, vol. 7, no. 1, 1995. [http://www.state.gov/www/regions/eur/bosnia/bosagree.html].

18. S. Berg and P. Shoup, *The War in Bosnia-Herzegovina* (Armonk, N.Y.: Sharpe, 1999).

19. D. Holley, "Croat Nationalists Imperil Goal of Unified Bosnia," *Los Angeles Times,* May 10, 2001, sec. A1, p. 5.

20. "The returns proceeded slowly in the first few postwar years because of ethnic mistrust and violence. But this year, 30,236 people returned to the Muslim-Croat federation and 17,899 to the Serb republic. Another 2,314 people returned to Brcko, a northern district run by the central government. Of nearly 1.5 million refugees the war produced, 778,651 have been registered by the UNHCR as having returned in the past six years." "Bosnia:

UN Agency Reports Significant Increase in Returning Refugees," *AP World-News*, Oct. 9, 2001.

21. North Atlantic Treaty Organization, "SFOR Organization," Mar. 6, 2002. [http://www.nato.int/sfor/organisation/sfororg.htm].

22. The UN was excluded because of American pique at the UN's restrictions on the conduct of war termination.

23. S.C. Res. 186, UN SCOR, 19th sess., 1098th mtg., UN Doc. no. S/5575 (1964).

24. These efforts are typified by "bicommunal" programs funded by both the United States and nongovernmental organizations like the Institute for Multitrack Diplomacy. The United States allocates $15 million annually in economic support funds "to bring peace to Cyprus" in the words of Sen. Olympia Snowe; those funds go to economic and social development projects as well as training in practical fields. Other initiatives have brought Turkish and Greek Cypriots together for training in conflict management. For more information, see Embassy of the United States of America, "The Cyprus Peace Process" [http://www.americanembassy.org.cy/cyprus.htm], and Institute for Multitrack Diplomacy, "Initiatives: Cyprus" [http://www.imtd.org/initiatives-cyprus.htm].

25. Independent International Commission in Kosovo (IICK), *The Kosovo Report: Conflict, International Response, Lessons Learned* (New York: Oxford University Press, 2000). See also M. Zucconi, "The European Union in the Former Yugoslavia," in A. Chayes and A. H. Chayes (eds.), *Preventing Conflict in the Post-Communist World: Mobilizing International and Regional Organizations* (Washington, D.C.: Brookings Institution, 1996).

26. IICK, *The Kosovo Report.*

27. S.C. Res. 1199, UN SCOR, 53rd sess., 3930th mtg., UN Doc. no. S/RES/1199 (1998).

28. S.C. Res. 1160, UN SCOR, 53rd sess., 3968th mtg., UN Doc. no. S/RES/1160 (1998).

29. S.C. Res. 1160. See also S.C. Res. 1207, UN SCOR, 53rd sess., 3944th mtg., UN Doc. no. S/RES/1207 (1998).

30. IICK, *The Kosovo Report.*

31. S.C. Res. 1244, UN SCOR, 54th sess., 4011th mtg., UN Doc. no. S/RES/1244 (1999), sec. 10. See also IICK, *The Kosovo Report.*

32. IICK, *The Kosovo Report.*

33. B. Boutros-Ghali, "An Agenda for Peace," UN Doc. no. A/47/277-S/2411 (1992), in Chayes and Chayes, *Planning for Intervention*, p. 33. See also J. M. Shalikashvili, "Foreword," in A. J. Goodpaster, *When Diplomacy Is Not Enough: Managing Multinational Military Interventions* (New York: Carnegie Commission on Preventing Deadly Conflict, 1996) [http://wwics.si.edu/subsites/ccpdc/pubs/dip/dipfr.htm].

34. The history of the Bosnian war is a classic example. The United States disagreed with its allies and undermined the European proposals embodied in the proposed Vance-Owen agreement yet several years later drove an agreement at Dayton that was not materially different. In Rwanda, failure of political agreement among potential interveners frustrated UN action until

after the genocide. See S. A. Power, *A Problem from Hell: America in the Age of Genocide* (New York: Basic Books, 2002).

35. Confidential interview with a senior diplomat, Aug. 2001.

36. Chayes and Chayes, *Planning for Intervention*, pp. 91–92.

37. Confidential interview with a UN official, Aug. 2001, notes on file with author.

38. D. Chigas, with E. McClintock and C. Kamp, "Preventing Diplomacy and the Organization for Security and Cooperation in Europe: Creating Incentives for Dialogue and Cooperation," in Chayes and Chayes, *Preventing Conflict.*

39. Confidential interviews with senior U.S. commanders following the Gulf War, spring and summer 1991.

40. J. Moore, *The UN and Complex Emergencies* (Paris: RISD, 1996); N. Ball with T. Halevy, *Making Peace Work: The Role of the International Development Community Policy* (Baltimore: Johns Hopkins University Press, 1996).

41. Compare the situation in El Salvador: C. Cervenak, *Learning on the Job: Organizational Interaction in El Salvador, 1991–1995* (Cambridge, Mass.: Conflict Management Group, 1997).

42. Ball, *Making Peace Work;* Moore, *UN and Complex Emergencies;* L. Rohter, "Guatemala Foes Now Train for Peace," *New York Times,* Mar. 11, 1997, p. A3.

43. R. Ullman, "Introduction: The World and Yugoslavia's Wars," in R. Ullman (ed.), *The World and Yugoslavia's Wars* (New York: Council on Foreign Relations, 1996).

44. It brings together OHR, UNHCR, the Commission for Real Property Claims for Refugees and Displaced Persons (CRPC), SFOR, the European Commission (EC), ECHO, the World Bank, UNMIBH, OSCE, the United Nations Development Programme (UNDP), the International Management Group (IMG), the International Organization for Migration (IOM), and the U.S. and German governments.

45. See M. J. Dziedzic and R. B. Oakley (eds.), *Policing the New World Disorder: Peace Operations and Public Security* (Washington, D.C.: National Defense University Press, 1998).

46. The Executive Committee on Peace and Security, which meets biweekly, is made up of the heads of the Department of Peacekeeping Operations, the Department of Humanitarian Affairs, the Department of Political Affairs, UNHCR, UNDP, and other UN agencies or departments.

47. *Report of the Panel on United Nations Peace Operations* ("Brahimi Report"), UN Doc. no. A/55/305-S/2000/809 (New York: United Nations, 2000); Annan, *Report of the Secretary General.*

48. Nadler, "Concepts"; Chandler, *Strategy and Structure;* Kanter, Stein, and Jick, *Challenge of Organizational Change;* Powell and DiMaggio, *New Institutionalism;* L. Gulick, "Notes on the Theory of Organization," in L. Gulick and L. Urwick (eds.), *Papers on the Science of Administration* (New York: New York Institute of Public Administration, 1937); J. P. Kotter, *Leading Change* (Boston: Harvard Business School Press, 1996); E. H. Schein, *Organizational Culture and Leadership,* 2nd ed. (San Francisco: Jossey-Bass, 1992); M. Hammer and J. Champy, *Reengineering the Corporation: A Manifesto for Business Revolution* (New York: HarperCollins, 1993).

49. K. Annan, statement to the Special Meeting of the UN General Assembly on Reform, New York, July 16, 1997. [http://www.un.org/reform/track2/sgstatmn.htm].

50. Chayes and Chayes, *Planning for Intervention.*

51. T. Seybolt, *The Success and Failures of Humanitarian Coordination in Somalia* (Cambridge, Mass.: Conflict Management Group, 1999); R. Oakley and J. L. Hirsch, *Somalia and Operation Restore Hope* (Washington, D.C.: United States Institute of Peace Press, 1995).

52. S. Rosegrant and M. D. Watkins, *A "Seamless" Transition: United States and United Nations Operations in Somalia, 1992–1993.* Kennedy School of Government Case Program no. C09-96-1324.0 (Cambridge, Mass.: Kennedy School of Government, Harvard University, 1996).

53. C. Seiple, *The U.S. Military/NGO Relationship in Humanitarian Interventions* (Carlisle, Pa.: Peacekeeping Institute, U.S. Army War College, 1996).

54. M. Bowden, *Black Hawk Down: A Story of Modern War* (New York: Atlantic Monthly Press, 1999).

55. Chayes and Chayes, *Planning for Intervention.*

Chapter Nine

The Culture of Corruption in the Postconflict and Developing World

Glenn T. Ware and Gregory P. Noone

Corruption in postconflict societies has emerged as one of the most serious obstacles to recovery.[1] War-torn societies, particularly those that have engaged in civil war or ethnic violence, emerge with their infrastructure destroyed or damaged; food, medicine, and even water is lacking, and the flow of basic goods and services has been disrupted. Corruption may begin to flourish in the early phases of reconstruction when the international community is providing emergency humanitarian assistance and large sums of money are pouring in. The diversion of funds can deliver a devastating blow to those regions, which teeter on the edge of reconstructing a viable nation or a return to conflict. Moreover, academic and policy analysts "have found that corruption is an activity that is increasingly difficult to disentangle from the broader effects of large-scale fraud, organized, 'disorganized' or business crime, and international theft."[2]

Note: The views expressed in this chapter are those of the authors and do not represent the views of the United States government, the Department of Defense, the United States Navy, or the United States Institute of Peace, which does not advocate specific policies. The authors would like to thank Diana Noone, Parth Chanda, Amanda Kosonen, Antonia Chayes, Martha Minow, and Lauren Guth for the assistance they provided in the writing of this chapter. Gregory Noone would also like to express his gratitude and appreciation to his wife for her timeless efforts.

In order to determine the most effective ways to reduce the damaging effects of corruption, it is essential to understand its characteristics and the form of corruption that poses the greatest threat to postconflict societies. This chapter does not address the "petty" or "five and dime" corruption of low-level officials but rather the massive "state machinery" corruption that devours millions of dollars of precious hard currency desperately needed for recovery from violence.[3] We first discuss the characteristics of state machinery corruption. Next, we argue that the common theme that corruption in the developing world is "unsolvable" or "inevitable" because of its "cultural roots" is misguided. Culture alone does not cause or fuel state machinery corruption. We argue that greed, combined with opportunity, lies at the root of corruption and poses the most significant threat to stability in postconflict regions. The final section offers a variety of collective responses that can be taken by the international community to control corruption in postconflict and developing societies.

What Is Corruption?

Volumes of research and countless scholarly articles have been written on the forms and types of corruption from the perspective of different disciplines such as economics, law, sociology, business, and international trade.[4] Each focus is somewhat different. While legal observers focus on the need to establish a robust rule of law, economists may raise the issue of exploitation of economic rents. This chapter does not choose a single disciplinary perspective, nor does it analyze the differences among them. Rather, it tries to offer a realistic picture of the obstacles that state machinery corruption poses to the recovery of postconflict societies and suggests what the international community can do to combat it. In particular, our concern is the role of international financial institutions (IFIs) in both fostering and fighting corruption.[5]

Definitions

Corruption has been defined as "government officials abusing their power to extract [or] accept bribes from the private sector for personal benefit."[6] Other writers have defined it as the "subversion of the public interest or common good by private interests."[7] Another reasonable definition is that it is characterized by an official who "deviates from the formal duties of a public role because of private-regarding (personal, close family, private clique) pecuniary or status gains; or violates rules against the exercise of certain private-regarding behavior."[8] No single definition of corruption seems to capture the perspectives of different disciplines or the context in which it occurs.[9] For the purposes of this chapter, corruption is the "use of public office for private gain."[10] One writer compares the difficulty in quantifying corruption to the now common reference to pornography and states "you know it when you see it."[11] Definitions notwithstanding, "transnational corruption has become too 'grand' to ignore."[12] While definitions may illuminate both the context and the perspective of the writer, no perspective can afford to lose sight of corruption's impact. Bribery, extortion, fraud, embezzlement, cronyism, and nepotism are common manifestations of corruption.[13] Personal gain is society's loss. In this context, "it is useful to consider what private parties can 'purchase' from a politician or bureaucrat."[14] Corruption involves government contracts, government benefits, reduction in the payment of taxes, regulatory avoidance (thereby saving time), and influencing outcomes in the legal or regulatory process.[15]

Characteristics of Postconflict and Development Corruption

Until the proliferation of internal violence and civil wars of the 1990s, the focus of anticorruption analysis and efforts was on the developing world. The focus has been economic cost and legal inadequacy. There is little doubt that in any society, state machinery corruption "raises transaction costs and uncertainty in an economy" and is inefficient.[16] Furthermore, such widespread corruption threatens even the most basic rule of law that may exist, by demonstrating both the weakness of the criminal law system and disregard for property rights and contracts.[17] But traditional economic and legal analyses of corruption ignore a third and crucial impact of corruption particularly relevant to societies emerging from war. Widespread corruption stunts the development of capable institutions of government critical for long-term societal reconstruction, despite massive efforts of the international community to create them.

The IFIs and other donors pour money into these countries to support the full range of reconstructive activities. Every postconflict state has to repair or develop infrastructure: roads, schools, hospitals, public buildings, electricity, communications, and housing. In any endeavor of this nature, massive procurement of goods and services is necessary to undertake construction. The overwhelming and rapid influx of money creates an environment in which corruption flourishes. In the face of large amounts of aid funds, officials and politicians in postconflict societies may devote their efforts to obtaining larger and larger grants, often for personal gain, rather than working to improve conditions and operate a functioning government.[18] Even without corruption, nations ravaged by conflict tend to rely too much on international aid funding and the secondary employment and revenues from international workers. Widespread corruption increases this dependence even further, crippling any recovery to a self-reliant economy. The failure to develop and employ local resources, talents, and ideas will leave local institutions weak and incapable when external funding dries up.[19] If nepotism and patronage are rampant, if civil servants can live only by bribery, if jobs are sold or bartered, the incentives needed for the development of an adept civil service will be completely undermined.[20] In fact, "corruption embodies a 'jungle of nepotism and temptation' which has dangerous and tragic consequences, replacing the enthusiasm of the young . . . civil servant with disenchantment and cynicism."[21] Widespread corruption stifles the development of well-functioning government entities and in the process undermines government legitimacy.[22] The problem that many postconflict nations face is absorption capacity. Generally, after years of war, famine, decolonization, or general institutional decay, states do not have developed and functioning systems to manage or "absorb" incoming development and reconstruction funds. Banking systems have collapsed, financial management tools are nonexistent, buildings and infrastructure are often severely damaged, and technical expertise to manage multimillion-dollar construction projects is often limited. Moreover, donors do not provide supervisory staff to monitor the use of the money that they give to the fledgling governments. Even when a donor group does have sufficient controls on this money, ingenious schemes are implemented to siphon off these precious funds illegally.

International aid donors, nations, and nongovernmental organizations (NGOs) often have little capacity to ensure that the resources they are providing are used for their intended purposes. Diversion to offshore bank accounts is widespread. Funds designed for humanitarian assistance and reconstruction are often given directly to the recipient government's financial authorities without controls and with "almost unlimited discretion."[23] Temptation often overcomes duty. In a recent case in East Timor, no sooner did the turmoil end and the aid start to flow than investigators discovered a collusive scheme to funnel contracts to designated corrupt individuals. This scheme was implemented not only by the local citizens but also by a foreign national ostensibly there to help in the reconstruction.[24]

An informal survey of donor NGOs indicates that most lack an organic investigative capability. The lack of accountability and forensic structures in donor NGOs creates an environment conducive to fraud and corruption and makes donor NGOs susceptible to financial abuse and manipulation. Many are aware of their shortcomings. They have been surprisingly cooperative with and appreciative of World Bank investigations into fraud and corruption. Many are beginning to understand that without strong mechanisms to account for the disbursement of resources, aid can have unintended and often negative effects.[25] When corruption becomes evident, "donor fatigue" is accelerated as donors become disillusioned by the lack of positive results.

In addition to insufficient financial management, postconflict and many developing countries also lack sophisticated governmental compliance regimes and effective enforcement mechanisms to control and account for donated funds. Accordingly, the government lacks the capability to absorb financial aid. It cannot control vast amount of funds or hold officials accountable. They cannot prevent corruption or assure donors that funds will be used as intended. Reconstruction efforts in Bosnia provide an example of the corrupt diversion of international assistance, together with the loss of revenues from inadequate legal enforcement machinery and an incapable taxing function and antiquated bureaucratic machinery that thwarted international investment. An antifraud unit set up in 1999 by the United Nations' Office of the High Representative (OHR) discovered that at least $20 million of the $5 billion that Bosnia received in international aid between the end of the war in 1995 and the 1999 investigation had been stolen.[26] The antifraud investigation also discovered that $1 billion of Bosnian public funds were lost as a result of corruption.[27] An even more detailed report covering public corruption in Bosnia and anticorruption measures to combat this corruption can be found in a report by the Commission of International Legal Experts on Corruption and the Anti-Corruption Measures in the Federation of Bosnia and Herzegovina.[28]

Unfortunately, as money pours into a postconflict society, scant attention is paid to ensuring that funds can be managed and that the state machinery is capable of absorption and accountability. Instead, bureaucratic systems are rapidly set up to procure and manage multimillion-dollar construction projects, often involving hundreds of contracts.[29] In turn, the opportunity to engineer subsystems to divert funds can be ingeniously exploited by corrupt actors. Capital is siphoned away and personal bank accounts are set up in offshore banks in traditional safe haven areas, preventing the transition of a postconflict or developing nation into a healthy self-sufficient economy with a robust, functioning government. For example, Augustine Ruzindana, a member of parliament and chairman of the public accounts committee in Uganda, argued that in many parts of Africa, projects such as roads and factories were started and abandoned because of such corruption.[30] The schemes that are employed are not necessarily new but are built into the state system as a matter of bureaucracy, making it harder to uncover.[31]

The capital flight even deprives the country of the benefits of both international spending and private investment in the economy that the funds were designed to help. Moreover, state machinery corruption and the officials who create it form a labyrinth or an internal network. The government ministries throughout the country work in concert with one another and rapidly evolve into efficient money-siphoning machines. Often it is not just the state bureaucrats that profit from corrupt systems; the private companies and consultants receiving reconstruction and development contracts are complicit as well. Furthermore, there are cases in which staff of "international aid organizations share in or even initiate the corruption by taking bribes through project officials, [through] middlemen, or directly from the larger contractors to approve expenditures."[32] Recently, a World Bank staff member pleaded guilty to violating the Foreign Corrupt Practices Act for his role in accepting and funneling kickbacks to government officials and others.[33]

Large-scale construction contracts provide the most lucrative opportunity for corruption. In some countries, international funding received from IFIs or other donors is manipulated by a corrupt government minister rigging the tender process in order to ensure that contracts are awarded to designated contractors—often those in which his family owns shares. The scheme takes place when the bidding companies are "invited" to attend government planning sessions in preparation for bidding where government officials will brazenly announce what "commissions" are expected in exchange for being awarded a particular contract. After the contract award, a government ministry sets up a mechanism to siphon funds from the contract. For example, an invoice processing system may be created whereby invoices by contractors must flow through a maze of bureaucratic approvals within the ministry responsible for payment. At each step in the invoice process, a bribe is extracted from the contractor by the government official in order to pass the invoice on to the next stage in the process. This scheme multiplies the cost of a project because bidders must account for these "costs" by inflating their bids across the board or by substituting lower-quality goods than are called for under the contract. The end result is disastrous to the country since contracts are priced higher to account for the bribes, the bribes are funneled offshore, and the projects are littered with substandard materials to offset the bribe payments. The cycle of decay worsens when donors pour more money into the country to continue to prop up an eroding infrastructure and keep the country afloat.

As discussed earlier, corruption of the state machinery also serves to impede the development of capable governance and retards social reconstruction. Corruption inhibits good representation and accountability, weakens institutions, and protects "illicit advantages, in the process of weakening potential competitors and reformers."[34] In postconflict states particularly, the reconstruction of governance is hampered by official corruption in costly ways, including diminished support for the state among the citizenry. Ironically, corruption also shortens the transition time to enforced self-reliance by its contributors due to donor fatigue. A strong reciprocal association has been noted between better development outcomes and good governance.[35] Thus if official corruption impedes development, as it did in Haiti when necessary public savings for development did not exist because of government corruption, effective governance is made impossible.[36] But without effective governance, the temptations of state machinery corruption may be overwhelming. A well-publicized example of the effects of official corruption on governance is the government of Kazakhstan's reaction to revelations of its alleged corruption where $1 billion of state money was secretly siphoned into a Swiss bank account by the country's president. Political opposition leaders were arrested, newspapers and television stations were shut down, and journalists critical of the government were assaulted.[37] Neither the oppression of political opposition nor the silencing of the media is in any way a reflection of good governance. As previously pointed out, corrupt reliance on foreign aid, even more than honest dependence, hampers the development of local long-term solutions to a postconflict nation's problems. It penetrates the heart of the recovery process. It will create insuperable obstacles to the efforts to create coexistence among those who had committed violence against one another.

Cultural Connections with Corruption

There are well-known cultural differences around the globe with respect to standards of acceptable and unacceptable behavior. But widespread state machinery corruption is not explained by cultural differences. How should the international community concerned with rebuilding societies address the context of operative values and accepted practices? These questions are being raised from the Balkans to Africa to Afghanistan. A protracted debate surrounds the significance of cultural relativism in the phenomenon of corruption.[38] In some cultures, it is extraordinarily difficult to discern the line between a gift and a bribe.[39] There are genuine differences in perception and attitude about the point at which gift giving shades into bribery and corruption.[40] In some cultures, discomfort with impersonal, arms-length business relationships may actually help foster corruption. For example, in some African and Asian nations, the act of gift giving is an obligation that is "a pivotal aspect of common social interactions."[41] Gift giving, like loyalty to family and friends, is "embedded in the framework of society."[42] Acts acceptable in one society may be criminal offenses in another. There are studies indicating that one nationality may have a "higher limit" than others before considering an act to be corruption.[43] One observer notes that in Thailand, the acceptable limit on monetary gifts to government officials is considerably higher than in other states.[44] "In one obvious sense, corruption is socially defined: it is what the public in a country think it is. But public opinion is not monolithic. It is often divided, unstable, ambiguous and ignorant. Public awareness is often low, access to mass media is limited, and state censorship is common. The values of rural communities may be incommensurate with those of urban elites or there may be clashes between the opinions of different religious or ethnic groups."[45]

In the end, the strategic awarding of jobs, contracts, loans, and grants to the particular elite groups by those in power are manipulated for personal financial gain.[46] Even where ethnic division seems to foster favoritism, communal divisions are trumped by state machinery corruption.[47] Cultural differences may mark different thresholds between acceptable gifts and illegal bribes and may provide opportunities to create larger schemes to siphon off huge amounts of money. But considerable evidence suggests that substantial agreement exists across cultures with respect to what is considered truly corrupt behavior.[48] Cultural differences may make it difficult to erect precise universal boundaries between acceptable and unacceptable behavior, but there is universal disapproval of large-scale bribery and loss of substantial public funds to personal gain.[49]

Some degree of corruption flourishes in nearly every society and in every corner of the globe, despite vast cultural differences. The United States alone tallies over $600 billion a year lost to fraud, even with its effective law enforcement machinery.[50] The cultural relativist's argument that culture is to blame for corruption is not very persuasive.[51] Moreover, it inspires a passive stance toward the elimination of large-scale corruption. In short, the argument is unconvincing and unhelpful. Cultural differences are not the main problem. Culture may create complications in the development of enforceable international standards of acceptable behavior, but in the end they can be harmonized into an international regime that moves to eliminate state machinery corruption.[52] In our view, the focus should be on those officials who wield the power to divert resources from the society at large to enrich themselves.

International Responses to Corruption

The international community has been aware that corruption flourishes globally. However, the response from the IFIs, the predominant donors, has seemed slow and somewhat haphazard. In the case of the World Bank, the "*c*-word," as corruption was known, was considered a problem that could not be addressed by the institution because it was thought of as inherently "political."[53] Since Article IV, section 10, of the World Bank Articles of Agreement specifically prohibit political activity, defining anticorruption efforts as "political" had placed them outside the scope of its charter. This concept changed in 1996 when James Wolfensohn, president of the World Bank Group, determined that corruption was not a political issue but an issue of development and poverty. With that decision, the world's leading international organization had a significant restraint lifted and was free to attack the problem using a variety of mechanisms.

But even a determined attack by one international organization has proved to be a task of immense proportions. Corruption flourishes most in states with inadequate controls, poor compliance machinery, and insufficient enforcement mechanisms to deter state actors from conspiring with commercial enterprises to siphon millions of dollars of loans and credits intended to benefit their country. The issue has been where to start and then how to ensure an effective attack on corruption in states receiving vast quantities of international assistance.

The U.S. Congress has placed the burden on the IFIs supported by the United States. It demands a concerted effort to reduce fraud and corruption associated with its lending programs under the threat of withholding a portion of U.S. contributions. Public Law 106-429 states:

> Sec. 588 (a) Funding Conditions—Of the funds made available under the heading "International Financial Institutions" in this Act, 10 percent of the United States portion or payment to such inter-

national Financial Institutions shall be withheld by the Secretary of the Treasury, until the Secretary certifies to the Committee on Appropriations that, to the extent pertinent to its lending programs, the institution is . . .

(3) Taking steps to develop an independent fraud and corruption investigative organization or office.

The purpose of the legislation is to ensure that the money lent by the institution is used for the purposes for which it is intended. The World Bank Articles of Agreement state that loan proceeds shall go only for the purposes for which they are intended. Other IFIs have similar requirements in the charters or treaties that establish their existence. PL 106-429, Section 588, provides every incentive for the IFIs to establish effective, independent anticorruption surveillance programs. What the law does not stipulate, however, is what should become of the investigative findings that these anticorruption offices generate within the IFIs. Nor does the act prescribe what specific sanction the IFI should undertake when acts of fraud and corruption are uncovered in the lending programs. The act also does not impose a rigorous level of commitment from IFIs, stipulating only that they take "steps to develop" these bodies. Coupled with the fact that the act withholds only 10 percent of the United States' financial commitment, substantial as that amount may be, the law may be viewed as only a preliminary soft push to IFIs to start the process of enacting more rigorous fraud and corruption investigation and sanction tools.

The World Bank, even before the passage of P.L. 106-429, was well on its way to establishing a fraud and investigative function that meets the requirement of the public law. The World Bank conducts extensive investigations of allegations of fraud and corruption pertaining to projects funded or executed by the World Bank. When the World Bank obtains evidence that confirms that fraud or corruption has taken place, it has a variety of options at its disposal. First, it may debar any company that has been caught paying bribes in exchange for contracts awarded. As of this writing, the World Bank has debarred more than seventy companies and individuals for engaging in fraud and corruption in World Bank projects.[54] Second, it can suspend or cancel funding to a borrower country. Third, it can refer the evidence to a criminal prosecutor in any one of a number of countries that have the appropriate jurisdiction.[55] But unfortunately, the criminal justice system in many nations where corruption is rampant has been decimated or remains deficient. Unless adequate international attention and resources are devoted to creating effective justice systems, that option can ring hollow.

Because of the provisions of Section 588, many other IFIs are developing or have developed internal fraud and corruption investigation units. Currently, there are no formal agreements between the various IFIs to share fraud and corruption information or to act collectively on the basis of findings of an investigation by one IFI. Collective sanctioning among multilateral, bilateral, and regional development institutions, as well as donor agencies, would require express agreements among these institutions. IFIs might retain the right to autonomously review the findings of other institutions and make independent determinations while working to harmonize their rules defining corruption and the standards of proof required to find misconduct. Express agreements requiring cooperation rather than competition between IFIs would also minimize risks of noncooperation. It would be a powerful deterrent if the IFIs would act collectively to do so. For example, if the World Bank debarred ABC Construction Company from receiving World Bank–funded contracts in any borrowing country because of its corrupt practices, the deterrent effect would be magnified enormously if the other IFIs moved to debar ABC Construction Company also. Such punishment would be powerful. Moreover, if IFIs shared information on fraud schemes uncovered within particular governments, collective leverage could be brought to bear on the governments to take specific action to address these state corruption practices.

Such collective action against fraud and corruption of this sort would be an important new development by the crucial international lenders. But as Antonia Chayes points out in Chapter Eight, bureaucratic jealousy and "turf" battles make such coordination and cooperation difficult. Bureaucratic autonomy remains a strong force in every international organization. Moreover, a fear of politically motivated debarments also exists, along with the well-known competition among development agencies. Regional development agencies also have their bureaucratic jealousies. For example, one regional financial institution may prefer not to honor a debarment by another regional lender in cases where it might require favoring a business from another region. Such fear that business interests from a particular region were behind the sanction might lead to further suspicion of the collective sanctions approach.

Despite bureaucratic obstacles, there seems to be an emerging norm within the international community against large-scale corruption and fraudulent practices in postconflict and developing countries receiving large infusions of funds. Evidence for such a normative trend can be found in the growing number of multilateral and regional arrangements undertaken to harmonize both criminal and civil procedures and sanctions against corruption by nations who may be on the receiving end of international donations. These legal arrangements foster cooperation between nations to fight corrupt and fraudulent practices. Three international anticorruption conventions—the Organization of American States (OAS) Inter-American Convention Against Corruption, the Organization of Economic Cooperation and Development (OECD) Convention on Combating Bribery of Foreign Officials in International Business Transactions, and the Council of Europe Criminal Law Convention on Corruption—include scores of countries committed to fighting bribery and other corrupt practices.[56] While the conventions require varying degrees of legal harmonization from their signatories, all conventions maintain judicial control in the hands of each signatory country.[57] These conventions can also serve as models for harmonization of IFI anticorruption offices and for cooperation among them.

Some scholars and human rights activists have called for the International Criminal Court to handle cases of state machinery corruption by classifying it as a crime against humanity.[58] Such a grave designation is not widely subscribed to in the international or anticorruption community. While the trend for international criminal sanctioning of corruption is gaining momentum, it is clearly still considered the province of national judicial bodies.

Thus even if the IFIs police and enforce their loans and grants and assist other donors in that process, the failure of the international community to assist in the development of a robust rule of law means that corruption can flourish again and again in the same country. Part of the anticorruption effort must be the development of strong compliance and criminal justice systems in recipient countries. The effort to build a strong legal system is a herculean task. It involves the training of civil police, prosecutors, and judges and also extends to the provision of adequate prisons. It is costly and takes a long time. The international community has demonstrated neither the persistence nor the generosity to make the effort in all the countries that need such assistance.

There are some positive examples, however, including the U.S. Department of Defense's Defense Institute of International Legal Studies (DIILS), the U.S. Department of Justice's International Criminal Investigative Training Assistance Program (ICITAP) and Office of Overseas Prosecutorial Development, Assistance and Training (OPDAT), the United States Institute of Peace's Rule of Law program, the American Bar Association's Central and East European Law Initiative (CEELI) program, and the U.S. Agency for International Development, to name a few.[59]

Therefore, two sets of collective approaches need to be nurtured in order to ensure the success of the attack on corruption. The first is collective action by international lenders. NGOs' reliance on World Bank anticorruption findings points an encouraging path for international institutional lenders. As noted, it may be more difficult politically for regional lenders, and certainly bilateral donors, to accept the investigatory findings of IFIs. Nevertheless, they should be encouraged to do so and at least to copy the efforts and short-circuit wholly independent investigations. Although a collective sanctioning system might not work flawlessly in all cases, international normative forces exist to support its creation. The model of cooperation among regional organizations such as the OECD and the OAS provides the basic architecture for such a system of cooperation.

The second approach—that of harmonizing state criminal and civil codes toward more effective law enforcement—has already begun, as we have shown. Its scope must be deepened and widened so that the option of criminal sanctions is not a hollow alternative for the IFIs when it turns cases over to state prosecutors. But as also mentioned, the very nations that suffer from widespread state machinery corruption are the ones most deficient in their legal systems. Thus for state cooperation in law enforcement to be meaningful, the international donors must help provide struggling states with resources and other international institutions with technical assistance so that they can develop a strong rule of law.

Conclusion

Corruption in the postconflict environment is perhaps the most complex problem facing war-torn regions as they struggle for stability. It is enduring, complex, and debilitating for development. The myth of corrupt cultures should give way to the realization that it is the opportunity and greed of actors—and, state machinery corruption in particular—that stunts true progress. There may be no silver bullet to eradicate fraud and corruption in the postconflict world, but there is much more that the international community can do. The responsibility does not end with action by international organizations. A multidimensional attack is needed. The role of free and responsible media cannot be overlooked in this ongoing battle. Local and international NGOs, such as Transparency International, devoted to combating corruption and advocating financial and governmental transparency and accountability, are necessary throughout the developed and developing world alike.[60] Governments themselves must also strike a blow against corruption by establishing ombudsman offices, direct "hot line" access for complaints, competitive salaries for civil servants based on merit, and participation in international treaties that ban corrupt business practices.[61] Global efforts, by both large IFIs and small NGOs, as well as individual states, are necessary to eradicate corruption in postconflict societies. The effort to facilitate reconstruction of war-torn areas and efforts to provide the means for coexistence will be futile unless large-scale corruption is attacked more vigorously.

Notes

1. World Bank, *Helping Countries Combat Corruption* (Washington, D.C.: World Bank, 2000). "In a recent survey of more than 150 high ranking public officials and key members of civil society from more than 60 developing countries, the respondents ranked public sector corruption as the most severe impediment to development and growth in their countries." C. W. Gray and D. Kaufmann, "Corruption and Development," *Finance and Development*, Mar. 1998, p. 7. "Foreign investors still prefer to go to less corrupt countries, other things being equal. . . . Systematic research conducted recently by a number

of authors finds that the more corrupt a country, the slower it grows." S. Wei, "Corruption in Economic Development: Beneficial Grease, Minor Annoyance, or Major Obstacle?" Paper presented at the UNDP/Transparency International Thailand Workshop on Integrity in Governance in Asia, Bangkok, June-July 1998, pp. 16, 24.

2. A. Doig and S. McIvor, "Corruption and Its Control in the Developmental Context: An Analysis and Selective Review of the Literature." *Third World Quarterly*, 1999, *20*, 660. See also M. Hampton, *The Offshore Interface: Tax Havens in the Global Economy* (Old Tappan, N.J.: Macmillan, 1996), and M. Levi, *Regulating Fraud* (London: Tavistock, 1987).

3. See N. M. Rubin, "A Convergence of 1996 and 1997 Global Efforts to Curb Corruption and Bribery in International Business Transactions: The Legal Implications of the OECD Recommendations and Convention for the United States, Germany, and Switzerland," *American University International Law Review*, 1998, *14*, 257–320. "Petty" or "five and dime" forms of corruption occur in large bureaucracies and throughout organized society. An example would be paying the mechanic at the state motor vehicle inspection garage $20 to ensure that a vehicle passes the required inspection.

4. I.F.I. Shihata, "Corruption: A General Review with an Emphasis on the Role of the World Bank," *Dickinson Journal of International Law*, 1997, *15*, 451–485. See also A. Posadas, "Combating Corruption Under International Law," *Duke Journal of Comparative and International Law*, 2000, *10*, 345–414, and F. Heimann, "Combating International Corruption: The Role of the Business Community in Corruption and the Global Economy," in K. A. Elliot (ed.), *Corruption and the Global Economy* (Washington, D.C.: Institute for International Economics, 1998).

5. International financial institutions include the International Bank for Reconstruction and Development (IBRD), the International Financial Institution, the European Bank for Reconstruction and Development, and the African Development Bank, to name a few. The IBRD (World Bank) was established in 1944 at the Bretton Woods Conference to confront the destruction resulting from World War II and to promote economic development.

6. Wei, "Corruption in Economic Development," p. 4.

7. R. Williams, "New Concepts for Old," *Third World Quarterly*, 1999, *20*, 505.

8. O. Azfar, Y. Lee, and A. Swamy, "The Causes and Consequences of Corruption," *Annals of the American Academy of Political and Social Science*, 2001, *573*(42), 44. Nathaniel Leff defined corruption as "an extra-legal institution used by individuals or groups to gain influence over the actions of the bureaucracy. As such, the existence of corruption per se indicates only that these groups participate in the decision making process to a greater extent than would otherwise be the case." Quoted in Williams, "New Concepts for Old," p. 506.

9. "To date, no all purpose definition is available and there are grounds for believing that the search is futile. Corruption is complex and multifaceted and resists simple labeling. How corruption is defined depends on the context

in which it is located, the perspectives of the definers and their purpose in defining it. Different questions demand different responses and the choice of question depends on what it is we are trying to identify and understand." Williams, "New Concepts for Old," p. 512.

10. Gray and Kaufmann, "Corruption and Development," p. 7.

11. Wei, "Corruption in Economic Development," p. 4.

12. Rubin, "Convergence," pp. 259–260.

13. Article 1 of the Organization for Economic Cooperation and Development's Convention on Combating Bribery of Foreign Public Officials in International Business Transactions (effective Feb. 15, 1999), Treaty Doc. 105–43, 1997 U.S.T. Lexis 105, states that it is a criminal offense "for any person intentionally to offer, promise or give any undue pecuniary or other advantage . . . in order to obtain or retain business or any other improper advantage in the conduct of international business."

14. Gray and Kaufmann, "Corruption and Development," pp. 7–8.

15. Gray and Kaufmann, "Corruption and Development."

16. Gray and Kaufmann, "Corruption and Development," p. 8.

17. Azfar, Lee, and Swamy, "Causes and Consequences of Corruption," p. 46.

18. S. S. Gibson, "The Misplaced Reliance on Free and Fair Elections in Nation Building: The Role of Constitutional Democracy and the Rule of Law," *Houston Journal of International Law*, 1998, *21*, 1–49, citing M. Laurent, "Forces Against the Development of an Independent Judiciary in Haiti," *National Business Association Magazine*, Mar.-Apr. 1996, p. 13.

19. G. Anglade, "Rules, Risks, and Rifts in the Transition to Democracy in Haiti," *Fordham International Law Journal*, 1997, *20*, 1176–1214.

20. Wei, "Corruption in Economic Development."

21. R. Theobald, "So What Really Is the Problem About Corruption?" *Third World Quarterly*, 1999, *20*, 491.

22. Gray and Kaufmann, "Corruption and Development."

23. M. Lloyd, "Aid Summit Stresses Accountability," *Boston Globe*, Mar. 24, 2002, p. A6.

24. We base this statement on unpublished empirical fieldwork shared with us by fraud and corruption investigators.

25. M. B. Anderson, *Do No Harm: How Aid Can Support Peace—or War* (Boulder, Colo.: Rienner, 1999).

26. C. Hedges, "Leaders in Bosnia Are Said to Steal Up to $1 Billion," *New York Times*, Aug. 17, 1999, p. A1.

27. Hedges, "Leaders in Bosnia."

28. Commission of International Legal Experts on Corruption and Anti-Corruption Measures in the Federation of Bosnia and Herzegovina, *Final Report*, Feb. 25, 2002.

29. We base these conclusions on unpublished empirical fieldwork shared with us by fraud and corruption investigators.

30. A. Ruzindana, "The Importance of Leadership in Fighting Corruption in Uganda," in K. A. Elliot (ed.), *Corruption and the Global Economy* (Washington,

D.C.: Institute for International Economics, 1998). Ruzindana (p. 135) writes: "Ugandan president Yoweri Museveni describes how the dilution of drugs by corrupt medical staff led to the development of disease-resistant microbes."

31. W. M. Kramer, "Corruption and Fraud Stunt Third-World Growth," *White Paper,* 2002, *16*(3), 24–25, 43. Kramer's article provides a survey of fraud and corruption schemes in the developing world.

32. Kramer, "Corruption and Fraud," p. 24. Often the aid organization participates in corrupt practices not to profit but rather to ensure "security" with a payoff, however small.

33. "A World Bank Glass House?" *AFNWS,* Reuters Business Briefings, May 20, 2002.

34. M. Johnston, "Corruption and Democratic Consolidation," paper presented at the Conference on Democracy and Corruption, Princeton University, Mar. 1999.

35. D. Kaufmann, A. Kraay, and P. Zoido-Lobaton, *Governance Matters,* Policy Research Paper no. 2196 (Washington, D.C.: World Bank, 1999).

36. S. J. Schnably, "The Santiago Commitment as a Call to Democracy in the United States: Evaluating the OAS Role in Haiti, Peru, and Guatemala," *University of Miami Inter-American Law Review,* 1994, *25,* 393–483.

37. P. Baker, "New Repression in Kazakhstan; Journalists Targeted After President Implicated in Scandal," *Washington Post,* June 10, 2002, p. A12.

38. S. Schwenke, "The Moral Critique: Corruption in Developing Countries," *Journal of Public and International Affairs,* 2000, *11,* 137–156.

39. Schwenke, "Moral Critique."

40. S. R. Salbu, "Are Extraterritorial Restrictions on Bribery a Viable and Desirable International Policy Goal Under the Global Conditions of the Late Twentieth Century?" *Yale Journal of International Law,* 1999, *24,* 223–303. Businesses "in some countries are culturally less inclined to have arms-length economic relationships, which in turn may lead to more ingrained corruption." Wei, "Corruption in Economic Development," p. 14. "Largely due to cultural differences, what may be considered an illicit punishable payment in one country may well be permitted in another." J. Kim and J. B. Kim, "Cultural Differences in the Crusade Against International Bribery: Rice-Cake Expenses in Korea and the Foreign Corrupt Practices Act," *Pacific Rim Law and Policy Journal,* 1997, *6,* 557.

41. B. C. Harms, "Holding Public Officials Accountable in the International Realm: A New Multi-Layered Strategy to Combat Corruption," *Cornell International Law Journal,* 2000, *33,* 185.

42. Harms, "Holding Public Officials Accountable," pp. 185–186.

43. Wei, "Corruption in Economic Development."

44. Wei, "Corruption in Economic Development."

45. Williams, "New Concepts for Old," p. 506.

46. Theobald, "So What Really Is the Problem?"

47. Theobald, "So What Really Is the Problem?"

48. Azfar, Lee, and Swamy, "Causes and Consequences of Corruption."

49. Salbu, "Are Extraneous Restrictions . . . ?"

50. Association of Certified Fraud Examiners, *Report to the Nation: Occupational Fraud and Abuse* (Austin, Tex.: Association of Certified Fraud Examiners, 2002).

51. Schwenke, "Moral Critique."

52. Kim and Kim, "Cultural Differences."

53. J. D. Wolfensohn, speech at the Third Annual Conference of International Investigators, Washington, D.C., Mar. 7, 2002.

54. World Bank Group, "World Bank Listing of Ineligible Firms: Fraud and Corruption." [http://www.worldbank.org/html/opr/procure/debarr.html].

55. World Bank Group, "Procurement Guidelines," secs. 1.15 and 1.25. [http://www.worldbank.org/html/opr/procure/debarr.html#Procurement].

56. Organization of American States, Inter-American Convention Against Corruption, Treaty Doc. no. 105-39; Organization of Economic Cooperation and Development, Convention on Combating Bribery of Foreign Officials in International Business Transactions, Treaty Doc. no. 105-43, 1997 U.S.T. Lexis 105; Council of Europe, Criminal Law Convention on Corruption, ETS no. 173, entered into force July 1, 2002.

57. P. Henning, "Public Corruption: A Comparative Analysis of International Corruption Conventions and United States Law," *Arizona Journal of International and Comparative Law*, 2001, *18*, 793–865.

58. Harms, "Holding Public Officials Accountable."

59. For details of these programs, go to the following Web sites: http://www.dsca.osd.mil/diils; http://www.usdoj.gov/criminal/icitap; http://www.usdoj.gov/criminal/opdat.html; http://www.usip.org; http://www.abanet.org/ceeli/; and http://www.usaid.gov. See also A. Chayes and A. H. Chayes (eds.), *Planning for Intervention: International Cooperation in Conflict Management* (Cambridge, Mass.: Kluwer Law International, 1999).

60. For details on Transparency International, go to http://www.transparency.org.

61. Wei, "Corruption in Economic Development." In Singapore and Hong Kong, cabinet ministers' salaries are commensurate with those of the CEOs of large multinational firms, and both countries have "very low corruption levels." Wei, "Corruption in Economic Development," p. 18.

Part Four

Approaches

Chapter Ten

Education for Coexistence

Martha Minow

Two stories haunt me. I heard the first from Dr. James Orbinski,[1] the current president of Medecins Sans Frontières, or Doctors Without Borders, when he served as head of the group's mission in Rwanda as the genocide unfolded. When he learned that a hospital sheltered several hundred children but was under control of the Hutus, he went to the Hutu leader in charge and asked to take the children and transfer them to a safer place. The leader said no. Dr. Orbinski asked, "Do you have children?" "Why, yes," the leader replied, proudly pulling out photos. The physician returned to the situation at hand, and said, "But these are children too." The Hutu leader replied, "No, they are cockroaches." The next day, half of the children had been murdered.

A recent documentary film, titled *Promises*, tells the second story.[2] The film follows the separate lives of several children who live in and near Jerusalem; some are Israeli Jews, and some are Israeli Arabs. There is a Jewish boy who lives in one of the settlements, a religious Arab, two secular Jewish Israelis (twins), one grandchild of refugees still living in the camps, and one child of a Palestinian imprisoned by the Israelis as a security risk. Some of the children became curious about the others being filmed, and

Note: An earlier version of this chapter appeared in the *Arizona Law Review*, 2002, *44*, 1–29. The author appreciates the help offered by Dean Toni Massaro, Selma Paul Marks, Eileen Babbitt, Antonia Chayes, Daniel Shapiro, Joe Singer, Elizabeth Spelman, Margot Strom, Nienke Grossman, Gregg Comeau, and Gary Buccigross.

the filmmakers arranged for the twin Israelis, Yarko and Daniel, to meet several Palestinians in the refugee camp, twenty minutes from Jerusalem.

The film shows the children, in their early teens, overcoming initial awkwardness, sharing a meal, playing soccer, wrestling, and discussing how they felt after having met one another. Daniel, one of the Israelis, said he had never understood how anyone could support Hamas, the militant Palestinian organization, but based on this day, he understood. He concluded that he would, too, if he were in the situation of his new friends. Faraj, one of the Palestinian adolescent boys, started to cry. He said he feared the glimmerings of mutual understanding would disappear when the filmmakers left. The film ends with a follow-up visit with the same individuals, by then older teens. Daniel notes that the connections faded, although Faraj, the Palestinian friend, tried to keep in contact. For himself, the Israeli observed that he had other things to think about, like his own life, school, and soccer. Faraj, in the time since the earlier filming, looks hardened, hollow-eyed, resigned to a long political struggle that could extend through the lifetime of his future grandchildren.

What can prevent people from thinking of other people's children as cockroaches, worthy of extermination? What practical and psychological shifts are necessary for people to undertake the long-term work of overcoming prejudices and politicized differences? What, if any, opportunities for learning can help people seek the humanity of individuals despite persistent conflicts organized around group identities and political struggles? A common impulse after intergroup conflict—whether international, interethnic, or interracial—is to call for education. Education offers the chance to shape minds, hearts, and behaviors of succeeding generations. Educational responses express this hope: if we can educate young people to respect others, to understand the costs of group hatreds, to avoid stereotypes, to develop tools for resolving disputes, to choose to stand up to demagogues, and to be peacemakers, we might hope to prevent future violence.

After mass violence, the challenge is not to "return to normal" after the conflict, for normal is what produced the conflict. Two probing anthropologists crystallized this insight when they wrote:

"No glib appeal to 'our common humanity' can restore the confidence to inhabit each other's lives again. Instead, it is by first reformulating their notions of 'normality' as a changing norm that communities can respond to the destruction of trust in everyday life."[3] Educational change must be part of more comprehensive efforts to alter the conditions in which massive intergroup conflict arises.

Working with young people is especially crucial. Obviously, the future is in their hands. More subtly, studies of memory indicate that experiences formed in adolescence and early adulthood become the basis for the most enduring and most vivid memories over people's lifetimes, but the shape of any memory is affected by the stories the individual learned within the context of the present.[4] Thus adolescents who live through group conflict will likely hold on to those memories for the rest of their lives, but the meanings they attribute to those memories will be affected by the collective narratives they learn and by emerging needs and interests in their adult lives. To prevent revenge as the response to their past and to prevent dehumanizing people in other groups, educational experiences for adolescents could be vital. Moreover, studies of human development indicate that it is during adolescence that people first develop strong commitments to abstract ideals. The ideas that young people form about their national struggles will connect with their emerging notions of right and wrong, truth and fairness, identity and injustice that will deeply influence the rest of their lives.

Education for Coexistence

I will discuss five approaches to education for coexistence. Each grows from a particular assessment of what is needed to promote coexistence. Each also mirrors real political struggles, whether in geopolitics or internal issues, that reflect efforts to break the cycle of hatred and prejudice. I will draw, where possible, on evaluations of the four kinds of initiatives: education in conflict resolution; education through social contact, education in human rights, education in moral reasoning, and education in the histories of intergroup conflicts. How might each help promote coexistence in this fragile and sometimes terrifying world?

Conflict Resolution

A leading focus in education for coexistence is conflict resolution. Teaching conflict resolution to young people ranges from skill training in negotiation and mediation to studies of international peace-building efforts. These efforts try to strengthen students' own skills in resolving or transcending conflicts, to promote inclusive ideas of community, and to resist ethnic or nationalist indoctrination.[5]

Conflict resolution programs usually focus at least in part on developing students' skills to avoid violent conflict through negotiation and mediation. Experts believe that teaching students how to negotiate and communicate and how to mediate conflicts can enhance students' capacities to cooperate and to employ self-control, reducing incidents of aggression at school.[6] In the United States, 15 to 20 percent of public schools offer some version of conflict resolution instruction as part of social studies, peer mediation, or special programs aimed at developing mediation skills. Sustained programs, on the order of twenty-five lessons, have an effect, whereas brief programs introduced after a crisis are associated with no reduction of violence among the students.[7] It is less clear whether the programs genuinely strengthen students' abilities to handle conflicts generated because of racial, ethnic, or religious tensions. There is little evidence that these programs significantly improve school climate.[8]

Some programs involve students or mediators in their schools. Some efforts combine academic study of conflict resolution with skills training in communication and mediation. For example, one curriculum, known as Conflict and Communication, received support from George Soros's Open Society Institute for implementation in Central and Eastern European schools, implemented in Macedonia and Romania and piloted in other Eastern European countries.[9] Using practice exercises to generate experiences, the curriculum engages students in practicing a five-step conflict resolution strategy. The steps are (1) recognizing conflict, (2) examining your own feelings and those of others, (3) recognizing what you and others want from the conflict, (4) thinking of ideas to help both sides or parties get what they want at the same time, and (5) devising and acting on a plan to get there while strengthening the relationship with apparent opponents. Research suggests that such programs most profoundly affect the students who become mediators. It seems especially sobering to note at this moment that a notable concentration of peace-building education efforts have taken place in the Middle East. A thoughtful study by Mohammed Abu-Nimer identifies obstacles to peace-building education in the Middle East after the Oslo Accords.[10] He found that when peace education came into Palestinian schools, it meant an emphasis on the national liberation struggle continued without pursuing universal approaches for peace and reconciliation. Similarly, a politicized tilt affected Israeli educational materials, which avoid Palestinian issues, even when they attend to the needs for coexistence and peace among Arabs and Jews inside Israel.

Conflict resolution training and peace education risk may be of little use if they ignore the larger political frame within which concrete conflicts arise. Yet addressing the larger political frame embroils curriculum in the very disputes it seeks to reshape or transcend. Moving between interpersonal relations to intergroup relations requires more than analogizing the groups to individuals; it requires deep historical and political analysis and attention to the potentially multiple versions of the relevant histories without losing a moral compass. Programs that neglect dimensions of power and politics will be less likely to have relevance or staying power.

Intergroup Contact

Whereas conflict resolution programs seek to equip students as peacemakers and mediators, intergroup contact initiatives proceed by giving students positive experiences with people in other groups in order to overcome stereotypes through positive experiences while building relationships of equality and mutual acceptance.[11] In the United States, we are familiar with legally mandated programs of racial desegregation and voluntary school desegregation efforts. But there is also intensive short-term experiential learning, bringing together Palestinians and Israelis for a few weeks, teens from opposing sides in Northern Ireland, or suburban and urban adolescents in the United States.

As Cindy Cohen notes in Chapter Thirteen, studies of the effect of school desegregation in the United States have focused largely on the effects on prejudices, meaning negative attitudes formed on the basis of insufficient or erroneous information. Many of the studies show ambiguous findings in part because it is hard to ensure that meaningful interactions actually occur. Casual, superficial contact—such as passing one another in the cafeteria—is much less likely to affect attitudes than joint school projects or experiences on the same, not opposing, sports team. Cooperative work rather than competitive work tends to improve intergroup relationships.

Yet the setting for intergroup contact is often problematic. Adults oppose it. Schools resegregate informally or formally (such as through academic tracking in a formally desegregated school). In these circumstances, intergroup contact may actually be worse for intergroup relationships. Court-ordered desegregation, without thoughtful planning, can fail. Letting students choose where to sit in class or during lunch will lead many to segregate and may generate new feelings of distance, threat, or discomfort. Superficial contact can generate conflict rather than harmony. Studies show that white students tend to be more active and dominating in interracial groups without carefully planned programs that involve nonwhite children in teaching white children new skills.[12] The idea that social contact will naturally occur and inevitably lead to positive results is not borne out.

Carefully designed plans for cooperative work groups can have positive effects on intergroup relations. Early research demonstrated the value of joint tasks and experiences of interdependence while learning.[13] Robert Slavin, a scholar and school reformer, pioneered more recent studies on the effects of cooperative learning assignments in which students are graded as a team. Members of the multiethnic, multiracial teams are assessed in light of their own improvement over past performance, and that individual improvement is each student's contribution to the team's grade.[14] Efforts of this kind have improved both reported attitudes of the students and also chances for cross-group friendships.[15]

The national experiment in school desegregation encountered powerful resistance, no matter how successful it was in certain instances. Using social contact among students to improve race relations is too weak a tool, given white flight to the suburbs and private schools, segregated housing patterns, and the retreat of politicians and judges. As many parts of the country become majority-minority—especially with growth of the Hispanic population—the model of racial integration used by the courts was too limited in any case. The future may hold pockets of self-segregated white communities outside of urban districts, filled with Hispanic, African American, and Asian students, many of them immigrants. Because the racial differences also correlate so strongly with class differences, stereotypes about racial differences become intertwined with differences in economic power. The fate of school desegregation is a sobering caution to any society seeking to promote intergroup coexistence by relying on integrating students.

Legal and political barriers to integrating students of different religious and ethnic groups dominate the Middle East, Eastern Europe, Northern Ireland, and even Canada. Twenty years of efforts to create integrated schools joining Catholics and Protestants in Northern Ireland have resulted in thirty-seven schools attended by less than 10 percent of the student population.[16] That these schools are oversubscribed gives some indication of success, yet resistance from the government, the churches, and ultimately the broader public must explain the funding shortages and failure to meet the target goal of serving one-third of the student population by 2000.

An experiment in school integration in Israel is actually part of a larger coexistence effort. Jews and Palestinian Arabs who are Israeli citizens jointly established and collaboratively run the village Neve Shalom/Wahat al-Salam. The school is bilingual. Some in the region fear it, and others disapprove of it.[17] I admire it. By taking the ambitious step of integrating the entire town, this initiative does not rest the entire responsibility on the shoulders of children.

It is, however, highly unusual. Few people in settings of intense conflict or oppression create integrated communities. A more manageable but still courageous effort for intergroup contact emphasizes intensive short-term sessions, for a few days or a few weeks, usually removed from the home territory of members of each group. A leader in this approach is Seeds for Peace, a camp in Maine for Arab and Israeli teens who spend three weeks sharing cabins, sports, arts, and discussions of their region's conflicts.[18] Its participants are selected by their governments. Seeds of Peace has expanded to include youth from Eastern Europe in its summer camp, programs for Greek and Turkish youth from Cyprus, and a year-round center in Jerusalem to help its alumni maintain their friendships. Recognized and supported by political leaders in the region and in the United States, Seeds of Peace aims to empower children to break cycles of violence, to shatter negative images of members of opposing groups, and to engage in critical reflection about themselves and their world. Staff leaders assign students to tables, bunks, and sports teams with a deliberate plan for encouraging interaction among members of different groups. Campers are given a chance to meet once a week with individuals from their own group, accompanied with teachers and representatives of their ministries of education.

One counselor described how she invited her campers to name one "rose" and one "thorn" each night before sleeping. "Forcing my campers to summarize one positive and negative aspect of their day allowed them to recognize the wide spectrum of emotions that each day brought."[19] Usually, this led to discussions of bad meals, fun swims, lost sports competitions, or helpful conversations. One night, however, it led to a passionate debate over who should control Jerusalem. The counselor explained that her role was to serve as a neutral listener and, if necessary, a mediator, allowing the teens to converse; discussions of tense and conflictual issues indicates success in making the camp feel like a safe place. The counselor felt great relief as the campers quieted down for sleep.

Anecdotal accounts indicate that friendships do form through Seeds for Peace, and the intense experiences of coexistence affect what participants can imagine and hope for in the future. Daily events of shared meals, athletics, and arts seem more significant than the explicit conversations about the regional conflicts. Yet what happens if Seeds of Peace allows teens to develop close friendships only to send them back to their homes and schools where their newfound relationships and views are not appreciated or supported? Internet communication allows for even short-term friendships to continue, but the intense political conflicts at home can create treacherous loyalty dilemmas for participants.

The long-term effect of such initiatives is not documented, but they avoid the simplistic view that social harmony follows simply by putting antagonistic groups together. More thoughtful efforts join youth around shared interests and experiences while creating a sense of community.

Human Rights

Many education efforts aiming at peaceful coexistence focus on human rights as the curriculum. By articulating abstract principles about universal human liberty and equality and by building institutions and practices predicated on those principles, the human rights movement and human rights education seek to draw people away from specific conflicts, oppressions, and injustices through commitments to broad ideals. Placing individual dignity at the core, human rights education shares with human rights documents faith in the rule of law, the power of social movements, and potential of rights language to build reciprocal respect among people. The foundational belief of both human rights activists and human rights educators is that individuals, groups, nations, and the world can build a common language and set of institutions to improve the lives of all sharing aspirations of equality and liberty.

The United Nations itself and many nongovernmental organizations support human rights education as an ongoing activity.[20] The Office of the UN High Commissioner for Human Rights produced a teaching guide titled "ABC: Teaching Human Rights: Practical Activities for Primary and Secondary Schools," distributed through its Web site. The document recounts the United Nation's long-standing commitment to teaching about human rights and the resolution at the International Conference on Human Rights "to call upon all States to ensure that 'all means of education' be used to provide youth with the opportunity to grow up in a spirit of respect for human dignity and equal rights."

The early portions of the teaching guide resemble teaching materials on conflict resolution. They emphasize community, self-understanding, and self-esteem. Yet the teaching guide then turns to the foundational human rights documents in international law, laying out a long list of fundamental rights, and places them at the center of the educational program. The teaching guide explicitly links instruction in human rights to prevention of violent intergroup conflict: "The denial of human rights and fundamental freedoms not only is an individual and personal tragedy, but also creates conditions of social and political unrest, sowing the seeds of violence and conflict within and between societies and nations. As the first sentence of the Universal Declaration of Human Rights states, respect for human rights and human dignity 'is the foundation of freedom, justice and peace in the world.'"

The teaching guide, if adopted anywhere, actually immediately affects regular classroom instruction in many parts of the world. It rejects traditional, hierarchical instruction and calls for teaching methods that are consonant with the content of the human rights of freedom of expression and equality. This means exposing and foreclosing the hypocrisy of a lecture on freedom of expression that begins with the instructor directing the students to shut up; it also means turning to experiential and hands-on learning that would be alien to many teachers around the world.[21] Suggesting role-play exercises to engage students in devising their own human rights documents, the teaching guide also offers a "plain language" translation of the human rights declaration and conventions.[22] Frankly, this would be useful to adults trying to learn—or use—the international legal materials as well.

A great attraction of human rights education is its connection with the international institutions and practices of the human rights movement and the United Nations. Schools and teachers pursuing human rights education can feel part of this global effort and point to language and conceptions that at least aspirationally join every person in the network of mutual recognition, individual dignity, and equality. Starting with these ideas and materials, instruction can pursue a discourse less heated than ones immersed in particular ethnic and racial conflicts.

Yet does human rights education risk being too abstract to be accessible to students and too unrealistic to seem meaningful? My perspective from the United States may be particularly distorted. Human rights struggles have been central over the past twenty years to the democratic transitions in Eastern Europe and in the responses to violence in Bosnia and Kosovo, in Rwanda and the Sudan, across the Middle East, and in Argentina and Brazil. Ours is the nation that has not adopted the Convention on the Rights of the Child and failed to join the International Criminal Court, while scores of other nations have. The language of human rights may in fact feel more real elsewhere, and the quick spread of human rights education programs may join young people to growing national and international political movements rather than seeming to rest on their shoulders the task of making peace for the world.

Moral Reasoning

Without explicitly using international human rights documents, the fourth educational method for coexistence uses rights and abstract principles as a focal point for instruction in moral reasoning. Moral education—and civic and multicultural education—use varied curricula but share the assumption that direct instruction in tolerance and other values can and should proceed through the content of the curriculum.[23] In the United States, civic education has never generated a measurable impact on tolerance or attitudes toward others.[24] Perhaps this is due to the contrast between the typical instructional method and the content of the ideas; learning about free and open debate in settings where controversial and minority views are excluded as subversive or dangerous may strike students as hypocritical or simply boring.[25]

A Harvard University psychologist, Lawrence Kohlberg, developed a moral education curriculum emphasizing abstract reasoning and principles from the U.S. Constitution.[26] Kohlberg predicated his work on a theory that children move through stages of moral reasoning, parallel to the cognitive development theorized by Jean Piaget. Kohlberg hypothesized that as young people moved further in their moral reasoning capacities, they would develop a greater attachment to tolerance. To teach tolerance, therefore, teachers should help young people move up the stages of moral reasoning.[27] Scholars studied efforts to implement this idea in individual classrooms and in a series of more ambitious experiments to create entire schools as "just communities," managed in line with the moral principles of tolerance and democracy.[28] The studies found limited evidence that students' moral reasoning advanced, but schools could not sustain the commitments to becoming "just communities" after the studies ended and their graduate student helpers departed.[29] Mainly, though, researchers were not able to show much influence on children's moral maturity from the Kohlberg program.[30]

Kohlberg's work also comes under vigorous criticism from various quarters. Thomas Lickona argued that Kohlberg's work could not disentangle reasoning from content—and Kohlberg did not teach the right content.[31] Lickona urged schools to teach respect and responsibility as the central values and to engage moral feeling and acting as well as moral knowing to help each student develop a virtuous character.[32] Carol Gilligan found Kohlberg's work gender-biased and wrong to prefer individual rights over human relationships of care.[33]

Consonant with Gilligan's critique but pursuing an alternative understanding of children's growth, Howard Gardner developed a theory of multiple intelligences that emphasizes interpersonal intelligence as a contrast to cognitive and other dimensions of human capacity.[34] Daniel Goleman pursued a related line in his argument that tolerance education neglects the emotions, especially those that flow from beliefs; he suggests instead that educational programs help root out erroneous perceptions of threat that generate intergroup distrust and hostility.[35]

Multicultural education and tolerance education programs emphasize the strengths of a society composed of people with many cultures and the value of individual cultures. Which cultures are included and valued often becomes a politically charged question; in addition, poorly conceived and executed multicultural education turns into superficial exposures to the foods and holidays of different ethnic and religious groups without addressing either the roots of intolerance or the deeper reasons to respect others. Some programs directly seeking to combat racism, anti-Semitism, and other prejudices pursue a deeper route, but these have not received systematic evaluation.[36]

Moral education, multicultural education, and antibias education may each have promising elements in promoting tolerance and coexistence. Especially if they bridge cognitive and emotional dimensions, such instruction can equip students for more positive intergroup relations.[37] I wonder whether schools would do better to concentrate on curbing the discriminatory attitudes and behavior of teachers and students instead of trying to promote a general atmosphere of tolerance if real change is to happen through education.[38] This is the specific advice advanced by the Teaching Tolerance program of the Southern Poverty Law Center in its publication *Responding to Hate at School: A Guide for Teachers, Counselors, and Administrators*. The adults must take a stand against hateful materials and create an unwelcome environment for the expression of hatred and bigotry.[39]

Comparative History and Self-Reflection

Exemplified by a Massachusetts-based initiative named Facing History and Ourselves (FHAO), the fifth educational approach emphasizes inquiry into a period of one historical horror as a basis for involving students in thinking about their own situations and the importance of action to prevent violence and intergroup hatred.[40] The central goal is to promote young people's capacities for critical thinking, understanding, tolerance, caring and compassion, and action when needed to oppose injustice. FHAO develops curricular materials and intensive professional development and support for teachers. Teachers in public and private secondary schools work with the FHAO curriculum to provide students with an intensive look at the failure of democracy in the Weimar Republic, the rise of totalitarianism, and the genocide of World War II. Besides developing rigorous historical understanding, the classes seek to involve students in thinking about what it takes to prevent mass atrocity, what kinds of citizen participation are necessary to sustain democratic institutions, and what kinds of individual and collective actions are needed to resist the dehumanization of any individual or group.

Implemented since the late 1970s, FHAO's durability stems in part from its view that each teacher is a learner and a key to educational change. Through professional development activities organized in intensive two-day and weeklong workshops and conferences, FHAO invites teachers to engage with leading scholars, to debate historical and contemporary issues, and to explore creative pedagogical approaches involving the visual arts, poetry, and community service. One teacher reported that it was difficult to find the right words to describe a summer institute experience "in part because so many things took place, and on so many different levels. Alternately casting ourselves in the roles of teacher and student, we acquired information about the history itself; we explored our own feelings, beliefs, and assumptions about genocide, racism, violence, and resistance; and we became our own community while still representing diverse and separate communities back home."[41]

FHAO develops curricular materials that combine primary historical sources, works of fiction, and other readings. Through regional and international offices, the program supports teachers with pedagogical suggestions and access to resources such as films, guest speakers, and practice leading discussions about difficult issues; the teachers, in turn, adapt the materials for their own students and program. Recently, FHAO has developed programs in Eastern Europe and South Africa.

Students are invited to reflect on the choices made by historical actors and on their own personal choices, to see the dangers of indifference and consequences of stereotypes and hatred, and to learn from positive models of people who have made a real difference. One important tool is the student journal: students are expected to write reflections about the readings and class discussions and in so doing exercise a developing vocabulary for writing and speaking about dealing with human differences.

FHAO has consistently undertaken self-evaluations and sought out external evaluations.[42] External evaluations show that participating students demonstrate increased knowledge of historical content, greater capacity for moral reasoning, empathy, social interest, and improved self-perception. One study indicates that FHAO students strengthen key competencies in interpersonal and intergroup relations, increased relationship maturity, decreased fighting behavior, and diminished racist attitudes and insular ethnic identities relative to comparison students.[43] Observers suggest that the program helps adolescent students break out of a sense of isolation by experiencing themselves as members of a community of learners, engaged in important and challenging critical work.[44]

Increasingly in the United States, refugee and immigrant students participate in FHAO courses, and they frequently report that the course helps them address their own often violent and disturbing prior experiences. A Cambodian refugee named Kim wrote, "I don't want to hold my anger inside of me any more. . . . Since I've been involved with Facing History, I've become more outspoken about racial hatred and my past. . . . Facing History has helped me to speak out more for myself and others. It's made me realize that I have something important to say. It's made me realize that I am not alone." Aida, a Bosnian immigrant, explained that in the historical inquiries in FHAO, "the people were not someone we didn't know. They were you and I; they were like us. So what happened to them we soon realized could happen to anyone." Alice, a teacher, explained that "students look at examples in history when humanity has failed so they can see how humanity can thrive." A student named Eric concluded that "the message that came from my Facing History class was clear: all of us must speak out against injustice."[45]

When It's Dark Enough

I reviewed a variety of educational programs and sorted them into the five categories I have discussed here. It could be that the coexistence education models simply share certain predicates with much of American law. They share an acknowledgment that deep and intense conflicts between people are inevitable but an optimism that the right procedures, experiences, principles, reasoning, or reflection can prevent the worst kinds of violence and abuse. They share a commitment to the particular, the contextual, the lived experiences of the students themselves with an eye on principles or ideals that reach beyond the particular, the factual. In law school, we pursue this through the case method. In education for coexistence, the cases include the lives of the participants.

Conflict resolution and peacemaking, social contact, human rights education, moral reasoning, and comparative history for personal reflection: the five approaches each in different ways invite participants to acknowledge the harsh reality of antagonisms while aspiring to mitigate them. Education for coexistence is now a prime priority for the United Nations and for nations emerging from massive conflict; in various versions, it has vital importance for societies that seem more distant from immediate clashes. Education for coexistence is barely a recognizable phrase, and yet it inspires brave efforts undertaken all over the world.

The educational efforts I have described offer ingredients that could make a real difference, though taken alone, they each have notable shortcomings. Conflict resolution and peace education can equip individuals with useful tools for mediating disputes and defusing their own conflicts. Yet without a fuller political and moral framework, such programs may fail to cultivate students' abilities to know when to stand up in opposition to mistreatment or abuse of others or of themselves. If amplified by historical case studies and moral inquiry, insights worked out in conflict resolution theory and practice could equip students to prevent escalations of local conflicts while also developing substantive commitments to justice and fairness.

Similarly, human rights education and moral reasoning instruction each risk operating too abstractly to engage students' hearts and affect their aspirations and commitments. Abstract, inclusive moral vocabularies risk operating at a level of remoteness that does not connect with messy problems and therefore does not seem worthwhile to people living in the mess. Young people meant to learn human rights or moral reasoning might find them inaccessible or unmemorable. A review of moral instruction suggests that detailed and rich language, grounded in particular narratives and echoed by practiced ritual, is more likely to have a durable effect on children than purely cognitive instruction.[46] If connected with hands-on conflict resolution activities and applications to rich historical contexts, education in both human rights and moral reasoning could motivate students and secure the kinds of lasting lessons that result when cognitive and emotional learning come together. Joint classes in subjects of practical importance—subjects such as computer technology or physics—could also provide occasions for common constructive experiences, but this has not been a focus for coexistence efforts in the past.

Three barriers seriously jeopardize education for coexistence. The first is the students' own experiences of trauma. Trauma, if left unacknowledged and untended, shuts down many people's capacity to care about others. Trauma can also create the context for fantasies (or realities) of revenge. The second is the perpetuation of narratives of victimization or entitlement for the nation or group. When these are the materials of imagination and memory, people will find it difficult to summon the generosity and humility to reach for coexistence. The third is the absence of sufficient conditions, on the ground, to establish safety, hope, or freedom from discrimination or jeopardy for some or all of the participants.

The first two barriers can, with some difficulty, be addressed through education. Especially in places where children have witnessed massive violence, their trauma requires careful attention. This does not necessarily mean individual psychotherapy. Educational initiatives and support for the survivors' capacities, as a group, to mourn and rebuild can take priority. Humanitarian workers in Beirut during armed conflict reminded themselves of what children need with the acronym STOP: structure, time, talk, organized activities, and parents. Priority should be given to restoring educational services and health services.

The second obstacle is the perpetuation of narratives of victimization or entitlement for the nation or group. It is difficult, if not impossible, to teach coexistence to students who are simultaneously learning from history texts that stoke desires for revenge or preserve lopsided versions of the past. The narratives of history taught to young people conflate factual or partial descriptions with attitudes about the past. Should previous governmental treatment of minority groups be ignored, celebrated, or condemned? Should the nation's conduct during wartime be ignored, celebrated, or condemned? Which of the competing versions of ethnic conflicts should make it into the textbooks—or can a framework emerge that acknowledges the competing versions without abandoning the project of telling factual history? Initiatives to revise textbook treatment of national histories, to offer multiple narratives about recent ethnic conflicts, and to examine previously suppressed or ignored accounts of the negative experiences of minority groups attempt to address these issues.

History revision projects aimed at students offer stories of the past intended to influence current students' self-understandings and future orientations. One approach is to revise textbooks and other teaching materials to resist one-sided versions of conflicts or to replace chauvinistic or militaristic themes. Some efforts instead seek to redress silence about conflicts. After World War II, revising the history taught to students in Germany became a focus of attention for the Allies and a subject of considerable controversy between the Americans and the Soviets. It took a full two years after the war ended for new texts, written by German scholars under Allied oversight, to emerge. Even then, the treatment of the war in German schools remained a subject of contention and revision for decades, apparently mirroring and in turn influencing cycles of grief, denial, and acknowledgment over several generations. As difficult as that experience may have been, subsequent developments in international law restrain outside nations from directing the educational reforms of nation states following violent conflict.[47]

Working with historians to build richer, truer accounts, educational projects can involve young people in gathering oral histories to preserve and report the histories of ordinary people whose perspectives have been traditionally neglected. This kind of work can engender a sense of pride among disadvantaged groups and respect for diversity among students, as well as enhance appreciation for multiple perspectives and experiences that belong in the collective story of the society or nation.[48]

The third obstacle—actual or perceived lack of conditions necessary to secure safety, hope, or freedom from discrimination—is the most difficult. How can young people be expected to take the risks of empathizing with others, trying to become peacemakers, building friendships in integrated settings, and believing in human rights or moral ideals if their own world cannot ensure them of safety or supply them with hope? The circularity of the problem of peace is its apparent doom. Without peace, how can people try to make it? Without mutual respect, how can people try to risk it?

Here I have only an aphorism from historian Charles Beard, who described one of the lessons of history: "When it is dark enough, you can see the stars."[49]

I opened this chapter with two haunting stories; I close with two bright images, in the dark. The first is a children's television show. The American public television experiment, *Sesame Street,* showed that preschool children can learn reading and interpersonal skills by watching entertaining shows informed by high-quality educational research. Inspired in part by this effort, a team of Israeli, Palestinian, and Jordanian writers and producers has developed new versions of *Sesame Street* for Israeli, Palestinian, and Jordanian audiences. The creators found the idea of one street, shared by members of different groups, simply implausible. So the show instead relies on visits between residents of different streets. The show's development has been stymied by violent conflict and diplomatic failures, but the show has also found support at the highest levels of diplomacy and government.[50]

The second image I learned from a Kenyan teacher who leads coexistence efforts across Africa. She told me that a workshop in Rwanda in the summer of 2002 engaged a group of Hutu and Tutsi women in a dance, matching one Hutu and one Tutsi and tying their hands together with a thread. As one moved, so the other had to, and they practiced learning to move harmoniously. They performed the result gracefully and then sat back, marveling at what they'd done.[51]

Notes

1. J. Orbinski, speech given at the Conference on Justice, Memory and Reconciliation, Monk Centre for International Studies, University of Toronto, Feb. 16, 2000, by the leader of the Nobel Prize–winning Medecins Sans Frontières.
2. The film was produced and directed by Justine Shapiro and B. Z. Goldberg.
3. V. Das and A. Kleinman, "Introduction," in V. Das and others (eds.), *Remaking a World: Violence, Social Suffering, and Recovery* (Berkeley: University of California Press, 2002), p. 23.
4. D. L. Schacter, *Searching for Memory: The Brain, the Mind, the Past* (New York: Basic Books, 1996).
5. See D. Sandole, "Strengthening Transitional Democracies Through Conflict Resolution," *Conflict Resolution Education,* 552 Annals 125 (1997).
6. A. Tugend, "Peaceable Playgrounds: Do Conflict Resolutions Deliver on Their Promise?" *New York Times,* Nov. 11, 2001, p. 18. A University of Washington study indicated a 29 percent decline in fighting incidents at schools and a 20 percent decline in verbal incidents in six schools teaching conflict resolution, compared with a 41 percent increase in violent incidents and 22 percent increase in verbal incidents in schools without such programs.
7. Tugend, "Peaceable Playgrounds."
8. Tugend, "Peaceable Playgrounds." See also W. S. Haft and E. R. Weiss, "Peer Mediation in Schools: Expectations and Evaluations," *Harvard Negotiation Law Review,* 1998,*3,* 213–270.
9. See D. Shapiro, *Conflict and Communication: A Guide Through the Labyrinth of Conflict Management* (Budapest: Open Society Institute, 1995). Thanks to Daniel Shapiro for conversations about the curriculum and the topics it reflects.
10. M. Abu-Nimer, *Dialogue, Conflict Resolution, and Change: Arab-Jewish Encounters in Israel* (Albany: State University of New York Press, 1999); M. Abu-Nimer, "Education for Coexistence in Israel: Potential and Challenges," in M. Abu-Nimer (ed.), *Reconciliation, Justice, and Coexistence: Theory and Practice* (Lanham, Md.: Lexington Books, 2001).
11. W. P. Vogt, *Tolerance and Education: Learning to Live with Diversity and Difference* (Thousand Oaks, Calif.: Sage, 1997). The idea of social contact as a basis for positive outcomes began with Gordon Allport's work. See G. W. Allport, *The Nature of Prejudice* (Boston: Beacon Press, 1954).
12. E. Cohen and others, "The Center for Interracial Cooperation: A Field Experiment," *Sociology of Education,* 1976, *49,* 47–58.
13. See E. Aronson, C. Sikes, N. Blaney, C. Stephin, and M. Snapp, *The Jigsaw Classroom: Building Cooperation in the Classroom* (Thousand Oaks, Calif.: Sage, 1978); M. Sherif and others, *Intergroup Conflict and Cooperation: The Robber's Cave Experiment* (Norman: University of Oklahoma Book Exchange, 1961); and E. Staub, "Breaking the Cycle of Genocidal Violence: Healing and Reconciliation," in J. Harvey (ed.), *Perspectives on Loss: A Sourcebook* (Bristol, Pa.: Taylor & Francis, 1998).
14. See R. Slavin, "Cooperative Learning: Applying Contact Theory in Desegregated Schools," *Journal of Social Issues,* 1985, *41,* 45–56.
15. W. P. Vogt, *Tolerance and Education.* See also R. Slavin, "Cooperative Learning:

Theory, Research, and Practice," 1990, and R. Slavin, "Cooperative Learning: Applying Contact Theory."

16. E. Cairns and M. Hewtone, "The Impact of Peacemaking in Northern Ireland on Intergroup Behaviour." [http://construct.haifa.ac.il/~cerpe/book/cairns.pdf]. See also E. Cairns, "The Role of the Contact Hypothesis in Peacemaking in Northern Ireland: From Theory to Reality" [http://construct.haifa.ac.il/~cerpe/papers/cairns.html]; and A. M. Gallagher, *Majority Minority Review 1: Education in a Divided Society* (2nd ed.) (University of Ulster: Colerzine, 1995). See also E. Cairns and I. J. Toner, *Children and Political Violence in Northern Ireland: From Riots to Reconciliation* (Oxford: Blackwell, 1966), esp. pp. 215–223, documenting the gap between those who in theory support integrated education in Northern Ireland and those actually sending their children to integrated schools.

17. For information, go to http://nswas.com/index.html. Another group, Hand in Hand, tried to foster the development of integrated bilingual schools for Jews and Arabs in Israel; see "Teaching the Language of Peace." [http://www.handinhand12.org/TheLangu/TheLangu.html].

18. Its founder has written a book describing Seeds of Peace. See J. Wallach, *The Enemy Has a Face: The Seeds of Peace Experience* (Washington, D.C.: United States Institute of Peace Press, 2000). See "Seeds of Peace: Empowering Children of War to Break the Cycle of Violence." [http://www.seedsofpeace.org].

19. M. Terc, "Sowing the Seeds of Peace," 2000. [http://www.abroadviewmagazine.com/archives/fall_00/seeds.html].

20. See, for example, United Nations Office of the High Commissioner for Human Rights (UNHCHR), "ABC: Teaching Human Rights: Practical Activities for Primary and Secondary Schools" [http://www.unhchr.ch/html/menu6/2/abc.htm]; Human Rights Education Associates [http://www.hrea.org]; and the Human Rights Resource Centre [http://hrusa.org].

21. "Already implicit above is the idea—central to this booklet—that teaching about human rights is not enough. The teacher will want to begin, and never to finish, teaching for human rights. Students will want not only to learn of human rights, but learn in them, for what they do to be of the most practical benefit to them. That is why the main part of the text consists of activities. The purpose of the activities is to create opportunities for students and teachers to work out from the basic elements that make up human rights such as life, justice, freedom, equity, and the destructive character of deprivation, suffering and pain—what they truly think and feel about a wide range of real world issues."

22. This version is based in part on the translation of a text prepared in 1978 for the World Association for the School as an Instrument of Peace by a research group at the University of Geneva led by Professor Leonardo Massarenti. In preparing the translation, the group used a basic vocabulary of twenty-five hundred words in use in the French-speaking part of Switzerland. Teachers may adopt this methodology by translating the text of the Universal Declaration into the language in use in their region.

23. Vogt, *Tolerance and Education*.

24. Vogt, *Tolerance and Education.*
25. Vogt, *Tolerance and Education.*
26. See F. Power, A. Higgins, and L. Kohlberg, *Lawrence Kolhberg's Approach to Moral Education* (New York: Columbia University Press, 1989).
27. Vogt, *Tolerance and Education.*
28. See Power, Higgins, and Kohlberg, *Lawrence Kohlberg's Approach.*
29. Vogt, *Tolerance and Education.* For a picture of the implementation problems, see J. Reimer and C. Power, "Educating for Democratic Community: Some Unresolved Dilemmas," in R. Mosher (ed.), *Moral Education: A First Generation of Research and Development* (New York: Praeger, 1980).
30. See J. Leming, "Curricular Effectiveness in Moral Values Education," and R. Enright and M. Levy, "Moral Education Strategies," in M. Pressley and I. Levin (eds.), *Cognitive Strategy Research: Educational Applications* (New York: Springer-Verlag, 1983).
31. See T. Lickona, *Educating for Character: How Our Schools Can Teach Respect and Responsibility* (New York: Bantam Books, 1991). See also E. R. De Roche and M. M. Williams, *Character Education: A Guide for School Administrators* (Lanham, Md.: Scarecrow Press, 2001).
32. Lickona, *Educating for Character.* See also J. D. Hunter, *The Death of Character: Moral Education in an Age Without Good or Evil* (New York: Basic Books, 2000). Hunter rejects the individualism and abstract universalism of moral education such as Kohlberg's in favor of education grounded in particular moral or religious traditions. This is part of a more general criticism of contemporary American culture for encouraging selfishness and undermining ideas about restraint and personal sacrifice.
33. C. Gilligan, *In a Different Voice: Psychological Theory and Women's Development* (Cambridge, Mass.: Harvard University Press, 1982).
34. H. Gardner, *Multiple Intelligences: The Theory in Practice* (New York: Basic Books, 1993).
35. D. Goleman, *Emotional Intelligence: Why It Can Matter More Than IQ* (New York: Bantam Books, 1995).
36. Vogt, *Tolerance and Education.*
37. Vogt, *Tolerance and Education.*
38. See A. Cabrera and A. Nora, "College Students' Perceptions of Prejudice and Discrimination and Their Feelings of Alienation," *Review of Education, Pedagogy, and Cultural Studies,* 1994, *16,* 387–409. Analogously, I have argued that altering the conditions that make students think it is permissible to engage in hate speech would be more productive than regulating hate speech. See M. Minow, *Breaking the Cycles of Hatred* (Princeton, N.J.: Princeton University Press, 2003), and M. Minow, "Speaking and Writing Against Hate," *Cardozo Law Review,* 1990, *11,* 1393–1408.
39. Teaching Tolerance, *Responding to Hate at School: A Guide for Teachers, Counselors, and Administrators* (Montgomery, Ala.: Southern Poverty Law Center, 1999).
40. See M. Fine, "The Politics and Practice of Moral Education: A Case Study." Ed.D thesis, Harvard Graduate School of Education, 1991.

41. Margot Stern Strom, a former teacher who founded FHAO, wrote that FHAO encourages young people "to understand different perspectives and to express their own ideas without becoming mired in relativism." M. S. Strom, "Do I Have to Know Where I'm Going in Order to Start?—Or Do We Make the Road as We Go?" Paper presented at Theological Opportunities Program Spring Symposium, Harvard Divinity School, Cambridge, Mass., Mar. 2002.

42. See, for example, M. Brabaeck and others, "Human Rights Education Through the 'Facing History and Ourselves' Program," *Journal of Moral Education*, 1994, *23*, 333–347; M. Lieberman, *Evaluation Report 78508D to the Joint Dissemination Review Panel* (Brookline, Mass.: Facing History and Ourselves Resource Center, 1986); M. T. Glynn and others, *American Youth and the Holocaust: A Study of Four Major Holocaust Curricula* (New York: National Jewish Resource Center, 1982); B. Bardidge, "Things So Finely Human: Moral Sensibilities at Risk in Adolescence," in C. Gilligan, J. V. Ward, and J. M. Taylor (eds.), *Mapping the Moral Domain: A Contribution of Women's Thinking to Psychological Theory and Education* (Cambridge, Mass.: Harvard University Press, 1983); and D. Barr and others, "Improving Intergroup Relations Among Youth: A Study of the Processes and Impact of the Facing History and Ourselves Program," Final Report to the Carnegie Corporation of New York, Facing History and Ourselves, and the Group for Study of Interpersonal Development, 1998.

43. D. Barr and others, "Improving Inter-group Relations Among Youth."

44. D. Barr and others, "Improving Inter-group Relations Among Youth."

45. D. Barr and others, "Improving Inter-group Relations Among Youth."

46. Hunter, *Death of Character.*

47. G. P. Wegner, "Germany's Past Contested: The Soviet-American Conflict in Berlin over History Curriculum Reform, 1945–48," *History of Education Quarterly*, 1990, *30*(Spring), 1–16.

48. Cynthia Cohen wrote a workbook explaining how oral history projects can be devised to serve these purposes. C. Cohen, *Working with Integrity: A Guidebook for Peacebuilders Asking Ethical Questions* (Waltham, Mass.: International Center for Ethics, Justice, and Public Life, Brandeis University, 2001).

49. C. Beard, quoted in H. R. Mayes, *An Editor's Treasury*, Vol. 2 (New York: Atheneum, 1968), p. 1312.

50. Personal discussion with Eli Evans, president of the Revson Foundation.

51. Personal discussion with Atema Eclai, Mar. 19, 2002.

Chapter Eleven

Coexistence and Repair

Elizabeth V. Spelman

The desire to fix things is as powerful and important a force in human affairs as the desire to create and to destroy. The very possibility of coexistence in the aftermath of violence, death, and dislocation depends on some kind of basic repair and restoration of persons, places, institutions, and services. Yet insofar as coexistence between conflicting parties is conceived of as something considerably more modest than the kind of robust repair suggested by the goal of reconciliation, projects of coexistence seem to require constraints on the reparative impulse. Because coexistence appears, then, both to invite and to check the reparative impulse, some degree of clarity about the nature of repair—what it aims at and the skills it requires—will be useful. But examination of the politics of repair also seems in order: Who conceptualizes, authorizes, and executes the kinds of intervention that various forms of repair entail? Rehearsing some of the prominent features of repair can help clarify the meaning, conditions, and goals of coexistence; at the same time, exploring coexistence makes particularly vivid the many forms repair can take and the complex skills repair often involves—including the capacity to judge just how far and in what direction repair can and should go.

Note: Many thanks to Antonia Chayes and Martha Minow for the invitation to learn about coexistence and for inspired editorial advice. Portions of this essay are borrowed from Elizabeth V. Spelman, *Repair: The Impulse to Restore in a Fragile World* (Boston: Beacon Press, 2002).

Homo reparans: A Partial Portrait

Repair is ubiquitous, something humans engage in every day and in almost every dimension of our lives. Perhaps the most obvious kinds of repair are those having to do with the inanimate objects with which we surround ourselves—the clothes crying out for mending, the automobiles for fixing, the buildings for renovating, the works of art for restoring. But our bodies and souls are also by their very nature subject to fracture and fissure, for which we seek homely household recipes for healing and consolation, or perhaps the expert ministrations of surgeons, therapists, and other menders and fixers of all manner of human woes. Moreover, relationships between individuals and among nations are notoriously subject to fraying and being rent asunder. From apologies and other informal attempts at patching things up to courts of law, conflict mediation, and truth and reconciliation commissions, we try to reweave what we revealingly call the social fabric. No wonder, then, that the reparative skills of people are always and everywhere on call, that *Homo sapiens* is also *Homo reparans:* we, the world we live in, and the objects and relationships we create are by their very nature things that can break, decay, unravel, fall to pieces.

Our reparative repertoire is vast, something readily and richly attested to by sources ranging from *Reader's Digest* stories about legendary handymen[1] to essays in professional philosophy journals on the ethics of environmental restoration;[2] from Dave Barry's sendups of men's delusions about their superior repairing skills[3] to legal treatises weighing monetary reparations against the work of truth and reconciliation commissions;[4] from *The You Don't Need a Man to Fix It Book: The Woman's Guide to Confident Home Repair*[5] to *Tikkun,* the journal emblazoned with the Hebrew phrase *tikkun olam,* "to repair the world." Daily newspapers around North America and Western Europe tell us that the "hardest task" in the Middle East is "repairing the lost trust,"[6] that a former news anchor is finding some obstacles to "repairing her image,"[7] that Pope John Paul II has been continuing his "efforts to mend historical rifts,"[8] that voter apathy in the United States is evidence that "a fraying political fabric needs repairing,"[9] that the hardest skill required of family members is "the emotional work of forging, deepening or repairing family relationships."[10] A poster boy for the U.S. Air Force is depicted in a recruiting ad as having these ambitions: "Make the U.S. Olympic Team. Make my own decisions. Get an education. Be a hero to someone. Show people I can fix anything."

H. reparans also can be found wondering whether sometimes it isn't the better part of wisdom to leave the flaws, the fragments, the ruins alone: restorers of *Gone With the Wind* had to decide whether a flaw in the original film should "be fixed or retained as an intrinsic part of the original masterpiece";[11] a syndicated columnist counsels her readers that "you don't have to be abused or betrayed to have a bad marriage—a marriage that cannot be fixed, even with the help of all the therapists on the Upper West Side, or all the preachers in Louisiana."[12]

The English language is generously stocked with words for the many preoccupations and occupations of *H. reparans*: *repair, restore, rehabilitate, renovate, reconcile, redeem, heal, fix,* and *mend*—and that's just for starters. Such linguistic variety is not gratuitous. These are distinctions that make a difference. Do you want the car repaired so that you can continue to commute to work? Or do you want it restored so that you can display it in its original glory? Is a patch on that jacket adequate, or do you insist on invisible mending, on having it look as if there never were a rip to begin with? Should that work of art be restored or simply conserved? Why do some ecologists want to preserve an environment rather than try to repair the damage done to it? Does forgiveness necessarily restore a ruptured relationship or simply allow its resumption? What does an apology achieve that monetary reparations cannot—and vice versa? What is thought to be at stake for citizens of the new South Africa in the contrast between restorative and retributive justice—between the healing promised by a truth and reconciliation commission and the punishment exacted through an adversarial court system?

As crucial as such distinctions are, the family of repair activities shares the aim of maintaining some kind of continuity with the past in the face of breaks or ruptures in that continuity. They involve returning in some manner or other to an earlier state—to the bowl before it was broken, to the friendship before it began to buckle under the weight of suspicion, to the nation before it was torn apart by hostility and war. Even though taking superglue to the bowl repairs it without fully restoring it to its preshattered condition, both repairer and restorer want to pick up a thread with the past. Their work thereby appears to involve something distinctly different from the original creation of the bowl but also from its accidental or deliberate destruction, its abandonment, or the serendipitous retrieval of its shards for flowerpot filler. In a similar fashion, there is a difference between putting a friendship back together and simply letting it hobble on, decisively ending it, or making a new friend altogether.

In short, as varied as the activities of *H. reparans* are, they appear to be notably different from other kinds of relations to or attitudes toward the past. Creators start anew; they do not repair what already exists (though there is good reason to question too neat a distinction between creating and repairing); destroyers want to get rid of what's there, not somehow rescue it; noninterferers neither help nor hinder but simply allow things to degenerate or decay; replacers figure it's not possible or worthwhile to repair but want to have the kind of thing in question; *bricoleurs* collect and make use of pieces of the past but do not try to return them to an earlier function.

Repair wouldn't be necessary if things never broke, never frayed, never splintered or fell to pieces—or if we didn't care that they did, either because we just felt no connection to or investment in them or because even though we did care for them, we found it perfectly acceptable to replace them. A world in which repair was not necessary would either be filled with unchanging unbreakable eternal objects (a version, perhaps, of Plato's world of Forms) or be a junk heap of things, people, and relationships abandoned when they no longer functioned in the requisite manner. To repair is to acknowledge and respond to the fracturability of the world in which we live in a very particular way—not by simply throwing our hands up in despair at the damage or otherwise accepting without question that there is no possibility of or point in trying to put the pieces back together but by engaging mind, hand, and heart (sometimes in exquisite combination) to recapture an earlier moment in the history of an object or a relationship in order to allow it to continue.

H. reparans has been known to take great satisfaction in exercising the capacity to repair and great pride in what the result of such exercise can do for broken-down cars, torn retinas, and frayed partnerships. Indeed, sometimes we take greater pleasure in having a well-repaired object than an unbroken one, prefer (if we're lucky enough to have options) living in a neighborhood of renovated houses to one in which the buildings are all spanking new, enjoy a friendship that has known apology and forgiveness more than one protected from the risks of being rent. We seem to welcome the sentiment that things are stronger in the broken places (though this is probably not a good motto for, say, an airline).

At the same time, a voracious appetite for fixing can lead to poor judgment about what is and is not desirable or even possible to repair. Pride in our repairing abilities may push us into believing that whatever has been broken can be and ought to be fixed. Recognition of occasions on which such a belief is wrongheaded can provide, on the one hand, comic relief: "I was able, thanks to my experience as a homeowner and my natural mechanical sense, to get pieces of insulation deep into my nose."[13] On the other hand, tragic grief over irreparable loss—for example, the death of a child—reminds us of how much there is that cannot be undone, how thoroughly inappropriate the confidence that there is nothing that can't be fixed. Still, we do not always mourn what we cannot repair. Sometimes the irreparable has been the source of complex delights, as we might learn from the reflections of Rose Macauley and others on the pleasure in historical ruins[14] or fascination with what the title of one book calls *Demolition: The Art of Demolishing, Dismantling, Imploding, Toppling and Razing.*[15]

Coexistence and Reparative Projects

The language of repair, not surprisingly, generously dots the landscape of the literature on coexistence, and many of the features of repair I have outlined are clearly in evidence. In Chapter Eight of this book, for example, Antonia Chayes sadly reminds us of the multiple forms and locations of brokenness left in the wake of interethnic conflict and hence of the call for repair in so many dimensions of human life: people themselves are in "tattered" condition; care must be given to "how societies are put back together"; outsiders may feel an obligation to "help heal the rift between those who have done violence to one another." There are both "physical and social elements that would be involved in rebuilding a peaceful society": repair of the infrastructure is in order, including "water, power, roads, transportation, and the like," and the means of "communication would have to be restored."

As is also clear from Chayes's analysis, the various members of the family of repair terms are not synonymous, and the differences among them often mark crucial distinctions. For example, while Chayes refers to coexistence as itself a "tool for the international community to use in the process of helping heal and reconstruct societies decimated by internal conflict," she, like many others, thinks it important to emphasize that the kinds of repair, restoration, or reconstruction that constitute coexistence are not the same set that would constitute a real reconciliation among formerly warring groups. Advocates of coexistence may want to help repair relations between conflicting parties, but surely they do not want and indeed fear the restoration of an earlier state of affairs in which the parties were in mortal combat. Similarly, as Chayes points out, local police would not be simply restored to their former positions, but "would have to be retrained or replaced."

The Humility and the Arrogance of Repair

Repair appears to be such a modest activity, especially in comparison with the boldness of creation and destruction, that its own kind of assertiveness, indeed, its own kind of arrogance, may often go unnoticed. After all, repair is in one sense quite conservative: it makes it possible for what has existed in the past to continue into and beyond the present. Repair gets the car running again, the marriage back on its legs, the community able to resume civil functioning. But in order to bring about this link to the past, in order to undo the damage, repair has to do something about those breakdowns, ruptures, and collapses. In this sense, repair is interventionist, a characteristic that family members implicitly note when they wonder whether they ought to let the surgeons try one more repair or simply leave their loved one to "die a natural death." Curators of historical buildings have been taught by authorities in the field to think of options before them in terms of degrees of intervention: "We can . . . classify levels of intervention according to a scale of increasing radicality, thus: (1) preservation; (2) restoration; (3) conservation and consolidation; (4) reconstitution; (5) adaptive reuse; (6) reconstruction; (7) replication."[16]

In bowing deeply toward the past, allowing a previous condition to dictate what needs to be done, repair requires the kind of humility that according to Lewis Mumford is a hard-earned achievement of *H. sapiens:*

> . . . In dealing with the forces of nature, man's animism got him nowhere. He might attribute willful mischief to a pot that leaked or to a basket that came apart when it was filled, . . . but he could not come to terms with these recalcitrant objects by any amount of sympathetic communication. Eventually, he would have to overcome his anger or indignation sufficiently to patch the leak or reweave the badly woven osier, if he wants to make it perform its function. That humility before the object, that respect for function, were essential both to man's intellectual and his emotional development.[17]

And yet repair is also presumptuous in its insistence that a given point in the history of something or a given condition of something is more important than any other point or condition; for while repair in one sense honors the past by paying homage to an earlier moment, in another sense it erases the past by undoing much of what has happened in the meantime. Hence the conflicts, for example, between preservers of historical sites and those who would repair and restore them, over what moment of history ought to be the community's focus: should the crumbling gas chambers at Birkenau "be restored, [be] somewhat restored or be allowed to fade into oblivion"?[18]

The Politics of Repair

To repair, then, is to enact a complicated attitude toward the past and the preexistent: repair is conservative but also interventionist, humble but also presumptuous; it honors some moments in the past while erasing others. It always signals a decision to devote resources and energies to keeping something going rather than abandoning it or replacing it. The case of Birkenau makes clear what also emerges from studies of efforts to create communities in coexistence: decisions to undertake repair are often morally or politically fraught. In Chapter Four, Diana Chigas and Brian Ganson report that those willing to try to repair interethnic relations in Kosovo have been regarded by some parties to the conflict between Serbs and Albanians as "traitors"—as if to say that there are some relationships one should not even think of mending. The call to heal souls and spirits after the conflict is over can be rife with social and political meaning. Holocaust survivor Jean Amery worried that the "natural" process through which time might heal the wounds inflicted on him by the Nazis and their collaborators would destroy what was left of his own moral compass and erode the passion with which he demanded a full acknowledgment of and accounting for the atrocities sanctioned by and too hastily buried by the German people. He sought out a means of repair that would not in his eyes be morally and politically compromising.[19]

Indeed, the very authority with which one asserts what the damage is, where it is, and what it would take to repair it can itself reflect or represent an attempt to subvert existing social, political, and economic relations. The humor of Dave Barry often implicitly turns on such a point. One day, when the ceiling started to leak, his wife "suggested that maybe there was water sitting on the roof and leaking into the house, but I knew, as an experienced guy of the male gender, that she was wrong. I knew the problem was the plumbing."[20]

In a much more serious vein, James Baldwin famously argued that the racial conflict endemic in American life cannot come close to being fixed until the nation begins to focus not on how blacks are to mend their ways but on how thoroughgoing a repair job whites need. Baldwin clearly did not think that African Americans are flawless. But he was insistent that America cannot be restored to—or rather, hope finally to achieve—its promise of justice and equality if the white soul is not thought of as a major repair site. The steady diet of white supremacy—itself the product in part of deep and unsettling fears—that has been fed to most whites from birth has meant that "they have destroyed and are destroying hundreds of thousands of lives and do not know it and do not want to know it."[21] Although Baldwin's analysis in *The Fire Next Time* brought him positive acclaim from an influential part of the white population in the 1960s (part of the book was published originally in *The New Yorker*, and Baldwin was featured on the cover of *Time*), it seems likely that many whites did and would resist and repudiate Baldwin's analysis of the sites of damage systematic racism entails.

Baldwin's words also have a haunting poignancy in the early moments of the twenty-first century. For almost the same words have been heard since (and indeed long before) the events of September 11, 2001: Do American citizens know about the acts of violence and destruction carried out in our name and with the support of our tax dollars day after day around the world? Do we want to know? Is it precisely a measure of the perverse immunity provided by our country's power that we haven't had to? And how will what we do and don't know, what we choose to know and choose not to know, affect our judgment of how and where to repair a world made ever more fragile by the threat of terrorism?

The international community's recognition that coexistence may be a much more appropriate goal than reconciliation—the very recognition that undergirds initiatives to explore the meaning of and prospects for coexistence—would itself seem to reflect an implicit awareness that third-party intervention in the name of repair carries its own presumptions about where the damages are and how best to mend them. As Antonia Chayes makes clear in Chapter Eight, even the rhythm of restorative projects can be a site of implicit or explicit struggle between outside organizations and the battered communities to whom they present themselves as helpers.

Education for Repair and the Prospects of Coexistence

Any close examination of repair invites us to ask not only about who has the authority to make such decisions and carry out such projects but also about who has the requisite skills to do so. The busy life of *H. reparans* is very instructive in this regard: the many kinds of repair jobs humans engage in typically require a hearty and complex combination of knowledge, skills, and judgment.

Even what appear to be straightforward instances of repair engage many human capacities simultaneously. Take, for example, Willie, a crackerjack mechanic in rural upstate New York carefully and lovingly described in Douglas Harper's *Working Knowledge: Skill and Community in a Small Shop*.[22] Willie—we never learn his last name—specializes in Saab automobiles, but he also works on tractors, furnaces, and other equipment necessary for life in a remote and seasonally snowbound part of the United States. Though to their dismay many auto mechanics have been reduced more or less to parts changers, Willie has a lifetime of experience with many kinds of engines and machinery, deep knowledge of the materials he works with, and the ability to correct flaws in the original designs of the cars and tractors his customers leave for him to work his minor miracles on. An ingenious *bricoleur,* Willie is always figuring out ways to use miscellaneous odds and ends, what others discard as useless junk, to extend the life of an engine or the career of a door. People rely on Willie to find a way to fix things that others have given up as having fallen into hopeless disrepair.

Like crackerjack auto mechanics, skillful art restorers have a deep knowledge of the materials they work with: "To do her job, a restorer needs technical expertise backed by knowledge drawn from a variety of fields—spectroscopy, chemistry, and materials science, to name a few. Manual dexterity worthy of a neurosurgeon and nerves of steel also help. Just to figure out what she is trying to do requires knowledge of the work she is dealing with and its art historical context, as well as critical acuity, and delicacy of discrimination."[23]

But unlike Willie, art restorers can't even think of redesigning a creator's or designer's original work; they surely should not contemplate making use of just any old paint that might be around. They need richly informed judgment to know the difference between welcome signs of aging in a painting and changes that are considered damaging to the integrity and identity of the work.

If the kind of repair involved in auto work and art restoration involves specific kinds of knowledge, skill, and judgment, so does that undertaken in apology. As Nicolas Tavuchis reminds us, when an apology works well, it not only helps resolve conflicts, but it also restores social and moral order by reaffirming the importance of preserving the explicit and implicit rules by which we live together. Apology is an act made possible by certain conventions governing the use of language to acknowledge responsibility for and express genuine sorrow over what one has done while refraining from offering excuses or justifications for it. Such an act is likely to backfire in the absence of certain kinds of knowledge and judgment: an apology rings hollow if one doesn't know or hasn't bothered to inquire into the nature of the harm one has caused; it requires judgment that what one has done is "an apologizable offense and not . . . something else, for example, an occasion for terminating [a] friendship or an injustice beyond apology."[24]

South Africa's Truth and Reconciliation Commission was built on the assumption that the desired reconciliation was not possible in the absence of efforts to learn a great deal about the country's history of violence, secrecy, and inhumanity—much more than could be gleaned in the confines of a court of law. Both gathering such knowledge and figuring out just what to do with it called on and continue to call on considerable skill and judgment: How much and what kind of knowledge will provide healing? How much and what kind of knowledge of who did what to whom might in fact be destructive of both individuals and the larger society?

Perhaps it's obvious that repair of all kinds—of the objects around us; of our relationships with family, friends, and colleagues; of connections among peoples—requires a rich mix of knowledge, skill, and judgment. But recognition of this can be lost or obscured in the calls for repair and restoration and healing and reconciliation with which we are surrounded. What do would-be repairers need to know and to be able to do, how do they need to be able to think, in order to "repair the lost trust" in the Middle East, to repair professional "images," to "mend historical rifts," to engage in the "emotional work of forging, deepening, or repairing family relationships"? What cognitive and emotional resources has that poster boy for the Air Force who can "fix anything"? One of the reasons why reading Dave Barry on men, tools, and the wonderful world of male repairing fantasies is so instructive is that the humor in the situations he describes depends on the huge discrepancy between his reparative ambitions and his actual flimsy knowledge, pathetic skills, and dreadful judgment: "I was able, thanks to my experience as a homeowner and my natural mechanical sense, to get pieces of insulation deep into my nose."

Whatever their natural inclinations, people need training to become expert auto repairers or plumbers or art restorers. But there are many forms of repair—especially those involving fractures between people—that cannot be done by specialists. You can have the rip in your dress repaired by a seamstress, but you can't have someone else apologize for you. Marriages can be helped by those not in the marriage, but surely they cannot be fixed unless both partners are party to the repair. So the question of who needs the requisite knowledge, skill, and judgment to carry out the repair cannot always be finessed by turning the repair job over to specialists.

Indeed, some critics of our faltering criminal justice system have urged that resolution of conflicts resulting from one person's harming another be taken as much as possible out of the hands of lawyers and judges and juries and be left to small collectives of citizen repairers. In Milwaukee, for example, the district attorney's office might allow a criminal case of theft to be dealt with not by putting the alleged offender in court and then perhaps in jail but by having the offender, the parties harmed, and members of the larger community engage in a joint repair job. Among their tasks would be to describe the nature of the injuries inflicted, the nature and location of repair needed in response, and the roles of the victim, offender, and community in mending the rips in the social fabric the conflict has brought about.[25]

Conclusion: Coexistence and the Work of Repair

Coexistence among formerly conflicting parties will be short-lived if they do not have, develop, or desire to put to use the complex skills involved in describing and addressing the multiple reparative tasks before them. After all, coexistence, like any other state of human affairs, must not only be constructed but also be continually maintained and repaired. Especially where living with conflict and violence, or the justified fear of them, has long defined the rhythm of everyday life, such construction, maintenance. and repair skills are not likely to have been developed. Indeed, they are not likely to have been developed even in relatively peaceful countries where turning to the law to define and fix conflict has long been a way of life. Resolution of ethnic conflict would appear to be an example of the kind of repair that requires participants in the conflict to be directly involved. Others cannot do the repair work for them, and they must agree on what is to be repaired. But what if the very conditions at issue militate against their calling on or even having developed the kinds of knowledge, skills, and judgment such repair would require? Part of the challenge facing advocates and agents of coexistence is helping conflicting parties find routes by which the challenges of such repair (where what constitutes repair is something other than revenge) might come to be seen as more pressing and more engaging than the habits of destruction. Even then, the desire to repair doesn't count for much in the absence of the skills it takes.

But how do people acquire the requisite knowledge, skills, and judgment to carry out the repair work they end up wanting or needing to do and for which they cannot and should not in the end turn to handy experts?

Nicholas Tavuchis addresses this head-on in a section of his book *Mea Culpa* called "The Pedagogy of Apology." He reminds us that of course children have to *learn* to apologize. Given the complex structure of apology, that means much more than learning to say "I'm sorry" in certain situations. For the apology will never be genuine unless the apologizer understands the harm that has been done, recognizes her or his culpability in bringing about that harm, and actually feels sorrow for having done what she or he did. Learning about apology also involves learning what kinds of harms to oneself entitle one to ask for or expect an apology, acquiring "a sense of righteous anger and indignation."[26] We all need instruction in what Tavuchis refers to as "the delicate arts of pacification and conciliation"[27]—practices that become even more difficult in settings where among the differences between the parties involved are culturally distinct notions of what is and is not forgivable.

The task of acquiring the knowledge, skills, and judgment it takes to engage in the work of repair is complicated by the fact that one is continuously called on to decide whether repair is possible or even appropriate. Indeed, the successful exercise of any skill entails knowing the limits of its deployment: sometimes, after all, *H. reparans* is *persona non grata*.

For example, Lawrence Langer is one of several analysts who have noted that the language of repair occurs quite often in interpretations of the testimonies of Holocaust survivors, and he has done much to identify and try to undermine what he takes to be its inappropriately redemptive logic.[28] The experiences of Holocaust survivors, he worries, have been preempted by the reparative impulse evident in what Langer finds not in the oral testimonies of the survivors themselves but in the eagerness of many interviewers and interpreters to find reparative motifs.[29] Langer's work on the testimonies is an urgent and sustained plea to bracket off the language of repair typically found in interpretations of survivors' accounts of what they endured and still continue to experience. A survivor's memories "create a break in the chain of her life that telling cannot mend"; memory becomes "a monument to ruin rather than reconstruction."[30] "The unappeasable experience is part of [survivors'] inner reality, and though the optimistic American temperament winces at the notion," survivors know that what they have survived "is an event to be endured, not a trauma to be healed."[31] Indeed, Langer thinks that it is only when we are deprived of the consoling hopefulness of the language of repair that we might be motivated "to intercede in situations of atrocity before they have spent their energy, leaving negotiated 'reconciliation' as the only practical course of action."[32]

Langer's cautionary remarks about assuming that repair is always possible and that the desire to help repair is always welcome don't necessarily extend to the forms of repair that concern those involved in projects of coexistence. Still, no examination of the prospects for coexistence after ethnic conflict can be complete without considering whether there might be at least some conflicts that are not likely to benefit from the exercise of humankind's considerable repairing skills. Such a conclusion seems to have been reached, or in any event reported on, in *Aggression and Conflict: A Cross-Cultural Encyclopedia.*[33] The entry for "Ethnic Conflict" describes the many forms ethnic conflict takes (legal, religious, and so on), the various aims of the conflicting parties (separatist, irredentist, and the like), and typical causes of such conflict (repression by the dominant party, a global economy that exacerbates already existing economic exploitation, and so forth). A final section of the entry, "Managing and Resolving Ethnic Conflicts," begins with the following sobering assessment: "Many experts now believe that most ethnic conflicts are uniquely resistant to resolution and that the international community and national governments would be wiser to invest their resources in trying to manage and control these conflicts rather than in trying to resolve them. Recent experience suggests that this is sound advice—while conflict resolution efforts do sometimes produce formal accords, they rarely yield long-term peace and harmony. Ethnic conflicts in Cyprus, Northern Ireland, Bosnia, and Sri Lanka and northwest India have all been 'settled' by accords, but the conflicts quickly flared up anew and continued."[34]

The entry concludes with a list of some of the reasons ethnic conflicts seem so resistant to resolution: the fierce strength of ethnic solidarity, the fact that the stakes are considered high enough to kill and die for, intense and sustained feelings that get in the way of rational deliberation and judgment, the paucity of examples of harmonious multiethnic nations, and the fact that resolution of such conflict remains a matter internal to the nation or people involved, with international intervention restricted mostly to peacekeeping and rescuing.

But reports from the field suggest that even after the fiercest and bloodiest of conflicts, members of different ethnic groups can sometimes inch their way into repairing or rebuilding the kinds of social and economic ties that allow them to coexist. The "co" in *coexistence* means existing *together,* not just side by side; the "existence" entails not simply being alive but having a characteristically human life, one that involves not only living in accordance with specific norms and values but also living with and through the material objects in connection with which those values are experienced (shelter, food, clothing, and art, for example). Students of the reparative impulse in human affairs can't help but be struck by the fact that sometimes the repair work that people do putting back together the physical infrastructure—rehabilitating schools or fixing sewer systems, for example—seems to prepare them in some way for the delicate work of mending social relations. For example, in Chapter One, Aneelah Afzali and Laura Colleton cite projects in which "physical rebuilding can be a valuable handmaiden to social and psychological rebuilding in postconflict societies."

Such transfer of repairing skills from one dimension of human life to another—from the fixing of material objects to the mending of human relationships—is not something that can be taken for granted. For one thing, while buildings can't be violated by attempts to repair them (except in the sense that their structural integrity might be compromised), there are moral constraints on attempts to repair others, to "straighten them out," against their will or in the name of a better way of doing things. Moreover, just because Willie, for example, has the skills, knowledge, and judgment to be a Saab mechanic *extraordinaire* doesn't mean he must be a good mediator of human conflict, any more than skillful diplomats must be excellent tailors. Perhaps the lesson to be learned from struggles to coexist is not that people who can fix roads can mediate conflict but rather that people who can begin to fix roads together might also thereby begin to lay the basis for patching up (and maybe only just that) their severely tattered relationships. But putting it that way might obscure the fact that being able to fix things together already requires a considerable level of interaction and trust. As Afzali and Colleton remind us, unless formerly conflicting parties agree that providing clean water, for example, is a priority, they can hardly be expected to function well as co-repairers of sewer systems. Even in an intimate relationship such as marriage, questions such as what needs repair and what doesn't, who can and should do repair, and who can't and shouldn't constitute ready points of contention.

When former combatants join in the repair of objects that make ongoing existence possible for both of them—fixing houses, rebuilding schools, mending roads, restoring water pipes—it's not because they've become or are about to morph into conflict mediators. But their willingness and capacity to do such basic yet necessary work together—not avoiding conflict, but also not allowing it to tear them apart—suggests that they've already begun the hard labor of coexistence.

Notes

1. P. Walsh, "Mr. Rhoades's Neighborhood," *Reader's Digest,* Jan. 1995, pp. 62–66.
2. For example, R. Elliot, "Ecology and the Ethics of Environmental Restoration," in R. Attfield and A. Belsey (eds.), *Philosophy and the Natural Environment* (Cambridge: Cambridge University Press, 1994).
3. D. Barry, "The Tool Man Cometh," *Ellsworth American,* June 27, 1997, pp. 9–10.
4. M. Minow, *Between Vengeance and Forgiveness: Facing History After Genocide and Mass Violence* (Boston: Beacon Press, 1998); E. Yamamoto, *Interracial Justice: Conflict and Reconciliation in Post–Civil Rights America* (New York: New York University Press, 1999).
5. J. Webb and B. Houseman, *The You Don't Need a Man to Fix It Book: The Woman's Guide to Confident Home Repair* (New York: Doubleday, 1973).
6. *International Herald Tribune,* Oct. 7, 1996, p. 11.
7. *New York Times,* May 22, 1995, p. A10.
8. *Daily Hampshire Gazette,* May 22, 1995, p. 32.
9. *Wall Street Journal Europe,* Aug. 30–31, 1996, p. 8.
10. A. R. Hochschild, "There's No Place like Work," *New York Times Magazine,* Apr. 20, 1997, p. 55.
11. A. Pollack, "Digital Film Restoration Raises Questions About Fixing Flaws," *New York Times,* Mar. 16, 1998, p. D1.
12. K. Pollitt, "What's Right About Divorce," *New York Times,* June 27, 1997, p. A29.
13. Barry, "Tool Man Cometh," p. 9.
14. R. Macauley, *Pleasure of Ruins* (New York: Walker, 1966).

15. H. Liss and the Loizeaux Family of Controlled Demolition, Inc., *Demolition: The Art of Demolishing, Dismantling, Imploding, Toppling and Razing* (New York: Black Dog and Leventhal, 2000).

16. J. M. Fitch, *Historic Preservation: Curatorial Management of the Built World* (Charlottesville: University Press of Virginia, 1990), p. 46.

17. L. Mumford, *Art and Technics* (New York: Columbia University Press, 1952), p. 42.

18. J. Perlez, "Decay of a 20th Century Relic: What's the Future of Auschwitz?" *New York Times,* Jan. 5, 1994, p. A6.

19. J. Amery, "Resentments," in J. Amery, *At the Mind's Limits: Contemplations by a Survivor of Auschwitz and Its Realities* (New York: Schocken Books, 1986).

20. Barry, "Tool Man Cometh," p. 9.

21. J. Baldwin, *The Fire Next Time* (New York: Dell, 1963), p. 15.

22. D. Harper, *Working Knowledge: Skill and Community in a Small Shop* (Berkeley: University of California Press, 1987).

23. C. Elgin, "Restoration and Work Identity," in C. Elgin, *Between the Absolute and the Arbitrary* (Ithaca, N.Y.: Cornell University Press, 1997), p. 105.

24. N. Tavuchis, *Mea Culpa: A Sociology of Apology and Reconciliation* (Stanford, Calif.: Stanford University Press, 1991), p. 25.

25. See D. Lerman, "Restoring Justice," *Tikkun,* Sept.-Oct. 1999, pp. 11–13.

26. Tavuchis, *Mea Culpa,* p. 65. Tavuchis doesn't mention it, but here he echoes Aristotle's view that among the moral virtues young people must acquire is learning to be angry at the right people, in the right amount, at the right time, and in the right way.

27. Tavuchis, *Mea Culpa,* p. 2.

28. L. Langer, *Holocaust Testimonies: The Ruins of Memory* (New Haven, Conn.: Yale University Press, 1991); L. Langer, *Preempting the Holocaust* (New Haven, Conn.: Yale University Press, 1998).

29. Langer also finds evidence of the logic of redemption and salvation in some of the written testimonies of survivors, the message of which is belied by the less guarded, less narratively structured and guided accounts that they give orally. Of Jean Amery, for example, he says that "his writing constitutes the reconciliation or the integration whose success oral testimony dramatically disputes." Langer, *Holocaust Testimonies,* p. 91.

30. Langer, *Holocaust Testimonies,* pp. 50, 146.

31. Langer, *Preempting the Holocaust,* p. 72.

32. Langer, *Preempting the Holocaust,* p. 67.

33. D. Levinson, *Aggression and Conflict: A Cross-Cultural Encyclopedia* (Santa Barbara, Calif.: ABC-CLIO, 1994).

34. Levinson, *Aggression and Conflict,* p. 56.

Chapter Twelve

Religion as an Aid and a Hindrance to Postconflict Coexistence Work

Marc Gopin

The post–Cold War era is characterized by two countervailing trends. One trend is unprecedented economic integration and cultural homogenization, especially at the hands of materialist culture associated with the Western forms of investment, media, advertising, and entertainment. But the other trend is unprecedented cultural and religious fractionalization. People the world over are rebelling against the materialistic homogenization, searching out the roots of their identity, exploring the uniqueness of their background and its original systems of meaning. It is not an age of a new world order but one of great social, cultural, and psychological uncertainty in the context of an overwhelming and almost overpowering economic integration of the world.

Many people turn to religion now—but in divergent ways. Paradoxically, it is a time when we witness both great creativity in religious life and an unparalleled invigoration of old patterns of belief and practice. On the one hand, people engage in new explorations of religion or secular perspectives, sometimes completely independent from traditional religious authority, dogma, or law. This trend grows as diverse peoples of all faiths mix together, especially in large cosmopolitan centers; as women participate in unprecedented levels in public religious life; and as liberal states enable free religious inquiry and experimentation. Yet at the same time, partly in reaction to these trends, others express extreme enthusiasm for traditional religious practices and beliefs as ways to oppose state or secular authorities or global secular culture. The first trend of creative exploration includes multifaith communication and cooperation never equaled in human history. This, too, is transforming modern life and creating a common global culture. Thus while the fractionizing character of religious revivalism is more noticeable and sometimes more violent, a quiet revolution of integration is taking place as well.

Religion is thus one of the most salient phenomena likely to cause massive violence in this century. But religion will also play a critical role in constructing a global community of shared moral commitments and vision. Religion's visionary capacity and its inculcation of altruistic values have given birth to extraordinary leaders, such as Mahatma Gandhi, Martin Luther King Jr., the Dalai Lama, and Bishop Desmond Tutu, who have in turn had a dramatic effect on pushing the global community toward ever-greater commitments to human rights and compassion for human and nonhuman life, regardless of race or citizenship. Less well known globally, but equally revolutionary in their context, are people such as Badshah Khan, the nonviolent Islamic leader of the Pathans; Rabbi Abraham Joshua Heschel, of U.S. civil rights era fame; Dorothy Day, one of the preeminent Catholic peacemakers of the twentieth century; and many others. In other words, religion has helped set the stage for a fully functioning global moral community that may take a very long time to fully materialize, but that is unquestionably closer to fruition than it was a century ago. There have always been exclusive religious visions of a peaceful world. Never before in history, however, have so many leaders and adherents been inspired to work for a truly inclusive vision that is multicultural and panreligious.

The contraindications to this trend are painfully apparent in the murders and tortures of recent history and the religiously motivated contributions of financial support for brutal regimes. Since September 2001, no one can forget the power of radical religious zealots to kill an unprecedented number of civilians, astonishing in their willingness to commit suicide for the sake of otherworldly gains. Suicide is the most difficult of all security breaches, because it calls into question every human being one sees and what he or she may be carrying around, literally or figuratively. And let not the al-Qaida network obscure the fact that Timothy McVeigh, the Oklahoma City bomber, was deeply influenced by a paranoid and bizarre form of Christian identity. Furthermore, religious murder used to take much longer to carry out due to poor technology, but the sum total of its effects historically, in terms of the great religious wars and crusades, is well known for its massive atrocities. At the same time, there is an unmistakable level of global commitment to shared values that is being upheld and defended every day by literally hundreds of government and nongovernmental agencies globally who adhere to and legally uphold the international agreements of the United Nations. Difficult as it is to imagine, the brutal abuses in places such as Bosnia, Kosovo, Tibet, and Burma would be even worse than they have been, were it not for this global consensus.

I consider here the paradoxical contributions of religion to the social order (or disorder) when there are at least some collective efforts under way to promote coexistence between enemy groups.

Learning from History:
Humility, Active Listening, and Ritual

Radical religion as a destabilizing and destructive force in human history was manifest from the earliest stages of monotheism. Biblically based monotheisms—Judaism, Christianity, and Islam—insist on the sacred nature of the Hebrew Bible, and in that book, the genocide of selected "idolatrous" nations is not only permitted but in fact commanded. Whether or not genocides actually took place after the Israelites entered the land of Canaan is hard to know, but the textual precedent for mass murder gave permission for centuries thereafter for the massacre of polytheistic natives wherever in the world they were encountered, the sad legacy of the successful Christian conquest of Europe, Africa, and the Americas. Theology was always invoked at the critical moment to justify the slaughter. It goes without saying that millions of believers abhorred this practice, but by and large, the organized hierarchy of religion was either silent or complicitous. From the crusades of the Middle Ages to turn-of-the-twentieth-century American decisions to Christianize the Philippines, the results were always the same: the deaths of hundreds of thousands of innocents fallen afoul of cynical theological constructs.

Islam's success was built on violent conquest as well, and the conquests continued well after Muhammad's death. The results were less bloody comparatively but quite intolerant by today's standards of civil rights, especially for polytheists. And there were occasional periods of extremism at the hands of radicals such as the Almohides and Almoravides, stained with the deaths of innumerable nonbelievers. Enslavement of polytheists and destruction of their own religions became the standard pattern, and some of this abuse continues to this day (in Sudan, for example).

Eastern and indigenous religions have had similar problems and by-products. Indigenous religions in and stemming from Africa were often predicated on the use of occult powers to destroy one's enemies, while wars and violence built on Buddhist or Taoist principles have been well known from Japan to Sri Lanka, especially in the twentieth century.

Religion had an important role to play in undergirding the neofascist and racist political movements in South Africa, Bosnia, and Rwanda. In each case, the complicity of leading religious figures or institutions was critical to the success of the oppression. Furthermore, at any number of times in the past quarter century, Israelis and Arabs came closer together, inching toward solutions, only to have religious extremists assassinate major leaders, including Sadat and Rabin, and slaughter hundreds in the most brutal fashion, creating political circumstances that stalemated all efforts. The majority of Jews now killed by Arabs in this war are being killed by heavily funded religious extremists, whereas the backbone of the settler presence in the West Bank continues to be the religious settlers and their ideological supporters in the Israeli government.

Yet it would be wrong to ignore the power of religion as a force for love and intergroup coexistence. Only the truly intolerant secularist would divorce the horrific evidence of religion's folly from the equally compelling evidence that the creative imagination of religious geniuses from Amos and Isaiah to Jesus, Rumi, and Gautama Siddharta have saved millions of people from their own worst impulses. In so doing, they made a more peaceful world than what might have been. In addition to the creation of peace-generating dogma, religion's inspiration has provided the world with political

geniuses such as Gandhi, King, and the Dalai Lama, who undoubtedly saved hundreds of thousands, if not millions, of lives by steer-
ing their constituencies to nonviolent resistance and constructive
ways of pursuing justice and peace.

What are the cognitive and emotional underpinnings of great
religious souls? What beliefs, practices, and mental disciplines an-
imate their extraordinary courage and creativity? And how can
these be put to use in coexistence work? As I explore more fully
elsewhere,[1] a series of beliefs and practices that become second nature, habits of the mind and heart to generate extraordinary par-
adigms of interpersonal behavior, can be of benefit to religious and
nonreligious actors alike.

Across diverse religions, great leaders have developed beliefs
in the connection or interrelatedness of all sentient life, the sa-
credness of each and every human being, and the possibility of
human change and evolution for the better, or repentance. Practices include a series of mental assumptions and concentrations
that lead to a habitual embrace of compassion, peace, justice,
mourning as a sacred task, forgiveness, and apology. Finally, the
extraordinary religious peacemakers understand the power and
importance of story, mythic structure, and above all, ritual as a
transformative act.

Despite the presence of such extraordinary religious figures
both in history and today, the fact is that we face some unprecedented circumstances of so many millions of religious people
bumping up against competitors in a crowded and confusing
world. The question then becomes how to take the best of religious
beliefs and practices and apply them to unprecedented levels of
interaction. Here is where the intellectuals of the world, those who
for centuries have been at the forefront of often courageous interreligious exploration, have done such a great disservice. They
have emphasized the skills that *they* have—and not others—and
overlooked the importance of skills that they sometimes lack. They
have emphasized ideas, words, abstract discussions of theology,
even comparative studies of myth, but not the single most important ingredient of coexistence: relationships and the emotional
bond that is the bedrock of all moral interactions. What is needed
globally is not just discussion and dialogue but building relationships, which can rest only in part on intellectual discussion and di-

alogue. Essential to building relationships in a world marked by conflict among groups aligned through religious identities are gestures and forms that have religious resonance.

Relationships depend on gestures of honor, shared understandings of civility, hospitality, generosity, expressions of regret, and shared defense against needless suffering. All of these characteristics of relationship building can and must be founded on religious sources, especially because extremists will bring their own readings of religious sources to deny the possibility or permissibility of relationships based on respect and equality.

Moral and religious leaders on all sides can play a crucial role in generating these relationships, but no peace process should be subverted or suffocated by leaders who are tyrannical, backward-looking, or self-serving. Creative conflict resolution, including religiously informed conflict resolution, must work with but also circumvent the kind of encrusted leadership that is part of the problem.

There is one trait that is more important than all the rest for peacemaking, and that is humility. The ability to listen to the soul of the other in silence emerges from the discipline of humility. I am reminded of the enthusiasm that Buddhist teachers receive when they come to Israel and how odd it is that these "polytheists" receive such a warm welcome, especially from Israeli youth. Young people always help us perceive what is missing in a culture, what its great weaknesses are. A young person has not yet had to buy into his or her culture or don any particular socioeconomic strait-jacket and therefore becomes an important barometer of tragic flaws in the prevailing culture. These Buddhist teachers practice silence, laugh at themselves in ways unthinkable to monotheistic hierarchies, and speak, above all and repeatedly, about humility and compassion for all living things. These leaders attract young disaffected Israelis in search of spiritual solace because of what is missing in life for many people of this region. Both Jewish and Arab youth in a tension-ridden state officially neither at war nor at peace rarely witness the gentleness, humanity, and noncombativeness displayed by these great Buddhist teachers.

It seems clear from a religious viewpoint that humility, silence, and the wisdom of compassionate listening respond to what has been wrong in the region of conflict. Ironically, these qualities have ample precedent in the monotheistic literature, both as recommended moral behavior and as deep religious experience.[2] Muslims, Jews, and Christians can find throughout Biblical and Qur'anic literature evidence that humility is a sine qua non of the human being's position before God. It is a quintessential act of faith.[3] In Judaism it is even portrayed as a divine attribute to be emulated,[4] and for all Abrahamic traditions, the great prophet of the Bible, Moses, is described as the humblest of all men.[5]

Silence may not seem as central in Judaism and Islam as it is in Buddhism, at least when it comes to prayer, and yet where do the monotheistic prophets and heroes receive their wisdom if not through silent listening in desert and wilderness?

With humility, silence, and listening, there is a happy coalescence of diverse religious traditions and the most avant-garde conflict resolution practice. The best peacemakers that I have watched work—the best social change makers in general—are people who understand silence, who value the power of orchestrating the evolution of human relationships without dominating those relationships or encounters. Such peacemakers are not afraid of open discussion and even welcome it, but they do not relish argumentation for its own sake. They do not see every conversation as a win-lose competition, and they do not mistake overall progress and success in their endeavors with the need to come out "on top" in every encounter and conversation, even in their peace efforts. This requires great personal discipline, a very long view of time and "outcomes," and a strong degree of personal inner peace. It also requires a deeply felt patience, a basic trust in humanity and the world, viewed over time, and a love of imperfect human beings as such.

The kind of silence that builds relationships is not actually total silence. The complete silence of strangers, even given in respect, may trigger suspicion or worries that behind the silence is disdain or behind the smile is hatred. Compassionate, active listening requires probing but subtle questions that indicate more to the other than mere respectful silence.

Many people I know who love peace have not internalized these values sufficiently and thus become bad peacemakers despite their best intentions. The task of evoking and inculcating these values and worldviews is something that could benefit from a fusion of spiritual values and training in conflict resolution. Till now, far

too much of the emphasis of conflict resolution has been on process, replicable processes for use in all contexts, as if peacemaking
were a General Motors car to be disassembled and shipped to all
parts of the world and reassembled regardless of circumstances. Not
only does that approach not work, but it is barbaric, for it ignores
the cultural context. It is far better to offer ways to encourage the
development of peacemakers in each culture and religion[6] and cultivate the peacemaking personality honored in various religious
traditions. The character of the peacemaker is a major concern in
religious literature, and it should be the same for conflict resolution theory and practice.

Finally, humility necessarily interlaces—as many emotive and
ethical gestures do—with the bestowal of dignity and honor. Human beings, particularly those who have suffered indignity and injury, crave the dignity of being heard and understood almost as
much as they need air to breathe and water to drink. In our rush to
economic and geographical negotiations of conflict, we constantly
forget this basic need. Leah Green's Compassionate Listening Project represents a conscious institutionalization of listening as peacemaking integrated with compassion and has specialized in bringing
groups to Israel to listen compassionately to the *entire* spectrum of
Jewish and Palestinian political and religious life.[7] This listening has
proved to be transformative for many participants and should be
studied further.

Some additional examples of innovative peacemaking and relationship building include shared study of sacred texts in Jerusalem, across enemy lines. The act of study becomes not only a
gesture of respect and reconciliation but also the basis of relationship building, shared mourning, and constructive argumentation. Rebuilding destroyed religious sites has been an important
part of reconciliation in Bosnia. The restoration of devastated or
abused cemeteries has proved to be of immense value, as has been
the visitation of sites of massacres, with the accompanying acknowledgment by word and deed of the pain of the other. In fact, much
of the successful Christian-Jewish reconciliation work of the past
thirty years has occurred at these very sites.

Such examples may seem hard to imagine in the heat of conflict. Yet in Jerusalem, just two days after Islamic extremist suicide
bombers destroyed the lives of dozens of Israeli teenagers, there

were shared celebrations of Ramadan and Hanukkah by those superior religious souls of the region who hold on, sometimes by a thread, to relationships and humanization of the other. The United States, Cambodia, and India have seen marching used in an opposite way as it has been in Ireland. Both for war and peace, marching is a sacred act. Marching together is a vital and ongoing means of reconciliation, from Maha Gosananda's walks to Gandhi's marches to marches retracing the path of slaves in Richmond, Virginia, and black and white members of Congress in the United States retracing the Freedom Marchers' treacherous journeys through the South. All of these marches have been deeply spiritual events, rituals of immense power and transformation for those who participated in or witnessed them.

Prayers became critical to some efforts to frame tough negotiations in Latin America, a way to make a moral space and presence in the midst of hard bargaining, a way to make an oasis of vision in the midst of the predictable and necessary tale of grievances and injuries. Increasingly, secular educational institutes, such as the Adam Institute in Israel,[8] have seen the value of overlaying their education for democracy and human rights with cultural and religious foundations that will appeal to the spiritual side of the youth who they are educating. These are just a few examples. A full documentation, a true telling of this global story, awaits.

A final example is close to my heart. That is an effort on the part of sheikhs and rabbis in Israel and Palestine to create a religious peace treaty, a symbol of peace, and a token cease-fire.[9] An Islamic concept, referred to as *hudna,* has had a history in the Middle East that allows for the possibility of coexistence. *Hudna* is a hotly debated topic because a religious cease-fire has the implication of a temporary cessation of hostilities, not true peace. Those of us who have worked on this religious treaty have believed that the power of religious symbolism as a force for even a temporary cessation of violence and hate would be enough to generate other symbolic gestures and further progress on the hard-core issues. It would give momentum to religion as a source of healing rather than hatred, which could be built on by further efforts. Most important, it would give a voice to religious leaders who have been threatened and silenced by the well-financed radicals supported by oppressive leaders around the Middle East.

We whistled in the wind for a long time. We met with as many diplomats as we could. We made the case for the wisdom of this path to politicians and seasoned diplomats. Many were persuaded but remained silent. We managed to get support in principle from a letter received from the president of the United States. We met with Palestinian Chairman Yasser Arafat on several occasions with really extraordinary results. As dubious and duplicitous a peace partner as he is, we felt that just getting the approval of the top leaders would generate new possibilities. It did and it has. The leaders are important, but the goal of their involvement should be to circumvent their intransigence and ultimately make their presence less important, historically speaking.

Despite the knee-jerk skepticism of many, we have now come to a situation in which key Arab businessmen, members of the Israeli Parliament, the Palestinian Legislative Council, the attorney general of Israel, and the president of Israel have publicly expressed interest in cultural and religious symbols of reconciliation and, specifically, interest in *hudna*. This is rather startling, considering that this is taking place in the midst of the *intifada* and in the immediate aftermath of September 11, 2001.

We have argued that such gestures have no business attempting to replace security cooperation and counterterrorism measures but that counterterrorism measures have no business trying to substitute for a means to change the one thing that perpetuates all wars: fear born of hatred. That requires trust, forgiveness, and many other treasures of the human mind that only the path of ritual and culture can truly provide.

Supporting Coexistence Through a Religious Lens

Here I will develop a series of suggestions for anyone who wants to promote coexistence among conflicting groups where religion plays a role in the conflict or where religious resources can help build peace.

1. *Recognize the paradox of religious hate and love, violence and prosocial values, and face the implications.* The most important step to take is to abandon naïve beliefs about religion that register it mentally as either a categorical positive or negative in terms of coexistence.

There may be political interests at work in either demonizing or lionizing religion, such as President Bush's recent attempts rhetorically to see Islam in only good terms. But for strategists of coexistence, it is critical to examine and understand how each religion involved in the conflict promotes countervailing values. One of the primary reasons that this is so important is that the adversary groups are generally very familiar with the worst and best in their religions, cleverly using both to strengthen the us-them dynamics of conflict and violence wherein the members of one's own group are the righteous victims and the others are only abusers. They will know when you are soft-pedaling religion and when you are covering up their own religious leaders' contributions to the conflict. This will not help matters. It is imperative to acknowledge fully both contributions to the war, the positive and the negative, and it is important to engage religion in a way that will be believable to inherently skeptical audiences.

2. *Rein in the damage of prejudices and hatred emanating from the texts and traditions of organized religion, as well as from religious leaders and representatives.* How does one contain the damage done by organized religions in the context of war? By stimulating and generating a public repudiation of the activities of some in the war, especially if and when they used particular symbols, traditions, or texts in the course of justifying or perpetrating any atrocities. Each use of religion for atrocity must be responded to hermeneutically in exactly the same fashion.

Religious leaders or representatives who were active during the war must be encouraged and, if possible, compelled to repudiate those same uses of religion during the war. They must reject and, if possible, disown actual religious perpetrators, especially those who committed atrocities in the name of religion.

If these leaders cannot or will not repudiate prior religious hermeneutics, then it is important to encourage alternative leaderships and courageous individuals who will engage in that repudiation. This is most successfully accomplished where there are third-party strategies to stimulate these reactions bilaterally and simultaneously or consecutively. These reactions should be accompanied by acknowledgments of the pain inflicted and apologies. This may take years, but the efforts must begin as soon as possible and on a small scale.

3. *Understand the paradoxes of hermeneutic variation with time and place. Understand the war within each religion both in the traditional way and in the contemporary setting.* If one understands in a deep way the hermeneutic variation of traditions and the war within communities over their values choices, one is in a much better position to strengthen those who are engaged in battles for the prosocial side of a religious tradition. It is important to know the substance of the debate as well as the players, because conflict resolution or coexistence third parties will then be in a better position to design appealing peace strategies that mesh nicely with each community's way of framing its choices morally and spiritually.

4. *Find the peacemakers, and strengthen them within and between communities.* Strengthening the peacemakers means helping them financially and spiritually. It means giving them whatever they need to persist. They should be the ones, for the most part, to explain their needs and what will make them more effective. But it is also the case that sometimes peacemakers are so far on the fringe that they are not necessarily adept at social influence. We must also keep in mind that in every corporate religious group there are peacemakers who leave the group and struggle from the outside and others who work from within. Mechanisms of support for religious peacemakers should always be so structured by third parties as to be ready for inclusion. This is particularly problematic historically for peacemakers who tend to be as exclusive as any other inbred groups. It is the job of third parties not to allow left-right or peace-violence divisions to become encrusted in religious communities. There should a highly elastic and creative process of ever-widening communication and creativity.

5. *Build alliances of new hermeneutics, interpretations, and symbols to support coexistence.* In the long run, with the work of local peacemakers, more possibilities of interreligious alliances can emerge and support new hermeneutics, new interpretations, and symbols of coexistence. The more varied each group's religious actors are, the more they will find their counterparts on the other side. Liberals will find liberals and conservatives will find conservatives, and out of a broadened coalition of those committed to coexistence will come a slow and steady defeat of those committed to violence.

6. *Focus on deeds more than dialogue, or make dialogue contingent on or interactive with a regime of righteous bilateral deeds.* Dialogue is

overrated. It may make a good platform for leaders to demonstrate their political importance, but it just as often generates skepticism, especially when it is engaged too soon. It is the rage of the masses that is the critical dynamic of religion and war, and that rage is not turned off like a spigot. It is true that leaders are critical symbols of social change, and fostering their relationship with one another is crucial. But we must not overrate the contribution of dialogue. The masses of people understand, in their wisdom, the evidence of reconciliation, acknowledgment, and repentance, in the realm of deeds rather than in the rhetoric of political manipulation.

7. *Understand and use the interaction of economics, psychology, power relations, and military reality, along with religious trends, to coordinate more effectively secular and religious efforts of peace, security, and development.* Efforts at religious coexistence work can be hampered by bureaucratic division of efforts and poorly integrated thinking about the nature of conflict. Just as deeds are crucial to true religious trust, development and poverty relief are at the heart of serious conflict resolution. These two insights can and should be integrated in the form of creative programs and joint activities that the warring communities design with the help of others. Similarly, religious healing and psychological recovery need to work hand in hand. Each must understand the peculiar approaches of the other and attempt a cooperative or parallel set of processes. The case is the same with security concerns. Issues of public safety, crime, and justice should be framed in terms of religious values wherever possible. This suggestion does not mean surrendering the public order to religious authority. At the end of the day, there is no peace when one religious community or another controls the military or judiciary or the public space. Most religious adherents around the world have come to understand that religion is at its best when it does not control the temporal space. Democracy and human rights ultimately depend on this principle. That having been said, there is no reason that the liberal forms of social order—judiciary, police, democracy—should not be hermeneutically framed in religious ways. Enough adherents around the world are actively engaged in this framing process—often in very deep ways—that this alliance of civil society need not be seen as the enemy of religion. This process must be aggressively funded the world over. We are engaged

not in a war of religions but rather a war within religions and civilizations over the future of civil liberties, particularly the freedom of women. It is my impression that most religious adherents want human rights and democracy, but not if it is perceived to be a means of crushing their identity or civilization. We need to work harder at making the case for a culture- and religion-friendly liberal social order. And we need the international corporations and representatives of capitalism to become an asset, not a liability, in this struggle.

8. *Face and focus on the tremendous psychological power of religion to stimulate mood swings, and use gestures of acknowledgment, apology, and repentance for reconciliation, but be prepared to combat the compelling contagion of righteous hatred.* Religion can produce powerful and irrational symbols of hatred, such as desecrations, libels, conspiracies, or devil discoveries. These can erupt in a highly charged situation in which some unscrupulous group in search of power can provoke and capitalize on symbolic religious rage. Be prepared with alternative and liberal healing symbols of religion, such as broadly publicized and filmed interfaith ceremonies of healing or restoration of a holy site that has been destroyed or desecrated.

9. *Explore and use the power of symbols to divide, unite, and reconcile.* The greatest danger that we face from religion today is its tremendous power to stimulate rage in massive numbers of people. Irresponsible clerics cannot resist the opportunity to capitalize on this power to actively fight world orders with which they see themselves unable to coexist. In a poverty of vision, these clerics have not yet reached the conclusions that millions of other clergy have about the modern world: that it is possible for religion to flourish even with Coca-Cola, MTV, and absolute freedom of choice by women and men. But the free-floating rage of millions of people waits, like a ripe fruit, for power-hungry individuals and institutions to trigger and appropriate. And then the sociopaths, the fascistic leaders and terrorists, come along as the great release of the rage. This was as true in the twentieth century, under the aegis of fascism and communism, as it is today under the aegis of fundamentalism.

It is our job to undermine that rage aggressively with compassion, acknowledgment, antipoverty plans, and inherent respect for cultural and religious diversity. If there is global religious rage, then a global Marshall Plan is necessary to quell it. Respect is the ultimate way to undermine the violent potential of religion and give voice to the majority in each religious tradition who tend to abhor the abduction of their religion by rage.

Religion can serve as the language for triggering rage or as the vehicle for cultivating relationships, active listening, and rituals of respect across difference. Religions can organize people into warring factions or instead sustain coexistence and development. Religions can divide or instead build bridges to peace.

Notes

1. M. Gopin, *Between Eden and Armageddon: The Future of World Religions, Violence and Peacemaking* (New York: Oxford University Press, 2000). See also M. Gopin, *Holy War, Holy Peace: How Religion Can Bring Peace to the Middle East* (New York: Oxford University Press, 2002).

2. See *Tractate Derekh Eretz Zuta* 1 and *Avot of Rabbi Nathan* 15; for a representative collection of rabbinic approaches to humility, see M. C. Luzzatto, *The Path of the Just*, trans. S. Silverstein (New York: Feldheim, 1969), ch. 22. There are numerous sources on silence and its relationship to understanding. See *Midrash Rabbah* (Margoliot ed.), Leviticus 16:5; *Midrash Tanhuma* (Warsaw ed.), *Va'ye'tseh* 6; *Otsar Midrashim Alpha Beta d'Ben Sira*, para. 19; *Tractate Derekh Eretz Zuta* 7; and *T. B. Pesahim* 99a.

3. See, for example, Qur'an 7:161; 57:16.

4. See *Midrash Rabbah*, Deuteronomy 7:12; and *Midrash Tanhuma* (Warsaw ed.), *Bereshit* 4, *Vay'erah* 8, *Ki Tisah* 15.

5. Numbers 12:3.

6. See M. Gopin, "The Religious Component of Mennonite Peacemaking and Its Global Implications," in C. Sampson and J. P. Lederach (eds.), *From the Ground Up: Mennonite Contributions to International Peacebuilding* (New York: Oxford University Press, 2000).

7. For more information, see the Compassionate Listening Project Web site at http://www.mideastdiplomacy.org/clp.html.

8. See Adam Institute for Democracy and Peace at http://www.adaminstitute.org.il/english/index.html.

9. For the full text of at least one proposed peace treaty, as well as an extensive analysis of it, see Gopin, *Holy War, Holy Peace*.

Chapter Thirteen

Engaging with the Arts to Promote Coexistence

Cynthia Cohen

Understanding an enemy is like understanding a poem.

In what sense might this be true? And if it were true, what implications might it have for the educational processes inherent in facilitating coexistence between former enemies?

In this chapter, I will first argue for the important similarities between the understanding of enemies and of poems and the relevance of this comparison to the challenges of promoting coexistence. Then I will illustrate how practitioners of coexistence and reconciliation effectively use a variety of artistic forms to address some of the central challenges for promoting coexistence in historically divided societies.

Starting Points

To apprehend something poetically means to be receptive to it, to open ourselves to the reverberations it creates in our beings. According to the French philosopher Gaston Bachelard, poetic images "react on [our] minds and in [our] hearts, despite all barriers of common sense. . . . At the level of the poetic image, the duality of subject and object is iridescent, shimmering, unceasingly active in its inversions. . . ."[1]

To understand a poetic image, we must pay attention to how it reverberates within us. Our attention "shimmers" back and forth between our own response and the image, constructing new meanings out of those reverberations. The image in the poem allows us to experience, perceive, or understand something previously unknown about ourselves. Conversely, it is by attending to what is evoked within us that we are able to understand the poetic image. Understanding a poem can alter a reader who enters into a state of receptivity to the poetic image, to its resonances and reverberations within the reader, and to the "unceasingly active" inversions between them. Bachelard refers to this kind of understanding of self and other *through* each other as "trans-subjectivity."[2]

The deepening of relationships between former enemies also involves a kind of trans-subjectivity, an epistemological interdependence that results from the features of enmity. Political psychologists theorize that children's sense of ethnic or national identity is created in part through the "externalization" of pleasurable and wholly good impulses onto symbols of the in-group. In a parallel process, unpleasurable phenomena or impulses labeled as "bad" are attached to symbols associated with the enemy. Vamik Volkan writes that "since our enemies . . . serve as a reservoir of our unwanted selves, they are unconsciously seen to some extent as being like us, although on a conscious level they should not seem to be the same as us since they contain our unwanted aspects—those characteristics we vigorously reject."[3]

To maintain an "enemy system," both adversaries are "locked into a permanent 'dance'" in which their apprehension of each other "is largely governed by projection."[4] Especially in cases of overt aggression, the stereotyped enemy is devalued through demonizing and dehumanizing attitudes and behaviors that allow us to avoid feeling guilty about inflicting injury and destruction. To justify our violence, we convince ourselves that the enemy is not only subhuman but also threatening—a force from which we must defend ourselves. Single incidents are taken as evidence that the total fabric of the enemy group is demoniacal. These beliefs are supported by members of our own group—family, friends, media, and political leaders[5]—with whom we are intersubjectively linked.

How is it possible to overcome this polarization? The psychological anthropologist Howard Stein writes that "transcendence of group-isms can only be accomplished, and always incompletely, as we are able to relinquish and integrate the inner splits between 'goodness' and 'badness' that have led us throughout history to dichotomize between idealized and disparaged groups. . . . Only by grieving over our own imperfectability and mortality can we begin to permit ourselves and others to be ambivalently, more fully, 'human, all too human,' and not people the social and supernatural world with saints and demons. Liberation begins with an understanding of what we need and use our indispensable enemies for."[6] Because enemies become receptacles for the negatively valued attributes of ourselves, to perceive our enemy more completely necessarily entails revising our understanding of ourselves as well. Shifting between self and other to remake images of each, the work of overcoming an enemy system mirrors the shimmering attention between the poetic image and our own response.

Because of the similarities between the qualities of presence inherent in aesthetic encounters and the sensibilities required of former enemies who seek to understand each other, the arts can be crafted to encourage the kind of movement between self and other that can help former adversaries overcome the challenges of forging relationships. The examples of coexistence intervention described later in the chapter demonstrate how engagement with the arts can encourage the intellectual and emotional attitudes and proclivities—such as receptivity, creativity, vitality, respect, and imagination—that are required for the difficult work of coexistence and reconciliation.

Why are these attitudes required? Let's take coexistence to refer to the point on a continuum of intergroup relations between the extremes of war, slavery, and apartheid, predicated on utter disregard for the other, and cooperation, characterized by recognition of interdependence. Coexistence refers to a threshold point where the individuals or groups shift from reciprocal hatred and injury to rudimentary, even grudging respect and then all further movement in the direction of cooperation, understanding, and reconciliation. Thus coexistence implies mutual participation in determining the degree and quality of interaction. Because intergroup relations can cascade backward in the direction of intolerance and violence, coexistence requires nourishing the attitudes, values, and capacities people need, not just to cease violence, but to build respect, understanding, and cooperation over time. This work of nourishing attitudes, values, and capacities—which could be viewed as educational work in the broadest sense—must focus on restoring and enhancing individual and collective capacities for intellectual, social, emotional, creative, and spiritual life. These capacities, often impaired by violence, are vital to sustaining both individual well-being and intergroup coexistence over time.

In conflict and postconflict situations, coexistence workers face several difficult challenges in engaging people in conversation or the planning of cooperative projects with their enemies or former adversaries. Many challenges result from the traumatic effects of violence. One difficulty is the mismatch between people's need to tell their stories and express their suffering and their former enemy's capacity to listen. In most cases of violent conflict, people on all sides have been traumatized in ways that limit their capacity to listen. A related challenge, especially in cases of extreme trauma or long-standing oppression, is that the experiences that most need recounting may not be readily accessible to language. Nondiscursive modes of expression may be the only route available to people as they seek to construct meaning from and gain power in relation to the violations they have experienced.

Other challenges involve the ways in which the dynamics of the conflict have become insinuated into the discourses of the various communities. The categories through which people perceive each other and articulate their experiences are likely to have become embedded within the stereotypes that have fueled reciprocal dehumanization. The constructs people use to discuss historical, geographical, and cultural phenomena are likely to be unacceptable to each other. Therefore, the most readily available modes of communication—the discourses of each community's regular conversation—can often exacerbate misunderstandings and perpetuate processes of reciprocal, symbolic injuring. Sometimes participants in coexistence activities sense this risk and become very polite. They thereby minimize the risk of injuring each other but also avoid addressing the issues that divide them.

Resistance to the learning required for coexistence can also arise because people often defend themselves against facing the suffering of their own communities and the suffering of others— suffering caused by actions in which they or the institutions of their country may be complicit. Normal tendencies to avoid confronting pain are exacerbated by the proximity in time to people's own traumas as well as feelings of shame, guilt, and rage.

People also bring to coexistence efforts defenses against learning ideas that can shatter their worldviews and compromise the meaning of symbols they hold sacred. Because in enmity relations, all positively valued qualities tend to be attributed to one's own group, the processes of rehumanizing an enemy often involve simultaneously acknowledging the shadow sides of oneself and one's group. These lessons come at a high price, not only in disruptions to the infrastructure of one's intrapsychic world but also in disruptions to relationships with cherished family members and friends. It is no wonder that people are resistant to such changes. The educational work of coexistence must reach beneath people's defenses but do so in respectful and gentle ways that support people to configure new patterns of meaning as old patterns become obsolete. Indeed, the work must be able to reach people whose worlds have been so shattered that they have lost faith in the potential benevolence of human creativity and lost the capacity or willingness to trust or even to discern when trust might be warranted. Finally—and this might be especially true for children who have grown up knowing only violence—many whom we seek to engage in coexistence efforts find it difficult to imagine another way of being. They don't have memories of the "time when we all got along." Overcoming or circumventing these challenges is a daunting task.

However, in artistic forms and processes, many coexistence practitioners find resources that are uniquely well suited to address them. Art—from paintings viewed by solitary museumgoers to participatory rituals of dance and drumming—can support movement toward coexistence for a variety of reasons:

Art is pleasurable and enlivening. If people are depressed, singing or creating with colors can provide energy for expression and engagement. If people are disoriented, the forms of rituals can provide support to sustain interactions and focus in spite of uncertainties. By engaging the senses and cognitive capacities, art can reach beneath people's defenses, circumventing the incompatibility of existing discourses.[7]

Art invites reciprocity. It involves people in reciprocal relationships of sensitivity toward others. A work of art is inherently other-regarding in a way that is rarely the case in political discourse or debate.

Art invites creativity. People tend to perceive the world through the categories of preexisting conceptual frameworks; artists, however, generally take the elements they apprehend in the world and bring them into relation in new ways. The ability to "see the world with fresh eyes," or imagine new configurations of the elements, needs strengthening in virtually every society, especially in societies where the sense of possibility has been blunted by violence.

Artists can serve as mediators. In divided communities where violence has impaired people's capacities to listen, artists can use the qualities of receptivity to facilitate expression, healing, and reciprocal understanding. The qualities of listening associated with aesthetic attention—alert but calm, emotional but cognitively aware, engaged but detached—are precisely the kinds of presence that can help people put their experiences into words. Also, artists' listening to those who have been traumatized by violence can begin to restore a victim's capacity and willingness to hear the stories and experiences of the other.

Contributions of the Arts to Coexistence Efforts

Both the arts and coexistence efforts are difficult to evaluate, yet it is possible to document the kinds of responses and conversations that are nourished by the creation, rehearsal, production, and witnessing of the work. The following examples focus on particular kinds of artistic expression: ritual, folk and traditional arts, music and cultural work, visual art, drama, and oral narrative mediated through art forms.[8] This very small sampling of the thousands of arts-related coexistence programs that exist in conflict regions and multiethnic societies illustrates the distinctive qualities of a range of approaches that use art to promote coexistence in postconflict societies.

Ritual

Structured within a framework of traditional symbols, participants in rituals enter moments when they are released from the normative demands of cultural scripts and where they enjoy the freedom associated with play. As Clifford Geertz puts it, ritual allows the "dreamed of" and the "lived in" orders to fuse.[9]

In the Tamil community of Sri Lanka, ritual is the focus of work used to help people, traumatized by violence and dislocation, develop or regain the communicative capacity to share their stories and join in a dialogue with their Sinhalese counterparts. A Tamil colleague from Sri Lanka, who is a drummer, healer, and lecturer in theater at Jaffna University, uses processes of ritual and theater to work with the Tamil community in the northern part of the country to help its members overcome trauma so that they are prepared both to express themselves and to listen to their enemies.

His example is instructive for several reasons. The work it describes relies on an adaptation of an expressive form—in this case, ritual—that is indigenous to the region and familiar to all parties involved. It illustrates the power of incorporating into coexistence efforts the expressive forms that are or were thriving in the communities involved in the conflict.[10] Also, this work takes place almost exclusively with people from only one of the communities in the conflict. Very often preparation for intercommunal exchanges—especially when it involves some degree of healing from trauma—is best accomplished in uninational or unicommunal sessions. In this instance, the ritual was designed to help participants overcome the trauma of violence and displacement by acknowledging and expressing their feelings. As people supported each other to enact their most frightening images, a community of trusting relations was built. As a result of the working through of feelings, the shared experience of the ritual, and the support people felt from each other, the participants developed the capacities for expression and for listening that they would need to participate in coexistence dialogues. My colleague, Kandasamy Sithamparanathan, explained:

In the early 1990s, our theater group conducted workshops in a very interior peasant village. We were not sure about these workshops, but when we began, people cried and expressed their feelings. At last they told how they found a different life here. We experienced very close relationships with these people. Our theater group recognized that the people themselves have inner energy and suppressed feelings. Henceforth, rather than use our theater skills to perform propaganda dramas (as we had earlier), we constructed rituals that invited people to express their feelings and thus build on their human resources.

The rituals take place in houses. It is as if the house has a life and a vibrancy of its own, and people can feel the house as they enter it. A lot of reverence is paid to the place. Flowers are brought in and placed on a white design. People remove their slippers and touch the ground. People have said that after entering this area, they have felt the house responding to them.

There are drummers inside the house. As people enter, they dance to the music and sway from side to side. As the music continues, people begin to dance faster. The dancing can become very frenzied and emotional. People manifest themselves in very different ways. One person was so rigid that he was frozen in place. Some people cry; others scream. People hit things.

The forms are similar to traditional rituals, although traditional rituals deal with supernatural powers. We believe in human leaders and the power of human interaction.

Sometimes people in the workshop see images involving someone else who is there. I might have a vision of you running up into a spiral, being chased by many people, and you would have no place to go. It's an aspect of the unconscious that manifests these images of other people. After these images come up, people sit together and talk about the images and what they have seen. After that, they act out what they have envisioned.

One girl saw an image of a ghost chasing her. The ghost had a torn mouth. She chose to express this using four or five people to show that one ghostly figure, because she didn't feel one person could adequately represent the ghost. She still had problems expressing the torn mouth. Usually, we use other materials like masks, but this girl, who was a senior in high school, felt she couldn't in any way express the torn mouth. This vision related to the political situation. Another time, a man described a vision in which the army was burning a couple's children right before their eyes. He was actually remembering an incident from when he was nine years old.

The rituals can go on for six days. People stay overnight, and we cook together. There are sessions for meditation. People talk among themselves and perform for each other. There is a closeness and intimacy that comes out of these interactions—a closeness that they have never felt before. In our culture, men and women don't touch each other, but after these workshops, there is no such inhibition, and people hold each other and support each other. Emotions are very intense—not sexually but in another way. We might start at seven in the morning and go until eight at night. The last day does not end. They don't go to sleep, staying up from Friday morning until Saturday morning, and then they leave for home.

People who participate in these workshops leave feeling stronger and more courageous. They come out with the feeling that they have been a part of a family. They are not ready to accept oppression or to oppress others. Going to a workshop like this gives them courage, and so they speak without fear. The change takes place because the people express themselves at a very deep level.

They are given the tools to express themselves and to bring forth all that they are holding inside. The workshops are a deliberate process through which they are able to bring their suffering, their fears, and their hopes out into the open.

In our theater group, we are all friends. Although there is a big age difference, we are all equals. We don't have that much schooling, but our minds are very clear and powerful, and our people are very energetic. Dancing and acting skills come to us very easily, but we have to develop the inner mind. We experience a very good life in our theater group. We offer something to everybody, and we enjoy that, even amid the chaos and oppression and everything. One of the major issues in Sri Lanka is that the Sinhalese people don't know what the Tamil people want. So now we have a project to get the Tamil viewpoint out. After Tamil people have participated in our ritual workshops, they are better able to express themselves.

Our goal is for the people on both sides to become better listeners. First, we develop listening skills through theater activities, working with each group separately. Then, using the new listening skills, we bring the two groups together for dialogue. Through participation in theater, people's minds are broadened. They begin to form a collective voice for peace. They become more willing to listen to Sinhalese people and their perspectives. This allows everyone to hear the other side and how people on that side perceive the situation. This is what we hope will happen in the exchanges we are planning.[11]

Folk and Traditional Arts

Many coexistence projects build on the folk arts and other traditional expressive forms of communities. Strengthening intergroup relations through folk arts makes sense for several reasons. Even when material resources are scarce, people still have their songs, stories, cooking styles, children's games, and perhaps gardens. These resources exist within the community, and community members themselves are the experts. Artists and folklorists who work with community lore can find ways to honor and dignify the knowledge that exists within communities, thereby strengthening people's confidence in their ability to reconstruct their lives and their relationships with others. They can also construct opportunities for people from different communities to come to know, respect, and begin to understand each other as they share aspects of their communities' knowledge and as they build on that understanding to create together songs, plays, quilts, festivals, and museums.

One particularly impressive folklore project is called Traditional Creativity in the Schools, run by the Centre for Creativity in Education and Cultural Heritage based in Jerusalem, under the direction of folklorist Simon Lichman. Using schools as the vehicle, its target population is Arab and Jewish school communities, including the children in each participating class, their families and teachers, and eventually the communities at large. According to Lichman's project description: "Through the folklore project we facilitate ongoing communication and the building of positive relationships between neighboring peoples. Our ultimate objective is that groups of Jews and Arabs (children, families, teachers), having worked together creatively for several years, develop a climate for coexistence, tolerance, and mutual respect. Arab and Jewish children learn more about their own folklore while receiving a window into each other's daily life and traditions, with family members helping to create a mosaic of community history and cultural heritage. Participating school staff are trained to run the program and become a working partnership."[12]

The program consists of weekly classwork on folklore and coexistence, conducted separately in paired Arab and Jewish schools in Israel. Each pair of schools participates for as long as eight years, with particular classroom pairings lasting at least two to three years. Students collect information from their own parents and grandparents, exploring their own community's traditions in play, food, oral history, and music. Parents and grandparents from both communities are thrilled to be asked to share this sort of knowledge, which is seldom reflected or acknowledged in the formal educational system and which children had previously tended to dismiss as irrelevant to modern life. Every six or eight weeks, the program sponsors a "joint activity day" in which participants from both Arab and Jewish communities are invited to the school in their roles as culture bearers. On one day, for instance, Israeli and Palestinian Arab and Jewish grandparents demonstrate different styles of hopscotch; on another day, different techniques for pickling food. Over the course of two or three years, the project facilitates cross-cultural, multigenerational social ties between people as individuals, as members of families, and as members of communities. The program is multifaceted, including teacher training and photography and multimedia exhibitions in each community, so that parents who are unable to participate in school-day activities can still become familiar with the project and have opportunities for social interaction. Children visit each other's houses of worship and learn about each other's holidays. "Unlike many folklore projects that focus on the preservation of tradition, this project shows participants how the wisdom of tradition, transmitted as ongoing and dynamic, can facilitate social cohesion."[13]

The approach of the Centre for Creativity in Education and Cultural Heritage is unusual because of the staff's sustained commitment to entire school communities. Here is Lichman's own assessment of the project's impact, written in light of the increased violence that has characterized the region since October 2000:

> Despite the radical disruption of normal contacts and the enormous strain of mutual suspicion, fear, and pain since the outbreak of violence in October 2000, the center continued to work intensively with the children and school staff in the Arab and Jewish Israeli schools separately. The first set of joint activities between the paired Jewish and Arab classes was postponed and rescheduled for after Ramadan, Hanukkah, and Christmas. We concentrated on the collection of folklore and on the way in which researching and understanding our own heritage and traditions influences our respect for, and sensitivity to, one another. In the Palestinian and Israeli communities, we have only been able to maintain telephone contact. In both the Palestinian-Israeli and Jewish and Arab Israeli programs, the teachers focused on developing their pupils' communication skills, encouraging them to see that dialogue, not violence, is the only way forward.

> Keeping the channels of communication open has been a primary task for the center. We have provided a forum for thinking through the devastating experience of this ongoing tragedy, offering support and guidance to parents and children in the communities as well as to the teaching staff. The children, parents, grandparents, and teachers worry about each other as the violent events unfold. During the first few months, we carried messages of goodwill between children, their families, and school staff in the Israeli Arab and Jewish communities; thus points of view and alternative perspectives could be expressed and heard. Many individuals regularly telephoned each other, and in response to the adult population's urgent need for direct contact, we set up meetings between Arab and Jewish parents and grandparents while their children could not travel to each other's schools.

It is precisely in times like these that the project's long-term, community-oriented approach has been paying off. While suffering the consequences of what is happening all around us, these paired Jewish and Arab communities have people on the other side whom they have come to know on a personal and positive level. For them it is harder to be carried along with so large a proportion of the population into stereotyping generalizations about "Jews" and "Arabs."

Even though the situation in the country has not yet settled, it has been possible to resume regular meetings between children in the Jewish and Arab Israeli schools because of the confidence they have in each other as partners working toward creating a safe society based on equality, dignity, and mutual respect.[14]

Music and Cultural Work

According to the philosopher Suzanne Langer, music is a kind of expression that makes apparent the forms of human emotions. We only need to watch a television show or a movie with the audio track muted to realize the extent to which music can be used to communicate the emotional significance of an interaction or the inner feelings of a character.

Music is perhaps the art form where the qualities of harmony, balance, and rhythm can be most readily apprehended. When elements appear in harmonic relationship to each other, we perceive unity in diversity. Just as musical expression can be used to mobilize people in the service of national interests and military readiness, it can be crafted to reveal and express commonalities across differences. When diverse groups of people—in some cases former adversaries—work with artists and facilitators to compose songs that give voice to their common aspirations, the processes of generating and performing the songs can offer the embodied experience of an imagined unity in diversity even before it is realized in politics or institutions.

One educator who draws on the educational potential inherent in music expression is the African American cultural worker Jane Sapp, now a senior fellow at the Center for Reflective Community Practice at the Massachusetts Institute of Technology and a visiting artist at Brandeis University's International Center for Ethics, Justice, and Public Life. Educated as a musician and folklorist, Sapp works to strengthen communities by helping groups of people become aware of their shared knowledge and how to use it as a source of strength for creating a future together. She refers to her interaction with communities as "cultural work," which, as she puts it:

> . . . focuses on what the community has, rather than what it does not have. People have their songs, stories, histories, cooking styles, and ways of being together. My work has been to take all the ways in which people have fashioned a life together and use it as a mirror. People can look in this mirror, look at themselves, and say: "This is the way we have created our lives together. Can we not continue to do that today? Can we not continue to be active participants in our own lives?" . . . People can know how to take that knowledge and recognize in it the building blocks for the future and for change.[15]

For twenty-five years, Sapp has worked in disenfranchised communities, including many African American communities in the poorest counties in the American rural South. Since 1989, Sapp has been based in Springfield, Massachusetts, where she directs several multicultural choruses and leads music workshops with young people deemed to be "at risk." She uses her art to bring people together and draw them out, and to engage them not simply in artistic expression but in a critical evaluation of the social and cultural issues that affect them.

In 1996, Sapp created Voices of Today, an after-school program that uses the arts to encourage teens to express their visions, hopes, and dreams for the future. She works with a multiracial group of low-income middle school students, many of whom were silent or disruptive in class. Sapp encourages the children to talk about their families, their schools, poverty, racism, and other pressing issues. She then sets their spoken and written words to music and teaches the children to sing their songs. In many cases, the children have gained a sense of self-discipline and direction that spills over into their academic work and their planning for their futures.

Several of Sapp's projects have, as a core component, the strengthening of intergroup relations. Recently, she directed a ten-day institute at Brandeis University, launching the Global Partnerships for Education project. Community-based educators from Haifa (Israel), Grenada, and refugee communities in Boston were linked with Brandeis faculty and students to experience and learn

Sapp's approach to cultural work and then fashion projects in their three communities. Through storytelling, visual art, poetry writing, the construction of timelines, and oral history interviews, participants explored their communities' cultural resources. They looked at these resources in terms of community, family, historical, intellectual, and aesthetic inheritances. Discussion focused on areas of disagreement and difference among participants as well as on commonalities and shared values.

Over the course of the ten days, in the context of this intensive community-building experience, each participant became more openly expressive. Conversations became deeper, more serious, and filled with more humor. The Haifa team, which included both Arab and Jewish Israelis, was able to draw on that reservoir of creativity and energy as they confronted their very different ideas about how to adapt the cultural work approach to a coexistence project in Haifa.

Toward the end of the institute, Sapp led the participants in the composition of a song that reflects and celebrates the ideas that had been generated by their time together.[16] She discusses her goals for the institute and the songwriting activity in particular:

> I have people compose a collective song so that they have a sense of what is possible. A key goal of cultural work is to look at what is possible, to remind ourselves that there are always possibilities. There are no dead-end streets in terms of our having the will to create a new world and change in our community. As my grandmother used to say, as long as you're living and breathing, there's possibility. Another reason for the song is to encourage creativity, to oil the imagination. This ensures that we don't reach a dead end, that we imagine something beyond the obstacles that we think we see, either in quality of life or changing relationships in our community. The ability to imagine that things can be different is very important.

> When you work with relationships and openly share your knowledge in a safe place, at some point people come together. Even with their differences in inheritances and experiences, people find a common humanity, a common will. When you listen to that song, you see that collective will, that collective vision, that common humanity that comes forth. We could not have done the song on the first day, and we couldn't have done it on the third. It was after the process that people came together and saw each other in different ways.[17]

Visual Arts

Like music and other performing arts, the two- and three-dimensional visual arts also create harmonies and rhythms through the interplay of disparate elements within bounded forms. In visual arts, elements are organized in space, each symbol replete with layers of meaning, enhanced by the relationships among them and by the resonance they evoke in their viewers. The beauty of a visual form—a sculpture or painting, a building or garden—can invite viewers to become aware of images and to linger as they are supported to encounter, reexamine, and reconsider symbols and their own processes of making meaning.

One artist who has explored the possibilities for reconciliation inherent in public art installations is Wen-ti Tsen, a Chinese American muralist, graphic designer, and sculptor. On the occasion of the millennium, he was given the opportunity to work with the Allied Arts Council of Yakima Valley, Washington, to create a public work of art that would bring together all segments of the community to "reflect on the last thousand years and to view the next thousand."[18] During early conversations between the artist and his local counterparts, the idea emerged for a project that would create a "sculptural plaza" for downtown Yakima that would bring into relationship the historical narratives, grievances, and contributions of the region's substantial European American, Native American, and Mexican communities, as well as its African American, Filipino American, and Japanese American minorities. The plaza would focus on the theme of water.

Relations among groups in the region exhibit signs of alienation and strain. For instance, tensions between the European American orchard owners and two waves of Mexican American laborers, only some of whom enjoy legal immigrant status, have resulted in a city that is ethnically segregated. The Native American community also remains quite separate from the city proper, with most members living on a reservation that represents one-tenth of their original land, established in a treaty signed in the 1830s. The local Japanese community was uprooted as a result of the Internment Act during World War II; a small portion has returned to work as truck farmers. A small black community came to the region to work in coal mines. According to the artist's report on the project, the plaza was to be created in such a way that it would be felt "owned by many people. Stories about lives would be told. Ways would be found that they could be heard."[19]

During 1999 and the first half of 2000, Tsen made three preparatory visits to the Yakima Valley. These visits, ranging in length from a few days to two months, introduced him to the city, region, economy, and landscape. He worked at county fairgrounds and in community colleges to produce murals depicting the people of the region. He also attended social events, Rotary Club meetings, city and town councils, schools, and art colleges. He was presented to the Yakama Indian nation in a powwow and did interviews with various media.

Tsen describes the creation of the installation:

The installation is called "The Water of Life." At one edge of the plaza are four large basalt blocks, from six to eight feet tall, each weighing four to seven tons, forming an arc. A sheet of water trickles on the face of each. This represents the elements in their natural state, water coming from the mountains. Viewed in a primary way, the piece refers to the irrigation water flowing from the Cascade Mountains, providing the life source for the agricultural economy of the Yakima Valley. A six-foot-high bronze case contains a glassed-in tank of water, with a bronze sculpture of a segment of the Cascade Range on top. This represents people's abilities to tap and transform nature into resource. The bronze sculpture that represents the Cascades is in direct alignment with the actual ridge toward the west, on which it is modeled.

Two concrete walls that slope from eight feet to six feet zigzag on two sides of the plaza like reaching arms. Set in the walls are thirty-six cases, twelve by twelve inches each, glazed on both sides. Each case holds a "power object" created by an artist or a community person in order to "redeem the past, reconcile the present, or imagine a good future." A selection committee of ten thoughtful and very articulate people from various cultural backgrounds chose the items to be represented in these "community walls" from ideas solicited from the community. They chose the forty pieces in a half-dozen congenial and provocative sessions. I wanted this to provide a process for the reclamation of something, a moment to rethink the past, assess the present, and take action toward the future.

Eight basalt columns sit around the open space in the middle. Seven columns serve as the pedestals for bronze casting of actual objects, tools used in the valley. The objects are a Singer sewing machine, a Yakama Indian basket with berries, a GI helmet, an irrigation crank, an apple-harvesting bag, a saddle, and a farmworker's short-handled hoe. The last column has an inscribed circle with a spring of water flowing from the center; this installation represents the spiritual.

In the front of the plaza, aligned with the Cascade water tank, is a two-by-two-by-four-foot bronze-plated box with a three-spout water fountain in front. A bronze sculpture of an apple orchard is set on the top. The size of the box replicates an apple harvest bin. The fountain is suitably sized for a child to romp in. A ring of light made of fiber optics with changing and circulating colors sits over the plaza. The movement and rhythm simulate those of the circular "friendship" dance at a powwow. It represents a coming together of the people and a healing of the nations.[20]

Throughout this project, Tsen understood his role to include a large measure of listening. In cases where different groups in the community did not respond to general requests for participation, dialogue sessions were established, set up at a place where people would feel at home. These visits meant that the project was informed by the ideas, experiences, and sensibilities of a broad diversity of the community, including nuclear waste scientists at a nearby plant and incarcerated teens. "The artist must subsume himself to what others want to say," Tsen explained. "The artist becomes others' tongues."[21]

Tsen also understood that his role was that of a mediator. He consistently stressed the importance of the process and the installation itself being fair to all of the different cultures of the region. In the context of a project sponsored by the nearly all-white local arts agency, this meant building up trusting relationships through small preliminary projects and through many conversations.

The original planners of the project envisioned the installation as celebrating water. From a white European perspective, they conceived of water as an economic resource. Through the development of irrigation systems, they had transformed water into wealth. The Native American community, however, referred to water in spiritual terms, as a God-given blessing, to be ritually sipped before meals. Tsen explained his role in relation to this difference in the following way:

Without arguing, we could add more layers of meaning to the symbolic representations in the public plaza. While being true to the original planners' desire for a public art installation of the highest quality, and celebrating water as a resource, we could create something cohesive around the idea of the circular movement of water. We could honor the Mexican community's contributions by focusing on labor, on actions, rather than on the products of that labor. And we could honor the Native American sensibilities by emphasizing nature itself. As an artist, I came with no dogma. I always sought to incorporate each new perspective, layering meaning upon meaning and representing the ambiguity of things. The installation as a whole and its various elements must be attractive enough to catch the eye of those who pass by, but the viewer must bring himself or herself to it. The more people engage with it, the more they get out of it.

The work conveys a quality of acceptance and fullness. Each person's and each community's feelings were accepted and valued. In this sense, there is a quality of forgiveness in the piece. Each element is viewed differently because it is in the context of the others, held within a series of concentric circles marked by the objects and by a path with benches that surrounds them.

The flowing water can be taken as a cleansing agent that could salve the splits and disdain the hurt that has inscribed the relationships among the communities of the region. In this sense, it is a symbol of reconciliation. The possibility of reconciliation is something that the artist must imagine. The form of the artwork must hold all of the elements in relation, and then it must become invisible so that people aren't noticing the form but perhaps just focusing on the object within one window. Because of the spirit of the piece, barriers are opened up. And because of the intensity of effort that has gone into the creation of the work, viewers can grasp the meaning with a relatively small amount of energy.[22]

Drama

One of the most important capacities required for coexistence and reconciliation is the ability to imagine the experiences of the "other" and in particular to empathize with the suffering of one's enemy. In Western literary and philosophical tradition, the correlation between drama and literature and the development of the human capacity for empathy is long-standing, having been articulated by Aristotle in his *Poetics*.

Drama (and literature) can be crafted to help us understand ourselves and our adversaries and the reality of our interdependence, in part because of the emotional space created by our awareness that we are viewing a "representation" of events and not the real events themselves. This space, which has not only emotional but also cognitive, psychological, and spiritual dimensions, is created when we apprehend a situation having stepped back from our own interests and purposes. Artists can make use of this space to help us understand things we have resisted knowing and to comprehend in ways that lead to ethical action.

The International Playback Theatre Network (IPTN) is an organization that uses the resources of theater to promote understanding, community, and coexistence. Lesley Yalen, program assistant at the Coexistence Initiative at Brandeis University, describes an IPTN workshop held at Search for Common Ground:

> Our group consisted of about fifty conflict resolution and coexistence practitioners from around the world—Burundi, Angola, Liberia, Sierra Leone, Macedonia, Ukraine, the Middle East, and the United States. The theater troupe consisted of five actors. The actors asked if anyone had a story to share. A young man from Burundi who did coexistence and reconciliation work with youth in Bujumbura raised his hand. He came up and sat in the "storyteller's seat" next to one of the actors. The actor asked him, "How does your story begin?"

> He told us about the work he had done to bring peace and reconciliation to his country. He talked about the delicate and tenuous nature of the relationships that had been built between Hutu and Tutsi. He told us about the day when there were rumors that the market in Bujumbura had been set on fire and that it was an ethnically motivated act and another round of conflict was likely to break out. He said that he wanted to check it out for himself; he was afraid that all of his hard work was collapsing before his eyes. Almost breathless, he described how getting to the market was very difficult because parts of the city were blocked off. When he arrived at the market, it was in flames. His mother called him on his cellular phone and cried, "The market is burning, the market is burning. Come home! There will be trouble!"

> However, he was determined to learn what was really going on and eventually discovered that the fire was not set as an act of ethnic hatred: some thugs with no political agenda had set it. Immediately he began calling the network of Hutu and Tutsi with whom he had been working. One by one, he spread the

word: "The Hutu did not do this. The Tutsi did not do this. This is nothing more than a common crime. Do not retaliate." To both sides, in a frenzied state of urgency, he did his best to stop the rumors' dangers of ethnic nationalism.

While the young man was telling his story, the actor from the theater troupe listened intently, prompting him with only one question: "And how does your story end?" The young man responded: "My group of Hutu and Tutsi youths did not fall apart." After he finished speaking, without any consultation, the theater troupe began to dramatize his story. The actors portrayed this story with a beautiful blend of literalism and abstraction. It was literal enough that we recognized everything we had just heard—the emotion, tone, pitch, and events. We saw the whole process, from the reconciliation work to the news of the fire to the frantic search for the truth to the panicked call from the mother to the realization of the truth and finally to the urgent attempt to stem the rising tide of anger and to stop the cycle of violence before it began.

The dramatization was also abstract in that it took the man's story to a deeper and more symbolic level. We recognized him in their portrayal, although he was not played by a man for the entire skit. We recognized the market and the city, though they only had five people with which to construct it. They did things symbolically—focusing on the essences of characters and events—but were true to the emotions he expressed. The audience was even brought into the scene as the fire. On cue, we raised our arms and made whooshing and crackling noises as one of the actors ran among us in fear and despair.

I am sure that everyone in the room was deeply moved. The most powerful part of this experience was observing my Burundian colleague as he watched the actors depict his story. He sat on the edge of his chair the entire time. His eyes were wide open and his mouth agape. He looked completely in awe. Afterward, when they asked him how it had been for him to watch their performance, he nodded his head and said: "You got it, exactly."

It was amazing that by listening, these actors were able to symbolize and artistically express his experience for him. They were able to dramatize it in a way that did not retraumatize him or call his decisions into question. Rather, they validated his experience and allowed the rest of us to experience a day in the life of a peacemaker in Burundi.[23]

Oral Narratives Mediated Through Art Forms

Eliciting oral histories is another way to facilitate communication across differences and to strengthen communities. During the 1980s, I directed a community organization devoted to strengthening intergroup relations through the processes of oral history and the arts. Our projects were based on the theory that through a sharing of life stories, community people would come to feel a sense of pride in their own cultures, appreciate their commonalities, and acknowledge (and perhaps begin to address) the dynamics of racial oppression and ethnic hatred that kept their communities divided from each other.

Artists, scholars, educators, and community people collaborate to make murals, drama, and curricular projects in multiethnic American neighborhoods, prisons, public housing developments, and teen empowerment programs. Our program was adopted by a rural women's association in Belize to strengthen a coalition of poor, rural Mayan, Garifuna, and Creole women involved in craft production and small-scale sustainable development projects. Adult literacy workers in Toronto adapted the model, and I used it in coexistence sessions with Arab and Israeli teens at Seeds of Peace.

The model emphasizes the importance of listening. Training sessions in oral history focus on helping people develop the quality of listening that is necessary to help people tell the stories they need and want to tell. By telling stories, cultivating thoughtful listening, and deploying artistic symbols that reach beneath people's defenses, oral history can help people reclaim dignity, imagine the possibility of forgiveness, and perceive the humanity of others.

As a community oral historian, I once joined Jane Sapp as part of a team of cultural workers leading a weeklong cultural camp for children and teens from the African American, Vietnamese, and white communities of Biloxi, Mississippi. The intention of the camp was to strengthen the community and to address racial tensions that were emerging as the African American community watched the Vietnamese newcomers leap ahead of them economically, supported by financial assistance for refugee resettlement from the U.S. government. The mornings were spent sharing songs and listening to tradition bearers from all three communities. We visited a Vietnamese shrimping boat, for instance, and listened to members of the African American clergy describe their experiences in the civil rights movement. It was my responsibility to lead a daily story-sharing session for the teenagers, all of whom were African American. Their Vietnamese and white agemates were busy at summer jobs, opportunities denied to them by patterns of racial discrimination in employment.

Twelve teenage African American residents of Biloxi shared stories with each other about being mistrusted or humiliated by white teachers at school and also about incidents in stores owned or operated by either white or Vietnamese adults. On the last day of the camp, before an audience of their parents and community leaders, the teens presented a dramatic scene based on their stories. It was set in a public school classroom. Each of the twelve performers wore a sign indicating the race of the person he or she represented. Kim, who portrayed a white teacher, set the scene by instructing the class to take out papers and pencils for term exams.

The teens portrayed five incidents in which the teacher discriminated against the African American and Vietnamese students in the classroom, all of which were based on their stories. In the first incident, the teacher invites the students to move around the classroom to do anything they need to do prior to the test. After allowing a white girl to get up to discard some trash, the teacher admonishes Dandrea, a black student, for being out of her seat. She demands that Dandrea retrieve her paper from the trash. "I ain't no trash digger," Dandrea refuses. "Now you go and sit down," instructs the teacher. In an aside to the audience, Dandrea holds her own: "I'm sitting down because I *want* to." In another incident, the white teacher accuses Darius of cheating. She tears his paper and sends him to the office—all enacted while two white students are visibly and audibly comparing answers with each other without consequence. Darius's body jolts with a frustration that is all too real. As Darius marches offstage, the teacher offers help to a white student while denying it to a Vietnamese student and then allows a white girl extra time to complete her exam, making excuses for her when the other students complain.

In the final moments of their presentation, the students portray a scene that was not anticipated. Through an invention of their imagination, they collectively confront the teacher, pointing out the unfairness of her prejudicial attitudes and racist behavior. And then, with large generosity of spirit, they imagine the white teacher as someone capable of reconciliation. She apologizes to Dandrea in front of the class and offers Darius the opportunity to take the exam again. She ends the play promising, "In the future, I'll treat everyone equally." As the teenagers leave the stage, Darius says under his breath, "We should take this play to the school board."

Before the cultural camp, the African American teenagers in Biloxi understood the dynamics of racism that pervaded their lives. They were also impressive storytellers, exploiting the vibrant colors and syncopated rhythms of African American vernacular to full advantage. What they were missing was support to take each other's stories seriously and the opportunity to understand their stories as part of a larger whole. The dramatic scene provided a structure that called for a resolution and an adult audience capable of and willing to take them seriously. Had their performance been part of an ongoing program or even a monthlong program, perhaps Darius would have led his friends in performing for the school board.

In any case, these teenagers from Biloxi now have in their repertoire of imaginable responses to the racism they encounter in their daily lives the possibility of supporting each other to confront racist behavior firmly but nonviolently, even when they experience it at the hands of an authority figure. They and their audience also have an image of a white person capable of apologizing, of committing herself to changing her racist ways. Hopefully, these constructs of their imaginations will serve them well in the future and enhance the quality of coexistence they are able to construct with their white and Vietnamese neighbors.

Reflections

The examples cited in this chapter illustrate how engagement with artistic forms and processes can help members of communities transcend narratives of powerlessness, imagine the experiences of the other, create expressions of their common humanity, and begin to develop metanarratives that can embrace particularities in a coherent and accepting whole. Yet the work can be difficult and trigger miscommunication and intense feelings.

In 1988, I collaborated with Feryal Abbasi Ghnaim, a Palestinian American colleague, fabric artist, and collector of Palestinian embroidery patterns. Together we created a project we called A Passion for Life: Stories and Folk Arts of Palestinian and Jewish Women. It was designed to use the Oral History Center's model to strengthen relations between the Jewish and Palestinian diaspora communities in the greater Boston area. The project involved interviewing eight folk artists and tradition bearers from the two communities and creating an exhibition of their artwork (embroidery, family photographs, children's toys, ritual objects, and the like) accompanied by written excerpts of their stories.

It proved to be more difficult than Feryal and I ever could have imagined at the outset. Sometimes it seemed to be little more than a snarl of ethical dilemmas, miscommunication, demanding relationships, and intense emotions. We struggled over language—terms like *1948, Holocaust, Israel,* and *Palestine. Holocaust* stimulated long and difficult discussions. We sometimes hurt each other in spite of our best intentions. At times both Feryal and I felt pressured by members of our families and communities to withdraw from the project. Key people from both communities chose not to participate or, in a couple of cases, backed out at the last minute. When I look back, it seems like a miracle that we ever managed to bring the eight women's stories under one roof, even for just a couple of months.

As I look back over A Passion for Life, I see an enormous landscape, still partly clouded by fear and confusion. It seems that what we were attempting was actually impossible. But all along, there were moments when the terrain would shift, creating new contours of possibility. These openings enlarged our imagination and deepened our yearning for reconciliation. These were the moments that sustained us in our work. One time Feryal and I were presenting at an open house. She showed her beautiful tapestry of a Palestinian woman, dressed in a traditional embroidered dress, holding aloft a large white dove. In the bird's beak is an envelope, carrying the following message:

> Women of the world: Women love peace to raise their children in, so why don't you make peace your number one goal? I as a Palestinian know intimately that there are two kinds of peace. (1) Peace that is built on the bodies of those brutalized and murdered to silence their calls for their just rights; (2) peace which comes from understanding a people's suffering, sitting down with them to genuinely solve and resolve their problems, so that justice and equality can be the code of the land, not death and suffering. Why don't we, women, raise our voices high and strong in the service of true peace to preserve our children, our future as human beings? I ask you to support my call for true peace for my people.

> We are not subhumans. We are people with history and civilization. We are mothers and fathers and children. We have had enough killing and diaspora. I smuggled my dreams in my hidden

wishes and crossed the ocean in hope for peace, for my Palestinian sisters who lost their children in wars and who have been widowed at an early age. I ask you for true peace for my people.[24]

I followed Feryal by reading an excerpt from the autobiography of Heda Margolius Kovaly in which she recounts the events of her life in Prague from 1941 through 1968:

> Three forces carved the landscape of my life. Two of them crushed half the world. The third was very small and weak, and, actually, invisible. It was a shy little bird hidden in my rib cage an inch or two above my stomach. Sometimes in the most unexpected moments the bird would wake up, lift its head, and flutter its wings in rapture. Then I too would lift my head because, for that short moment, I would know for certain that, somewhere beyond the line of my horizon there was life indestructible, always triumphant.
>
> The first force was Adolf Hitler; the second was Iosif Stalin. They made my life a microcosm in which the history of a small country in the heart of Europe was condensed. The little bird, the third force, kept me alive to tell the story.[25]

When I finished reading Kovaly's words, Feryal leaned over and pointed to the dove in her tapestry. "You see," she whispered, "it's the same bird."[26]

Notes

1. G. Bachelard, "Introduction," *The Poetics of Space,* trans. M. Jolas (Boston: Beacon Press, 1994), pp. xviii–xix.
2. Bachelard, "Introduction," p. xix.
3. V. Volkan, "An Overview of Psychological Concepts Pertinent to Interethnic and/or International Relationships," in V. Volkan, D. Julius, and J. Montville (eds.), *The Psychodynamics of International Relationships,* Vol. 1: *Concepts and Theories* (San Francisco: New Lexington Press, 1990), p. 38.
4. H. Stein, "The Indispensable Enemy and American-Soviet Relations," in Volkan, Julius, and Montville, *Psychodynamics of International Relationships,* p. 71.
5. R. Moses, "Self, Self-View, and Identity," in Volkan, Julius, and Montville, *Psychodynamics of International Relationships,* p. 53.
6. Stein, "Indispensable Enemy," pp. 86–87.
7. People's aesthetic sensibilities have been shaped by engagement with different expressive forms. In designing coexistence efforts, consider the aesthetic sensibilities and symbolic references of the cultures involved.
8. I have not included examples of film and media projects, although they also lend themselves to coexistence projects. Readers may consider *Peace of Mind,*

in which Palestinian and Israeli teens document their communities on video (information available at http://www.global-action.org), and *Long Night's Journey into Day*, an intimate inquiry into South Africa's Truth and Reconciliation Commission (information available at http://www.irisfilms.org/longnight).

9. C. Geertz, "Blurred Genres: The Refiguration of Social Thought," *American Scholar*, Spring 1980, pp. 165–179.

10. The importance of this point can hardly be overstated. Further elaboration on the importance of linking coexistence efforts to local knowledge and local cultural practices can be found in the work of John Paul Lederach, who emphasizes the importance of "elicitive strategies." This is also emphasized in the work of Search for Common Ground, a conflict resolution organization based in Washington, D.C. See J. Marks and E. Fraenkel, "Working to Prevent Conflict in Macedonia." [http://www.sfcg.org/Info/Articles/macedonia_negotjrnl.htm].

11. Kandasamy Sithamparanathan, interview, Nov. 1998. To my knowledge, the exchanges with Sinhalese counterparts described at the end of this passage have not taken place. However, the sessions as planned would have drawn on one of the particular attributes inherent in various art forms: communication by means other than the use of verbal expression.

12. Simon Lichman, personal communication, Aug. 2002. For further information, see "Building Bridges: The Experiential Approach." [http://www.us-israel.org/jsource/bridges/bbcontent.html].

13. Simon Lichman, personal communication, Aug. 2002.

14. Simon Lichman, personal communication, Aug. 2002.

15. J. Sapp, "Global Partnership for Education," International Center for Ethics, Justice, and Public Life, Brandeis University, Waltham, Mass., 2001, p. 7.

16. The song, "If Only We Believe," was written by participants in the Global Partnership for Education Institute, Brandeis University, June 2001, with direction from Jane Sapp. The lyrics are as follows:

The sky is full of dreams
The ground is full of struggle
Our voices set us free
If only we believe

The nightmare seems endless
And shadows fill our hearts
But we reach for possibility
And the courage to break free

CHORUS:
THROUGH STRUGGLE WE REACH THE SKY
TOGETHER WE DREAM OF JOY
WITH COURAGE WE GIVE OUR VOICE
FOR JUSTICE! FOR PEACE! FOR LIFE!

Within us all we have the power
To make a better future

To go forward for our children
We can learn! We can grow! We can love!

CHORUS

The sky is full of dreams
The ground is full of struggle
Our voices set us free
If only we believe . . .
If only we believe . . .
. . . If only we believe . . .

17. Jane Sapp, personal communication. For a detailed description of the application of Sapp's model in three different communities, see International Center for Ethics, Justice, and Public Life, "Global Partnership for Education," Sept. 10, 2001. [http://www.brandeis.edu/ethics/publications_resources/publications/GPE.pdf].
18. Wen-ti Tsen, "Artist's Report on the Project," unpublished report, Dec. 2000, p. 1.
19. Wen-ti Tsen, "Artist's Report on the Project," p. 1.
20. Wen-ti Tsen, personal communication, Feb. 2002.
21. Wen-ti Tsen, personal communication, Feb. 2002.
22. Wen-ti Tsen, personal communication, Apr. 2002.
23. Lesley Yalen, personal communication. For further information about IPTN, go to the Web site at http://www.playbacknet.org/iptn/index.htm.
24. Courtesy of Feryal Abbasi Ghnaim.
25. H. M. Kovaly, Under a Cruel Star: A Life in Prague, 1941–1958, trans. H. Epstein and F. Epstein (New York: Holmes & Meier, 1996), p. 5.
26. A detailed account of A Passion for Life can be found in Cynthia Cohen, "Removing the Dust from Our Hearts: A Search for Reconciliation in the Narratives of Palestinian and Jewish Women," NWSA Journal, 1994, 6, 197–233.

Chapter Fourteen

Fostering Coexistence in Identity-Based Conflicts
Toward a Narrative Approach
Sara Cobb

Violence marks a place where words no longer fit, where words are inadequate to express the hatred that flows from and fuels stories of victimization. Violence is a form of interaction in a context where "they" deserve to be victimized for what they have done to us or might do to us. Violence is the breeding ground for more violence, an endless cycle of victimization and countervictimization. And in the process, hope dies, giving birth to fear and vengeance.

Violence, from this perspective, punctuates a given interpretation of a set of events; it arises from and valorizes a story about who did what to whom and why. Violence is a chapter in what Allen Feldman calls an "origin myth."[1] Such myths are stories about the past that account for the violence of the present and forecast a particular future; they justify violence in the present and in the future as they preserve and embellish the story of the origin of the vio-

Note: This chapter is based on a paper prepared for a conference on coexistence funded by the United States Institute for Peace. It grew out of interviews I conducted in Rwanda along with Cindy Burns, Laura McGrew, Carlos Sluzki, and Juergen Wintermeyer, all of whom contributed substantially to my understanding of the relationship between narrative and coexistence. The work in Rwanda was funded by UNHCR as part of the Imagine Coexistence project, under the direction of Martha Minow at Harvard Law School.

lence, which is never a function of the acts of the storyteller, the narrator, but always a result of the acts of the "other." Origin myths externalize responsibility for violence at the same time that they call for violence as a response to victimization.

But to say that violence is a function of an origin myth is not to say that victims necessarily know the myth that gave rise to violence against them. We have only to consider the question that thousands of Americans have asked since September 11, 2001: "Why do they hate us?" Tragically, and prophetically, we do not need to know the origin myth that compelled the hijackers to end their lives, taking along thousands of others, to counter with violence. No matter the origin—for many Americans, the story begins on September 11, 2001; for others, it may have begun with the occupation of the West Bank—the violence to come will function to anchor the origin myth *of* each side *for* each side, regardless of the fact that there is little or no knowledge of the other's story.

There are other times when one side knows the story of the other but is not aware of the threshold beyond which violence is inevitable. In Rwanda, radio broadcasts that blamed Tutsi for national hardships had been active for at least two years prior to the genocide in 1994. The Tutsi knew the story told by Hutu officials, but they may not have expected that one day their Hutu neighbors, uncles, and brothers-in-law would take up machetes and act on that story. They may have thought that the force of local and marital ties would militate against adoption of the "official story," but they were wrong. But just as the Tutsi were unprepared for the official story to be adopted and enacted locally, no doubt the Hutu themselves were, after the fact, surprised as well that they had written themselves, as avengers and protectors, into the official story, as instruments of that story. Although we like to think that we are in charge of language, of narrative, all too often it is in charge of us, the tellers. We are, from this perspective, actors in stories we did not make, most often unwitting participants in the perpetuation of origins myths.

Trapped by the internal integrity of stories, parties in conflict are subjected to cycles of reciprocal violence. And unless these stories are transformed or evolved, they retain their coherence, collecting "data" that confirm the myth as events unfold. If there is to be an end to the cycle of violence, if there is to be an opening for building new relationships, if there is to be an opportunity to anchor a new civil society, one where rival groups interact and are more integrated, these origin myths must lose their totalitarian grip; they must be opened to new information, new plots, new character roles, and new themes. Yet it is precisely because narrative in the form of origin myths provides the basis for *identity* that these myths are so resistant to change and hence to conflict resolution.

This chapter deepens the work of those who have described intractable conflicts as identity-based conflicts.[2] These theorists presume that violence is a function of the efforts to protect and consolidate identity, which in turn serves to maintain and nourish intragroup relations while increasing the social, cultural, political, and economic boundaries between groups.[3] However, there is little work in this tradition that elaborates the practice of narrative transformation that is core to the formation and transformation of identity in ethnic conflict. Some research has examined how dominant conflict narratives are anchored and reproduced in cultural symbols.[4] However, this work has not addressed the pragmatics of narrative change processes. Vamik Volkan does address the transformation of narratives that are core to ethnic conflict, but he does so from a psychoanalytic perspective, requiring long-term therapeutic interventions not centered in narrative analysis itself.[5] Linking narrative process to identity production and transformation, this chapter argues that narrative is the location for analysis, intervention, and evaluation of conflict and its evolution. Drawing on du Toit,[6] I explore the relationship between narrative and identity to assist both the design and the evaluation of interventions that foster coexistence. It is my intention to contribute a theoretical frame with very practical tools that NGOs and international agencies can use in their work on the ground as they engage in efforts to reduce violent conflict and rebuild civil society.

Narrative and Identity Performance in Social Networks: A Systemic Framework for Coexistence Practice

As du Toit and others[7] have noted, identity is reproduced in daily interaction, in social groups. In Rwanda, there is a women's cooperative called Dusohenye, composed of both Hutu and Tutsi, some 350 women who are widows, mothers, grandmothers, daughters, friends, coworkers, and teachers. Their roles are varied and their relational histories complex: some Tutsi women are family members of Hutu women whose husbands, fathers, uncles, or brothers killed the family members of the Tutsi members of this group. While the genocide anchors the Tutsi as victims of the Hutu, the identity narratives of these group members, and of the group as a whole, are much more fluid and fuzzy. They are not just Tutsi women; they are widows, and the narrative of that identity is core to their daily performance as individuals and group members as they work in the agricultural coop or teach classes or care for children or build houses. But even this core narrative is performed in a variety of ways and shifts according to the age of the women; for some, it is a badge of courage; for others, a cross to bear. Nonetheless, the women share a general origin myth in the community that anchors them, alongside an identity as widows, with the pain and suffering related to being women, postgenocide. The result is that while there are core ethnic identities in this group—that is, they are branded by the story of the genocide—it is not a monolithic identity for either Hutu or Tutsi because of what du Toit calls "personal identity" that constantly destabilizes a dominant ethnic (origin) narrative.

Personal identities flourish where multiple kinds of narrative performance are permitted—specifically, movements between narrative positions as characters, as narrators, and as listeners. In the Dusohenye group, women developed a ritualized practice of sharing their suffering or "mourning together," which is what the name of the organization itself signifies. They adopted positions as narrators, telling their stories; as listeners, as others told of suffering; and as characters, in the reciprocal stories that were told about community life, before and after the genocide. If we follow du Toit's notion of identity as narrative performance, this group has inoculated itself against any uniform or dominant ethnicity narrative that could be pushed down from political elites who might want, as the Hutu government did, to consolidate power by fomenting a *simple* origin myth where historical violence is unidirectional and victimization is a call to revenge. In fact, it could be argued that it is when the personal identity, forged in daily interaction, across social networks, collapses into the singular ethnic identity, forged from the origin myth, that ethnic conflict will erupt. From this perspective, it is not only the presence of the origin myth that is predictive of cycles of violence but also the absence of variation in roles from which to perform and enact narratives, for it is that variation that supports what du Toit calls "narrative imagination":

> If identity is understood as the specific stories in which we live, then a large part of that identity has to do with the imagination. Not only do we imagine stories told to others about us or stories directed at us (the other has a virtual or imaginative presence in us), but also does each story in which we live and make sense of our particular lives contain some reference to future possibilities? As the mask of Greek theatre enables actors to participate in alternative identities, so does imagination prevent us from becoming victims of the dominant or current stories in which we live? Built into every story is the possibility of transcendence, the hope of something more that is immediately before us—the power of the creative and transformative imagination.[8]

We can see that narrative imagination is important in the maintenance of personal identity, as a challenge to ethnic identity, but how is it fostered? What conditions would favor this imagination? Again, turning to du Toit, she argues that this imagination is fostered by and through the presence of irony, in which speakers not only present their views but take what Mikhail Bahktin called "sideways glances" at their own or others' views.[9] These "glances" destabilize the frames for interpreting any story and leave us, as the audience, open to multiple interpretations of that story. They effectively present the voice of the other inside the story that is being narrated. The layering of meaning resulting from irony multiplies interpretive frameworks, for irony is a "wink" to listeners that there is more to the story than meets the eye or ear. As multiple interpretations for any story are permitted, the likelihood increases that personal identities will become more complex as people "play" with roles, narrator positions, and listening or witnessing functions. Again, this complexity militates against the uniformity of a given origin myth and in that way helps a community break the cycles of violence that are driven by singular, linear origin myths.

However, it is not only irony that increases the complexity of narrative performance; reflection does as well. Like irony, reflec-

tion brings to light the frames that are in use, the ways of understanding that are embedded in practice. However, unlike irony, reflection is most often directed by the narrator at the narrator's own
frames—speakers reveal areas of their story where *they* find the
story itself problematic or wonderful, questionable or worthy of
celebration. For example, when I asked a group of the leaders of
Dusohenye how they were able to maintain group coherence when
there were both Tutsi and Hutu women present in the group, they
told me a story about how they came together, sharing their stories
of suffering, noting that both Hutu and Tutsi women had suffered.
As part of this story, the speaker built in segments where she re-
counted her own uncertainty and fear when the group began, but
then she explained how she had learned from listening to others.
This reflection of her uncertainty functioned as a story that framed
the first story, as a reflection that established the character of the
speaker and her relation to others. As she told this story, other wom-
en nodded in approval and began to both smile and to whisper to
each other, elaborating how they too were uncertain in the beginning and they too had learned and grown. Both reflection and
irony are performances that increase narrative imagination, com-
plicate interpretive frames, and multiply speaker and listener roles
and positions. If, as du Toit has argued, narrative imagination demands attention to the role of the aesthetic in ethic conflict (the
form of the story), the "aesthetic can be . . . regarded as prerequisite
for the ethical: without a notion of . . . how things could be, there
is no possibility of saying how things should be."[10] I would go even
further and argue that the aesthetics of narrative identity performance is equivalent to the ethics of narrative performance; that is,
the nature of the stories that are told is a measure of the ethics of
the social context, for they forestall or permit variation, permuta-
tion, and progressive diversification of the social network. They either move social worlds toward emancipation and learning, building
connections to others, or they contribute to fear, repression, and social isolation.

In this vein, Carlos Sluzki has argued that some stories are "better" than others because they permit the evolution of the system,
while "worse" stories lead to the production of conflicts and the
maintenance of symptoms.[11] Given that story content is related to
the performance, I would like to extend du Toit's thesis, using

Sluzki's work, toward the construction of some guidelines for identifying better and worse stories or differentiating stories that increase narrative imagination from those that consolidate uniform ethnic frames for action or stories that foster coexistence from those stories that favor origin myths that fuel violence.

From Origin Myths to Coexistence Narratives

Stories based on origin myths are problematic not because they are not true or because they misrepresent the "facts" but because they are very "thin"—they are a shorthand version of history that is condensed precisely so it can authorize violence toward others. Extending the work of Sluzki, origin myths can be seen to have the following characteristic content in four specific areas:

Time

- The stories are focused on the past and are not likely to contain a description of the future.
- Descriptions of the past are more vivid and developed than those of the present.

Characters

- There are few roles or characters.
- The characters that are included are starkly portrayed as either victims (self, in-group) or victimizers (others).

Causality

- The stories feature a linear logic that attributes responsibility to the acts of the other, leading to passive, reactive positions for the speaker.

Values and Themes

- Overarching themes include hopelessness, suffering, justice, rights, vengeance, and in-group loyalty.

These features characterize origin myths. As they are performed, they call for *action* against the others and passive *reaction* to local conditions where often urgent needs for survival preempt opportunities for narrative imagination. Theoretically, the "flatter" the narrative, the fewer people will be engaged in the production of what du Toit calls "personal identity." Local variation of ethnic identity diminishes as the simplicity of the origin myth increases. In summary, I am arguing not only that there is a link between narrative performance and ethnic violence but also that the performance of personal identity, enhanced by reflection and irony, in local conditions, in multiple interactions, across sectors of the social network, decreases the control of the origin myth.

If these features of origin myths are indeed consistent with the lack of diversity in social networks, the insularity of intragroup relations, and the absence of cooperative intergroup interaction, then these features could be used as indicators of the continued threat of violence. Indeed, it would be possible to create a conflict assessment tool by assessing the narratives across multiple sectors of society (health, education, policy, business, social groups, artistic groups), as well as narratives at different levels (local, regional, national) to determine where there were thicker or thinner narratives, which would in turn provide a logic for initiating interventions: the more narrative imagination, the more established the conditions for coexistence; the less narrative imagination, the greater the need for intervention to support the development of coexistence.

In contrast, and again adapting the research on family narratives developed by Sluzki, the following characterize stories that signal the presence of narrative imagination and anchor a culture of coexistence:

Time

- The narratives contain accounts not only of the past but also of the present and the future.
- The present and the future are more richly described and figure more prominently than the past.

Characters

- There is a diverse array of characters in the narrator's accounts of his or her relation to others.

- The boundaries between victims and victimizers are blurred as "victims" transform themselves into "survivors" and transform victimizers into characters to be pitied for a host of historical, moral, and social reasons that are displayed in the narrative.
- The characters exhibit care for others, even those in groups or communities with which they are in conflict.

Causality

- Circular logic connects the actions of the narrator to the actions of others such that responsibility and agency are not externalized.

Values and Themes

- Overarching themes include hope, charity, justice, growth and development, participation, and learning.

Again, drawing on du Toit, we can hypothesize that these narratives emerge when there are interactions that allow for the expansion of particular and personal identity, rather than the uniform ethnic identity often mandated from above. Both irony and reflection are signs of, and generative of, these narratives. Moving from why to how, it becomes important to learn to foster coexistence, personal identity, and narrative imagination as a *method* for doing development, peacekeeping, or emergency shelter work in contexts where there has been identity-based conflict.

Thus origin myths, which reduce the proliferation of personal (contextualized) identity, have distinctive features that can be used both as predictions of violence, as dimensions for intervention, and as features for assessment of aid and development projects. However, as narrative is itself a reflexive phenomenon—talking about the story changes the story—assessment aimed at "discovering" or "assessing" origin myths would also function as intervention into those myths. As du Toit and many others have pointed out,[12] if our social worlds are a function of the stories we tell and perform, then exploration of those stories serves inevitably to elaborate them in new directions.[13] Furthermore, as narrative is itself a closed, coherent system, changes to any portion of a story generate changes in the entire system of meaning; thus conversations with people about the future, about the characters involved, or about core themes alter the meaning of the whole narrative. And it is this conversational practice, as a practice intended to increase narrative imagination, that I am suggesting is at the core of fostering coexistence.

By way of illustration, I describe two techniques that can be used to intervene in narrative performance to alter the stories that are told as a *way of working toward coexistence* rather than as a set of discrete projects that would be fostered.

Narrative Intervention and Evaluation: Fostering Performance of Coexistence

Narrative transformation has been the subject of much attention in the family therapy and organizational change literature and more recently in the mediation literature.[14] These arenas of narrative research are founded on the theoretical tenets of social constructionism and have led to the development of narrative intervention technologies such as reframing, positive connotation, negative explanation, circular questions, reflective questions, appreciative inquiry, and externalization. Here I describe two: circular questions and appreciative inquiry.

Circular Questions: A Technology for Fostering Narrative Imagination

Circular questioning is a technology that was developed in the 1980s in Milan, Italy, by systemic family therapists. As described and elaborated by other researchers,[15] circular questions create "news of difference" or new dimensions of difference. They ask for comparisons to be made along dimensions provided by the question itself. The comparisons can be temporal, calling for distinctions between time 1 and time 2, for example: *If I were to ask you how this crisis differs from the last one, what would you tell me?* or *From five years ahead, looking back on this time, what will you be able to see from there that you cannot see from where you are now?* They could be characterological: *Who in your group has seemed best able to manage the stress? How are they different from or similar to others in your group?* They could be relational: *If I were to ask your friend how this crisis has changed you, what would your friend tell me? If I were to stand in the shoes of the others, what one thing do you think they would want me to convey to you, something that you think they think you do not understand? How could you signal to them that you do understand?* These kinds of comparison questions "upload" new information into the story, and if this information is grounded in subsequent rounds of conversations, it will have a "shelf-life" longer than the conversation itself. This approach to narrative transformation follows the principles of chaos theory—the "butterflies" let loose in a given conversation influence future conversations in ways that we cannot predict; however, as long as the elements lean in the direction of the positive transformation associated with narrative imagination or coexistence, they will have a tendency to yield positive changes over time. Furthermore, as these questions lead to reflective practice, they support the emergence of a culture of reflection.[16] This, I suggest, breeds coexistence.

As du Toit has noted, ethnic identity is often constructed as a set of binary opposites (hardworking versus lazy, open versus sneaky), and the "flatter" the narrative, the less complex the system of differences. Circular questions open narrative to new dimensions of difference and are therefore extremely useful for fostering narrative change and imagination. For example, people engaged in identity-based conflict assign legitimacy to themselves along the same dimensions as they use to delegitimize the others: "We are hardworking; they are lazy" or "We never lied about what we were doing, but they have lied all along, sneaking rather than working in the open." Questions that open dimensions in affirmative directions will yield positive transformations over time:

- Toward temporal complexity: *I understand that you feel as though you have been cheated; if we jump ahead five years from now, and you look back on this time, what do you think you will have learned that will help you get through this, something that you would like perhaps to pass on to your son?* This question builds in a future orientation as a frame for understanding the present.
- Toward characterological complexity: *You have indicated that your daughter (or mother) is very sad from all these losses, but she keeps on going somehow. Do you have an explanation for that? What does this reflect about her spirit?* This question seeks to add another dimension to the traits that are reflected about the relative by the speaker, something beyond sadness.

- Toward causal complexity: *If I were to ask the others to name a couple of things that you folks did to really push their buttons, what might they tell me?* This question makes the implicate connection in the action-reaction cycle.
- Toward thematic complexity: *We have been talking here about some basic needs for survival, but I am very impressed that you have already survived—it must be more than luck, true?* This question seeks to open a new theme, beyond the one centered on survival.

Although the answers to circular questions cannot be predicted, neither do they have to be in order to be productive of narrative imagination or narrative transformation. If a shift in the narrative takes place on any of the dimensions, it will, over time, cause shifts in the narrative system as a whole. However, for a narrative shift to endure, it must be elaborated by more than the narrator—it must include the others with whom they regularly converse, the people in their network with whom they interact. Following this logic, narrative interventions are group interventions, not individual (therapeutic) sessions designed to promote individual healing. This, along with different predicates for the relationship between the intervener and the individuals in the community, separates the use of a narrative method in development, aid, and peacekeeping work from therapeutic efforts to promote individual healing.

Appreciative Inquiry: Fostering Narrative Transformation and Imagination

The second intervention strategy I offer for promoting narrative change is appreciative inquiry (AI). Developed by organizational change experts,[17] this mode of inquiry begins with the "heliotropic principle," which presumes that systems evolve toward the most positive image or description they have of themselves. This means that if systems evolve in concert with the descriptions they make of themselves, they will in fact become as good as the descriptions they make of themselves. However, as Cooperrider and others have noted, most systems have negative or problem-based descriptions of themselves, and as a result, their potential for positive growth is limited. So if planners, strategists, designers, and interveners could begin to support the system to develop more positive descriptions of itself, it would be able to grow and develop. Applied to conflict contexts, identity-based groups that have been engaged (as victims or victimizers) are in narrative systems where the descriptions about those systems are problem-focused. The "half-empty glass" saps the strength and resilience of the community, whereas "full" descriptions emphasize aspects of the community that orient it toward its own positive growth. Again, these questions can been understood within the aesthetic or "better-formed" narrative framework:

- Regarding time: *If we look back over the last few years, there were certainly times where things were better rather than worse. Can you describe some features that characterize those times?*
- Regarding character: *What have you learned about yourself that has helped you survive these hard times?*
- Regarding causality: *Given the fact that you and the others do not engage in violence all the time, what do you do differently in those times?*
- Regarding values and themes: *Seeing that participation is key to the success of this project, what are some lessons about participation that we need to remember in order to maximize the participation of others in this project?*

As these questions indicate, fostering narrative transformation is a very active process of inserting new dimensions of difference that can contribute to the affirmation of individuals and the system in which they are embedded. This is counterintuitive to most conflict practitioners, who are trained to worry about "neutrality"; they try *not* to "influence" or "bias" their "target populations." However, from the perspective of social constructionism, it is not possible not to influence the evolution of meaning when in conversation with others. Any participation, even participation that seeks to not influence, influences. Accordingly, becoming highly aware of the mode of influence is better than pretending to have no influence. Consider the problem-solving approach so central to conflict resolution practice. For that process to be successful, its first task is the reformulation of the problem, for it is difficult to generate solutions from inside the problem that do not reactivate the problem. Managing the process affects the content.[18] Circular questions and appreciative inquiry provide methods for participating in conversations that evolve origin myths toward narratives that support coexistence.

A Narrative Approach to Evaluation

As controversial as it may be to some to challenge the goal of neutrality by intervening parties, I suggest that to aspire to "objectivity" in program evaluation is similarly problematic. In this, I join Donna Mertens[19] and others who critique traditional evaluation methods that use "indicators" selected by funders or implementing agencies rather than using input from "target populations" (hence the name "target population"). Thus it is assumed by funders and implementing agencies that the evaluation measures an objective phenomenon that is stable, if not fixed and observable. However, as Mertens and others have noted, the field is itself contingent and fluid, such that indicators that are created far from the field will not likely be adequate to capture the complexity of a given project. Better evaluation efforts use both qualitative and quantitative measures and involve the parties affected by the project in the creation of the indicators and the design of methods for assessment. This model, consistent with a Freirian model of participatory action research (PAR),[20] presumes that the individuals affected by the intervention should have a say in the development and evaluation of the project; it takes as a core notion that those who have been marginalized need to be included in the strategies intended to reduce their marginality.

There are many versions of PAR in the evaluation literature, including Participatory Monitoring and Evaluation (PME) and Participatory Appraisal of Needs and Development in Action (PANDA). Within these, the transformative model that Mertens advocates is consistent with the narrative approach to identity conflicts as it seeks to include the marginal through the process of evaluation itself, aiming to transform the social systems through the evaluation process. Evaluation could well adopt qualitative assessment of the stories associated with a given project or program as part of intervention and evaluation.

Jessica Dart provides an extremely interesting strategy for the use of narrative in an evaluation process in what she calls the "story approach" to evaluation.[21] As it seeks to include the voices of multiple sectors in the evaluation of narratives, it is consistent with the PAR models. Stories are collected from the field, interpretations are attached to the stories by the evaluation team, and then sets of these interpretations with attached stories are selected for further interpretations, which are then circulated back to the field for conversation. This qualitative evaluation method calls attention to the nature of the experiences and stories that are being told and helps project directors and funders stay focused on the meaning that people are making about themselves and others in the course of the project.

This focus on narrative in evaluation is consistent with efforts to use narrative in building coexistence. Interventions that collect the stories of participants and invite them to tell new narratives of their past and future can be assessed in light of the social networks people identify before and after the interventions, as well as measures of the complexity of the narratives people tell. More diverse and extensive social networks and more complex narratives each enhance prospects for coexistence among previously conflictual groups.

Conclusion

If violence fills up the conversational space where words reside, emptying that space of violence requires filling that space with meaningful conversation. In this chapter, I have argued that meaning is a function of the stories that are told and that meaningful identities are just that—filled with meaning and generated not by wholesale reproduction of the dominant ethnic identity story but by the interactions that occur in local, particular, everyday settings. Following du Toit's argument, the thin, shrill narratives that anchor ethnic hatred leave little room for the daily negotiations of relationships, histories, and values that comprise personal identity. The richer the particular local narratives, the more complex the narrative performance and, according to du Toit, the more ethical the narrative claims. This narrative perspective provides a lens for (1) understanding the production of identity as both personal *and* ethnic; (2) designing interventions that provide a method of working on development, aid, and peacekeeping projects, one that fosters coexistence; and (3) performing project evaluation while focusing attention on the meaning-making process. I offer this narrative approach to fostering coexistence as a way to come to our sense making and to attend to what people are doing, as a practice in narrative process.

Notes

1 A. Feldman, *Formations of Violence: The Narrative of the Body and Political Terror in Northern Ireland* (Chicago: University of Chicago Press, 1991).

2. See, for example, J. Rothman, *Resolving Identity-Based Conflicts in Nations, Organizations, and Communities* (San Francisco: Jossey-Bass, 1997); J. P. Lederach, *Building Peace: Sustainable Reconciliation in Divided Societies* (Washington, D.C.: United States Institute of Peace, 1997); V. Volkan, *Blood Lines: From Ethnic Pride to Ethnic Terrorism* (New York: Farrar, Straus & Giroux, 1997); and V. Volkan, "The Tree Model: A Comprehensive Psychopolitical Approach to Unofficial Diplomacy and the Reduction of Ethnic Tension," *Mind and Human Interaction*, 2000, *10*, 142–206.

3. See D. Druckman, "Nationalism, Patriotism, and Group Loyalty: A Social Psychological Perspective," *Mershorn International Studies Review*, 1994, *38*, 43–68; S. Cross and R. Rosenthal, "Three Models of Conflict Resolution: Effects on Intergroup Expectancies and Attitudes," *Journal of Social Issues*, 1999, *55*, 561–580; and J. Rothman and M. Olson, "From Interests to Identities: Toward a New Emphasis in Interactive Conflict Resolution," *Journal of Peace Research*, 2001, *38*, 289–305.

4. T. Katriel and A. Shenhar, "Tower and Stockade: Dialogic Narration in Israeli Settlement Ethos," *Quarterly Journal of Speech*, 1990, *76*, 359–380.

5. Volkan, *Blood Lines*.

6. L. du Toit, "Cultural Identity as Narrative and Performance," *South African Journal of Philosophy*, 1997, *16*(3), 85–93.

7. C. Mattingly, *Healing Dramas and Clinical Plots: The Narrative Structure of Experience* (New York: Cambridge University Press, 1998).

8. du Toit, "Cultural Identity," p. 90.

9. G. S. Morson and C. Emerson, *Mikhail Bakhtin: Creation of a Prosaics* (Stanford, Calif.: Stanford University Press, 1990), p. 155.

10. du Toit, "Cultural Identity," p. 90.

11. C. E. Sluzki, "Transformation: A Blueprint for Narrative Changes in Therapy," *Family Process*, 1992, *31*, 217–230; C. E. Sluzki, "The Better-Formed Story," unpublished manuscript, 1994.

12. For an excellent description of narrative practice in therapy, see M. White and D. Epston, *Narrative Means to Therapeutic Ends* (New York: Norton, 1990). For a description of the role of language in large-scale organizational change projects, see F. Barrett, G. Thomas, and S. Hocevar, "The Central Role of Discourse in Large-Scale Change: A Social Construction Perspective," *Journal of Applied Behavioral Science*, 1995, *31*, 352–372.

13. J. Freedman and G. Combs, *Narrative Therapy: The Social Construction of Preferred Realities* (New York: Norton, 1996); D. Maines and J. Bridger, "Narratives, Community, and Land Use Decisions," *Social Science Journal,* 1992, *29,* 363–380.

14. J. Winslade and G. Monk, *Narrative Mediation: A New Approach to Conflict Resolution* (San Francisco: Jossey-Bass, 2000).

15. K. Tomm, "Interventive Interviewing, Part 2: Reflexive Questioning as a Means to Enable Self-Healing," *Family Process,* 1987, *26,* 167–183; C. Fleuridas, T. Nelson, and D. Rosenthal, "The Evolution of Circular Questions: Training Family Therapists," *Journal of Marital and Family Therapy,* 1986, *12,* 113–127.

16. For a description of reflective practice, see C. Argyris and D. A. Schön, *Organizational Learning II: Theory, Method, and Practice* (Boston: Addison-Wesley, 1996).

17. D. Cooperrider, "Positive Image, Positive Action: The Affirmative Basis of Organizing," in S. Srivastva and D. Cooperrider (eds.), *Appreciative Management and Leadership* (San Francisco: Jossey-Bass, 1990); F. Barrett and D. Cooperrider, "Generative Metaphor Intervention: A New Approach for Working with Systems Divided by Conflict in Defensive Perception," *Journal of Applied Behavioral Science,* 1990, *26,* 218–239.

18. S. Cobb and J. Rifkin, "Practice and Paradox: Deconstructing Neutrality in Mediation," *Law and Social Inquiry,* 1991, *16,* 35–62.

19. D. Mertens, "Inclusive Evaluation: Implications of Transformative Theory for Evaluation," *American Journal of Evaluation,* 1999, *20,* 1–14.

20. See P. Freire, *Pedagogy of the Oppressed* (New York: Seabury Press, 1970); P. Freire, *Education for Critical Consciousness* (New York: Continuum, 1973); P. Freire, "Creating Alternative Research Methods: Learning to Do It by Doing It," in B. L. Hall, A. Gillette, and R. Tandon (eds.), *Creating Knowledge: A Monopoly?* (Toronto: Participatory Research Network, 1982).

21. J. Dart, "A Story Approach for Monitoring Change in an Agricultural Extension Project," paper presented at the Conference of the Association for Qualitative Research, Melbourne, Australia, July 1999. [http://www.latrobe.edu.au/aqr/offer/papers/JDart.htm].

Chapter Fifteen

The Art of the Possible
Parallelism as an Approach to Promoting Coexistence
Lauren Elizabeth Guth

As we have seen throughout this volume, work in postconflict communities represents a very special set of opportunities and challenges, both for the previously warring parties and for outsiders endeavoring to aid in peace work and community healing. The kinds of hatreds that lead to mass violence of the sort concerned here do not dissipate quickly, making recovery from conflict particularly difficult. For years after the end of fighting, the emotional, legal, and political environment may remain hostile to any productive efforts toward the eventual repair and reconciliation of the community. Although joint work feeding into the "contact hypothesis" described in Chapter One generally appears to be the most usual course of action for furthering healing, it is not always feasible. Humanitarian workers and local leaders attempting to promote coexistence in these areas often face intransigent populations that are unable or unwilling to work jointly with former combatants toward a common goal. Rather than abandoning hope when this situation arises, I believe there exists another approach that should be considered: a notion termed *parallelism*. This expression describes working through separate but harmonized processes that can allow slow progress toward coexistence to occur.

Following a discussion of the term *parallelism* and a description of the notion in practice today in the United States and Europe, I will explore the case for the use of parallel processes, using as an illustration the establishment of the customs program in the Republic of Bosnia and Herzegovina after the war in the early 1990s there. Although parallelism may not always be the preferred method of action, it can, when partnered successfully with a capable third-party mediator, be an effective approach to long-term coordination of efforts when the proximity of the conflict inhibits parties from working jointly.

Definition and Examples of Parallelism

For the purposes of this chapter, I define parallelism as the process of allowing former combatants or adversaries to work through separate but harmonized institutions, structures, trainings, or activities toward a common goal in the hope of promoting cooperation and, in the case of postconflict communities, eventual healing, reconciliation, and joint work.

When I first began speaking with members of some of the international organizations present in Bosnia about the viability of using parallel institutions to promote coexistence, many individuals were confused by my use of the expression "parallel structures." The language of the international community in the Balkans defined parallel structures as the illegal, unconstitutional arrangements developed by the various ethnic groups during the war and perpetuated in its aftermath. These separate structures were used to encourage and promote the division of all governmental functions and services along ethnic lines in the hope that each group would one day govern its own ethnically distinct territory or even nation. Furthermore, these arrangements provided nonaccountable sources of funding for the continued ethnic separatist movements within Bosnia. Most authorities were vehement about the problems that these unconstitutional structures cause in the rebuilding of the nation and the belief that they must be eliminated in order for the nation to grow.

In light of this generally accepted definition, it became necessary to refocus my thought and to clarify my own understanding of parallel structures. It is admittedly a difficult concept to define in this situation. Given the reticence with which the notion of parallelism was received in Bosnia, I began to imagine a definition referring to relations among legally recognized governmental units, such as cities or states, rather than ethnic or other self-defined groups. This definition does fit the work of the customs officials in Bosnia with whom I spoke but unfortunately leaves no room for an exploration of parallel work at the grassroots level. Though it is currently unclear whether parallelism would work at that level, it would be foolhardy to so narrowly define the notion and thus reject out of hand the possibility that community organizations, many of which are themselves monoethnic, could effectively promote coexistence using such an approach. I then thought that the concept could perhaps be defined as between organizations—be they governmental or communitarian—committed to encouraging peace and cooperation. Yet this set of parameters does not fit the experience of the customs officials in Bosnia. Most of those individuals, and the association as a whole, opposed cooperation with each other and the eventual consolidation of the separate customs offices into a single national organization. Only when a third party committed to promoting coexistence (in this case, the European Union officials seconded to assist in the development of Bosnia's customs program) is with the organizations in question does this definition work. We shall see that in cases where parallelism has been successful, a committed third party has been involved.

One example of the successful applications of parallel structures can be found in the uniform state laws in the United States. In 1889, recognizing the problems caused by wide variations in state laws, the American Bar Association (ABA) decided to work toward uniformity of the laws in particular areas where states rather than the federal government have jurisdiction. By 1912, all states had appointed representatives for the National Conference of Commissioners on Uniform State Laws. The commissioners work as one body to propose and draft statutes in specific areas of law deemed suitable for consistency, such as commercial, family, and health law. They also act as advocates in their home jurisdictions for the adoption of each of the uniform or model acts. This arrangement of parallel or harmonized state laws effectively preserves the integrity and autonomy of each state while also promoting cooperation between the interdependent states.[1]

The harmonization of laws by the constituent nations of the European Union is another example of parallelism in action. In a variety of policy areas, the member states have adopted legislation proposed by the European Commission designed to harmonize laws and reduce barriers throughout the EU. This approach has been applied to a spate of issues from human rights to travel, but it is perhaps most readily apparent in the formation of the single market in Europe. The European Commission worked to harmonize the health, environmental, and safety requirements of all member states in order to eliminate legal impediments to the free flow of goods between nations. Again, this arrangement preserves the sovereignty of the individual nations while also encouraging effective collaboration between the members.

In both of these cases, the bodies in question were generally desirous of cooperation and increased efficiency, recognizing themselves as bound constituents of a larger whole (United States or European Union). However, they were also anxious not to lose any semblance of autonomy or identity. It is because of this dichotomy that rules could not be imposed from above and that parallelism was the appropriate methodology.

It should be noted before proceeding further that in neither of these examples was massive violence an immediate precursor to the environments in which parallel structures were used. The U.S. Civil War was more than twenty years in the past by the time the ABA began pushing for uniformity, and the first incarnation of the European Union was formed in 1950, five years after the end of World War II. Though both areas had been racked by conflict in relatively recent memory, each had had some time to recover. This raises the question, Can parallelism be successful in areas more recently affected by violence?

Conditions for Success

Before examining a current postconflict situation, let us look at a few of the factors that appear to be necessary for success when employing the parallelism approach. Initial evidence suggests that there are three elements that contribute in varying degrees of importance: a committed third party, professionalism, and economics.

The existence of a capable, funded, and patient third party to act as the glue that binds the main participants together is critical to the health of any effort involving parallel structures or actions. It is also the most important of the factors. Parallelism is recommended precisely because previously conflicting parties are unable or unwilling to work together. A mediating individual or organization is needed to bridge the gap, to facilitate movement along parallel tracks. I believe it is also crucial that the intervening party be perceived as fair and unbiased in order to effectively cause positive change. In the examples cited so far, though the state law commissioners and European Commission members were drawn from and represented the various jurisdictions of the separate parties, as distinct bodies they were viewed as professional organizations without prejudice for or against any particular constituent or faction. This perception of impartiality allows the conflicting or constituent parties to accept more readily the advice and work offered by the intervening organization.

Professionalism on the part of all players is another important aspect of parallelism. Though not explicitly defined as such, the word *professional* usually connotes a certain lack of prejudice and a degree of open-mindedness. To behave as a professional is, in common understanding, to hold oneself to a higher standard of decorum, to rise above pettiness and act without bias. Peter Haas and Anne-Marie Slaughter have both explored the notion that substate actors (professional associations) can and do make productive contacts that transcend national or other governmental boundaries while circumventing the politics that often are detrimental to such interactions.[2] This is the standard of behavior needed in cases attempting to use parallelism for coexistence and healing purposes.

It is almost without question that economics can play a significant role in encouraging former combatants to cooperate to some degree. Money is a powerful motivator, especially in communities destroyed by violence and suffering from a lack of income-generating opportunities. Reflecting on his experience with the customs program in Bosnia, one official stated, "I do not necessarily believe that we have invented a magic formula, but it appears to work. Of course, this might be partly due to the fact that customs revenue is extremely important for the budgets, and despite all the turbulence in Bosnia, the importance of having relatively stable customs revenue collection is recognized by all relevant parties."[3]

There are a variety of other factors that would certainly affect the viability of any effort to employ parallelism in a divided community, including knowledge of participation of the other in the same effort, a larger political environment that encourages or discourages healing, and short-term or long-term movement toward societal integration. In the case of Bosnia, most of the factors worked in favor of positive change: the participants are aware that their efforts are undertaken in parallel, and the political environment, though sometimes contentious, has been influenced by a strong international presence working for peace. Furthermore, the international commitment is also a long-term one, recognizing that healing and reconciliation cannot be accomplished overnight. Each of these issues and their effects calls for further research.

Before examining how all of these factors helped contribute to the comparatively successful use of parallelism to establish the customs program in Bosnia, one caveat must be addressed. As noted previously, parallel structures can sometimes be viewed as a divisive tool used to forestall and perhaps prevent the eventual healing and reconciliation sought for the community in question. A complaint I heard more than once while pursuing research in Bosnia is that slow parallel action only serves to allow the previously conflicting factions to drag their feet in an effort to outwait the international community's patience and involvement. It is a concern worth noting, as it can be expected that many in a community just torn by violence are hesitant to embrace any semblance of forgiveness or normalization of relations, the very ideas represented by work designed to draw participants closer together.

Customs as a Case Study in Parallel Institutions

The General Framework Agreement for Peace in Bosnia and Herzegovina (GFAP), concluded in December 1995 after the disintegration of Communist Yugoslavia, created the Republic of Bosnia, a nation composed of two separate "entities" virtually equal in size and power. The Federation of Bosnia is composed primarily of Bosniak Muslims and Croats and makes up the southern and western parts of the state. Republika Srpska governs the northern and eastern edges of the state and is predominately Bosnian Serb territory. In order to secure accord from all interested parties for the peace agreement, the GFAP gave the central government of Bosnia fairly weak powers while endowing both entities with great powers and government functions.

A nation in its own right for the first time, the Republic of Bosnia faced a divided population, a scarred countryside, an inexperienced government, and a new legal structure. Many institutions in Bosnia had to be created from scratch after the war. Included in this was an international customs policy and administration. Bosnia and Herzegovina had participated in the customs program of Yugoslavia when it existed and loosely patrolled the flow of goods between it and the other provinces of the country. However, as part of Yugoslavia, Bosnia had had no external borders. The new fledgling nation had no experience with implementing, operating, and regulating a national customs program. At the time of the signing of the GFAP, what passed for a customs program in the country was in complete disarray. Three separate, ethnically based customs services existed in Bosnia. Growing out of the prewar customs program, these illegitimate parallel services had individually adapted in the early 1990s to support the war efforts of each of the major ethnic groups. No standardization of tariffs or regulation existed, and each group pursued its own customs policy, depositing revenues into separate ethnic customs accounts. Bosnian Muslim and Bosnian Croat "officials" within the new federation were generally unwilling to communicate with one another, and neither group had any communication with Serb "officials" in Republika Srpska. There was no way effectively and efficiently to collect customs revenue for the Republic of Bosnia.

Annex Four of the GFAP established the Constitution for the Republic of Bosnia and Herzegovina and addressed the issue of the nation's customs program. The new constitution gave the responsibility and power of setting Bosnia's customs policy to the national government.[4] It did not, however, specify which level of government would be responsible for the administration of that customs policy and as stated in Annex Four, Article III, paragraph 3(a): "All governmental functions and powers not expressly assigned in this Constitution to the institutions of Bosnia shall be those of the Entities." Customs administration thus became an entity-level power. With this separation, the national government set and policed the legal framework of the customs program while the regulation and enforcement of the policy—controlling the flow of goods, collecting customs duties, and so on—rested in the hands of the entity governments. This division of power in a national customs program is fairly unusual.

Most nations have one customs policy and one customs administration, both overseen by the same level of government.

The division of power and responsibility outlined in the GFAP for the customs program would prove to be both difficult to maneuver and completely inefficient. The distinction meant that both the Federation of Bosnia and Republika Srpska could legally have individual customs administration services and that they did not necessarily have to work together. It also meant that the loosely parallel customs structures that existed between the Bosnian Muslims and Bosnian Croats within the Federation were considered unconstitutional and illegal. If customs administration was an entity power, the two groups would have to work together to decide on a federation system of customs administration.

Amending and correcting the customs program in Bosnia was to be a tremendous task, and the European Union stepped in to help. The EU has one customs policy for all members but separate, though interdependent, customs administration offices in each member state. At the time, this arrangement most closely paralleled the situation in Bosnia, thus making it the organization best suited to assist the new nation in implementing and operating its customs program. In Sarajevo on April 1, 1996, the European Union signed a memorandum of understanding with the central government of Bosnia to create the Customs and Fiscal Assistance Office (CAFAO). CAFAO, funded by the European Commission, was created to help implement the customs and tax-related provisions of the GFAP and develop an efficient and effective customs policy.[5] Through CAFAO, twenty to forty European customs and tax officers work with both the state and entity governments to help provide management, legal structural, training, procedural, computer, and investigation support. According to senior officials, CAFAO "has an advisory role to those local authorities dealing with customs and tax" issues, at both the state and entity level.[6] Because of this "advisory role," CAFAO cannot make or issue any binding decisions. Suggestions or recommendations are put forward on a case-by-case basis and "only implemented with the acceptance and cooperation of our local counterparts," the entity and state government actors. The official continued, "Generally speaking, we try to work alongside customs officers at all levels in a counterpart capacity and discuss their daily problems and suggest solutions as required. Representatives from CAFAO management regularly meet with relevant management representatives from Bosnia and entity-level authorities in order to try to sort out the problems not resolved at a lower level. CAFAO-provided advice is not always implemented in the shape and form given, however; over time things seem to eventually change in the direction as recommended." The only exception to this rule lies in the realm of employment policy. CAFAO officials do possess a great deal of influence over the hiring and firing of customs officials.

CAFAO recognized the importance of both uniting the unconstitutional customs structures within the Federation and bringing the two entity services together in some form. It would be impossible to have an efficient, effective, and legal customs program without those changes, but the organization faced an extremely difficult environment. Ethnic hatreds, as well as hopes for the eventual dissolution of Bosnia into further ethnic enclaves, remained strong after the war. Bosnian Muslims and Bosnian Croats would oppose any joint work in the Federation, and getting any cooperation from the Bosnian Serbs in the Republika Srpska seemed next to impossible.

CAFAO began its work in Bosnia by working within the Federation to unite the unconstitutional ethnic customs structures that existed. The initial work focused on confidence building and cooperative measures within the Federation "to establish and consolidate a unified Federation Customs Administration, comprising Bosniaks and Bosnian Croats."[7] With the law on its side, CAFAO quickly proposed the establishment of a single Federation revenue account for all customs duties, to replace the ethnically distinct accounts that previously existed. The organization also encouraged the "abolishment of ethnic lines of communication and management" and the introduction of a nondiscriminatory employment policy.[8] Furthermore, CAFAO officers worked steadily with the Bosniak and Croat members of the Federation Customs Administration to encourage high standards of professionalism. Referring to the merging of the separate Bosnian Muslim and Bosnian Croat structures within the Federation, one senior CAFAO official stated, "CAFAO has never ignored the ethnic problems, but on the other hand, we have never accepted and have repeatedly claimed that these problems should not be allowed to [affect] the professionalism of customs work."[9] Operating with virtually no powers of enforcement, the European body acted as an able mediator, slowly and patiently bridging the gap between the two sides through a combination of advice, management, and encouragement.

In 1997, CAFAO turned its attention from focusing solely on the consolidation of the Federation structures to working with customs administrations in both entities. Prior to this time, officials from the Federation of Bosnia and the Republika Srpska had little or no contact with each other, and movement of import and export goods between the entities was extremely difficult. Relations were so bad that officials from the opposing offices would not come together for joint management meetings with CAFAO, refusing even to drive into the other entity for these encounters. Some of the international organization's initial work in bringing the entities together involved literally transporting customs officials from one office to the other for joint meetings because the local officials refused to make the effort of their own accord.

From that humble beginning in 1997, CAFAO has worked with the entity customs administration offices on drafting nearly identical implementing legislation and regulations to reflect state-level policy and introducing customs enforcement capacities to ensure revenue compliance and generation while rooting out corruption. CAFAO has also placed a high premium on the importance of training the customs officials—together, if possible—and adopting a single customs computer system for the entire country. The organization has provided basic training, and some advanced training for managers, for officials in both entities. In recent years, it has had some success in offering joint training sessions but has as yet been unable to convince the entities of the benefits of establishing one training center for the country, rather than one training center for each entity. Finally, CAFAO has aided in the development of appropriate communication and management structures, strategic planning, and internal audit and reporting systems, all based on EU standards.

Six years after the start of CAFAO's work in Bosnia, much progress has been made. The entities have nearly identical legislation regarding customs implementation and regulation and identical computer systems. All customs authorities have undergone some training, often with their counterparts from the other entity. Officials of each administration interact frequently, and the flow of goods between the entities is unhindered. However, progress has been extremely slow and hard won. The entities still refuse to establish a joint training center, no matter how much sense it makes economically. They also refused to invest in a single computer system for the nation, instead agreeing to set up the same system individually. Likewise in the legislation department: the customs implementation and regulation laws are not 100 percent the same in the Federation of Bosnia and the Republika Srpska. They are close enough for all intents and purposes, but the refusal to adopt the same legislation is worth noting.

Most CAFAO officials believe that were they to leave today, the entity offices would begin to head down separate paths again. Authorities in each entity are much more willing to work with each other than before but generally do not reach out to one another without the guidance of CAFAO. The customs program in Bosnia and the work of CAFAO have made some tremendous strides since 1995, but the journey ahead is still quite long, albeit with some signs of hope. As one official put it, "Well, we may have to set up the meetings, but we don't have to pick anyone up anymore."[10]

The work of CAFAO was absolutely seminal in producing the positive changes that have occurred in the customs service of Bosnia since independence. Without the mediating organization and its constant work, advice, encouragement, and facilitation, the entity customs administration authorities would likely still be unwilling to even visit with each other, let alone work together to compose legislation and train customs officers. No doubt that the changes have often been frustratingly slow and incremental. It is thus a credit to the European Union's understanding that changes would not take hold overnight that CAFAO has been well funded and committed to working patiently with local officials until the work is done.

The development of parallel or harmonized systems within the customs service has paved the way for continued improvements and successes in the field of customs in Bosnia. Given the GFAP, neither CAFAO nor any other organization could legally force the entities to work together on customs administration, and given the difficult political climate in Bosnia, no organization could realistically expect the entities to work together on the issue. Though perhaps it would have been preferable to have the entities work jointly, because that was not possible, CAFAO did the next best thing: it harmonized the separate entity systems as much as possible in order to allow for future joint work. The greater the degree of similarity in legislation, computer systems, training materials, and office structures, the better the chances of joint work and, perhaps, the eventual merging of the separate systems into one national customs program.

When Is This Approach Useful?

Can parallelism and harmonization of processes be used effectively to promote coexistence? I believe that the answer is yes and that the case of the customs program in Bosnia is not an anomaly. Rather, there are characteristics of the situation that suggest that parallelism might be used successfully in other areas and at other levels. The questions we should now ask include the following:

Under what circumstances should parallelism be employed?

At what levels of power and organization is parallelism effective?

What are the benefits of this approach for individuals and for communities as a whole?

Parallelism is a valuable approach in any situation where joint work is impossible but peace and cooperation are desired. It is not—and should not be—the first option tried when operating in a postconflict setting. Experiences seem to suggest that positive interactions between former combatants lead more quickly to a humanizing of the other, forgiveness, and reconciliation. When there is an opportunity to promote coexistence through common work or activities and the participants are receptive to such advances, humanitarian workers and local leaders should encourage contact between the previously conflicting parties. Unfortunately, this is not always possible initially. When the conflict is still recent and the hatred still palpable, former combatants may not be able or willing to work together. In these times, parallelism is a choice tool. I would add, though, that parallelism can be successful only when it is accompanied by a mediating or coordinating party committed to working with the conflicting factions and slowly bringing them together over time. Without this neutral intervening organization bridging the gap and facilitating communication, there can be no real parallel movement.

The effectiveness of parallelism as an approach has been demonstrated at the level of government institutions and could be successfully applied to other such offices. Military organization and police training are but two examples of areas where joint work might initially be difficult but where harmonization of methods is critical. Beyond government institutions, however, I believe parallelism can have far-reaching effects at lower levels of organization, specifically at the level of professional associations of individuals. Given the professional belief in higher standards of decency and respectability, doctors, lawyers, accountants, and other professionals can be encouraged to respond to calls for parallel action and unbiased behavior in an effort to homogenize procedures and organizations. It is less clear whether parallelism could be effectively used at the grassroots level. I would surmise that if the mediating party were able to find a notion that engenders the same feeling as the idea of professionalism and encourages elevated standards of behavior among the members of the grassroots organizations, parallelism would be a valuable tool. This, however, remains to be seen and requires further investigation.

The benefits of employing parallelism as an approach are clear. Moving slowly and in parallel allows both space and time for healing to occur. In the immediate aftermath of conflict, individuals and communities need a space in which to allow anger to subside and for thoughts of peace and reconciliation to appear. Often this cannot be accomplished in the company of former combatants or adversaries. Working in parallel rather than jointly grants such a space for healing and helps build a sense of common goals.

Conclusion

Individuals and communities recovering from massive violence require time to heal. Hatred does not dissolve overnight, and previously conflicting parties may not be able to work jointly toward reconciliation for quite some time. In these cases, leaders attempting to promote coexistence may be best served by encouraging the use of parallel structures, institutions, or actions to spur healing. Such an approach is necessarily slow but can reap the long-term benefits of peace and reconciliation when used effectively.

Notes

1. National Conference of Commissioners on Uniform State Law [http://www.nccusl.org/nccusl/aboutus.asp].
2. See P. Haas, (ed.), *Knowledge, Power, and International Policy Coordination* (Columbia: University of South Carolina Press, 1997). See also A.-M. Slaughter, "A New World Order" (working title), Princeton University Press, forthcoming.
3. Interviews and exchanges with senior officials in the Law and Procedures division of the Customs and Fiscal Assistance Office, Bosnia, 2001.
4. Annex Four, Article III, Paragraph 1 of the General Framework Agreement states "Responsibilities of the Institutions of Bosnia. The following matters are the responsibility of the institutions of Bosnia: . . . c. Customs policy."
5. Customs and Fiscal Assistance Office (CAFAO), "CAFAO Programme to BiH," Report to the Republic of Bosnia, Sarajevo, Feb. 3, 2000.
6. Interviews and exchanges with senior officials in the Law and Procedures division of the CAFAO, 2001.
7. CAFAO, "CAFAO Programme to BiH."
8. CAFAO, "CAFAO Programme to BiH."
9. Interviews and exchanges with senior officials in the Law and Procedures division of the CAFAO, 2001.
10. Interviews and exchanges with senior officials in the Law and Procedures division of the CAFAO, 2001.

Afterword
Reflections on Coexistence
Michael Ignatieff

When thinking about coexistence, it is important to distinguish it clearly from reconciliation. I learned something about the contrast between coexistence and reconciliation from spending time in South Africa, watching the Truth and Reconciliation Commission conduct the amnesty hearings.[1] I came away from that experience feeling that reconciliation was altogether too sentimental a word to describe what was going on. What happened there was a difficult exchange in which victims had to grant amnesty to perpetrators simply to execute a political deal that allowed a transition to majority rule. The deal was hard for the victims, who had to watch as the perpetrators got amnesty. They were willing to do this for political reasons.

When we fail to distinguish clearly between coexistence and reconciliation, we end up sentimentalizing and depoliticizing the processes we are trying to understand. What was most impressive about the victims in the South African amnesty hearings was not their emotional intelligence, which was considerable, but their political intelligence. They understood the political content of that exercise, and in essence they said, "Our leaders have told us what the deal is, and we have to execute the deal. We have to bite our lip and let these people off in order to consolidate and guarantee democracy and majority rule." The Truth and Reconciliation Commission tended to describe this awareness, in the township populations, as

---

Note: Portions of this Afterword are adapted from Michael Ignatieff, *Blood and Belonging: Journeys into the New Nationalism* (New York: Farrar, Straus & Giroux, 1994).

reconciliation, but the authors in this collection have a better word: *coexistence.* It is a colder word and more rational too. *Reconciliation,* in contrast, is hot: emotional and sentimental, a meeting of hearts and minds, a forgiving and forgetting. I didn't see much forgiving or forgetting in the amnesty hearings, and I didn't see much empathy for the perpetrators. What I saw instead was awareness of political necessity: the sense that the white policemen belonged to a still powerful part of the state infrastructure; the sense that prosecution, rather than amnesty, would pit a newly established government against an old power structure that still had venom in its fangs; and finally, a sense that individual grievance and desire for justice or revenge had to subordinate itself to a greater good, namely, the secure transition to stable majority rule.

To be sure, reconciliation between individuals certainly occurs, a meeting of hearts and minds, and in South Africa, Christian faith often provided the vocabulary for such reconciliations. Reconciliation of a different kind also occurs, the coming to terms with facts. Reconciliation can mean simply acknowledging the world as it actually is, instead of fighting or opposing it. In this sense of the word, many whites came to be reconciled to majority rule, and many black victims came to be reconciled to the fact that their individual desires for vengeance and revenge would never be achieved. This meaning of reconciliation—being reconciled to the facts—has an intimate relationship with coexistence. The question is whether there is a priority relationship between the two. Must there be reconciliation before coexistence or coexistence before reconciliation? My experience in South Africa leads me to think you can have coexistence without any heart-to-heart reconciliation at all. Political enemies, historical antagonists, do not have to be reconciled before they can sit in the same room. You can coexist with people you cheerfully detest. You can coexist with people without forgetting or forgiving their crimes against you. Cold peace of many kinds does not require reconciliation of a personal kind. But reconciliation of the second kind—being reconciled to the world as it is—contributes to the sort of cold coexistence achieved in postconflict situations. Reconciliation in the first sense—a meeting of hearts and minds—might be a distant, second-order consequence of reconciliation in the second sense—accepting the world as it is.

It is only reconciliation in the second sense that assists coexistence. It needs to be added, however, that coexistence can go on without reconciliation in this second sense. Antagonistic groups can coexist without fully acknowledging or accepting the facts that require them to do so. Many South African whites may coexist with blacks because they have no choice but not because they fundamentally accept or are reconciled to their change of status. Many Serbs and Bosniaks coexist in the common institutions of Bosnia without being reconciled to each other, in either of the senses in which I have used the word. They never forgive or forget, nor do they fundamentally accept the realities—dictated by the Dayton Peace Accords—that oblige them to cooperate in shared institutions.

Another difficult issue is the relationship between coexistence and justice. What makes life difficult is not only choices between good and bad but choices between two goods. Coexistence is good. Justice is good. But in fact they are often on a collision course. For example, should there be prosecutions of people who committed war crimes in Bosnia? That may advance justice but make coexistence more difficult. Groups who feel scapegoated by international justice, like the Serbs, will be less willing to coexist with groups who construe themselves to be victims. Ordinary people in Bosnia find themselves asking, Which should matter more, that most people get along day by day or that guilty individuals see the inside of a prison cell? When the question is posed like this, as a choice between coexistence for the many and justice for the few, it seems easy to think that coexistence should trump justice, especially in cases where doing justice will tear open recently healed scar tissue. Yet there are cases where moral disgust about impunity is so strong in a victim community that it cannot coexist with the perpetrator community unless guilty individuals are punished. In such cases, doing justice works to further coexistence. Bringing Mladic and Karadjic to justice in Bosnia will probably further both goals: the Serbs are tired of the embarrassment of their impunity, and the Bosniaks feel that their arrest is a crucial demonstration of Western will to do justice. But everyone in Bosnia knows that impunity will not end if Mladic and Karadjic are behind bars. The country is simply full of unindicted war criminals on all sides, and there is nothing that The Hague will ever be able to do about it. Coexistence will have to take root in villages where victims and perpetrators share the same cafés, stores, and restaurants. The idea that justice is a precondition of co-existence is a perfectionist illusion. Coexistence is all about living with and even enduring injustice.

Still another perfectionist illusion is the idea that coexistence requires shared historical truth. On this view, groups formerly at war with each other cannot coexist, once conflict ceases, unless they begin to assemble a shared account of their tortured past. I am not sure that truth is a precondition for coexistence. This was driven home to me when I visited villages after the war between Croatia and Serbia in 1991 and 1992. These villages had previously coex-isted, and rates of intermarriage were high. Coexistence does not get more intimate than intermarriage. What made the eastern Slavonian plain, between Zagreb and Belgrade, such a tragic place in 1992 and 1993 is that everyone had a vivid memory of a coexis-tence that worked. Before the war, Serbs and Croats went to each other's baptisms, weddings, and funerals, even though the Serbs had painful historical memories of Jasenovac, the concentration camp run by the Croatian fascist regime of Ante Pavelic during World War II. Coexistence and intermarriage were quite compati-ble with these memories, or at least with memory on the Serb side and denial on the Croat side. As long as Tito's regime kept the peace in Yugoslavia, coexistence trumped both memory and de-nial. The regime did little to teach historical truth to either side. In fact, it encouraged the repression of memory and the continu-ation of denial. True, there was a museum at the Jasenovac con-centration camp site, but the dominant ethos of the Tito era in that region was "Brotherhood and Unity," the socialist slogan endless-ly repeated in order to consign the wartime experience of mutual ethnic slaughter to distant history. The highway that ran between Zagreb and Belgrade, through the Slavonian plain, was called the Highway of Brotherhood and Unity, and if highways can have ide-ological functions, this one's function was to symbolize the ethnic unity of the country under socialist single-party leadership.

Brotherhood and unity is now a cruel joke to the divided Serbs and Croats on the Slavonian plain. Outsiders like myself, who toured the region in late 1992, after ethnic war had set village against vil-lage and reduced Vukovar, the leading town of the region, to ruins, found ourselves saying that the coexistence created under broth-

329

erhood and unity was false. We argued that the rapidity with which coexistence was replaced by enmity and war proved that coexistence without truth was bound to be shallow. The conclusion we outsiders drew was that coexistence depends on some degree of shared historical truth, a common narrative of the painful past. Where such a common narrative is absent, the daily coexistence that develops is bound to be shallow, vulnerable to the first incident or atrocity that recalls the suppressed past.

Yet I wonder now whether shared or common narratives of historical events are actually possible between ethnic groups that have a history of slaughter or murder between them. Perhaps outsiders were setting the bar too high when we concluded that the fragility of coexistence in the eastern Slavonian plain was due to the absence of genuine historical truth. Maybe the reality was different. Each side knew what the other side had done. Each side knew what *it* had done. There was no lack of knowledge. It is not obvious to me that knowing more, sharing more, would have prevented the collapse of coexistence. This idea depends on what may be a sentimental fiction about societies at peace, namely, that they are at peace because everyone shares the same historical narrative or the same relationship to historical truth. The United States is a society at peace, but can it honestly be said that American blacks and whites share the same sense of historical truth about slavery? In the United States, what may matter much more than shared truth is that the institutions of the law keep certain promises, and provide some measure of equal protection. To be sure, they do so imperfectly, as anyone even slightly acquainted with the American criminal courts will know, and each race will probably have rather different estimates of whether these institutions perform adequately. But the two peoples coexist, and they do so not because they share historical truth or even the same estimate of whether the institutions keep their promises but because they share the same belief that they *ought* to coexist. They coexist, moreover, not because they like or understand each other very well but because cooperation rewards each group sufficiently for individuals to believe that continued coexistence is worthwhile. What matters, in this version of coexistence, is not shared truth about the past but common insertion in a social division of labor and shared belief that common institutions *should* function in a certain way and provide equal protection to both groups.

If we apply this thought to the Yugoslav case, what do we find? With the death of Tito, the institutions of the Yugoslav state began to crumble, and the economy began to fall apart. Institutional expectations could not be sustained. As the Croatians moved toward national independence in 1990, Serbs had good reason to ask themselves whether a Croatian state would safeguard their fundamental interests, and the Serbian regime in Belgrade had good reason to stir up these fears and suspicions of possible Croatian independence. To be sure, the past's malign hold did play a role in heightening these fears and suspicions, for any Serb knew that the last time Croatia had enjoyed independence, its rulers had put Serbs in concentration camps. But the real problem was not divided memories about the past but the slow collapse of common institutions and the demise of equal protection before the law or what passed for this under the Tito regime.

What I observed, during the immediate aftermath of the Serb-Croat war of 1991, was that the very protagonists of the conflict, the Serb and Croat villagers who fought each other so bitterly, did so without losing keen, even tragic memories of successful coexistence in the past. War did not obliterate the truth of coexistence, any more than war showed up the illusion of coexistence. Once the killing started, villagers sometimes only 250 meters apart were in dugouts firing mortar shells at each other by night. And then they'd pick up the two-way radio and talk to the people they were fighting and say, "So you married that girl? How many children you got?" I spent a night in one such Serb dugout listening to these and other conversations. And then they would fire at each other. You could say to these people, "You're fighting people with whom you're talking and with whom you have strong memories of coexistence! How do you get out of this obviously absurd situation?" They would have no difficulty agreeing that the situation was absurd. But in their analysis, it was a collective action problem. Each individual actor may see it as rational to coexist and cooperate with former antagonists. Each would have economic reasons to cooperate. Each would have memories of working together. Each would have memories of going to each other's weddings and funerals, and each would have nostalgia to return to that. It would simply be rational to do so. But individual intentions had no possible collective outcome as long as each side was firing at the other, and the political leadership on each side was making individual collaboration of any sort impossible.

If I am right—that coexistence is a collective action problem—then I think that political leadership and institutional bargains are essential to creating the conditions in which individuals can find it rational to coexist. Coexistence cannot proceed in the absence of two conditions: a political deal between antagonists and a security deal to ensure safety on all sides. Coexistence cannot be created through all the good intentions of nongovernmental organizations, willing to work at the grassroots and talk with individuals to help them understand how terrible it is to hate other people and how rational it would be to coexist. The people know that already. Their problem is that they cannot get a collective frame of action in which these individual intentions can produce an actual result. Small, well-intended, incremental NGO interventions tap into heartfelt forms of sentimentality about the benefits of coexistence, but without the frames of security and political agreement, they will not work. Resolving the collective action problem of generating a security and political framework is the critical precondition that enables individual good intentions to translate into good deeds.

It follows that you can't create coexistence by preaching tolerance. People don't need lectures on tolerance. They need institutions that guarantee the security bargain between ethnic groups that will allow tolerant behavior to be rewarded. To take the example of Macedonia, outsiders sometimes think the problem is that Macedonians are somehow more intolerant of each other than citizens from multiethnic societies like Canada or the United States. Actually, the problem is not tolerance but something else. There is no political agreement between the two competing ethnic groups in Macedonia as to the fundamental identity of the country as a political unit. There are lots of tolerant, multicultural Macedonians on all sides of the ethnic divide, but until there is a clear constitutional settlement, maintained by the political parties, that defines and entrenches the rights of both groups to equal participation in the life of the country, tolerant behavior by individuals cannot do anything to resolve the ever-tightening political tension in that country.

Another issue in thinking about coexistence is the relationship between trust and time. The old cliché tells us that time heals all wounds. This suggests that communities need time for coexistence to develop. In reality, time and coexistence have a paradoxical and even perverse relationship. Don't bank on time because it may do you no favors. Certainly, the more time that communities live peacefully side by side, the more likely it is that they will keep on doing so into the future. Yet the disturbing message from the Balkans is that time sometimes makes old wounds worse. The most startling example of this is the often rabid nationalism of Balkan exiles or refugees, especially those who left in 1945 and who played an important role in stoking hatreds back home. Some of the most furious Balkan nationalism I have ever encountered was not in the Balkans itself but in meeting halls in Toronto, where Serbs and Croats, removed from the primal scene of their enmities by fifty years of peace and four thousand miles of distance, seemed to relive these hatreds in all their original, incandescent fury. You would have thought that half a century of peaceful exile and a new start would cause the flames of mutual dislike to die down. You would be wrong. In many ways, as these groups assimilated into the Canadian pattern of life, as parents watched their children growing up without strong ethnic identities, they reacted with a violent reassertion of the original, primal identity, circa 1945. In the Balkans itself, the same pattern of violent reversion could also be seen among the young paramilitaries on all sides who, before the war, were unlikely to have ever seen the inside of a mosque, a church, or an Orthodox cathedral and who now manned barricades proudly displaying the insignia of their particular religion. A lifetime of secular antireligious instruction in the Tito period, specifically designed to root out ethnic intolerance and religious fanaticism, was obliterated at the first exchange of gunfire.

Time does not build trust because time does not necessarily heal old wounds. What matters more than time, it seems to me, is the real performance of institutions. If ethnic groups can be obliged—as they were by the Dayton Accords—to cooperate, even against their will, in common institutions of government, this pattern of cooperation will lead, in time, to the emergence of cautious, limited patterns of interethnic trust. Time alone heals nothing. Institutional cooperation, the learning that goes on when ethnic groups find themselves rewarded for cooperation, can do much more.

Finally, I have learned that the international community plays a crucial but delicate role in promoting coexistence after ethnic conflict. The question is whether international actors can facilitate coexistence by intervening—or whether our interventions by their very nature usurp responsibility for the process. We become part of the problem and not part of the solution in ways we do not intend. No coexistence will develop in Kosovo unless there is a political dynamic led by political elites who say, "We, not the international community, are responsible for the protection of the Serb minority." Until this happens, the Serbs will never be safe. Yet the international community confiscates local capacity instead of building responsibility. There's a perverse potential logic by which the international interveners come in to adjudicate disputes and then take away local responsibility for resolving disputes. Postimperial coexistence is about doing yourselves out of a job, giving yourselves nothing to do, ending your contract, going home, handing it over, not being there in five years, not making a career out of it, not becoming essential, not becoming an irreplaceable linchpin in a coexistence dynamic. The test of success is when you're not needed. And getting to that seems to be the central challenge for international coexistence work.

Note

1. See M. Ignatieff, "Introduction," in J. Edelstein, *Truth and Lies: Stories from the Truth and Reconciliation Commission in South Africa* (New York: New Press, 2001). See also A. Krog, *Country of My Skull: Guilt, Sorrow, and the Limits of Forgiveness in the New South Africa* (New York: Times Books, 2000), and M. Minow, *Between Vengeance and Forgiveness: Facing History After Genocide and Mass Violence* (Boston: Beacon Press, 1998).

About the Editors

Antonia Chayes is an adjunct lecturer in public policy at Harvard University's Kennedy School of Government and vice chair of Conflict Management Group. She has served as undersecretary of the United States Air Force and on the board of directors of United Technologies for more than two decades. With her late husband, Abram Chayes, she is the author of several books, including *Planning for Intervention: International Cooperation in Conflict Management* (Kluwer Law International, 1999) and *The New Sovereignty: Compliance with International Regulatory Agreements* (Harvard University Press, 1995).

Martha Minow is a professor at Harvard Law School, where she has taught since 1981. Her books include *Between Vengeance and Forgiveness: Facing History After Genocide and Mass Violence* (Beacon Press, 1998) and *Breaking the Cycles of Hatred* (Princeton University Press, 2003).

335

About the Contributors

Aneelah Afzali is completing her law degree at Harvard Law School and holds a bachelor of arts degree from the University of Oregon. She served as a primary editor for the *Human Rights Journal* at Harvard Law School and will work for Heller Ehrman in Seattle upon graduation.

Eileen F. Babbitt is assistant professor of international politics and codirector of the Center for Human Rights and Conflict Resolution at Tufts University's Fletcher School of Law and Diplomacy.

Cynthia Burns has held a variety of staff positions with and is currently serving as senior protection officer of the Office of the United Nations High Commissioner for Refugees.

Diana Chigas is a fellow at the Center for Human Rights and Conflict Resolution, an adjunct assistant professor at the Fletcher School of Law and Diplomacy, Tufts University, and a senior associate at Conflict Management Group. She has written a number of articles on negotiation and conflict management.

Sara Cobb is the director of the Institute for Conflict Analysis and Resolution at George Mason University. Through her research, she elaborates discourse and narrative analysis of conflict transformation processes.

Cynthia Cohen is director of coexistence research and international collaborations at Brandeis University's International Center for Ethics, Justice and Public Life. Prior to working at Brandeis, she founded and directed The Oral History Center, a Boston-based community-based arts and humanities organization.

Laura Colleton is completing her law degree at Harvard Law School and holds a bachelor of arts degree from the University of Notre Dame. She served as a primary editor of the *Human Rights Journal* at Harvard Law School.

Brian Ganson advises international corporations and organizations on conflict and negotiation. He is an adjunct professor of international negotiation at the Fletcher School of Law and Diplomacy at Tufts University.

Marc Gopin is visiting associate professor of international diplomacy at Tufts University's Fletcher School of Law and Diplomacy and author of *Between Eden and Armageddon* (Oxford University Press, 2000) and *Holy War, Holy Peace* (Oxford University Press, 2002).

Lauren Elizabeth Guth is currently working toward her law degree at Boston College Law School. Prior to attending graduate school, Lauren worked at Conflict Management Group, after graduating from Williams College.

Michael Ignatieff is the Carr Professor of Human Rights Policy at the Kennedy School of Government, Harvard University. His most recent book is *Blood and Belonging: Journeys into the New Nationalism* (Farrar, Straus & Giroux, 1994).

Elizabeth McClintock is director of programs for Conflict Management Group. In her work, she has designed and implemented training and consulting programs for public and private sector organizations in the United States, Canada, Europe, Asia, Australia, and Africa.

Laura McGrew has worked with the United Nations High Commissioner for Refugees in Rwanda.

Gregory P. Noone is a lawyer in the training department of the United States Institute of Peace and is an adjunct professor at Roger Williams University School of Law. He served on active duty as a U.S. Navy judge advocate for more than a decade.

Sadako Ogata, former UN High Commissioner for Refugees (1991–2000), currently serves as Prime Minister Koizumi of Japan's Special Representative for Afghanistan, cochairs the Commission on Human Security, and is a Ford Foundation scholar in residence.

Carlos E. Sluzki is a research professor at George Mason University with joint appointments at the School of Public Policy and the Institute for Conflict Analysis and Resolution, and clinical professor of psychiatry and behavioral sciences at George Washington University Medical School in Washington, D.C.

Marc Sommers is a research fellow at Boston University's African Studies Center, serves as the Youth at Risk Specialist for CARE, Inc., and USAID's Basic Education and Policy Support Activity (BEPS), and regularly consults on conflict negotiation, emergency and peace education, human rights, forced migrant, urban migrant, and security issues. He is the author of *Fear in Bongoland: Burundi Refugees in Urban Tanzania* (Berghahn Books, 2001).

Elizabeth V. Spelman teaches philosophy at Smith College, where she is the Barbara Richmond 1940 Professor in the Humanities. Her most recent book is *Repair: The Impulse to Restore in a Fragile World* (Beacon Press, 2002).

Sven M. Spengemann is working on a doctoral dissertation at Harvard Law School, in the area of international law and governance. He holds master's of law degrees from Harvard University and from the College of Europe in Belgium.

Ilija Todorovic is currently head of the Legal Protection Unit at UNHCR/Banja Luka, BiH, and has been with UNHCR for some nine years. He is also a U.S.-licensed attorney and holds a master's degree in international relations.

Glenn T. Ware is senior legal adviser for the Department of Institutional Integrity at the World Bank. In this capacity, he conducts international fraud and corruption investigations involving projects funded or executed by the World Bank in all parts of the world.

Index